D0558436

THE JUSTIFICATION OF THE GOOD

170
S689j
29.99

THE JUSTIFICATION OF THE GOOD

An Essay on Moral Philosophy

by

Vladimir Solovyov

Translated from the Russian by
Nathalie A. Duddington, M.A.

Edited and Annotated by
Boris Jakim

Foreword by
David Bentley Hart

San Diego Christian College
2100 Greenfield Drive
El Cajon, CA 92019

WILLIAM B. EERDMANS PUBLISHING COMPANY
GRAND RAPIDS, MICHIGAN / CAMBRIDGE, U.K.

First Published 1897 in Russian as
Opravdanie dobra: Nravstvennaya filosofiia
English translation © 1918 by The Macmillan Company, New York

This edition © 2005 by Wm. B. Eerdmans Publishing Co.
All rights reserved

Wm. B. Eerdmans Publishing Co.
255 Jefferson Ave. S.E., Grand Rapids, Michigan 49503 /
P.O. Box 163, Cambridge CB3 9PU U.K.

Printed in the United States of America

10 09 08 07 06 05   7 6 5 4 3 2 1

ISBN 0-8028-2863-9

www.eerdmans.com

Dedicated to my father,
the historian Sergey Mikhailovich Solovyov,
and to my grandfather,
the priest Mikhail Vasil'evich Solovyov,
with a living and grateful recognition of an eternal bond

Contents

INTRODUCTION   Moral Philosophy as an Independent Science

Contents

PART I

The Good in Human Nature

CHAPTER I The Primary Data of Morality

(as in shame) but to living beings like himself. — Pity cannot be the
result of human progress, for it exists among the animals also. — Pity
is the individual psychological root of the right social relations

CHAPTER II   The Ascetic Principle in Morality

pleasure of another contains the approval of that pleasure, which may, however, be evil. — Participation in it may therefore be good or evil according to the object of the pleasure. — Since the co-rejoicing may itself be immoral, it cannot in any case be the basis of moral relations. — Answer to certain objections the false principle of egoism, which contradicts the absolute truth of the altruistic principle

CHAPTER IV   The Religious Principle in Morality

CHAPTER V   Virtues

same truth demands from its very nature a different attitude to our lower nature (the ascetic attitude), to our neighbours (the altruistic attitude), and to the supreme principle (the religious attitude). — Opposition between the absolute inner necessity or the binding nature of truth and its accidental and conditional character as a sufficient motive of human actions. — Hence the desire to replace the conception of the moral good or unconditional duty by the conception of happiness or of the unconditionally desirable

PART II

The Good Is from God

CHAPTER 1   The Unity of Moral Principles

Contents

CHAPTER II   The Unconditional Principle of Morality

actually comes to be in the history of the world. — Proof of the rational necessity of the process. A mollusc or a sponge cannot express human thought and will, and a biological process is necessary for creating a more perfect organism; in like manner the supreme thought and will (the Kingdom of God) cannot be revealed among semi-animals, and requires the historical process of making the forms of life more perfect

CHAPTER III   The Reality of the Moral Order

PART III

The Good through Human History

CHAPTER I   The Individual and Society

Contents

CHAPTER III Abstract Subjectivism in Morality

CHAPTER IV The Moral Norm of Social Life

Contents

CHAPTER VII   The Economic Question from
the Moral Point of View

Contents

CHAPTER VIII   Morality and Legal Justice

CHAPTER IX   **The Meaning of War**

Contents

Contents

activity of man and his whole-hearted devotion to God are equally necessary; but the two can be combined only if the two spheres of life (the religious and the political) and their two immediate motives (piety and pity) are clearly distinguished — corresponding to the difference in the immediate objects of action, the final purpose being one and the same. — Fatal consequences of the separation of the Church from the state and of either usurping the functions of the other. — The Christian rule of social progress consists in this, that the state should as little as possible coerce the inner moral life of man, leaving it to the free spiritual activity of the Church, and at the same time secure as certainly and as widely as possible the external conditions in which men can live worthily and become more perfect

Foreword

I

Within the unforgiving confines of a relatively brief life (1853-1900), Vladimir Solovyov contrived not only to produce a prodigiously varied body of brilliant (if not infrequently eccentric) work, but also to explore most of the regions of modern religious disenchantment and re-enchantment. Indeed, such was his extraordinary precocity, in both wisdom and folly, that the latter accomplishment could still be claimed for him had he died far younger than he did — perhaps just as he was crossing the threshold of manhood. Raised in a devout and erudite household (his father was the great historian Sergei Solovyov), he was all of twelve when he began to entertain "Protestant" doubts regarding the ancient pieties of the Orthodox Church, and by the age of fourteen — when he suffered his great crisis of faith and embraced atheism — he had by his own account passed through phases of deism and pantheism. This all might have amounted to little more than the typical ferment of a bright but callow mind in the case of someone less gifted or less passionate than Solovyov; but for the young Vladimir it was a severe probation of the soul, and for the next two years he wandered spiritually through all the fields and meadows of nihilist negation, materialism, and radicalism (which in the Russia of the time, one should note, were particularly floriferous fields and meadows). He was as unreserved in his intellectual enthusiasms at this point in his development as he would prove to be in all those that followed, even cultivating in his personality something of the fashionably demoniacal nihilist style of the age (to the point that his school friend, Lev Lopatin, saw him as having become a kind of "satan"). In short, the young Vladimir embarked early on the intellectual and moral course of the radical Russian *"intelligentsia,"* and might well have followed it to one of its conventional ends (however terrible or absurd) had his nimble and fitful mind not alighted on a new discovery.

It was Spinoza, implausibly enough, who ultimately rescued Solovyov (now having attained to the hoary antiquity of sixteen) from his atheism and set him on the path back toward Christian belief. Spinoza's philosophy excited his imagination, if for no other reason than that it suggested to his mind the possibility of a "theology" that was also a system of nature, a "science" of cosmic unity and of the harmony of divine and creaturely being. Soon he was immersing himself in Hegel's absolute idealism, and (retreating a little) in Kant's transcendental idealism, and (drifting forward toward the cliff's edge) in Schopenhauer, and (most importantly, I would argue) in Schelling, until, after a passage through Hartmann, he emerged as a Christian philosopher, acquainted with all the postures and passions of religious doubt and spiritual defiance, convinced of the philosophical coherence of Christian faith, and animated by an irrepressible conviction. He was eighteen.

It may seem to serve little purpose to rehearse the intellectual convulsions of the young Solovyov's capacious, agile, but definitely adolescent mind, especially in an introduction to one of his last and most mature works; I would argue, though, that his early experience of doubt and rejection of God, and the elliptical course he took in his recovery of faith, marked Solovyov's thought for life. If nothing else, those years of estrangement from the Church — occurring as they did at the dawn of adult consciousness, when the mind is still susceptible of the profoundest impressions — as well as the necessity of rediscovering his Christianity through an alien medium, made it a certainty that Solovyov's understanding of his faith would never be entirely conventional. And it would be false to suggest that Solovyov's return to the faith was entirely orthodox, or that it did not involve often intense flirtations with much of the esoteric flotsam of the late nineteenth century: theosophy, spiritualism, Qabbalism, Gnosticism, the *Corpus Hermeticum,* automatic writing, alchemy, the ideas of Jacob Boehme, and so on. At this period of his development, Solovyov had voyaged far toward the opposite extreme of Russian intellectual styles, and could scarcely have arrived at a greater remove from the conventional nihilism to which he had so lately adhered. It is easy to imagine that here, too, his development might have stalled, and then sent him along the ordinary path of the post-Romantic Russian occultist or visionary. He would have been a considerable adornment to the silver age's vatic milieu of opiates and ectoplasm, had he allowed himself to sink into its opulent twilight, and would perhaps be remembered now as the most credible figure in that continuum that comprised Scriabin, and Madame Blavatsky, and so many others, that bore fruit in Russian Symbolism and secreted poison in

Russian hermeticism, and that exercised a subterranean influence in the works of Berdyaev, and Merezhkovsky, and even Nabokov. Fortunately, however, Solovyov's philosophical sophistication was too great, and his nature too earnest, for the esoteric impulse to prevail. None of these *arcana* was sufficiently attractive to his intellect to entice him far away from Christian orthodoxy, and none exercised sufficient sway over his imagination to mark it in more than passing fashion; but the pattern inaugurated in Solovyov's thinking in those years was one of faith as discovery, as always something strange and fabulous, to be approached by hidden paths; and from this sprang not only the disorienting quality of some of his thought but also a great deal of its fecundity. It was also, at first, a pattern of speculative audacity and exotic fascinations, and even perhaps of a kind of mystical experience — if not ecstasy, at least elation. And it was during this period, when his mind was capable of many things to which a more settled nature would not have been hospitable, that Solovyov had his experience (intellectual but also, apparently, personal) of the divine Wisdom or Sophia.

It is crucial to take account of this experience, I would argue, if one is really to appreciate the governing logic of *The Justification of the Good;* for even though it is a text composed in the comparatively sober style of Solovyov's last years, when the divine Sophia, as an explicit *dramatis persona,* had more or less vanished from his writings, it is ultimately a "sophianic" book (and therein, arguably, lies its genius). The figure of Sophia, admittedly, arouses more than a little suspicion among even Solovyov's more indulgent Christian readers, and some would prefer to write her off as a figment of the young Solovyov's dreamier moods, or as a sentimental souvenir of his youthful dalliance with the Gnostics. To his less indulgent readers, she is something rather more sinister. And indeed it is difficult to know what exactly to make of the two visions of Sophia that Solovyov had in 1875 — the first in the British Museum, the second in the Egyptian desert — or the earlier vision he had at the age of nine. But it is important to note that, in Solovyov's developed reflections upon this figure (and in those of his successor "Sophiologists," Pavel Florensky and Sergei Bulgakov), she was most definitely *not* an occult, or pagan, or Gnostic goddess, nor was she a fugitive from some Chaldean mystery cult, nor was she a speculative perversion of the Christian doctrine of God. She was not a fourth hypostasis in the Godhead, nor a fallen fragment of God, nor a literal world-soul, nor an eternal hypostasis who became incarnate as the Mother of God, nor most certainly the "feminine aspect of deity." Solovyov possessed too refined a mind to fall prey to the lure of cultic mythologies or childish anthropomorphisms, despite his interest in Gnosticism (or at least in its special pathos); and all such characterizations of the figure of

Sophia are the result of misreadings (though, one must grant, misreadings partly occasioned by the young Solovyov's penchant for poetic hyperbole).

In truth, the divine Sophia is first and foremost a biblical figure, and "Sophiology" was born of an honest attempt to interpret intelligibly the role ascribed to her in the Wisdom literature of the Old Testament, in such a way as to complement the Logos Christology of the Fourth Gospel, while still not neglecting the "autonomy" of creation within its very dependency upon the Logos. Solovyov's Sophia stands in the interval between God and world, as an emblem of the nuptial mystery of Christ's love for creation and creation's longing for the Logos. Sophia is the divine Wisdom as residing in the non-divine; she is the mirror of the Logos and of the light of the Spirit, reflecting in the created order the rational coherence and transcendent beauty in which all things live, move, and have their being. She is also, therefore, the deep and pervasive Wisdom of the world who, even as that world languishes in bondage to sin, longs to be joined to her maker in an eternal embrace, and arrays herself in every palpable glory and ornament to prepare for his coming, and by her loveliness manifests her insatiable yearning.

Another way of saying this is that Sophia is creation — and especially human creation — as God eternally intends, sees, loves, and possesses it. The world is created in the Logos and belongs to him, shines with the imperishable beauty of the Father made visible in him, and in the Logos nothing can be found wanting; thus one may say that he, in his transcendence, eternally possesses a world, and that the world, in its immanence, restlessly longs for him. And yet another way of saying this is that Sophia is humankind (which contains within itself all the lower orders of creation) as God eternally chooses it to be his body, the place of his indwelling, and in his eternity this humanity is perfect and sinless, while in our world it is something toward which all finite reality strives, as its eschatological horizon. One can thus speak of an eternal Christ: the Logos as forever turned toward a world, a world gathered to himself from before all the ages just as — in time — we see the world gathered to him in his incarnation. Here Solovyov is following a line of thought with quite respectable patristic pedigrees: seen thus, as the body of the Logos (the *totus Christus* in its eternal or eschatological aspect), Sophia is scarcely distinguishable from the eternal *Anthropos* of whom Gregory of Nyssa writes in *On the Making of Humanity*. She is not another hypostasis as such, but is the personal and responsive aspect of the concrete unity of a redeemed creation united to — and so "enhypostatized" by — Christ; or, looked at from below (so to speak), the "symphonic" totality of created hypostases perfectly joined to Christ. She is thus indeed a kind of intelligence in the created order (analogous to the intelligence of the spiritual world of which Augustine speaks in *The Confessions*), and she is beauty, and order, and eros, but only insofar as she personifies the answer of creation to God's call, the beloved's response to the lover's address; far from a kind of Romantic pantheism, what she represents is creation's desire for God, its insufficiency in itself, its eternal vocation to be the vessel of his glory and the tabernacle of his indwelling presence. She is, in other words, a figure for the active longing of creation and for its accomplished rest; she is both passion and repose, ardent expectation and final peace. She is still God's Wisdom, but as mirrored in the intricacy, life, unity, and splendor of created being, and in the unity and love of the Church.

At the heart, then, of Solovyov's Sophiology is Christology. He works from the conviction that the end of creation is the deified humanity of Christ, which in the Kingdom of God will divinize humankind and will (as Paul promises in Romans 8) transform the entirety of the created order. If this is so, then the ultimate purpose for which humanity was fashioned is to be joined to the Logos in the incarnation. It is only in this sense that one *might* say that the Mother of God somehow embodies Sophia: in Mary the human openness to the advent of God reaches its purest and most selfless expression; she perfectly embodies the consent of humanity — and of all creation — to the power of God's Spirit, and so is the full flowering of nature's longing to become fruitful with the Logos — to become the temple of divine glory. It is the Mother of God's "sophianic" transparency before divine love that makes of her the highest exemplar of humanity waiting upon (but not of itself accomplishing) the arrival of "divine humanity" or "Godmanhood" (*Bogochelovechestvo* or, in Greek, *theandria*).

This latter concept, which was the theme of Solovyov's most famous early work — the *Lectures on Divine Humanity* (1878-1881) — is an inseparable concomitant of the idea of Sophia; grounded in Chalcedonian Christology, it refers to humanity's "divine destiny," so to speak, the purpose for which God brings into being a creature fashioned in his image and likeness. Humanity exists, for Solovyov, that there might be divine humanity; the end of our existence, and its whole meaning, is to be deified in Christ. Thus the incarnate Logos is the one true man precisely in that he is the God-man. Nothing could be more alien, then, to Solovyov's thought than a more "dialectical" approach to the work of God in Christ that would treat the incarnation of the Word as an interruption of nature and history; between the eternal Word of God and the humanity he assumes, the relationship is — from all eternity — one of "divine organism": the fittedness of human nature to the divine, the "supralapsarian" orientation of humanity toward union with the divine nature and of the divine Son toward union with his creature. For this reason, the God-man does not appear among us simply as a word of contradiction, even when he convicts us of our sin, but as the fulfillment of our nature in what lies beyond our nature, the end toward which we are drawn in being awakened from nothingness, though it is an end we can never, in ourselves, achieve.

This last point must be especially stressed, for while Solovyov believes that the progress of human creativity — cultural, political, and spiritual production — constitutes a kind of "development" toward divine humanity, and that both nature and history unfold for the express purpose of giving birth to the God-man, he is quite adamant in his insistence that humanity is not intrinsically capable of its divine end. As he makes clear in the present work, and even more strikingly in his final work, *Three Conversations Concerning War, Progress, and the End of History, Including a Short Story of the Antichrist* (1900), the highest pinnacle that humankind unaided can attain is that of the man-god — the hero, or emperor, or Great Beast — but the God-man can come into being only from God's side; only the infinite can join the finite to itself, and while grace does indeed perfect nature, it remains nonetheless *grace.* True, sometimes Solovyov's emphasis upon our participation in the work of divinization (especially in some of its quainter, more prognostic moments) can appear to confuse natural teleology and supernatural eschatology; and, like every serious philosopher of his time, Solovyov is always engaged in a subtle struggle with the ghost of Hegel; but, in the end, he is quite explicit in denying that the God-man *evolves,* even though evolution is a sort of "posterior premise" for the incarnation of the Logos. Rather, the whole of natural and human history is merely that process whereby the Word of God prepares to appear "within his own." And thus, for Christian reflection, all human labor — physical, intellectual, cultural, political, economic, artistic — should be understood as the sphere of our consent to what has happened in Christ, our participation in the process by which that event will become a universal and cosmic reality for all of creation in the Kingdom of God, our creative "discovery" of our divine vocation in Christ, and a reverent preparation of the earth for the advent of a victory and a redemption that — in Christ — have already come to pass.

II

If Sophia is God's world as eternally conceived in his Logos, and if divine humanity is the crown and consummation of creation, and if then this world in its every order is an aspiration to that divine world, then any ethics worthy of Christian culture will be one whose concern is total: it must proceed from a rationale found not merely in the conscience or dignity of the autonomous subject, nor in a gross estimation of material needs and desires, nor in a purely social economy of civic duty; it will have the form of service to the entire cosmos as summed up in and brought about through human action. It is through humanity that the glory of God will be revealed in all of creation, as Paul says, and this truth is the principle that governs Solovyov's ethical philosophy. Not that — in *The Justification of the Good* — this is by any means immediately obvious.

In a letter of 1884 to Aleksandr Kireev, Solovyov confessed his inability to write a system of ethics in abstraction from theological commitments; he could not, he said, erect any fast partitions in his mind between ethics and religion, or between religion and revelation, or between revelation and the Church. However, *The Justification of the Good,* which Solovyov wrote between 1894 and 1897 (and soon revised for its second edition), has every appearance of being just such a system; it certainly does not begin from any explicitly theological claims, but takes as its point of departure an examination of three moral feelings that Solovyov regards as innate in us and primary in our experience of the world and ourselves: shame (especially sexual shame), pity (whence come altruism and kindness), and reverence (the fear of God). The argument seems to begin, that is, from a set of purely human constants, which would also seem to place the entire project within the scope of one (vaguely Rousseauian) strand of modern ethical theory. Nonetheless, Solovyov's is genuinely a morality of the Good, in the most purely Platonic sense: it is not an ethics of affectivity, much less a consequentialist or utilitarian calculus, nor certainly any kind of ethics of the self-positing ego or "the moral law within" (as regards this last, Solovyov directs some of his more piercing animadversions at the preposterous purism of Kantian ethics); rather, Solovyov's reason for undertaking an examination of these three moral feelings is to demonstrate through them that the *idea* of the Good always acts as a cause upon us, within the most primordial promptings of our moral and social natures. The very presence within us of these three forms of moral sentiment reveals the power exerted over us by a transcendent law that will not accommodate itself to the savagely circumscribed rationality of evolution or survival or natural need. He also argues to great effect that all the paths by which we might seek to elude the claim of the Good upon us — solipsism, absolute causalism, and so forth — invariably lead into mires of incoherence where no sane soul can long survive. However, even though Solovyov believes that the Good governs us — whether we will it or not — through the idea of the Good we harbor within ourselves — whether we are aware of it or not — he still asserts that an ethics can be justified only from the human consciousness of the Good. As he argues in his preface (in one of those strikingly ingenious aperçus that are scattered liberally throughout the text), mere submission to extrinsic authority, without any understanding of the rational warrant for its dictates, is not really obedience, but is in fact the most brutish kind of voluntarism; rather than an inner response to the greater authority of the Good, it is a purely arbitrary decision to submit, and so is a triumph of will over reason.

Solovyov devotes the first part of his book to a kind of phenomenology of these three irreducibly prior moral feelings, whose purpose is to demonstrate that each of them reveals a moral interval between the human soul and mere nature. Morality's first stirrings, then, are not primarily social, though its ends undoubtedly are; it begins from the experience of a certain rational dignity and vocation, an intrinsic remoteness of the soul from its own material conditions that — far from separating it from its fellows — binds it ever more securely to them. All one's loyalties to organic attachments larger than the self — social, moral, amorous — necessarily follow from this experience of one's own native worth, this sense of alienation from one's own physical "identity." But, because this sense of the spirit's inviolable elevation over matter apprises us of the Good acting within us as a higher law, it also makes us conscious that the virtues we possess in ourselves have no intrinsic merit (the fidelity of the self to itself cannot be the ground of morality), but are good only insofar as they serve the Good beyond us.

The first feeling, shame, is the form in which we experience our initial moral awakening, a sense we cannot easily banish of something degrading in our enslavement to our animal nature; it is what, even if only dimly at first, alerts us to an inner spiritual dignity, and to a moral consciousness that refuses to submit to the exigencies of physical existence. The book's treatment of shame, incidentally, includes a number of passages on sexuality; and it is as well to acknowledge here that, to some readers, Solovyov's evident repugnance at sexual intercourse may seem more than a little morbid, and his hope that some future generation of the race will eliminate the need for the whole humiliating ceremony may seem more than a little absurd. However, before we take too much pride in our modern disdain of excessive pudency, we should remind ourselves that Solovyov is touching upon a phenomenon — sexual shame — of which a great many cultures have been poignantly aware, and that he nevertheless affirms the goodness of sexual love and the bearing of children; what inspires horror in him is what he sees as the demeaning subjugation of love and fertility to reproduction's merciless law of the displacement of one generation by another, which he believes involves a guilty impiety toward the generations of one's fathers (whom one implicitly wills away when one yields to the imperative of new life), and a tragic scattering of the fertility of love to the sublime indifference of *thanatos* — a kind of sowing of life in death. Whether one entirely shares Solovyov's almost neurasthenic aversion to the very idea of the sexual act, one must grant that he goes some considerable way toward identifying certain of the more occulted elements within sexual shame.

In any event, in shame we discover our moral nature through our relation to that which is, in some sense, *beneath* us (animality, natural process, and so forth), and this inspires us to seek the transfiguration — the spiritualization — of our corporeality and of the material world. We discover our moral nature through our relation to what is *equal* to us in the second feeling, pity. It is this sentiment that, progressively throughout history, human civilization attempts to embody in humane laws and rational economy, and that makes us aware that the ground of morality is not, as Schopenhauer asseverated, a metaphysical identity between ourselves and all others (for then we should feel not *pity* but only indignation or pain), but the irreducible difference of ourselves from all others. And we discover our moral nature through what is *above* us in our reverence, our piety, our need to venerate and adore, to offer thanks and confess our guilt. Early on, the religious impulse naturally and correctly, says Solovyov, takes the form of ancestor worship — gratitude and indebtedness to those through whom we receive life and all the cultural and material benefits bequeathed to us from earlier generations — which becomes in time worship of the gods, and ultimately an awareness of and awe before the transcendent God from whom all being flows.

As much, however, as Solovyov situates his ethical philosophy in these innate and seemingly "subjective" feelings, what makes the first part of this book such a tour de force is the seamless development of his argument toward the "objective" form of human morality: the God-man. Each of the three primary moral sentiments necessarily seeks expression in the cultural, political, and religious forms of human society, and thereby strives toward its own particular perfection. From this labor to attain the Good, as it announces itself within our most aboriginal feelings, comes the dynamism of history. From it also comes an ever greater awareness of the *moral* enormity of death — the futility to which death reduces every spiritual aspiration and every human project — and the consequent discovery that the secret logic of the ethical is one of resurrection: the restoration of all things, the Kingdom of God, the divinization of humanity. It is clear that Solovyov sees the course of human history as unfolding toward the Kingdom; but it is equally clear that he does not see this development in strictly linear terms, as though the Kingdom were merely the natural and inevitable conclusion of social evolution. Rather, he believes that humanity must necessarily arrive at a certain level of civilization and a certain state of spiritual refinement before God can reveal himself — and reveal the true end of humankind — in the incarnation and, finally, in the transfiguration of all things in Christ; and, for Christ to be seen clearly as the light of the world, every possibility of moral, religious, and aesthetic creativity must be passed through by humanity as a whole. The Good acts as a kind of *primum mobile* in history, drawing all of creation onward to its ideal end, prompting lower nature to strive after the higher, and the human will to translate its (sophianic) longing into concrete historical forms. The sheer cosmic scope of this vision of ethics finds its loveliest expression in Solovyov's elegant redaction of the *principium plenitudinis,* his doctrine of the five Kingdoms; each of these Kingdoms — the mineral, vegetal, animal, human, and divine — says Solovyov, is "translated" and exalted in the next. Each, in order, comprises one moment in the development of creation toward its union with the divine: to be, to live, to be conscious, to be rational, to be perfect. Plants absorb the nutrients of the earth and transform them into vitality; animals absorb the world not only as food but in varying degrees of consciousness; humanity raises the world up into rational reflection; and finally the God-man (as reason, Logos, incarnate) actively realizes the perfect moral order of all things in himself. The great chain of being has, in a sense, been given eschatological depth; the world-process gathers the universe into a living and diverse unity, and humanity gathers it again into rational and ordering thought, and the God-man gathers it together into its ultimate reality — the infinite moral order: universal resurrection. Thus, when the Kingdom comes, it does not abolish any of the lower orders of existence, but rather puts them in their proper places within the unity of the Logos.

In any event — not to anticipate the entire argument of Part I — what the reader should keep constantly in mind is that the underlying logic of Solovyov's justification of the idea of the Good, governing every step of his argument, is that of high Chalcedonian Christology. His point of departure may consist in the most minimal ethical conditions imaginable — human feelings — but his aim throughout is to demonstrate that the sources of morality within humanity can have no ultimate end but the union of the human and the divine in Christ, who is himself the full reality and concrete ideal of all ethical truth. Solovyov emphatically insists that human nature does not contain, nor can it give rise to, the *real* infinity of perfection that the idea of the Good in us adumbrates; but, by virtue of a universal meaning inherent in rational nature, humanity contains the *possibility* of such perfection, a "capacity" for the divine, an openness to what it could never, of itself, attain. Human perfection, he says, cannot be merely human; for the human is nothing but the preparation for — not the cause of — the divinely human. Jesus is not the "last word" of the human kingdom — he is not the man-god — but the first Word of the Kingdom of God — the God-man. And all history culminates in the new humanity born spiritually from Christ, whose triumph over every moral evil in the course of a life perfectly devoted to the Father, and triumph over the ultimate physical evil of death at Easter, is nothing less than the revelation within time of the eschatological Kingdom for which creation restlessly yearns. This then, for Solovyov, is the new foundation for all ethics: the essential moral task of humanity is to accept Christ, to see everything in the light of his Spirit, to seek to give form to the Spirit's presence in all human works, and to cultivate a "Marian" will within every soul, able truly to say, "Be it unto me according to thy Word." In practical terms, says Solovyov, this means that it is necessary to establish a Christian — and discern the anti-Christian — approach to every sphere of existence. For Christ has withdrawn from history, and given time over to his Spirit, that we might in all our works and ways learn to consent to what he has accomplished, obedient to his command: "Be ye perfect."

III

Part II of *The Justification of the Good* is the "practical" complement to the "theoretical" investigations of Part I. Here Solovyov's argument descends from the general to the particular, as it attempts to delineate precisely what the peculiarly Christian form of every area of moral endeavor is. This section of the book requires little introduction; depending on the reader's temperament, it is either the most substantial or the most time-bound portion of the text. Some of Solovyov's prescriptions, viewed in long retrospect, certainly appear a bit anachronistic (there is an especially grim irony in his expressions of hope for a united *Christian* Europe). As a whole, however, these pages abound in *trouvailles* and moments of penetrating insight: Solovyov's interpretations of Buddhism and Platonism, his reading of *Antigone* as a drama reflecting the transition of Western culture from clan to state, his sober defense of the state, his judicious rejection of pacifism, his novel treatment of marriage, his defense of property and inheritance as having spiritual significance, his rejection of both cosmopolitan internationalism and nativist nationalism, and so on.

Perhaps the most interesting portions of this part of the book (at least, given certain of the special preoccupations of modern theology) are those that deal with political economy. Here Solovyov undertakes a Christian critique of both classical capitalist liberalism and classical theoretical socialism by treating them not merely as dialectical extremes between which he hopes to chart a middle course, but as two sides of the same materialist heresy. If one were to seek analogies to Solovyov's own political economic vision, one might look to the distributism of Belloc and Chesterton, or to certain aspects of the American Southern agrarian movement, or to various Catholic schools of subsidiarity, or to that grand suspicion of materialist modernity — always solicitous of the local and the fragile — found in thinkers like Russell Kirk or Wendell Berry; but Solovyov's thought is more audacious than most Christian political theories because it is so indissolubly bound to the theology of divinization. "The absolute value of man," he writes, "is based, as we know, upon the *possibility* inherent in his reason and his will of infinitely approaching perfection or, according to the patristic expression, the possibility of becoming divine [θέωσις]." It is from this principle that he develops his three maxims of economic reform: that material wealth is not the correct goal of economic activity; that workers have a limitless dignity and are thus not to be made instruments of production; and that Christians have a responsibility to the earth. He accepts that a Christian society should guarantee a minimum degree of stability and subsistence for all persons, but he rejects the redistribution of wealth in favor of a broad distribution of property (the proximity to distributism is here especially obvious). Neither capitalism nor socialism, in his view, can answer to the spiritual dignity of the human world of production and community; he seems to regard the choice between them as a choice between individualist and collectivist nihilisms, which can at best parody either Christian freedom or Christian charity, but which can arrive at no real end other than a "passive disintegration" of society into individual units of will or an authoritarian social violence that elevates envy above gratitude or generosity. If classical liberalism separates the economic sphere from the moral, socialism confuses them, and both are degrading to the spirit. As far as Solovyov is concerned, laissez-faire economics has no place in any but a dying culture, in which the organic unity of a nation is progressively disintegrating; but the socialism of Saint-Simon, for instance, is at home only in a society in which the law of the Good has been displaced by material law. Indeed, socialism is even more monomaniacally economist than capitalism; at least plutocratic ethics recognizes institutions somewhat separate from and independent of the purely economic, like the Church and the state, but socialism really cannot. Socialism reduces human existence to the same base interests (though under the category of production rather than wealth) as does the most pitiless capitalism, and so — finally — there is no *inner* opposition between the two: "consistent socialism," he remarks, "is certainly not an antithesis to, but the extreme expression, the crowning stage of the one-sided bourgeois civilization."

I dwell on this part of Solovyov's argument not simply to enter a brief in its behalf, but to call attention, again, to the underlying logic of his argument as a whole. Today there are many who might argue for models of Christian capitalism and Christian socialism who would dismiss Solovyov's remarks as remnants of sincere but obsolete negotiations with industrial-age ideology (though I suspect that, if honest, such apologists would still find aspects of his critique quite solvent, at least of a certain subtle alliance between corporate and state power in liberal societies, and of the mutually profitable accommodation struck between them). What is most of interest here is *why* Solovyov is so uncompromising in his (final) rejection of the modern world's two dominant forms of economic and political discourse, and in favor of *what*. The answer is quite clear: he rejects any approach to social, political, or moral order that he sees as inimical to the communal life of the Church, which is in his view the culmination of all "moral organization." True, he defends both state and Church — as necessarily complementary structures of "pity" and "piety" — but it is a Christian state of which he speaks, embraced within the Church and legitimated thereby. We find, at the end of Solovyov's great ethical treatise, that the Good is grace, which does not abolish the natural institutions of nation, law, or civic order, but transforms them into regions of spiritual labor. Outside the Church, however, the only morality of which these institutions are capable is a negative morality: that is, the morality of legal rights, defense against one's neighbors, the negative liberty of equal protection and unprejudiced jurisprudence (all of which is admirable, as far as it goes). Only the Church realizes the unconditional value of each person in a "positive" morality, an association of rational souls reborn in the God-man, striving together to manifest in their works of love the Kingdom of God revealed in Christ.

At the last, then, Solovyov's letter to Kireev is not belied by the ethical "system" of *The Justification of the Good,* but confirmed. Just as Solovyov's investigations of the human constants at the ground of moral consciousness necessarily culminate in Christology, so his considerations of the practical particulars of ethical existence necessarily culminate in ecclesiology. For Christian thought, the whole of morality — not merely for human society, but for the whole of history and nature — is found ultimately only in the relation between Christ and his bride the Church.

IV

This edition of *The Justification of the Good* reproduces the English edition of 1918, in the translation of Nathalie A. Duddington. Between that edition and this, no English version of the text has appeared. Duddington was born in Russia but was a British subject, and was a philosopher in her own right with a deep understanding of Russian philosophy in its many forms. She was also a translator of works by S. L. Frank and Nikolai Lossky. The text has been scrupulously edited by the indefatigable Boris Jakim, who has made a few minor modifications in the translation, and who has provided explanatory footnotes throughout.

Solovyov refers to several of his own works in the text. Mindful of this, Jakim has provided the following bibliography of Solovyov's major philosophical and religious works, with both their Russian and English titles, and with references to the English translations currently available.

DAVID BENTLEY HART

Krizis zapadnoi filosofii: Protiv pozitivistov, 1874. Translated by Boris Jakim as *The Crisis of Western Philosophy: Against the Positivists.* Hudson, N.Y.: Lindisfarne Press, 1996.

Filosofskie printsipi tsel'nogo znaniia [*The Philosophical Principles of Integral Knowledge*], 1877.

Kritika otvlechennykh nachal [*The Critique of Abstract Principles*], 1877-1880.

Chteniia o Bogochelovechestve, 1877-1881. Translated by Peter Zouboff as *Lectures on Divine Humanity.* Edited by Boris Jakim. Hudson, N.Y.: Lindisfarne Press, 1995.

La Russie et l'Eglise universelle, 1888. Translated from the French by H. Rees as *Russia and the Universal Church.* London: Centenary Press, 1948.

Dukhovnye osnovy zhizni [*The Spiritual Foundations of Life*], 1884. Translated (from the French) by Donald Attwater as *God, Man, and the Church: The Spiritual Foundations of Life.* Milwaukee: Bruce Publishing, 1938; London: James Clarke, 1938, 1973.

Smysl liubvi, 1892-1894. Translated by Jane Marshall as *The Meaning of Love.* London: Centenary Press, 1945. Revised edition: West Stockbridge, Mass.: Lindisfarne Press, 1985.

Osnovy teoreticheskoi filosofii [*Foundations of Theoretical Philosophy*], 1897-1899.

1

Part I translated by Vlada Tolley and James Scanlan in vol. 3 (pp. 99-134) of *Russian Philosophy*, 3 vols. Chicago: University of Chicago Press, 1965.

Opravdanie dobra: Nravstvennaya filosofiia [*The Justification of the Good*], 1897.

Tri razgovora o voine, progresse, i kontse istorii, i kratkaya povest' ob Antikhriste, 1900. Translated by Alexander Bakshy as *Three Conversations Concerning War, Progress, and the End of History, Including a Short Tale of the Antichrist.* London, 1915. Revised edition: Hudson, N.Y.: Lindisfarne Press, 1990.

Solovyov's Preface to the Second Edition

The object of this book is *to show the Good as truth and righteousness,* that is, as the only right and consistent way of life in all things and to the end, for all who decide to follow it. I mean the Good *as such;* it alone justifies itself and justifies our confidence in it. And it is not for nothing that before the open grave, when all else has obviously failed, we call to this essential Good and say, "Blessed art thou, O Lord: teach me thy justification."[1]

In the individual, national, and historical life of humanity, the Good justifies itself by its own good and right ways. A moral philosophy, true to the Good, having discovered these ways in the past, indicates them to the present for the future.

When, in setting out on a journey, you take up a *guide-book,* you seek in it nothing but true, complete, and clear directions with regard to the route chosen. This book will not persuade you to go to Italy or Switzerland if you have decided to go to Siberia, nor will it provide you with money to traverse the oceans if you can only pay the fare down to the Black Sea.

Moral philosophy is no more than a systematic guide to the right way of life's journey for men and nations; the author is only responsible for his directions being correct, complete, and coherent. But no exposition of the moral norms — *i.e.,* of the conditions for attaining the true purpose of life — can have any meaning for the man who consciously puts before him an utterly different aim. To indicate the necessary stations on the road to the better, when the worse has been definitely chosen, is not merely a useless but an annoying and even insulting thing to do, for it brings the bad choice back to

---

1. Here the King James translation has been modified to make it agree with the Russian Bible. Cf. Psalm 119.2. — *Editor's note.*

lii

one's mind, especially when in our inmost heart the choice is unconsciously and in spite of ourselves felt to be both bad and irrevocable.

I have not the slightest intention of preaching virtue and denouncing vice; I consider this to be both an idle and an immoral occupation for a simple mortal, since it presupposes an unjust and proud claim to be better than other people. What matters, from the point of view of moral philosophy, are not the particular deviations from the right way, however great they may be, but only the general, definite, and decisive *choice* between two moral paths, a choice made with full deliberation. The question may be asked whether every man makes such a choice. It certainly is not made by people who die in their infancy, and, so far as clear consciousness of self is concerned, many grown-up people are not far removed from babes. Moreover, it should be noted that even when conscious choice has been made, it cannot be observed from outside. The distinction of principle between the two paths has no empirical *definiteness*, and cannot be practically *defined*. I have seen many strange and wondrous things, but two objects have I never come across in nature: a man who has attained perfect righteousness, and a man who has become utterly evil. And all the pseudo-mystical cant based upon external and practically applicable divisions of humanity into the sheep and the goats, the regenerate and the unregenerate, the saved and the damned, simply reminds me of the frank words of the miller —

> Forty years have I lived
> And everywhere have I been,
> But copper spurs on water pails
> I have never seen.[2]

At the same time I think of the lectures I heard long ago at the University on embryology and zoology of the invertebrate. These lectures enabled me, among other things, to form a definite conception of two well-known truths, namely, that at the lowest stages of organic life no one but a learned biologist, and sometimes not even he, can distinguish the vegetable from the animal forms, and that at the early stages of the intra-uterine life only a learned embryologist can tell, and not always with certainty, the embryo of man from the embryo of some other creature, often of a distinctly unpleasant one. It is the same with the history of humanity and with the moral world. At the early stages the two paths are very close together, and outwardly indistinguishable.

---

2. From Pushkin's poem "Scenes from the Days When Knighthood Was in Flower." — *Editor's note.*

But why, it will be asked, do I speak, with regard to the moral world, of the choice between *two* paths only? The reason is, that in spite of all the multiplicity of the forms and expressions of life, one path only leads to the life that we hope for and renders it eternal. All other paths, which at first seem so like it, lead in the opposite direction, fatally draw farther and farther away from it, and finally become merged together in the one path of eternal death.

In addition to these two paths that differ in principle, some thinkers try to discover a third path, which is neither good nor bad, but natural or animal. Its supreme practical principle is best expressed by a German aphorism, which, however, was unknown both to Kant and to Hegel: *Jedes Tierchen hat sein Plaisirchen.*[3] This formula expresses an unquestionable truth, and only stands in need of amplification by another truth, equally indisputable: *Allen Tieren fatal ist zu krepieren.*[4] And when this necessary addition is made, the third path — that of animality made into a principle — is seen to be reduced to the second path of death.[5] It is impossible for man to avoid the dilemma, the final choice between the two paths — of good and of evil. Suppose, indeed, we decide to take the third, the animal path, which is neither good nor bad, but merely natural. It is natural for animals, just because animals do not decide anything, do not choose between this path and any other, but passively follow the only one upon which they have been placed by a will foreign to them. But when man *actively* decides to follow the path of moral *passivity,* he is clearly guilty of falsehood, wrong, and sin, and is obviously entering not upon the animal path, but upon that of the two human paths which proves in the end, if not at the beginning, to be the path of eternal evil and death. It is indeed easy to see from the first that it is *worse* than the animal path. Our younger brothers are deprived of reason, but they undoubtedly possess an inner sense; and although they cannot consciously condemn and be ashamed of their nature and its bad, mortal way, they obviously suffer from it; they long for something better which they do not know but which they dimly feel. This truth, once powerfully expressed by St. Paul (Rom. 8:19-23), and less powerfully repeated by Schopenhauer, is entirely confirmed by observation. Never does a human face bear the expression of that profound, hopeless melancholy which, for no apparent reason, overshadows sometimes the faces of animals. It is impossible for man to stop at the animal self-satisfaction, if only because animals are not in the least self-satisfied. A conscious human being cannot be

---

3. "Every little beast has its little pleasures." — *Editor's note.*

4. "Every beast is fated to drop dead." — *Editor's note.*

5. The pseudo-superhuman path, thrown into vivid light by the madness of the unhappy Nietzsche, comes to the same thing. See below, Preface to the First Edition.

an animal, and, whether he will or no, he must choose between two paths. He must either become higher and better than his material nature, or become lower and worse than the animal. And the essentially human attribute which man cannot be deprived of consists not in the fact that he becomes this or that, but in the fact that he *becomes*. Man gains nothing by slandering his younger brothers and falsely describing as animal and natural the path of diabolical persistence in the wrong — the path which he himself has chosen, and which is opposed both to life and to nature.

What I most desired to show in this book is the manner in which the one way of the Good, while remaining true to itself, and, consequently, justifying itself, grows in completeness and definiteness as the conditions of the historical and natural environment become more complex. The chief claim of my theory is to establish in and through the unconditional principle of morality the complete inner connection between true religion and sound politics. It is a perfectly harmless claim, since true religion cannot force itself upon any one, and politics is free to be as unsound as it likes — at its own risk, of course. At the same time moral philosophy makes no attempt to guide particular individuals by laying down any external and absolutely definite rules of conduct. If any passage in the book should strike the reader as 'moralising' he will find that either he has misunderstood my meaning or that I did not express myself with sufficient clearness.

But I have done my best to be clear. While preparing this second edition I read the book over five times in the course of nine months, every time making fresh additions, both small and great, by way of explanation. Many defects of exposition still remain, but I hope they are not of such a nature as to lay me open to the menace, "Cursed be he that doeth the work of the Lord halfheartedly."[6]

Whilst I was engaged in writing this book I sometimes experienced moral benefit from it; perhaps this is an indication that the book will not be altogether useless for the reader also. If this should be the case it will be enough to justify this 'justification of the good.'

VLADIMIR SOLOVYOV
MOSCOW, December 8, 1898

6. Jeremiah 48:10. Here the King James translation has been modified to make it agree with the Russian Bible. — *Editor's note.*

Solovyov's Preface to the First Edition

A PRELIMINARY CONCEPTION
OF THE MORAL MEANING OF LIFE

Is there any meaning in life? If there is, is that meaning moral in character, and is its root in the moral sphere? In what does it consist, and what is its true and complete definition? These questions cannot be avoided, and there is no agreement with regard to them in modern consciousness. Some thinkers deny all meaning to life, others maintain that the meaning of life has nothing to do with morality, and in no way depends upon our right or good relation to God, men, and the world as a whole; the third admit the importance of the moral norms for life, but give conflicting definitions of them, which stand in need of analysis and criticism.

Such analysis cannot in any case be dismissed as unnecessary. At the present stage of human consciousness the few who already possess a firm and final solution of the problem of life *for themselves* must justify it *for others*. An intellect which has overcome its own doubts does not render the heart indifferent to the delusions of others.

I

Some of those who deny the meaning of life are in earnest about it, and end by taking the practical step of committing suicide. Others are not in earnest, and deny the meaning of life solely by means of arguments and pseudo-philosophic systems. I am certainly not opposed to arguments and systems, but I am referring to men who regard their philosophising as a thing *on its own account,* which does not bind them to any concrete actions or demand any practical realisation. These men and their intellectual exercises cannot be taken seriously. Truths like the judgment that the angles of a triangle are together equal to two right angles remain true quite independently of the person who utters them and of the life he leads; but a pessimistic valuation of life is not a mathematical truth — it necessarily includes the personal, subjective attitude to life. When the theoretical pessimist affirms as a real objective truth that life is evil and painful, he thereby expresses his conviction that this is so for *every one*, including himself. In that case, why does he go on living and enjoying the evil of life as though it were a good? It is sometimes urged that instinct compels us to live in spite of the rational conviction that life is not worth living. But this appeal to instinct is vain. Instinct is not an external mechanically compelling force, but an inner condition which prompts every living creature to seek certain states which appear to it to be pleasant or desirable. The fact that in virtue of his instinct the pessimist finds pleasure in life seems to undermine the basis of his pseudo-rational conviction that life is evil and painful. He may say that the pleasures of life are illusory. What, however, can be the meaning of these words from his point of view? If one recognises the positive meaning of life, many things may be dismissed as illusory in comparison, as drawing our attention away from the chief thing. St. Paul could say that by comparison with the kingdom of heaven, which is won through a life of renunciation, all carnal affections and pleasures are as dung and rubbish in his eyes. But a pessimist who does not believe in a kingdom of heaven, and attaches no positive significance to a life of renunciation, can have no standard for distinguishing illusion from truth.

From this point of view everything is reduced to the state of pleasure or of pain which is being actually experienced; but no pleasure while it is being experienced can be an illusion. The only way to justify pessimism on this low ground is childishly to count the number of pleasures and pains in human life, assuming all the time that the latter are more numerous than the former, and that, therefore, life is not worth living. This calculus of happiness could only have meaning if arithmetical *sums* of pleasures and pains actually existed, or if the arithmetical difference between them could itself become a sensation; since, however, in actual reality sensations exist only in the concrete, it is as absurd to reckon them in abstract figures as to shoot at a stone fortress with a cardboard gun. If the only motive for continuing to live is to be found in the surplus of the pleasurable over the painful sensations, then for the vast majority of men this surplus is a fact: men live and find that life is worth living. With them, no doubt, must be classed such theoreticians of pessimism who talk of the advantages of non-existence, but in reality prefer any kind of existence. Their arithmetic of despair is merely a play of mind which they themselves contradict, finding, in truth, more pleasure than pain in life, and admitting that it is worth living to the end. From comparing their theory with their practice one can only conclude that life has a meaning and that they involuntarily submit to it, but that their intellect is not strong enough to grasp that meaning.

Pessimists who are in earnest and commit suicide also involuntarily prove that life has a meaning. I am thinking of conscious and self-possessed suicides, who kill themselves because of disappointment or despair. They supposed that life had a certain meaning which made it worth living, but became convinced that that meaning did not hold good. Unwilling to submit passively and unconsciously — as the theoretical pessimists do — to a different and unknown meaning, they take their own life. This shows, no doubt, that they have a stronger will than the former, but proves nothing as against the meaning of life. These men failed to discover it, but what did they seek it in? There are two types of passionate men among them: the passion of some is purely personal and selfish (Romeo, Werther), that of others is connected with some general interest which, however, they separate from the meaning of existence as a whole (Cleopatra, Cato of Utica). Neither the first nor the second care to know the meaning of universal life, although the meaning of their own existence depends upon it. Romeo killed himself because he could not have Juliet. The meaning of life for him was to possess that woman. If, however, this really were the meaning of life, it would be wholly irrational. In addition to Romeo forty thousand gentlemen might find the meaning of their life in possessing that same Juliet, so that this supposed meaning would forty thousand times contradict itself. Allowing for difference in detail, we find the same thing at the bottom of every suicide: life is not what *in my opinion* it ought to be, therefore life is senseless and is not worth living. The absence of correspondence between the arbitrary demands of a passionate nature and the reality is taken to be the result of some hostile fate, terrible and senseless, and a man kills himself rather than submit to this blind force. It is the same thing with persons belonging to the second type. The queen of Egypt, conquered by the world-wide power of Rome, would not take part in the conqueror's triumph, and killed herself by means of a poisonous snake. Horace, a Roman, called her a great woman for doing it, and no one would deny that there is a grandeur about her death. But if Cleopatra was looking to her own victory as to a thing that ought to be, and regarded the victory of Rome as simply the senseless triumph of an irrational force, she, too, took her own blindness to be a sufficient reason for rejecting the truth of the whole.

The meaning of life obviously cannot coincide with the arbitrary and changeable demands of each of the innumerable human entities. If it did, it would be non-meaning — that is, it would not exist at all. It follows, therefore, that a disappointed and despairing suicide was not disappointed in and despaired of the meaning of life, but, on the contrary, of his hope that life might be meaningless. He had hoped that life would go in the way he wanted it to, that it would always and in everything directly satisfy his blind passions and arbitrary whims, *i.e.* that it would be senseless — of *that* he was disappointed and found that life was not worth living. But the very fact of his being disappointed at the world not being meaningless proves that there is a meaning in it. This meaning, which the man recognises in spite of himself, may be unbearable to him; instead of understanding it he may only repine against some one and call reality by the name of a 'hostile fate,' but this does not alter the case. The meaning of life is simply confirmed by the fatal failure of those who reject it: some of them (the theoretic pessimists) must live *unworthily*, in contradiction to their own preaching, and others (the practical pessimists or the suicides) in denying the meaning of life have actually to deny their own existence. Life clearly must have a meaning, since those who deny it inevitably negate themselves, some by their unworthy existence, and others by their violent death.

II

"The meaning of life is to be found in the æsthetic aspect of it, in what is strong, majestic, beautiful. To devote ourselves to this aspect of life, to preserve and strengthen it in ourselves and in others, to make it predominant and develop it further till superhuman greatness and new purest beauty is attained, this is the end and the meaning of our existence." This view, associated with the name of the gifted and unhappy Nietzsche, has now become the fashionable philosophy in the place of the pessimism that had been popular in recent years. Unlike the latter, it does not require any criticism imported from outside, but can be disproved on its own grounds. Let it be granted that the meaning of life is to be found in strength and beauty. But, however much we may devote ourselves to the æsthetic cult, we shall find in it no protection, nor the least hope of protection, against the general and inevitable fact which destroys this supposed independence of strength and beauty, and renders void the divine and absolute character they are alleged to possess. I mean the fact that the end of all earthly strength is impotence, and the end of all earthly beauty is ugliness.

When we speak of strength, grandeur, and beauty there rises to the mind of every one, beginning with the Russian provincial schoolmaster (see Gogol's *Inspector-General*) and ending with Nietzsche himself, one and the same image, as the most perfect historical embodiment of all these æsthetic qualities taken together. This instance is sufficient.

"And it happened after that Alexander, son of Philip, the Macedonian, who came out of the land of Chittim, had smitten Darius, King of the Persians and Medes, that he reigned in his stead, the first over Greece, and made many wars, and won many strongholds, and slew the kings of the earth, and went through to the ends of the earth, and took spoils of many nations, insomuch that the earth was quiet before him, whereupon he was exalted, and his heart was lifted up. And he gathered a mighty strong host, and ruled over countries, and nations, and kings, who became tributaries unto him. And after these things he fell sick, and perceived that he should die" (Book I of the Maccabees).[1]

Is strength powerless before death really strength? Is a decomposing body a thing of beauty? The ancient embodiment of beauty and of strength died and decayed like the weakest and most hideous of creatures, and the modern worshipper of beauty and of strength became in his lifetime a mental corpse. Why is it that the first was not saved by his strength and beauty, and the second by his cult of it? No one can worship a deity which saves neither those in whom it is incarnate, nor those who worship it.

In his last works the unhappy Nietzsche turned his views into a furious weapon against Christianity. In doing so he showed a low level of understanding befitting French free-thinkers of the eighteenth century rather than modern German savants. He looked upon Christianity as belonging exclusively to the lower classes, and was not even aware of the simple fact that the Gospel was from the first received not as a doubtful call to rebellion but as a joyful and certain message of sure *salvation,* that the whole force of the new religion lay in the fact that it was founded by 'the firstborn from the dead' (Col. 1:18), who had risen from the dead, and, as they firmly believed, secured eternal life to His followers. To speak of slaves and pariahs in this connection is irrelevant. Social distinctions mean nothing when it is a question of death and resurrection. Do not 'the gentle' die as well as 'the simple'? Were not Sulla the Roman aristocrat and dictator, Antiochus the king of Syria, and Herod the king of Judæa eaten up by worms while still alive? The religion of salvation cannot be the religion for slaves and 'Chandalas'[2] alone — it is the religion for all, since all need salvation. Before beginning to preach so furiously against equality, one ought to abolish the chief equaliser — death.

---

1. 1 Maccabees 1:1-5. — *Editor's note.*

2. "Chandals" or "chandalas" originally referred to Indians of the lowest caste, "untouchables." — *Editor's note.*

Nietzsche's polemic against Christianity is remarkably shallow, and his pretension to be 'antichrist' would be extremely comical had it not ended in such tragedy.[3]

The cult of natural strength and beauty is not directly opposed to Christianity, and it is not Christianity that makes it void, but its own inherent weakness. Christianity does not by any means reject strength and beauty, but it is not satisfied with the strength of a dying invalid or the beauty of a decomposing corpse. Christianity has never preached hostility to or contempt for strength, grandeur, or beauty *as such*. All Christian souls, beginning with the first of them, rejoiced at having had revealed to them the infinite source of all that is truly strong and beautiful, and at being saved by it from subjection to the false power and grandeur of the powerless and unlovely elements of the world. "My soul doth *magnify* the Lord, and my spirit hath rejoiced in God my Saviour. . . . For He that is *mighty hath done to me great* things; and holy is His name. . . . He hath *shewed strength* with His arm; He hath scattered the proud in the imagination of their hearts. He hath put down the mighty from their seats, and exalted them of low degree. He hath filled the hungry with good things, and the rich He hath sent empty away."[4] It is obvious that the contempt here is only for the false, imaginary strength and wealth, and that humility is not the absolute ideal or the final end but only the necessary and the right way to heights unattainable to the proud.

Strength and beauty are divine, but not in themselves: there is a strong and beautiful Deity whose strength is never exhausted and whose beauty never dies, for in Him strength and beauty are inseparable from the good.

No one worships impotence and ugliness; but some believe in the eternal strength and beauty which are conditioned by the good and which *actually* liberate their bearers and worshippers from the power of death and corruption, while others extol strength and beauty which are taken in the abstract and are illusory. The first doctrine may be waiting for its final victory in the future, but this does not make things any better for the second; it is conquered already, it is always being conquered — it dies with every death and is buried in all the cemeteries.

---

3. It will be remembered that after passing through a mania of greatness this unfortunate writer fell into complete idiocy.

4. Luke 1:46-47, 49, 51-53. — *Editor's note.*

III

The pessimism of false philosophers and of genuine suicides inevitably leads us to recognise that life has a meaning. The cult of strength and beauty inevitably shows that that meaning is not to be found in strength and beauty as such, but only as conditioned by the triumphant good. The meaning of life is in the good; but this opens the way for new errors in the definition of what precisely we are to understand by the good.

At first sight there appears to be a sure and simple way of avoiding any errors in this connection. If, it will be urged, the meaning of life is the good, it has revealed itself to us already and does not wait for any definition on our part. All we have to do is to accept it with love and humility, and subordinate to it our existence and our individuality, in order to make them rational. The universal meaning of life or the inner relation of separate entities to the great whole cannot have been invented by us; it was given from the first. The firm foundations of the family have been laid down from all eternity; the family by a living, personal bond connects the present with the past and the future; the fatherland widens our mind and gives it a share in the glorious traditions and aspirations of the soul of the nation; the Church, by connecting both our personal and our national life with what is absolute and eternal, finally liberates us from the limitations of a cramped existence. What, then, is there to trouble about? Live in the life of the whole, widen on all sides the limits of your small self, 'take to heart' the interests of others and the interest of all, be a good member of the family, a zealous patriot, a loyal son of the Church, and you will know the good meaning of life in practice and have no need to seek for it and look for its definition. There is an element of truth in this view, but it is only the *beginning* of truth. It is impossible to stop at this — the case is not so simple as it looks.

Had life with its good meaning assumed at once, from all eternity, one unchanging and abiding form, then there would certainly be nothing to trouble about. There would be no problem for the intellect, but only a question for the will — to accept or *unconditionally* to reject that which has been unconditionally given. This was precisely, as I understand it, the position of one of the spirits of light in the first act of the creation of the world. But our human position is less fateful and more complex. We know that the historical forms of the Good which are given to us do not form such a *unity* that we could either accept or reject them as a whole. We know also that these forms and principles of life did not drop down ready made from heaven but were developed in time and on earth. And knowing that they had *become* what they are, we have no rational ground whatever for affirming that they are finally and wholly fixed, and that what is given at the moment is entirely completed and ended. But if it is not ended, it is for us to carry on the work. In the times prior to ours the higher forms of life — now the holy heritage of the ages — did not come to be of themselves but were evolved through men, through their thought and action, through their intellectual and moral work. Since the historical form of the eternal good is not one and unchanging, the choice has to be made between many different things, and this cannot be done without the critical work of thought. It must have been ordained by God Himself that man should have no external support, no pillow for his reason and conscience to rest on, but should ever be awake and standing on his own legs. "What is man, that Thou art mindful of him? and the son of man, that Thou visitest him?"[5] Piety itself forbids us to despise in ourselves and in others that which God Himself respects, for the sake of which He remembers and visits us — namely, the inner, unique, and invaluable dignity of man's reason and conscience. And those who are guilty of such contempt and seek to replace the inner standard of truth by an external one, suffer natural retribution in the fatal failure of their attempt. The concrete, clear, and consistent minds among them — minds that cannot be content with vague phrases — accomplish with remarkable rapidity a direct descent from the certain to the doubtful, from the doubtful to the false, and from the false to the absurd. "God," they argue, "manifests His will to man externally through the authority of the Church; the only true Church is our Church, its voice is the voice of God; the true representatives of our Church are the clergy, hence their voice is the voice of God; the true representative of the clergy for each individual is his confessor; therefore all questions of faith and conscience ought in the last resort to be decided for each by his confessor." It all seems clear and simple. The only thing to be arranged is that all confessors should say the same thing, or that there should be one confessor only — omnipresent and immortal. Otherwise, the difference of opinion among many changing confessors may lead to the obviously impious view that the voice of God contradicts itself.

As a matter of fact, if *this* individual or collective representative of external authority derives his significance merely from his official position, all persons in the same position have the same authority which is rendered void by their contradicting one another. And if, on the other hand, one or some of them derive their superior authority in my eyes from the fact of my confidence in them, it follows that I myself am the source and the creator of my highest authority, and that I submit to my own arbitrary will alone and find in it the meaning of life. This is the inevitable result of seeking at all costs an *external*

---

5. Psalm 8:4. — *Editor's note.*

support for reason, and of taking the absolute meaning of life to be something that is imposed upon man from without. The man who wants to accept the meaning of life on external authority ends by taking for that meaning the absurdity of his own arbitrary choice. There must be no external, formal relation between the individual and the meaning of his life. The external authority is necessary as a transitory stage, but it must not be preserved for ever and regarded as an abiding and final norm. The human ego can only expand by giving inner heartfelt response to what is greater than itself, and not by rendering merely formal submission to it, which after all really alters nothing.

IV

Although the good meaning of life is greater than and prior to any individual man, it cannot be accepted as something ready made or taken on trust from some external authority. It must be understood by the man himself and be made his own through faith, reason, and experience. This is the necessary condition of a morally-worthy existence. When, however, this necessary subjective *condition* of the good and rational life is taken to be its essence and purpose, the result is a new moral error, namely, the rejection of all historical and collective manifestations and forms of the good, of everything except the inner moral activities and states of the individual. This moral *amorphism* or *subjectivism* is the direct opposite of the doctrine of the conservative practical humility just referred to. That doctrine affirmed that life and reality in their given condition are wiser and better than man, that the historical forms which life assumes are in themselves good and wise, and that all man has to do is reverently to bow down before them and to seek in them the absolute rule and authority for his personal existence. Moral amorphism, on the contrary, reduces everything to the subjective side, to our own self-consciousness and self-activity. The only life for us is our own mental life; the good meaning of life is to be found solely in the inner states of the individual and in the actions and relations which directly and immediately follow therefrom. This inner meaning and inner good are naturally inherent in every one, but they are crushed, distorted, and made absurd and evil by the different historical developments and institutions such as the state, the Church, and civilisation in general. If every one's eyes were open to the true state of things, people would be easily persuaded to renounce these disastrous perversions of human nature which are based in the long run upon compulsory organisations, such as the law, the army, etc. All these institutions are kept up by intentional and evil deceit and violence on the part of the minority, but their existence chiefly depends upon the lack of understanding and self-deception of the majority which, besides, employ various artificial means for blunting their reason and conscience — wine, tobacco, etc. Men, however, are beginning to realise the error of their ways, and when they finally give up their present views and change their conduct, all evil forms of human relations will fall to the ground; evil will disappear as soon as men cease to resist it by force, and the moral good will be spontaneously manifested and realised among the formless mass of 'wandering' saints.

In its rejection of different institutions moral amorphism forgets one institution which is rather important — namely, death, and it is this oversight which alone renders the doctrine plausible. For if the preachers of moral amorphism were to think of death they would have to affirm one of two things: either that with the abolition of the law courts, armies, etc., men will cease to die, or that the good meaning of life, incompatible with political kingdoms, is quite compatible with the kingdom of death. The dilemma is inevitable, and both alternatives to it are equally absurd. It is clear that this doctrine, which says nothing about death, contains it in itself. It claims to be the rehabilitation of true Christianity. It is obvious, however, both from the historical and from the psychological point of view, that the Gospel did not overlook death. Its message was based in the first place upon the resurrection of one as an accomplished fact, and upon the future resurrection of all as a certain promise. Universal resurrection means the creation of a perfect form for all that exists. It is the ultimate expression and realisation of the good meaning of the universe, and is therefore the final end of history. In recognising the good meaning of life but rejecting all its objective forms, moral amorphism must regard as senseless the whole history of the world and humanity, since it entirely consists in evolving new forms of life and making them more perfect. There is sense in rejecting one form of life for the sake of another and a more perfect one, but there is no meaning in rejecting form as such. Yet such rejection is the logical consequence of the anti-historical view. If we absolutely reject the forms of social, political, and religious life, evolved by human history, there can be no ground for recognising the organic forms worked out by the history of nature or by the world process, of which the historical process is the direct and inseparable continuation. Why should my animal body be more real, rational, and holy than the body of my nation? It will be said that the body of a people does not exist, any more than its soul, that the idea of a social collective organism is merely a metaphor for expressing the totality of distinct individuals. If, however, this exclusively mechanical point of view be once adopted, we are bound to go further still and say that in reality there is no individual organism and no individual soul, and that what exists are merely the different combinations of elementary particles of matter, devoid of all qualitative content. If the principle of form be denied, we are logically bound to give up the attempt to understand and to recognise either the historical or the organic life or any existence whatever, for it is only pure nothing that is entirely formless and unconditional.

V

I have indicated two extreme moral errors that are contradictory of one another. One is the doctrine of the self-effacement of the human personality before the historical forms of life recognised as possessing external authority — the doctrine of passive submission or practical quietism; the other is the doctrine of the self-affirmation of the human personality against all historical forms and authorities — the doctrine of formlessness and anarchy. The common essence of the two extreme views, that in which, in spite of the opposition between them, they agree, will no doubt disclose to us the source of moral errors in general, and will save us from the necessity of analysing the particular varieties of moral falsity, which may be indefinite in number.

The two opposed views coincide in the fact that neither of them takes the good in its essence, or *as it is in itself,* but connects it with acts and relations which may be either good or evil according to their motive and their end. In other words, they take something which is good, but which may become evil, and they put it in the place of the Good itself, treating the conditioned as the unconditional. Thus, for instance, it is a good thing and a moral duty to submit to national and family traditions and institutions in so far as they express the good or give a definite form to my *right* relation to God, men, and the world. If, however, this condition is forgotten, if the conditional duty is taken to be absolute and 'the national interest' is put in the place of God's truth, the good may become evil and a source of evil. It is easy in that case to arrive at the monstrous idea recently put forth by a French minister: "It is better to execute twenty innocent men than to attack *(porter atteinte)* the authority of a national institution." Take another instance. Suppose that instead of paying due respect to a council of bishops or to some other ecclesiastical authority, as a true organ of the collective organisation of piety, from which I do not separate myself, — I submit to it unconditionally, without going into the case for myself. I *assume* that this particular council *as such* is an unfailing authority, and consequently I recognise it in an external way. And then it turns out that the council to which I submitted was the

Robber Council of Ephesus,[6] or something of the kind, and that owing to my wrong and uncalled-for submission to the formal expression of the supposed will of God, I have myself suddenly become a rebellious heretic. Once more evil has come out of the good. Take a third instance. Not trusting the purity of my conscience and the power of my intellect, I entrust both my conscience and reason to a person vested with divine authority and give up reasoning and willing for myself. One would think nothing could be better. But my confessor proves to be a wolf in sheep's clothing, and instils in me pernicious thoughts and evil rules. Once more, the conditional good of humility, accepted unconditionally, becomes an evil.

Such are the results of the erroneous confusion of the good itself with the particular forms in which it is manifested. The opposite error, which limits the nature of the good by rejecting the historical forms of its expression, comes to the same thing. In the first case the forms or institutions are taken to be the absolute good, which does not correspond to truth and leads to evil. In the second case these forms and institutions are unconditionally rejected, and therefore are recognised as unconditionally evil, which is again contrary to the truth, and cannot therefore lead to anything good. The first maintains, for instance, that the will of God is revealed to us through the priest *only;* the second affirms that this never happens, that the Supreme will *cannot* speak to us through the priest, but is revealed solely and entirely in our own consciousness. It is obvious, however, that in both cases the will of God has been left out of account and replaced, in the first instance, by the priest, and in the second by the self-affirming ego. And yet one would think that there could be no difficulty in understanding that once the will of God is admitted, it ought not to be constrained, limited, or exhausted for us either by us ourselves or by the priest. The will of God may speak both in us and in him, but its only absolute and necessary demand is that we should inwardly conform to it and take up a good or right attitude to everything, including the priest, and indeed putting him before other things for the sake of what he represents. Similarly, when the first say that the practical good of life is wholly contained in the nation and the state, and the second declare the nation and the state to be a deception and an evil, it is obvious that the first put into the place of the absolute good its conditional manifestations in the nation and the state, and the second limit the absolute good by rejecting its historical forms. In their view the re-

---

6. At the Council of Ephesus (449), Dioscurus, the Patriarch of Alexandria, succeeded in imposing upon the church the language of "monophysitism," which ascribed to Christ a divine — but not a human — nature. In 451, the Fourth Ecumenical Council (at Chalcedon) condemned monophysitism as a heresy. — *Editor's note.*

jection is unconditional, and the good is conditioned by it. But it ought to be obvious that the true good in this sphere depends for us solely upon our *just and good relation to the nation and to the state,* upon the consciousness of our debt to them, upon the recognition of all that they have contained in the past and contain now, and of what they must still acquire before they can become in the full sense the means of embodying the good that lives in humanity. It is possible for us to take up this just attitude to the Church, the nation, and the state, and thus to render both ourselves and them more perfect; we can know and love them in their true sense, in God's way. Why, then, should we distort this true sense by unconditional worship, or, worse still, by unconditional rejection? There is no reason why, instead of doing rightful homage to the sacred forms, and neither separating them from, nor confusing them with, their content, we should pass from idolatry to iconoclasm, and from it to a new and worse idolatry.

There is no justification for these obvious distortions of the truth, these obvious deviations from the right way. It is as clear as day that the only thing which ought to be unconditionally accepted is that which is intrinsically good in itself, and the only thing which ought to be rejected is that which is wholly and essentially evil, while all other things ought to be either accepted or rejected according to their actual relation to this inner essence of good or evil. It is clear that if the good exists it must possess its own inner definitions and attributes, which do not finally depend upon any historical forms and institutions, and still less upon the rejection of them.

The moral meaning of life is originally and ultimately determined by the good itself, inwardly accessible to us through our reason and conscience in so far as these *inner* forms of the good are freed by moral practice from slavery to passions and from the limitations of personal and collective selfishness. This is the ultimate court of appeal for all external forms and events. "Know ye not that we shall judge angels?" St. Paul writes to the faithful.[7] And if even the heavenly things are subject to our judgment, this is still more true of all earthly things. Man is in principle or in his destination an *unconditional* inner form of the good as an unconditional content; all else is conditioned and relative. The good as such is not conditioned by anything, but itself conditions all things, and is realised through all things. In so far as the good is not conditioned by anything, it is *pure;* in so far as it conditions all things, it is *all-embracing;* and in so far as it is realised through all things, it is all-powerful.

If the good were not pure, if it were impossible in each practical question

7. 1 Corinthians 6:3. — *Editor's note.*

to draw an absolute distinction between good and evil, and in each particular case to say *yes* or *no*, life would be altogether devoid of moral worth and significance. If the good were not all-embracing, if it were impossible to connect with it all the concrete relations of life, to justify the good in all of them, and to correct them all by the good, life would be poor and one-sided. Finally, if the good had no power, if it could not in the end triumph over everything, including 'the last enemy death,'[8] — life would be in vain.

The inner attributes of the good determine the main problem of human life; its moral meaning is to be found in the service of the pure, all-powerful, and all-embracing good.

To be worthy of its object and of man himself, such service must be *voluntary,* and in order to be that it must be conscious. It is the business of moral philosophy to make it an object of reflective consciousness, and partly to anticipate the result which our reflection must attain. The founder of moral philosophy *as a science,* Kant, dwelt upon the first essential attribute of the absolute good, its purity, which demands from man a formally unconditional or autonomous will. The pure good demands that it should be chosen for its own sake alone; any other motives are unworthy of it. Without repeating what Kant has done so well with regard to the question of the formal purity of the good will, I have paid particular attention to the second essential attribute of the good, namely, its all-embracing character. In doing so I did not separate it from the other two attributes (as Kant had done with regard to the first), but directly developed the rational and ideal content of the all-embracing good out of the concrete moral data in which it is contained. As a result, I obtained not the dialectical moments of the abstract Idea, as in Hegel, nor the empirical complications of natural facts, as in Herbert Spencer, but complete and exhaustive moral norms for all the fundamental practical relations of the individual and the collective life. It is its all-embracing character alone which justifies the good to our consciousness; it is only in so far as it conditions all things that it can manifest both its purity and its invincible power.

VLADIMIR SOLOVYOV

---

8. 1 Corinthians 15:26. — *Editor's note.*

Moral Philosophy as an Independent Science

I

The subject-matter of moral philosophy is the idea of the *good;* the purpose of this philosophical inquiry is to make clear the content that reason, under the influence of experience, puts into this idea, and thus to give a definite answer to the essential question as to what *ought to be* the object or the meaning of our life.

The capacity of forming rudimentary judgments of value is undoubtedly present in the higher animals, who, in addition to pleasant and unpleasant *sensations,* possess more or less complete *ideas* of desirable or undesirable objects. Man passes beyond single sensations and particular images and rises to a universal rational *concept* or idea of good and evil.

The universal character of this idea is often denied, but this is due to a misunderstanding. It is true that every conceivable kind of iniquity has at some time and in some place been regarded as a good. But at the same time there does not exist, nor ever has existed, a people which did not attribute to its idea of the good (whatever that idea might be) the character of being a universal and abiding *norm* and ideal.[1] A Red Indian who considers it a virtue to scalp as many human heads as possible, takes it to be good and meritorious, not for one day merely but for all his life, and not for himself alone, but for every decent man. An Eskimo whose idea of the highest good is the greatest possible

---

1. In these *preliminary* remarks, which are merely introductory, I intentionally take the idea of the good in its original complexity, *i.e.* not merely in the sense of the moral worth of our actions, but also in the sense of objects which are generally regarded as desirable to possess or to enjoy ("all one's goods," etc.). Some doctrines deny that there is any such distinction, and I cannot presuppose it before the matter has been subjected to a philosophical analysis.

supply of putrid seal and cod-fish fat, undoubtedly regards his ideal as of universal application; he is convinced that what is good for him is also good for all times and all people, and even for the world beyond the grave; and if he be told of barbarians to whom putrid fat is disgusting, he will either disbelieve that they exist or will deny that they are normal. In the same way, the famous Hottentot who maintained that it is good when *he* steals a number of cows and bad when they are stolen *from* him, did not intend this ethical principle for himself only, but meant that for *every* man the good consisted in successful appropriation of other people's property, and evil in the loss of one's own.

Thus even this extremely imperfect application of the idea of the good undoubtedly involves its formal universality, *i.e.* its affirmation as a norm for all time and for all human beings, although the content of the supposed norm (*i.e.* the particular answers to the question, What is good?) does not in any way correspond to this formal demand, being merely accidental, particular, and crudely material in character. Of course the moral ideas even of the lowest savage are not limited to scalped heads and stolen cows: the same Iroquois and Hottentots manifest a certain degree of modesty in sexual relations, feel pity for those dear to them, are capable of admiring other people's superiority. But as long as these rudimentary manifestations of true morality are found side by side with savage and inhuman demands, or even give precedence to the latter, as long as ferocity is prized above modesty, and rapacity above compassion, it has to be admitted that the idea of the good, though preserving its universal form, is devoid of its true content.

The activity of reason which gives rise to ideas is inherent in man from the first, just as an organic function is inherent in the organism. It cannot be denied that alimentary organs and their functions are *innate* in the animal; but no one takes this to mean that the animal is born with the food already in its mouth. In the same way, man is not born with ready-made ideas, but only with a ready-made faculty of being conscious of ideas.

The rational consciousness in virtue of which man possesses from the first a universal idea of the good as an absolute norm, in its further development gradually supplies this formal idea with a content worthy of it. It seeks to establish such moral demands and ideals as would in their very essence be universal and necessary, expressing the inner development of the universal idea of the good and not merely its external application to particular material motives foreign to it. When this work of human consciousness developing a true content of morality attains a certain degree of clearness and distinctness, and is carried on in a systematic way, it becomes *moral philosophy* or *ethics*. The different ethical systems and theories exhibit various degrees of completeness and self-consistency.

II

In its essence moral philosophy is most intimately connected with religion, and, in its mode of knowledge, with the theoretical philosophy. It cannot at this stage be explained what the nature of the connection is, but it is both possible and necessary to explain what *it is not*. It must not be conceived of as a one-sided *dependence* of ethics on positive religion or on speculative philosophy — a dependence which would deprive the moral sphere of its special content and independent significance. The view which *wholly* subordinates morality and moral philosophy to the *theoretical* principles of positive religion or philosophy is extremely prevalent in one form or another. The erroneousness of it is all the more clear to me because I myself at one time came very near it, if indeed I did not share it altogether. Here are some of the considerations which led me to abandon this point of view; I give only such as can be understood before entering upon an exposition of moral philosophy itself.

The opponents of independent morality urge that "only true religion can give man the strength to realise the good; but the whole value of the good is in its realisation; therefore apart from true religion ethics has no significance." That true religion does give its true followers the strength to realise the good, cannot be doubted. But the one-sided assertion that such strength is given *by religion alone,* though it is supposed to be made in the higher interests of religion, in truth, directly contradicts the teaching of the great defender of faith, St. Paul, who admits, it will be remembered, that the heathen can do good according to the natural law. "For when the Gentiles," he writes, "which have not the law, do by nature the things contained in the law, these, having not the law, are a law unto themselves: which show the work of the law written in their hearts, their conscience also bearing witness, and their thoughts the meanwhile accusing or else excusing one another."[2]

In order to receive the power for realising the good, it is necessary to have a conception of the good — otherwise its realisations will be merely mechanical. And it is not true that the whole value of good is in the fact of its realisation: the *way* in which it is realised is also important. An unconscious automatic accomplishment of good actions is beneath the dignity of man and consequently does not express the human good. The human realisation of the good is necessarily conditioned by a consciousness of it, and there can be

---

2. ὅταν γὰρ ἔθνη τὰ μὴ νόμον ἔχοντα φύσει τὰ τοῦ νόμου ποιῶσιν, οὗτοι νόμον μὴ ἔχοντες ἑαυτοῖς εἰσιν νόμος· οἵτινες ἐνδείκνυνται τὸ ἔργον τοῦ νόμου γραπτὸν ἐν ταῖς καρδίαις αὐτῶν, συμμαρτυρούσης αὐτῶν τῆς συνειδήσεως καὶ μεταξὺ ἀλλήλων τῶν λογισμῶν κατηγορούντων ἢ καὶ ἀπολογουμένων. Romans 2:14-15.

consciousness of the good apart from true religion as is shown both by history and by everyday experience, and confirmed by the testimony of so great a champion of the faith as St. Paul.[3]

Further, though piety requires us to admit that the power for the realisation of the good is given from God, it would be impious to limit the Deity with regard to the means whereby this power can be communicated. According to the witness both of experience and of the Scriptures, such means are not limited to *positive* religion, for even apart from it some men are conscious of the good, and practise it. So that from the religious point of view also, we must simply accept this as true, and consequently admit that in a certain sense morality is independent of the positive religion and moral philosophy of a creed.[4]

A third consideration leads to the same conclusion. However great our certainty of the truth of our own religion may be, it does not warrant our overlooking the fact that there exist a number of religions, and that each of them claims for itself to be the only true one. And this fact creates in every mind that is not indifferent to truth a desire for an objective justification of our own faith — for such proof in favour of it, that is, as would be convincing not only to us but also to others, and, finally, to all. But all the arguments in favour of religious truth which are universally applicable amount to a single fundamental one — the ethical argument, which affirms that our faith is morally superior to others. This is the case even when the moral interest is completely concealed by other motives. Thus in support of one's religion one may point to the beauty of its church services. This argument must not be dismissed too lightly. Had the beauty of the Greek service in the cathedral of St. Sophia not impressed the envoys of Prince Vladimir of Kiev as much as it did, Russia would probably not have been Orthodox now.[5] But whatever the

3. What St. Paul says of the Gentiles of his time is no doubt applicable to men who in the Christian era were unable to accept Christianity either because they had not heard of it or because it had been misrepresented to them. And when they do good they do it according to the natural law "written in their hearts."

4. Of course, what is here denied is dependence in the strict sense, *i.e.* such a relation between two objects that one of them is entirely presupposed by the other and cannot exist apart from it. All I maintain so far is that ethics is not in *this sense* dependent upon *positive* religion, without at all prejudging the question as to the actual connection between them or their mutual dependence *in concreto*. As to the so-called natural or rational religion, the very conception of it has arisen on the ground of moral philosophy and, as will be shown in its due course, has no meaning apart from it. At present I am only concerned with the view which has, of late, become rather prevalent, that the moral life is wholly determined by the dogmas and institutions of a positive religion and must be entirely subordinate to them.

5. According to tradition, in the year 988 Prince Vladimir of Kiev, taking counsel of his en-

importance of this side of religion may be, the question is, in what precisely does the æsthetic value of one service as compared with another consist? It certainly does not lie in the fact that its form and setting should be distinguished by any kind of beauty. Beauty of form as such (*i.e.* the perfection of the sensuous expression of anything) may attach to the most diverse objects. A ballet, an opera, a military or an erotic picture, a firework, may all be said to have a beauty of their own. But the introduction of such manifestations of the beautiful, in however small a degree, into a religious cult, is rightly censured as incompatible with its true dignity. The æsthetic value of a religious service does not then lie merely in the perfection of its sensuous form, but in its expressing as clearly and as fully as possible the spiritual contents of true religion. These contents are in part dogmatic, but chiefly ethical (in the wide sense) — the holiness of God, His love for men, the gratitude and the devotion of men to their Heavenly Father, their brotherhood with one another. This ideal essence, embodied in the persons and events of sacred history, finds, through this sacred historical prism, new artistic incarnation in the rites, the symbols, and the anthems of the Church. The spiritual essence of religion appeals to some men only as thus embodied in the cult, while other men (whose number increases as consciousness develops) are able, in addition, to apprehend it directly as a doctrine; and in this case again the moral side of religious beauty clearly predominates over the dogmatic side. The metaphysical dogmas of true Christianity, in spite of all their inward certainty, are undoubtedly above the level of ordinary human reason, and therefore have never been, nor ever can be, the *original* means of convincing non-Christians of the truth of our religion. In order to realise the truth of these dogmas by faith, one must already be a Christian; and in order to realise their meaning in the sphere of abstract thought, one must be a philosopher of the school of Plato or of Schelling. And as this cannot be possible for every one, all that remains for persuading people belonging to other religions of the truth of our faith is its moral superiority.[6] And indeed, in the disputes between the different branches of one and the same religion, as well as between different religions, each side seeks to justify its own faith by means of moral and practical arguments. Thus Roman Catholics most readily quote in their own favour the solidarity and the energetic work of their clergy, united by the

---

voys, converted from his native paganism to Byzantine Christianity and decreed the destruction of all the idols of the old faith, the renunciation by all his subjects of their former beliefs, and their baptism as Christians. — *Editor's note.*

6. One of my critics — heaven judge him! — took me to mean that that religion is true to which the greatest number of good people belong. I wish he had suggested some method for such moral statistics!

religious and moral power of the papal monarchy, the unique moral influence of their clergy on the masses of the people, the part the Pope plays as the defender of universal justice and the supreme judge and peacemaker; and they especially point to the multitude of *works of charity* in their missions at home and abroad. Protestants, who originally separated off from the Roman Church precisely on the ground of *moral* theology, claim in their turn as their essential advantage the moral loftiness and purity of their doctrine which liberates the individual conscience and the life of the community from many practical abuses and from slavery to external observances and to traditions, in their view, senseless. Finally, the champions of Orthodoxy in their polemic against Western Christianity generally have recourse to moral accusations. They accuse the Roman Catholics of pride and love of power, of striving to appropriate for the head of their Church that which belongs to God as well as that which belongs to Caesar; they accuse the Roman Catholic clergy of fanaticism, of loving the world and of cupidity, make it responsible for the sin of persecuting heretics and infidels. Like the Protestants they lay stress on three main charges — the Inquisition, Indulgences, and Jesuit morality; and finally, independently of the Protestants, they bring against the Roman Catholics the charge of moral fratricide which found expression in the arbitrary legalization (without the knowledge of the Eastern Church) of local Western traditions. The moral charges they bring against Protestantism are less striking but just as serious. They accuse it of individualism which does away with the Church as a concrete moral whole, they reproach it with destroying the bond of love not only between the present and the past of the historical Church (by rejecting the traditions), but also between the visible and the invisible Church (by rejecting prayers for the dead, etc.).

Without going into theology or pronouncing on the value of or the need for such disputes[7] I would only draw attention to the fact that neither of the disputants rejects the moral principles proclaimed by the other side, but simply tries to turn them to his own account. Thus when the Roman Catholics boast of works of charity which especially characterise their Church, neither their Protestant nor their Greco-Russian opponents would say that charity is a bad thing; they would merely argue that the Roman Catholic charitable institutions serve the purposes of ambition, and, being thus vitiated by extraneous elements, more or less lose their moral worth. In answer to this, the Roman Catholics, for their part, would not say that ambition is a good thing or that Christian charity must be subordinate to worldly considerations, but

---

7. Concerning the reproach of 'moral fratricide,' see my article "The Dogmatic Development of the Church" in *Pravoslavnoe Obozrenie*, December 1885, pp. 727-98.

would, on the contrary, repudiate the charge of ambition and argue that power is not for them an end in itself but only a necessary means for carrying out their moral duty. Similarly when the Orthodox — as well as the Roman Catholics — reproach the Protestants with their lack of filial piety and their contempt for the Patristic tradition, no sensible Protestant would urge that tradition ought to be despised, but would, on the contrary, try to prove that Protestantism is a return to the most honourable and ancient traditions of Christianity, freed from any false and pernicious admixture.

It is clear, then, that the disputing parties stand on one and the same moral ground (which alone renders dispute possible), that they have the same moral principles and standards, and that the dispute is merely about their application. These principles do not as such belong to any denomination, but form a general tribunal to which all equally appeal. The representative of each side says in fact to his opponent simply this: "I practise better than you the moral principles which you, too, wish to follow; therefore you must give up your error and acknowledge that I am right." The ethical standards, equally presupposed by all denominations, cannot themselves, then, depend upon denominational differences.

But morality proves to be just as independent of the more important religious differences. When a missionary persuades a Muhammadan or a heathen of the moral superiority of the Christian teaching he evidently presupposes that his listener has the same moral standards as his own, at least, in a potential form.

This means that the norms which are common both to the Christian and to the heathen, and are 'written' in the latter's heart, are altogether independent of positive religion. Besides, in so far as all positive religions, including the absolutely true one, appeal in the disputes to the universal moral norms, they admit that in a certain sense they are dependent upon the latter. Thus during a judicial trial both the right and the wrong party are equally subordinate to the law; and inasmuch as they have both appealed to it, they have acquiesced in such subordination.

III

Moral philosophy has then a subject-matter of its own (the moral norms) independent of particular religions, and even in a sense presupposed by them; thus on its objective or real side it is self-contained. The question must now be asked whether on its formal side — as a science — moral philosophy is subordinate to theoretical philosophy, especially to that part of it which examines the claims and the limitations of our cognitive faculty. But in working out a moral philosophy, reason simply unfolds, on the ground of experience, the implications of the idea of the good (or, what is the same thing, of the ultimate fact of moral consciousness) which is inherent in it from the first. In doing this, reason does not go beyond its own boundaries; in scholastic language its use here is *immanent,* and is therefore independent of this or of that solution of the question as to the *transcendent* knowledge of things in themselves. To put it more simply, in moral philosophy we are concerned with our inward relation to our own activities, *i.e.* with something that can *unquestionably* be known by us, for it has its source in ourselves. The debatable question as to whether we can know that which belongs to other realms of being, independent of us, is not here touched upon. The ideal content of morality is apprehended by reason which has itself created it; in this case, therefore, knowledge coincides with its object (is adequate to it) and leaves no room for critical doubt. The progress and the results of this process of thought answer for themselves, presupposing nothing but the general logical and psychological conditions of all mental activity. Ethics makes no claim to a theoretical knowledge of any metaphysical essences and takes no part in the dispute between the dogmatic and the critical philosophy, the first of which affirms, and the second denies, the reality, and consequently the possibility, of such knowledge.

In spite of this formal and general independence of ethics from theoretical philosophy, there are two metaphysical questions which may *apparently* prove fatal to the very existence of morality.

The first question is this. The starting point of every serious speculation is the doubt as to the objective validity of our knowledge: Do things exist as they are known to us? The doubt about our knowledge gradually leads us to doubt the very existence of that *which is known, i.e.* of the world and all that is in it. This world is made up of our sense perceptions which the understanding unites into one coherent whole. But is not the perceived merely our sensation and the connectedness of things merely our thought? And if this be so, if the world as a whole be only my presentation, then all the beings to whom I stand in the moral relation prove also to be nothing but my presentations, for they are inseparable parts of the presented world, given in knowledge like everything else. Now moral rules, or at least a considerable number of them, determine my right relation to other people. If other people do not exist, do not these moral rules themselves become objectless and unrealisable? This would be the case if the non-existence of other human beings could be known with the same indubitable certainty which attaches to moral precepts in their sphere. If while my conscience definitely compelled me to act morally in relation to certain objects, theoretical reason proved with *equal definiteness* that these objects did not exist at all, and that therefore rules of action relating to them were meaningless — if practical certainty were thus undermined by *equal* theoretical certainty, and the categoric character of the precept were negated by the indubitable knowledge of the impossibility of carrying it out — then indeed the position would be hopeless. But in truth there is no such conflict between two *equal* certainties, and there cannot be. Doubt as to the independent existence of external things is not, and can never become, certainty of their non-existence. Suppose it were proved that our senses and our understanding are untrustworthy witnesses as to the existence of other beings, the untrustworthiness of the witnesses merely makes their testimony doubtful, but does not make the opposite true. Even if it were positively proved that a given witness had falsely testified to a fact which in reality he had not witnessed at all, it would be impossible to conclude from this that the fact itself never existed. *Other* witnesses might vouch for it, or indeed it might not have been witnessed by any one and yet be a fact. Our senses and our intellect tell us of the existence of human beings other than ourselves. Suppose that investigation were to show that this is false, and that these means of knowledge warrant the existence of objects as *our representations* only and not their existence as independent realities — which we consequently begin to doubt. But to go further and replace our former certitude of the existence of other beings by the certitude of the opposite and not merely by doubt would be possible only on the supposition that whatever is not actually contained in our senses and our thought cannot exist at all. This, however, is quite an arbitrary assumption, for which there is neither logical ground nor any reasonable foundation.

If we cannot in relation to the existence of other selves go further than doubt, we may rest satisfied about the fate of moral principles; for theoretical doubt is evidently insufficient to undermine moral and practical certainty. It must also be remembered that critical doubt is not the final point of view of philosophy, but is always overcome in one way or another. Thus Kant draws the distinction between phenomena and noumena (appearances and things in themselves), restoring to the objects of moral duty as noumena the full measure of independent existence which as phenomena they do not possess. Other thinkers discover new and more trustworthy witnesses of the existence of the external world than sense and thought (Jacobi's immediate *faith*, Schopenhauer's *Will* which is experienced as the root of our own reality, and, by analogy, of that of other beings), or they work out a system of a new and more profound speculative dogmatism which re-establishes the objective significance of all that is. (Schelling, Hegel, and others.)

But however great the force and the significance of the critical doubt as to the existence of other beings may be, it has bearing merely on one aspect of morality. Every ethical precept as such touches upon the object of the action (other men) only with its outer end, so to speak; the real root of it is always within the agent and cannot therefore be affected by any theory — whether positive or negative — of the external world. And the external aspect of the moral law which links it to the object belongs, properly speaking, to the sphere of legal justice and not of morality in the narrow sense. As will be shown in due course legal justice depends upon morality and cannot be separated from it, but this does not prevent us from clearly distinguishing the two spheres. When one and the same action, *e.g.* murder, is condemned equally by a criminologist and by a moralist, they both refer to one and the same totality of psychological moments resulting in the material fact of taking life, and the conclusions are identical, but the starting point and the whole train of reasoning are entirely different and opposed in the two cases. From the legal point of view, what is of primary significance is the objective fact of murder — an action which violates another person's rights and characterises the culprit as an abnormal member of society. To make that characteristic full and complete, the inner psychological moments must also be taken into account, first and foremost among them being the presence of criminal intention, the so-called *animus* of the crime. But the subjective conditions of the action are of interest solely in their relation to the fact of murder, or in causal connection with it. If a man was filled with murderous desires all his life, but his subjective mental state found no expression in actual murder nor attempt at one, nor in any violence, that person in spite of all his diabolical malice would not come within the range of the criminologist as such. On the contrary, from the moral point of view, the slightest emotion of malice or anger, even though it never expressed itself in action or speech, is in itself a direct object of ethical judgment and condemnation; and the fact of murder from this point of view has significance not on its material side, but simply as an expression of the extreme degree of the evil feeling which throughout all its stages is deserving of moral condemnation. For a criminologist murder is an infringement of right or a loss unlawfully inflicted upon the victim and upon the social order. But from the purely moral point of view, being deprived of life is not necessarily a loss, and may even be a gain for the victim; murder is an unquestionable loss for the murderer alone, not as a fact, but as the culminating point of the malice which is in itself a loss to a man in so far as it lowers his dignity as a rational being. Of course, from the ethical point of view, too, murder is worse than a mere outburst of anger. But this is simply because the former involves a greater degree of the same evil passion than the latter, and it is certainly not because one is a harmful action and the other merely a feeling. If with the firm intention of causing death to his enemy a man stabs a wax effigy, he is from the moral point of view a full-fledged murderer, though he has killed no one and interfered with no one's rights; but for this very reason, from the legal point of view his action is not even remotely akin to murder, and is at most an insignificant damage to another person's property.

Extreme idealism which recognises the subject's inner states as alone real does not deny that there exist qualitative differences between these states, expressing a greater or lesser degree of activity in the self. Therefore from this point of view also our actions, in spite of the illusory character of their object, preserve their full moral significance as indicative of our spiritual condition. If, for example, the feeling of anger or malice indicates like every other *passion* the *passivity* of the spirit or its inward subordination to illusory appearances, and is in that sense immoral, it is clear that the degree of immorality is directly proportionate to the strength of the passion or to the degree of our passivity. The stronger the passion, the greater passivity of the spirit does it indicate. Therefore a passion of anger leading to premeditated murder is more immoral than a passing irritability, quite apart from the theoretical question as to the illusory character of external objects. Even from the point of view of subjective idealism, then, bad actions are worse than bad emotions which do not lead to actions.

The conclusion that follows from this is clear. If the universe were merely my dream, this would be fatal only to the objective, the external side of ethics (in the broad sense), and not to its own inner sphere; it would destroy my interest in jurisprudence, politics, in social questions, in philanthropy, but it would not affect the individually moral interests or the duties to myself. I should cease to care about safeguarding the rights of others, but would still preserve my own inner dignity. Not feeling any tender compassion for the phantoms surrounding me, I should be all the more bound to refrain from evil or shameful passions in relation to them. If it be opposed to moral dignity to bear malice against a living human being, it is all the more so against a mere phantom; if it be shameful to fear that which exists, it is still more shameful to fear that which does not exist; if it be shameful and contrary to reason to strive for the material possession of real objects, it is no less shameful and far more irrational to entertain such a desire with regard to phantoms of one's own imagination. Quite apart from the theory that all that exists is a dream, when in the ordinary way we dream of doing something immoral we feel ashamed of it even after awakening. Of course if I dream that I have killed some one, on waking I am not so much ashamed of my action as pleased at its having been only a dream; but of the vindictive feeling experienced in the dream I am ashamed even when awake.

In view of all these considerations, the following general conclusion seems inevitable. Theoretical philosophy (namely, the critique of knowledge) may engender doubt as to the existence of the objects of morality, but it certainly cannot create a conviction of their non-existence. The doubt (which, however, is disposed of, in one way or another, by the theoretical philosophy itself) cannot outweigh the certainty which attaches to the testimony of conscience. But even if it were possible to be certain of the non-existence of other beings (as objects of moral activity), this would affect only the objective side of ethics, leaving its own essential sphere altogether untouched. This conclusion sufficiently safeguards the independence of moral philosophy with regard to the first point raised by the critique of knowledge. The second difficulty arises in connection with the metaphysical question of the freedom of will.

IV

It is often maintained that the fate of moral consciousness depends upon this or that view of the freedom of will. It is urged that either our actions are free or they are determined, and then it is affirmed that the second alternative, namely, determinism, or the theory that all our actions and states happen with necessity, makes human morality impossible and thus deprives moral philosophy of all meaning. If, they say, man is merely a wheel in the world machine, it is impossible to speak of moral conduct. But the whole force of the argument depends upon an erroneous confusion between mechanical determinism and determinism in general — a confusion from which Kant himself is not altogether free. Determinism in general merely affirms that everything that happens, and therefore all human conduct, is *determined* (*determinatur* — hence the name of the theory) *by sufficient reasons, apart* from which it *cannot* take place, and *given* which it happens with *necessity*. But although the general concept of necessity is always identical with itself, necessity as actual fact varies according to the sphere in which it is realised; and corresponding to the three chief kinds of necessity (with reference to events and actions) there may be distinguished three kinds of determinism: (1) *mechanical determinism,* which certainly is exclusive of morality; (2) *psychological determinism,* which allows for some moral elements but is hardly compatible with others; (3) *rationally ideal determinism,* which gives full scope to the demands of morality.

Mechanical necessity is undoubtedly present in phenomena, but the assertion that it is the only kind of necessity that exists is simply a consequence of the materialistic metaphysics which would reduce all that is to mechanical movements of matter. This view, however, has nothing to do with the conviction that everything that happens has a sufficient reason which determines it with necessity. To regard man as a wheel in the world machine, one must at least admit the existence of such a machine, and by no means all determinists would agree to this. Many of them regard the material world merely as a representation in the mind of spiritual beings, and hold that it is not the latter who are mechanically determined by real things, but that phenomena are mentally determined in accordance with the laws of the inner life of the spiritual beings, of which man is one.

Leaving metaphysics for the present on one side and confining ourselves to the limits of general experience, we undoubtedly find already in the animal world inner psychological necessity essentially irreducible to mechanism. Animals[8] are determined in their actions not merely externally, but also from within, not by the push and pressure of things, but by impelling motives, *i.e.* by their own ideas. Even granting that these motives are caused by outer objects, they nevertheless arise and act in the animal's mind in accordance with its own nature. This psychological necessity is of course not freedom, but it cannot be identified with mechanical necessity. Where Kant attempts to identify the two, the erroneousness of his contention is betrayed by a curiously unfortunate comparison he makes. In his words the freedom of being determined by one's own ideas is in truth no better than the freedom of a roasting-jack which being once set going produces its movements by itself. Not only Kant, who was opposed to any kind of hyloism (animation of matter), but the most poetically minded *Natur-philosoph* would certainly not ascribe to such an object as a roasting-jack the power of spontaneously producing its movements. When we say that it turns by itself we simply mean that, owing to the force of the impetus it has received, it continues to move alone. The words "by itself" mean here "without the help of any new additional agent" — the same as the French *tout seul*[9] — and in no way presuppose that the object

---

8. In a certain sense of course the same may be said of plants and even of the different parts of the inorganic world, for there does not exist in nature pure mechanism or absolute soullessness; but in these preliminary remarks I wish to keep to what is indisputable and generally understood. Concerning the different kinds of causality or necessity in connection with the problem of the freedom of will see in particular Schopenhauer, *Grundprobl. des Ethik* and *Wille in der Natur*. I have given the essence of his views in my *Critique of Abstract Principles*, chap. ix.

9. In the Polish language the word *sam* has kept only this negative sense — alone without the others (the derivative *samotny* = lonely); in the Russian and the German languages both meanings are possible, and if the positive (the inner, spontaneous causality) is given, the negative (absence of any other cause) is presupposed, but not *vice versa*. Thus the word *samouchka* (self-taught) denotes a man who has himself been the cause of his education and who studied alone without the help of others. The two meanings are here combined as in similar words in

moved contributes anything of itself to the movement. But when we say of an animal that it moves by itself, we mean precisely its inward participation in producing movements. It flees from an enemy or runs towards food, not because these movements have been externally communicated to it beforehand, but because at that moment it experiences fear of the enemy or desire for food. Of course these psychological states are not free acts of will, nor do they immediately produce bodily movements; they merely set going a certain mechanism which is already there, fitted for the execution of certain actions. But the special peculiarity which does not allow of animal life being reduced to mere mechanism is that, for the normal interaction between the animal organism and the external environment to take place, the latter must take for the animal the form of a motive and determine the animal's movements in accordance with its own pleasant or unpleasant feelings. The presence or absence of the capacity for feeling which is inseparably connected with the two other faculties of willing and of representing — *i.e.* the presence or absence of an inner life — is the most important difference that we can conceive. And if we grant the presence of this inner life in the animal and deny it to a mechanical automaton, we have no right to identify the two as Kant does.[10]

The psychical life as manifested in the different species and in individual animals (and in man) presents qualitative differences which enable us, for instance, to distinguish between the ferocious and the meek, the brave and the cowardly, etc. Animals are not aware of these qualities as either good or bad; but in human beings the same qualities are regarded as indicating a good or a bad nature. There is a moral element involved here, and experience unquestionably proves that good nature may develop and bad be suppressed or corrected; we already have here a certain object for moral philosophy and a problem of its practical application, though of course there is as yet no question as to the freedom of will. The final independence of ethics from this metaphysical problem is, however, to be discovered not within the sphere of psychical life which is common to man and animal, but within the sphere of human morality proper.

---

other languages, *e.g.* the German *Selbsterziehung* or the English *self-help*. But when we say that a roasting-jack moves by itself *(sam, Selbst)*, the word has merely the negative meaning that at the present moment nothing external is pushing the object. But it is certainly not meant that the jack is the spontaneous cause of its movements; the cause is wholly contained in the previous impetus, external to the object.

10. The logical right to doubt the presence of a mental life in animals must be based upon the same grounds upon which I doubt the existence of minds other than my own (see above). An exact solution of this purely theoretical problem is impossible in the domain of ethics and is not necessary for it; it is a question for epistemology and metaphysics.

V

Just as in the animal world psychological necessity is superadded to the mechanical without cancelling the latter or being reduced to it, so in the human world to these two kinds of necessity is added the ideally rational or *moral necessity*. It implies that the motives or sufficient reasons of human actions are not limited to concrete particular ideas which affect the will through pleasant or unpleasant sensations, but may be supplied by the universal rational idea of the good acting upon the conscious will in the form of absolute duty or, in Kant's terminology, in the form of a categorical imperative. To put it more plainly, man may do good apart from and contrary to any self-interested considerations, for the sake of the good itself, from reverence for duty or the moral law. This is the culminating point of morality, which is, however, quite compatible with determinism and in no way requires the so-called freedom of will. Those who affirm the contrary ought first to banish from the human mind and language the very term "moral necessity," for it would be a *contradictio in adjecto* if morality were possible only on condition of free choice. And yet the idea expressed by this term is not only clear to every one, but follows from the very nature of the case. Necessity in general is the absolute dependence of an action (in the broad sense, *effectus*) upon a ground which determines it, and is therefore called sufficient. When this ground is a physical blow or shock, the necessity is mechanical; when a mental excitation, the necessity is psychological; and when the idea of the good, it is moral. Just as there have been futile attempts to reduce psychology to mechanics, so now an equally futile attempt is made to reduce morality to psychology, *i.e.* to show that the true motives of human action can only be mental affections and not a sense of duty — in other words, to prove that man never acts for conscience' sake alone. To prove this is, of course, impossible. It is no argument to say that the moral idea is comparatively seldom a sufficient ground for action. Plants and animals are only an insignificant quantity as compared with the inorganic mass of the earth; but no one could conclude from this that there are no fauna and flora on the earth. Moral necessity is simply the finest flower on the psychological soil of humanity, and for this reason it is all the more important for philosophy.

Everything that is higher or more perfect presupposes by its very existence a certain freedom from the lower, or, to speak more exactly, from the exclusive domination by the lower. Thus the capacity of being determined to action by means of ideas or motives means freedom from the exclusive domination by material impact and pressure — *i.e.* psychological necessity means freedom from mechanical necessity. In the same way moral necessity, while wholly retaining its necessary character, means freedom from the lower, psychological necessity. If a person's actions can be determined by the pure idea of the good or by the absolute demands of moral duty, it means that he is free from the overpowering influence of emotions and may successfully resist the most powerful of them. But this *rational freedom* has nothing in common with the so-called freedom of will which means that the will is determined by nothing except itself, or, according to the incomparable formula of Duns Scotus, "nothing except the will itself causes the act of willing in the will" *(nihil aliud a voluntate causat actum volendi in voluntate)*. I do not say that there is no such freedom of will; I only say that there is none of it in moral actions. In such actions will is determined by the idea of the good or the moral law which is universal and necessary, and independent of will both in its content and in its origin. It may be thought, however, that the act itself of accepting or not accepting the moral law as the principle of one's will depends on that will alone, and that this explains why one and the same idea of the good is taken by some as a sufficient motive for action and is rejected by others. The different effects are due, however, in the first place, to the fact that one and the same idea has for different people a different degree of clearness and completeness, and secondly, to the unequal receptivity of different natures to moral motives generally. But then all causality and all necessity presuppose a *special* receptivity of given objects to a certain kind of stimuli. The stroke of a billiard cue which moves a billiard ball has no effect whatever on a sun ray; juicy grass which excites irrepressible longing in a deer is not, as a rule, a motive of willing in a cat, and so on. If the indifference of the sun ray to the strokes of a cue or the dislike of vegetable food by a carnivorous animal be regarded as a manifestation of free will, then, of course, man's good or bad actions must also be considered arbitrary. But this is simply a gratuitous introduction of misleading terminology.

For the idea of the good as duty to become a sufficient reason or motive for action, a union of two factors is necessary: sufficient clearness and fulness of the idea itself in consciousness and sufficient moral receptivity of the subject. Whatever the one-sided schools of ethics may say, it is clear that the presence of one of these factors in the absence of the other is insufficient for producing the moral effect. Thus, to use a Biblical example, Abraham, who had the greatest moral receptivity but an insufficient knowledge of what is contained in the idea of the good, decided to kill his son. He was fully conscious of the imperative form of the moral law as the expression of the higher will, and accepted it implicitly; he was simply lacking in the conception of what may and what may not be a good or an object of God's will — a clear proof that even saints stand in need of moral philosophy. In the Bible Abraham's decision is regarded in two ways — (1) as an act of religious devotion and self-sacrifice, which brought to the patriarch and his posterity the greatest blessings, and (2) as involving the idea that God's will is qualitatively indifferent — an idea so erroneous and so dangerous that interference from above was necessary in order to prevent his intention being carried out. (I need not here touch upon the connection of the event with heathen darkness nor upon its mysterious relation to Christian light.) In contradistinction to Abraham, the prophet Balaam, in spite of his being fully conscious of the right course, was led by his vicious heart to prefer the king's gifts to the decree of the Divine will and to curse the people of God.

When the moral motive is defective in the one respect or the other, it does not operate; and when it is sufficient in both respects it operates with necessity like any other cause. Suppose I accept the moral law as a motive for action solely for its own sake, out of reverence for it and without any admixture of extraneous motives. This very capacity to respect the moral law so highly and so disinterestedly as to prefer it to all else is itself a quality of mind and is not arbitrary, and the activity that follows from it, though rationally *free,* is entirely subject to moral *necessity* and cannot possibly be arbitrary or accidental. It is free in the relative sense, free from the lower mechanical and psychological necessity, but it is certainly not free from the inner higher necessity of the absolute good. Morality and moral philosophy are entirely based upon rational freedom or moral necessity, and wholly exclude from their sphere irrational unconditional freedom or arbitrary choice.

In order that the conscious choice of man might be determined by the idea of the good with full inward necessity and have a *sufficient* motive, the content of this idea must be sufficiently developed; the intellect must present the idea to the will in its full force — and to do this is precisely the function of moral philosophy. Thus ethics is not only compatible with determinism, but renders the highest form of necessity possible. When a man of high moral development consciously subordinates his will to the idea of the good, which is completely known to him and has been fully thought out, it is clear that there is no shadow of arbitrariness in his submission to the moral law, but that it is absolutely necessary.

And yet there is such a thing as an absolute freedom of choice. It is found not in the moral self-determination, not in the acts of the practical reason where Kant sought it, but just at the opposite pole of the inner life. At present I can only indicate my meaning partially and imperfectly. As already said, the good cannot be the direct object of arbitrary choice. Granted the requisite degree of understanding and of receptivity on the part of the subject, its own excellence is quite a sufficient reason for preferring it to the opposite principle, and there is here no room for arbitrary choice. When I choose the good, I do so not because of my whim but because it is good, because it has value, and I am capable of realising its significance. But what determines the opposite act of rejecting the good and choosing the evil? Is such choice entirely due to the fact that, as a certain school of ethics supposes, I do not know evil and mistakenly take it for the good? It is impossible to prove that this is *always* the case. A sufficient knowledge of the good in combination with a sufficient receptivity to it *necessarily* determines our will in the moral sense. But the question still remains whether an insufficient receptivity to the good and a receptivity to evil is merely a natural fact, or whether it depends on the will, which in this case, having no rational motive to determine it in the bad direction (for to submit to evil rather than to good is contrary to reason), is itself the ultimate cause of its own determination. For a rational being there can be no objective reason for loving evil as such, and the will therefore may only choose it arbitrarily — on the condition, of course, that there be full, clear consciousness of it; for when there is only half-consciousness, the bad choice is sufficiently explained by a mistake of judgment. The good determines my choice in its favour by all the infinite fulness of its positive content and reality. This choice is therefore *infinitely* determined; it is absolutely necessary, and there is no arbitrariness in it at all. In the choice of evil, on the contrary, there is no determining reason, no kind of necessity, and therefore infinite arbitrariness. The question then assumes the following form: given a full and clear knowledge of the good, can a rational being prove to be so unreceptive to it as to reject it utterly and unconditionally and choose the evil? Such lack of receptivity to the good that is perfectly known would be something absolutely irrational, and it is only an irrational act of this description that would truly come under the definition of absolute freedom or of arbitrary choice. We have no right *a priori* to deny its possibility. Definite arguments for or against it may be found only in the obscurest depths of metaphysics. But in any case, before asking the question whether there can exist a being who, with a full knowledge of the good, may yet arbitrarily reject it and choose the evil, we must first make clear to ourselves all that the idea of the good contains and involves. This is the task of moral philosophy which is thus seen to be presupposed by the metaphysical question as to the freedom of will (if this question is to be treated seriously), and certainly not to depend upon it.[11] Before going into any metaphysics we

11. A considerable part of my theoretical philosophy will be devoted to the inquiry into the problem of free will. So far, it is sufficient for me to show that this problem has no immediate bearing upon moral philosophy, which is concerned with the conception of the good, whether

can and must learn what our reason finds to be the good in human nature, and how it develops and expands this natural good, raising it to the significance of absolute moral perfection.

---

the good be regarded as an object of arbitrary choice or as a motive which necessarily determines the acts of rational and moral beings. In what follows I shall always mean by human freedom, individual freedom, etc., either moral freedom, which is an ethical *fact,* or political freedom, which is an ethical *postulate,* without any more referring to the absolute freedom of choice, which is merely a metaphysical *problem.*

PART I

The Good in Human Nature

CHAPTER I

The Primary Data of Morality

I

However convincing or authoritative a moral teaching may be, it will remain fruitless and devoid of power unless it finds a secure foundation in the moral nature of man. In spite of all the differences in the degree of spiritual development in the past and in the present, in spite of all the individual variations and the general influences of race, climate, and historical conditions, there exists an ultimate basis of universal human morality, and upon it all that is of importance in ethics must rest. The admission of this truth does not in any way depend upon our metaphysical or scientific conception of the origin of man. Whether the result of a long evolution of animal organisms or an immediate product of a higher creative act, human nature, with all its characteristic features — the most important among them being the moral features — is in any case a fact.

The distinctive character of the psychical nature of man is not denied by the great representative of the evolutionary theory. "No doubt the difference in this respect (between man and other animals) is enormous, even if we compare the mind of one of the lowest savages, who has no words to express any number higher than four, and who uses hardly any abstract terms for common objects or for the affections, with that of the most highly organised ape. The difference would, no doubt, still remain immense, even if one of the higher apes had been improved or civilised as much as a dog has been in comparison with its parent-form, the wolf or jackal. The Fuegians rank amongst the lowest barbarians, but I was continually struck with surprise how closely the three natives on board H.M.S. *Beagle*, who had lived some years in England, and could talk a little English, resembled us in disposition and in most of our mental faculties."[1]

Further on Darwin declares that he entirely agrees with the writers who hold that the greatest difference between man and animals consists in the moral sentiment,[2] which he, for his part, regards as innate and not as acquired.[3] But carried away by his desire — within certain limits a legitimate one — to fill up the 'immense' distance by intermediary links, Darwin makes one fundamental error. He regards all human morality as in the first instance *social,* thus connecting it with the social instincts of animals. Personal or individual morality has, according to Darwin, merely a derivative significance, and is a later result of historical evolution. He maintains that the only virtues which exist for savages are those that are required by the interests of their social group.[4] But one simple and universal fact is sufficient to disprove this contention.

There exists one feeling which serves no social purpose, is utterly absent in the highest animals, but is clearly manifested in the lowest of the human races. In virtue of this feeling the most savage and undeveloped man is *ashamed* of — *i.e.* recognises as *wrong* — and conceals a physiological act which not only satisfies his own desire and need, but is, moreover, useful and necessary for the preservation of the species. Directly connected with this is the reluctance to remain in primitive nakedness; it induces savages to invent *clothes* even when the climate and the simplicity of life make them quite unnecessary.

This moral fact more sharply than any other distinguishes man from all the other animals, for among them we find not the slightest trace of anything approaching to it. Darwin himself, discussing as he does the religious instinct of dogs, etc., never attempts to look to animals for any rudiments of shame. And indeed, not to speak of the lower creatures, even the highly-endowed and well-trained domestic animals are no exception. The noble steed afforded the prophet in the Bible a suitable image for depicting the shamelessness of the dissolute young men of the Jerusalem nobility;[5] the loyal dog has of old been rightly considered a typical example of utter shamelessness; and among the wild animals, the creature which in certain respects is still more developed, the monkey, affords a particularly vivid instance of unbridled cynicism, all

1. Darwin, *The Descent of Man* (beginning of chap. iii).
2. *Ibid.,* chap. iii.
3. *Ibid.,* the answer to Mill.
4. *Ibid.,* on social virtues.
5. See Jeremiah 5:8. — *Editor's note.*

the more apparent because of the monkey's external likeness to man, and its extremely lively intelligence and passionate temperament.

As it is utterly impossible to discover shame among animals, naturalists of a certain school are compelled to deny it to man. Not having discovered any modest animals, Darwin talks of the shamelessness of the savage peoples.[6] From the man who went round the world on his ship *Beagle* we might expect the positive and definite evidence of an eye-witness; but instead he merely makes a few brief and unsupported remarks, convincing to no one. Not only savages but even the civilised peoples of Biblical or Homeric times may strike us as shameless, in the sense that the feeling of shame which they undoubtedly possessed did not always express itself in the same way, nor extend to all the details of everyday life with which it is associated in our case. So far as this goes, however, there is no need to appeal to distant places and times: people who live side by side with us, but belong to a different class, often consider permissible things of which we are ashamed. And yet no one would contend that the feeling of shame was unknown to them. Still less is it possible to make any general deductions from cases of absolute moral deficiency which are found in the annals of crime. Headless monsters are sometimes born into the human world, but nevertheless a head remains an essential feature of our organism.

To prove his contention that primitive man is devoid of shame, Darwin also briefly refers to the religious customs of the ancients, *i.e.* to the phallic cult. But this important fact is rather an argument against him. Intentional, exaggerated shamelessness — shamelessness made into a religious principle — evidently presupposes the existence of shame. In like manner the sacrifice by the parents of their children to the gods certainly does not prove the absence of pity or of parental love, but, on the contrary, presupposes it. The main point about these sacrifices is that *loved* children were killed: if that which was sacrificed were not dear to the person who gave it, the sacrifice would be of no value and would lose its character of sacrifice. (It is only later, as the religious feeling became weaker, that this fundamental condition of all sacrifice came to be avoided by means of different symbolical *substitutes*.) No religion at all, not even the most savage one, could be based upon a mere absence of shame, any more than upon a mere absence of pity. False religion as much as the true presupposes the moral nature of man, and does so in the

---

6. *The Descent of Man*. When dealing with savages even serious scientists sometimes show remarkable thoughtlessness. The other day I saw an amusing instance of it in the writings of the anthropologist Brocke. He affirms that the aborigines of the Andaman Islands wear no clothes; for, he says, one cannot regard as such a thin belt with a piece of leather attached to it. I think one could with more ground deny the essential function of clothes to the European dress-coat.

very demand for its perversion. The demoniac powers, worshipped in the bloody and dissolute cults of ancient heathendom, were nurtured and lived by this real perversion, by this positive immorality. These religions did not require merely the natural performance of a certain physiological act. No, their essence was the intensification of depravity, the overstepping of all bounds imposed by nature, society, and conscience. The religious character of the orgies proves the extreme importance of this circumstance. If they involved nothing beyond natural shamelessness, what could be the source of the strained, the perverted, the mystical element in them?

It is obvious that it would not be necessary for Darwin to use such unconvincing indirect arguments in support of his view could he produce any trustworthy facts to show the presence of even rudimentary modesty among animals. But there are no such facts, and shame undoubtedly remains, even from the external and empirical point of view, the distinguishing characteristic of man.

II

The feeling of shame (in its fundamental sense) is a fact which absolutely distinguishes man from all lower nature. No other animal has this feeling in the least degree, while in man it has been manifested from time immemorial and is subject to growth and development.

But that which is involved in this fact gives it a further and a far deeper significance. The feeling of shame is not merely a distinctive feature whereby man is separated off for external observation from the rest of the animal world; in it man actually separates himself from material nature, his own as well as that external to him. In being ashamed of his own natural inclinations and organic functions, man proves that he is not merely a material being, but is something other and higher. That which is ashamed separates itself in the very mental act of shame from that of which it is ashamed. But material nature cannot be foreign to or external to itself. Hence if I am ashamed of my material nature, I prove by that very fact that I am not identical with it. And it is precisely at the moment when man falls under the sway of the material nature and is overwhelmed by it that his distinctive peculiarity and inner independence assert themselves in the feeling of shame, in and through which he regards the material life as something other, as something foreign to himself, which must not dominate him.

Even if individual cases of sexual shame were to be found among animals, it would simply be a premonition of the human nature. For in any case it is clear that a being who is ashamed of his animality *in that very fact* proves himself to be more than a mere animal. No one who believes the story of the speaking ass of Balaam ever denied, on that ground, that the gift of rational speech is a characteristic peculiarity of man as distinct from other animals. But still more fundamental in this sense is the meaning of sexual shame.

This fundamental fact of history and of anthropology — unnoticed or intentionally omitted in the book of the great modern scientist — had been noted three thousand years before in an inspired passage in a book of far more authority: "And the eyes of them both were opened [at the moment of fall] and they knew that they were naked; and they sewed fig leaves together, and made themselves aprons. And they heard the voice of the Lord God . . . and Adam and his wife hid themselves from the presence of the Lord God amongst the trees of the garden. And the Lord God called unto Adam, and said unto him, *Where art thou?* And he said, I heard Thy voice in the garden, and I was afraid, because I was naked; and I hid myself. And He said, Who told thee that thou wast naked?"[7]

At the moment of fall a higher voice speaks in the depth of the human soul, asking: Where art thou? where is thy moral dignity? Man, lord of nature and the image of God, dost thou still exist? And the answer is at once given: I heard the Divine voice and I was afraid of laying bare my lower nature. *I am ashamed, therefore I exist;* and not physically only, but morally — I am ashamed of my animality, therefore I still exist as man.

It is by his own action and by testing his own being that man attains to moral self-consciousness. Materialistic science would attempt in vain to give, from its point of view, a satisfactory answer to the question asked of man long ago: "Who told thee that thou wast naked?"

The independent and ultimate meaning of the sense of shame would be explained away if this moral fact could be connected with some material gain for the individual or for the species in the struggle for existence. In that case shame could be accounted for as a form of the instinct of animal self-preservation — individual or social. But there is no such connection.

The feeling of shame associated with the sexual act might be useful to the individual and to the species as a preventive against the abuse of this important organic function. In the case of animals which follow their instincts we do not find any injurious excesses; but in the case of man, owing to a superior development of the individual consciousness and will, excesses become possible; and against the most dangerous of them — the abuse of the sexual instinct — a useful check is provided in the feeling of shame which develops

---

7. Genesis 3:7-11. — *Editor's note.*

under the general conditions of natural selection. This is a plausible argument, but it is not really valid. To begin with, it involves an inner contradiction. If the strongest and the most fundamental of instincts — the instinct of self-preservation — is powerless to prevent man from dangerous excesses, how could this be done by a new and derivative instinct of shame? And if the instinctive promptings of shame do not have sufficient influence over man, which is really the case, no specific utility can attach to shame, and it remains inexplicable from the utilitarian and materialistic point of view. Instead of checking the excesses, which are a violation of the normal order, it itself simply proves to be an additional object of such a violation — *i.e.* an utterly useless complication. Connected with this is another consideration which contradicts the utilitarian view of shame, — the fact, namely, that this feeling manifests itself most clearly before entering upon sexual relations: shame speaks most clearly and emphatically *virginibus puerisque,*[8] so that if shame had a direct practical significance, so far from being useful, it would be detrimental both to the individual and to the species. But if shame has no practical effect even when it is felt most, no subsequent effect can be expected from it. So long as shame is felt there can *as yet* be no question of sexual abuse; and when there is abuse, it is *too late* to speak of shame. The normal person is sufficiently safeguarded from dangerous excesses by the simple feeling of satisfied desire, and an abnormal person or one with perverted instincts is least of all noted for his sense of shame. Thus, speaking generally, where shame might, from the utilitarian point of view, be useful, it is absent, and where it is present it is of no use at all.

In truth the feeling of shame is excited not by the abuse of a certain organic function, but by the simple exercise of that function: the natural fact is itself experienced as shameful. If this is a manifestation of the instinct of self-preservation, it is so in quite a special sense. What is being safeguarded here is not the subject's material welfare, but his highest human dignity; or rather that dignity evinces itself as still safe in the depths of our being. The strongest manifestation of the material organic life calls forth a reaction on the part of the spiritual principle which reminds the personal consciousness that man is not merely a natural fact, that he must not as a passive instrument serve the vital purposes of nature. This is only a *reminder,* and it rests with the personal rational will to take advantage of it. As I have already said, this moral feeling has no direct real effect, and if its promptings are in vain, shame itself gradually disappears and is at last completely lost.

It is clear, then, that even if it were true that individual persons or entire

8. "To maidens and lads" (in Horace, *Odes,* Book III, 1). — *Editor's note.*

tribes are devoid of shame, this fact would not have the significance ascribed to it. The unquestionable shamelessness of individual persons as well as the questionable shamelessness of entire peoples, can only mean that in these particular cases the spiritual principle in man which lifts him above material nature is either still undeveloped or is already lost — that this particular man or this particular group of men have either not yet risen above the bestial stage or have once more returned to it. But the hereditary or acquired animality of this or that person or persons cannot destroy or weaken the significance of the moral dignity of man, which with the enormous majority of people clearly asserts itself in the feeling of shame — a feeling absolutely unknown to any animal. The fact that infants at the breast, or the mute, are, like animals, unable to speak, does not in any way diminish the significance of language as the expression of a distinctive, purely human rationality, not found in other animals.

III

Apart from all empirical considerations as to the genesis of the feeling of shame in humanity, the significance of that feeling lies in the fact that it determines man's ethical relation to his material nature. Man is ashamed of being dominated or ruled by it (especially in its chief manifestation), and thereby asserts his inner independence and his superior dignity in relation to it, in virtue of which he must possess and not be possessed by it.

Side by side with this fundamental moral feeling determining the right attitude toward the lower, material principle in each of us, there exists in human nature another feeling which serves as a basis for a moral relation to other human, or, speaking generally, to other living beings that are like us — namely, the feeling of pity.[9] The essence of it lies in the fact that a given subject is conscious in a corresponding manner of the suffering or the want of others, *i.e.* responds to it more or less painfully, thus more or less exhibiting his solidarity with the others. The ultimate and innate character of this moral feeling is not denied by any serious thinker or scientist, if only because the feeling of pity or compassion — in contradistinction to that of shame — is present, in its rudimentary stage, in many animals,[10] and consequently from

9. I use the simplest term, the most usual in technical works on the subject being the terms *sympathy* or *compassion*.

10. A number of facts showing this are to be found in works of descriptive zoology (particularly in Brehm's *Life of Animals*), and also in the literature on animal psychology that has of late been considerably developed.

no point of view can be regarded as a later product of human development. Thus if a shameless man reverts to the brute stage, a pitiless man falls lower than the animal level.

The close connection of the feeling of pity with the social instincts of men and animals cannot be doubted owing to the very nature of that feeling. In its essence, however, it is an individual moral state, and even in the case of animals it is not reducible to social relations, much less so in the case of man. If the need for a social unit were the only foundation of pity, that feeling could be experienced only towards creatures that belong to one and the same social whole. This is generally but by no means always the case, at any rate not among the higher animals. Numerous facts of the tenderest love[11] between animals (both wild and domestic) belonging to different and sometimes remote zoological groups are well known. It is very strange that in the face of this fact Darwin should maintain — without adducing any evidence to prove his contention — that among savage peoples sympathetic feelings are limited to members of one and the same narrow group. Of course among the cultured nations, too, most people show real sympathy chiefly towards their own family and most intimate friends, but the individual moral feeling in all races may transcend — and did do so of old — not only these narrow limits, but all empirical limits altogether. To accept Darwin's contention unconditionally would be to admit that a human savage cannot attain to the moral level sometimes reached by dogs, monkeys, and even lions.[12]

The sympathetic feeling can grow and develop indefinitely, but its ultimate essence is one and the same among all living beings. The first stage and the fundamental form of all solidarity in the animal kingdom and in the human world is parental (and in particular maternal) love. This is the simple root from which spring all the complexity and multiplicity of the internal and external social relations; and it is here that we see most clearly that the individually-psychological essence of the moral bond is no other than pity. For no other mental state can express the original solidarity of the mother with her weak, helpless, *piteous* offspring wholly dependent upon her.

---

11. Love in the purely psychological sense (apart from the materially sexual and the æsthetic relation) is firmly established, permanent pity or compassion (sympathy). Long before Schopenhauer the Russian people identified these two things in their language: "to love" and "to pity" are one and the same for them. One need not go so far, but it cannot be disputed that the fundamental subjective manifestation of love as a moral feeling is pity.

12. It is obvious, of course, that such cases with regard to wild animals can be properly observed only when the animals are in captivity. It is very probable indeed that the sympathetic feelings in question are awakened chiefly in captivity.

IV

The feelings of shame and of pity essentially determine our moral attitude in the first place to our own material nature, and in the second to all other living beings. In so far as a man is modest and pitying he stands in a moral relation 'to himself and to his neighbour' (to use the old terminology); shamelessness and pitilessness, on the contrary, undermine the very roots of his character. Apart from these two feelings there exists in us a third one, irreducible to the first two, and as ultimate as they; it determines man's moral attitude not to his own lower nature and not to the world of beings similar to him, but to something different recognised by him as the *higher;* as that which he can be neither *ashamed* of, nor feel *pity* for, but which he must *revere.* This feeling of reverence *(reverentia),* or of awe (piety, *pietas),* before *the higher* forms in man the moral basis of religion, and of the religious order of life. When abstracted by philosophical reflection from its historical manifestations, it constitutes the so-called 'natural religion.' The ultimate and the innate character of this feeling cannot be denied for the same reason that the innateness of pity is not seriously denied by any one. In a rudimentary form both the feeling of pity and of reverence are found among animals. It is absurd to expect to find among them religion in our sense of the term. But the general elementary feeling upon which human religion is ultimately based — namely, the feeling of reverence and awe in the presence of something higher — may unconsciously spring up in creatures other than man. In this sense the following remarks must be said to be true: "The feeling of religious devotion is a highly complex one, consisting of love, complete submission to an exalted and mysterious superior, a strong sense of dependence, fear, reverence, gratitude, hope for the future, and perhaps other elements. No being could experience so complex an emotion until advanced in his intellectual and moral faculties to at least a moderately high level. Nevertheless, we see some distant approach to this state of mind in the deep love of a dog for his master, associated with complete submission, some fear, and perhaps other feelings. The behaviour of a dog when returning to his master after an absence, and, as I may add, of a monkey to his beloved keeper, is widely different from that towards their fellows. In the latter case the transports of joy appear to be somewhat less, and the sense of equality is shown in every action."[13] The representative of the scientific evolutionary view admits then that in the quasi-religious relation of

---

13. Darwin, *op. cit.,* end of ch. iii. Darwin had been speaking before of the intellectual side of religion — of the acknowledgment of an invisible cause or causes for unusual events. He finds this too among the animals.

the dog or of the monkey to a higher being (from their point of view) there is, in addition to fear and self-interest, a moral element and one quite distinct from the sympathetic feelings which these animals exhibit in relation to their equals. This specific relation to the higher is precisely what I call reverence; and if one admits it in dogs and monkeys it would be strange to deny it to man, and to deduce human religion from fear and self-interest alone. These lower feelings undoubtedly contribute to the formation and the development of religion. But the ultimate basis of it is the distinctive religiously moral feeling of man's reverent love for is more excellent than himself.

V

The fundamental feelings of *shame, pity,* and *reverence* exhaust the sphere of man's possible moral relations to that which is below him, that which is on a level with him, and that which is above him. *Mastery* over the material senses, *solidarity* with other living beings, and inward voluntary *submission* to the superhuman principle — these are the eternal and permanent foundations of the moral life of humanity. The degree of mastery, the depth and the extent of solidarity, the completeness of the inward submission vary in the course of history, passing from a lesser to a greater perfection, but the principle in each of the three spheres of relation remains one and the same.

All other phenomena of the moral life, all the so-called virtues, may be shown to be the variations of these three essentials or the results of interaction between them and the intellectual side of man. *Courage* and *fortitude,* for instance, are undoubtedly exemplifications — though in a more external and superficial form — of the same principle, the more profound and significant expression of which is found in shame, — the principle, namely, of rising above and dominating the lower material nature. Shame (in its typical manifestation) elevates man above the animal instinct of *generic* self-preservation; courage elevates him above another animal instinct — that of *personal* self-preservation. But apart from this distinction in the object or the sphere of application, these two forms of one and the same moral principle differ more profoundly in another respect. The feeling of shame necessarily involves a condemnation of that with which it is associated: that of which I am ashamed is declared by me, in and through the very act of being ashamed, to be bad or wrong. But a courageous feeling or action, on the contrary, may simply express the nature of a given individual, and, as such, contains no condemnation of its opposite. For this reason courage is found among animals, having in their case no moral significance. As the function of obtaining and assimilating food gets more complex and developed it becomes in some animals the destructive predatory instinct which may sometimes outweigh the instinct of self-preservation. This domination of one instinct over another is precisely what is meant by animal courage. Its presence or absence is simply a natural fact, not inwardly connected with any self-valuation. No one would think of saying that hares or hens are ashamed of their timidity; courageous animals when they happen to be afraid are not ashamed of it either — nor do they boast of their courage. In man, too, the quality of courage as such is essentially of that character. But owing to our higher nature and to the intervention of the intellectual elements this quality acquires a new meaning which connects it with the root of the distinctly human morality — with shame. Man is conscious of courage not merely as the predominance of the predatory instinct, but as the power of the spirit to rise above the instinct of personal self-preservation. The presence of this spiritual power is recognised as a virtue, and the absence of it is condemned as *shameful*. Thus the essential kinship between shame and courage is seen in the fact that the absence of the second virtue is condemned in accordance with the standard set by the first: a lack of courage becomes the subject for shame. This does not apply with the same force to other virtues (charity, justice, humility, piety, etc.); their absence is generally condemned in a different way. And when in judging other people's feelings and actions, malice, injustice, haughtiness, impiety strike us rather as hateful and revolting than as shameful; the latter definition is specially restricted to cowardice and voluptuousness,[14] *i.e.* to such vices which violate the dignity of the human personality as such, and not its duties to others or to God.

The inner dependence of other human virtues upon the three ultimate foundations of morality will be shown in due course.

VI

Of the three ultimate foundations of the moral life, one, as we have seen, belongs exclusively to man (shame), another (pity) is to a large extent found among animals, and the third (awe or reverence for the higher) is in a small degree observed in some animals. But although the rudiments of moral feeling (of the second and third kind) are found in the animal world, they differ

---

14. A complex wrong-doing like treason is recognised both as revolting and as shameful for the same reason, in so far as treason includes cowardice which prefers secret treachery to open enmity.

essentially from the corresponding feelings in man. Animals may be good or bad, but the distinction between good and evil as such does not exist for their consciousness. In the case of man this knowledge of good and evil is given immediately in the feeling of shame that is distinctive of him, and, gradually developing from this first root and refining its concrete and sensuous form, it embraces the whole of human conduct in the form of conscience. We have seen that within the domain of man's moral relation to himself or to his own nature, the feeling of shame (which has at first a distinctly sexual character) remains identical in form whether it is opposed to the instinct of generic or of individual self-preservation: a cowardly attachment to the mortal life is as *shameful* as giving oneself up to the sexual desire. When from the relation to oneself as a separate individual and a member of a genus we pass to the relations to other people and to God — relations infinitely more complex, varied, and changeable, — the moral self-valuation can no longer remain a simple concrete sensation. It inevitably passes through the medium of abstract thought and assumes the new form of *conscience*. But the two facts are no doubt essentially the same.[15] Shame and conscience speak different languages and on different occasions, but the meaning of what they say is the same: *this is not good, this is wrong, this is unworthy.*

This is the meaning of shame; conscience adds to it the analytic explanation, "if you do this wrong or unlawful thing, you will be guilty of evil, sin, crime."

The voice of conscience, in determining as good or as evil our relations to our neighbours and to God, alone gives them a moral significance which otherwise they would not possess. And as conscience is simply a development of shame, *the whole* moral life of man in all its three aspects springs, so to speak, *from one root* — a root that is distinctly human and essentially foreign to the animal world.

If the ultimate foundation of conscience is the feeling of shame, it is clear that animals which are devoid of this more elementary feeling cannot possess the more complex development of it — conscience. The presence of conscience in them is sometimes deduced from the fact that animals which have done something wrong look guilty. But this conclusion is based on a misunderstanding — on a confusion, namely, between two facts which, as we know from our own experience, are essentially distinct. The moral state of being reproached by conscience, or the state of repentance, has an analogy in the in-

---

15. The expressions *mnie stydno* ('I am ashamed') and *mnie soviestno* ('I am conscience-stricken') are used in the Russian language as synonymous, and, indeed, from the nature of the case it is impossible to draw a sharp line of demarcation between the two mental states.

tellectual sphere in the consciousness of mistake or miscalculation, *i.e.* of an act which from the utilitarian or the practical point of view is purposeless or *unprofitable* and is followed by a feeling of dissatisfaction with oneself. These two facts are similar in form, and both express themselves externally as *confusion* (physiologically as the flushing of the face). But although they sometimes coincide, their nature is so different that often they exist separately and even directly exclude one another. Thus, for instance, when the mayor in Gogol's *Inspector General* is terribly indignant with himself for having been deceived by Khlestakov and not having deceived the latter instead, or when a card-sharper in sudden confusion curses himself for not having been clever enough at cheating, such self-condemnation obviously has nothing to do with the awakening of conscience, but rather proves an inveterate absence of conscience. Intellectual self-condemnation is undoubtedly present in the higher animals. When a well-brought-up dog is so keenly conscious of its own misdemeanours that it actually tries to conceal them, this certainly proves its intelligence, but has no relation whatever to its conscience.

VII

The highest moral doctrine can be no other than a complete and correct development of the ultimate data of human morality, for the universal demands involved in them cover the whole sphere of possible human relations. But it is precisely the *universality* of these relations that forbids us to stop at establishing their existence as simply given in our nature and renders a further development and justification of them necessary.

The primitive, natural morality we have been considering is no other than the reaction of the spiritual nature against the lower forces — fleshly lust, egoism, and wild passions — which threaten to submerge and overpower it. The capacity for such a reaction makes man a moral being; but if the actual force and the extent of the reaction are to remain indefinite, it cannot, as such, be the foundation of the moral order in the human world. All the actual manifestations of our moral nature are merely particular and accidental in character. Man may be *more or less* modest, compassionate, religious: the universal norm is not given as a fact. The voice of conscience itself speaks *more or less* clearly and insistently, and can (in so far as it is a fact) be binding only to the extent to which it is heard in each given case.

But reason, which is as innate in man as the moral feelings, from the first puts to his moral nature its demand for universality and necessity. Rational consciousness cannot rest content with the accidental existence of relatively good feelings from which no general rule can be deduced. The primary distinction between good and evil already implies an idea of the good *free from any limitations,* containing in itself an *absolute* norm of life and activity. In the form of a postulate the idea of the good is inherent in human reason, but its actual content is determined and developed only through the complex work of thought.

From the ultimate data of morality we inevitably pass to the general principles which reason deduces from them, and which have in turn played the foremost part in the different ethical theories.

CHAPTER II

The Ascetic Principle in Morality

I

The fundamental moral feeling of shame psychologically contains man's negative relation to the animal nature which seeks to overpower him. To the strongest and most vivid manifestation of that nature the human spirit, even at a low stage of development, opposes the consciousness of its own dignity: I am ashamed to submit to the desire of the flesh, I am ashamed to be like an animal, the lower side of my nature must not dominate me — such domination is shameful and evil. This self-assertion of the moral dignity — half-conscious and unstable in the simple feeling of shame — is worked up by reason into the *principle of asceticism*.

The object of condemnation in asceticism is not material nature as such. From no point of view can it be rationally maintained that nature considered objectively — whether in its essence or in its appearances — is evil. It is usually supposed that the so-called Oriental religions, which are noted for extreme asceticism, are specially characterised by their identification of the principle of evil with physical matter, in contradistinction to true Christianity, which finds the source of evil in the moral sphere. But, strictly speaking, such identification is not to be found in any system of Oriental philosophy or religion. It is sufficient to mention the three most typical systems of India, the classical country of asceticism — the orthodox Brahmin Vedanta,[1] the independent Sankhya, and, finally, Buddhism.

1. It assumed its present form only about the time when Buddhism disappeared from India (VIII and XIII centuries A.D.), but the fundamental conceptions involved in it are to be found as early as the ancient Upanishads.

According to the Vedanta, evil is illusion of the mind, which takes material objects for entities separate from one another and from the self, and takes the self to be an entity separate from the one absolute Being. The cause of this illusion is the one ultimate Spirit itself (Paramâtman) which suddenly, in a moment of incomprehensible blindness or ignorance (Avidya), conceived the possibility of something other than itself, desired that other, and thus fell into an illusory duality, from which sprang the world. This world does not exist on its own account (as external to the One) but is erroneously taken so to exist — and therein lie the deception and the evil. When a traveller in the wood takes the chopped-off branch of a tree for a snake, or, *vice versa,* a snake for a branch of a tree, neither the image of the snake nor of the branch is in itself evil: what is evil is the one being taken for the other, and both being taken for something external to the self. The ignorant think that their evil works are distinct from the one Reality. But the evil deed, the evil doer himself, and the false thought about their separateness are all part of the one absolute and ultimate Spirit in so far as it *partly*[2] is in *the state of ignorance.* Its self-identity is re-established in the thought of the wise ascetics who by mortifying the flesh have conquered in themselves the illusion of separateness and learnt that *all is one.* According to such a system of thought evil clearly cannot belong to material nature, for that nature is regarded as non-existent. Its reality is acknowledged in another important Indian system — in the independent or atheistic Sankhya. In it the pure spirit (Purusha), existing only in the multitude of separate entities, is opposed to first matter or nature (Prakriti). But the latter is not as such the principle of wrong or of evil: evil (and that only in the relative sense) is in the abiding connection of the spirit with it. These two elements *must* be connected, but only in a *transient* fashion: nature must be the temporal means, and not the purpose, of the spirit. The paralysed man who can see (the spirit) must make use of the blind athlete (nature), on whose shoulders he can attain the end of his journey; but once the end is reached, they must part. The end of the spirit is self-knowledge — that is, knowledge of itself as distinct from nature. But if the spirit is to learn that it is distinct from nature, it must first know nature — and this is the only justification of the connection between the two. Nature is the dancer, spirit the spectator. She has shown herself, he has seen her, and they may part. The ascetic who resists natural inclinations is simply the wise man who refrains from using means which are no longer necessary once the

---

2. Some Hindu books determine the 'part' of ignorance arithmetically as forming one-fourth (or, according to others, one-third) of the Absolute. Probably in order that the relation may remain unaltered the birth of the ignorant is equalised by the enlightenment of the wise.

end has been reached. Orthodox Brahmanism affirms that only the One exists, and that there is no other (the principle of *Advaiti* — of unity or indivisibility). The Sankhya philosophy admits the existence of 'the other' — *i.e.* of nature — but maintains that it is foreign to the spirit, and, once a knowledge of it has been attained, unnecessary. Buddhism reconciles this duality in a general indifference: spirit and nature, the One and its other are equally illusory. 'All is empty'; there is no object for will; the desire to merge one's spirit in the absolute is as senseless as the desire for physical enjoyment. Asceticism is here reduced to a mere state of *not willing.*

Turning from the Hindu systems to a different type of philosophy developed in Egypt, we find that the striking and original form it finally received in the gnosticism of Valentinus's school, involved a conception of the natural world as mixed and heterogeneous in character. The world is, in the first place, the creation of the evil principle (Satan), secondly, the creation of the neutral and unconscious Demiurge who is neither good nor evil, and thirdly, it contains manifestations of the heavenly Wisdom fallen from higher spheres. Thus, the visible light of our world was taken by the thinkers in question to be the smile of Sophia remembering the celestial radiance of the Pleroma (the absolute fulness of being) she had forsaken. Materiality as such was not, then, regarded by the Gnostics as evil; light is material and yet it is a manifestation of the good principle. Matter is not created by Satan because it is in itself evil, but, on the contrary, it is evil only in so far as it is created by Satan, *i.e.* in so far as it manifests or externally expresses the inward nature of evil — in so far as it is darkness, disorder, destruction, death — or, in a word, chaos.

The Persian system of thought (Manicheism), which is more pronouncedly dualistic, no more identifies material nature with evil than does the Egyptian gnosis. The natural world contains the element of light, which proceeds from the divine kingdom of the good; this element is manifested in the phenomena of light and is also present in vegetable and animal life. The highest godhead is imagined by the Manicheans in no other form than that of light.

None of these 'Oriental' systems, then, is guilty of the meaningless identification of evil with material nature as such. But the contention that *there is evil in the material nature of the world and of man* would be granted by all the earnest thinkers both of the East and the West. This truth does not depend upon any metaphysical conception of matter and nature. We ourselves share in material nature and can know from our own inner experience in what respect nature can, and in what respect it cannot, satisfy the demands of the spirit.

II

In spite of Plotinus's well-known assertion to the contrary, the normal man of the highest degree of spiritual development is not in the least ashamed of being a corporeal or material entity. No one is ashamed of having an extended body of a definite shape, colour, and weight; that is, we are not ashamed of all that we have in common with a stone, a tree, a piece of metal. It is only in relation to characteristics we have in common with beings which approach us most nearly and belong to the kingdom of nature contiguous to us, that we have the feeling of shame and of inner opposition. And this feeling shows that it is when we are essentially in contact with the material life of the world and may be actually submerged by it, that we must wrench ourselves away from and rise above it. The feeling of shame is excited neither by that part of our corporeal being which has no direct relation to the spirit at all (such as the above-mentioned material qualities which the spirit has in common with inanimate objects), nor by that part of the living organism which serves as the chief expression of the specifically human rational life — the head, the face, the hands, etc. The object of shame is only that part of our material being which, though immediately related to the spirit, since it can inwardly affect it, is not an expression or an instrument of the spiritual life, but is, on the contrary, a means whereby the processes of purely animal life seek to drag the human spirit down into their sphere, to master and overpower it. The reaction of the spiritual principle, which finds an immediate expression in the feeling of shame, is evoked by material life thus encroaching upon the rational being of man and seeking to make him into a passive instrument of or a useless appendage to the physical process. The rational affirmation of a certain moral norm assumes psychologically the form of fear to violate it or of sorrow at having violated it already. The norm logically presupposed by the feeling of shame is, when expressed in its most general form, as follows: *the animal life in man must be subordinate to the spiritual.* This judgment is apodictically certain, for it is a correct deduction from fact and is based on the logical law of identity. The very fact of man's shame at being merely animal proves that he *is not* a mere animal, but is also something else and something higher; for if he were on the same or on a lower level, shame would be meaningless. Looking at the matter from the formal side alone it cannot be doubted that clear consciousness is better than blind instinct, that spiritual self-control is better than the surrender to the physical process. And if man unites in himself two different elements related as the higher and the lower, the demand for the subordination of the latter to the former follows from the very nature of the case. The fact of shame is independent of individual, racial, and other peculiarities; the demand contained in it is of a *universal* character; and this, in conjunction with the logical *necessity* of that demand, makes it in the full sense of the term a moral *principle.*

III

Man, like the animals, participates in the life of the universe. The essential difference between the two lies simply in the manner of the participation. The animal, being endowed with consciousness, shares inwardly and psychically in the processes of nature which hold it under their sway. It knows which of them are pleasant or unpleasant, it instinctively feels what is detrimental to itself or to the species. But this is true only with reference to the environment which immediately affects the animal at a given time. The world process as a *whole* does not exist for the animal soul. It can know nothing of the reasons and ends of that process, and its participation in it is purely passive or instrumental. Man, on the other hand, passes judgment on the part he takes in the world process, both with reference to the given events that affect him as *psychological motives,* and to the general principle of all activity. That principle is the idea of worth or of lack of worth, of good or of evil, and it can itself become the ground or the motive of human activity. This higher consciousness or inward self-valuation places man in a definite relation to the world process as a *whole,* the relation, namely, of actively participating in its purpose; for in determining all his actions by the idea of the good, man shares in the universal life *only in so far as its purpose is the good.* But since this higher consciousness as a fact grows out of the material nature and exists, so to speak, at its expense, that lower nature or the animal soul in man is naturally opposed to it. There thus arise two conflicting tendencies in our life — the spiritual and the carnal.[3] The spiritual principle, as it immediately appears to our present consciousness, is a distinct tendency or process in our life, directed towards realising in the whole of our being the rational idea of the good. Likewise the carnal principle with which in our inner experience we are concerned, is not the physical organism nor even the animal soul as such, but merely a tendency excited in that soul, and opposed to the higher consciousness, seeking to overpower and to drown in the material process the beginnings of spiritual life.

---

3. This is a fact of our inner experience, and neither its psychological reality nor its ethical significance depends upon the metaphysical or any other view which may be taken of the essence of spirit and matter.

In this case material nature is indeed evil, for it tries to destroy that which is worthy of being and which contains the possibility of something different from and better than the material life. Not in itself but only in this bad relation to the spirit, man's material nature is what in scriptural terminology is called *the flesh*.

The idea of 'flesh' must not be confused with the idea of 'body.' Even from the ascetic point of view body is the temple of the spirit; bodies may be 'spiritual,' 'glorified,' 'heavenly,' but 'flesh and blood cannot inherit the kingdom of heaven.'[4] Flesh is excited animality, animality that breaks loose from its bounds and ceases to be the matter or the hidden (potential) foundation of the spiritual life — as the animal life ought to be both on its physical and on its mental side.

At the elementary stages of his development man is a spiritual being potentially rather than actually; and it is just this potentiality of a higher spiritual life, manifested as self-consciousness and self-control in opposition to blind and uncontrolled physical nature, that is endangered by fleshly lust. Flesh, *i.e.* matter which has ceased to be passive and is striving for independence and infinity, seeks to attract the spiritual power to itself, to drag it in and absorb it into itself, increasing its own power at its expense. This is possible because, as incarnate, as actually *manifested* in the concrete man, spirit, or rather the life of spirit, is only a transformation of material existence (more immediately, of the animal soul), although in their ideal essence spirit and matter are heterogeneous. Regarded concretely, spiritual and material being are two kinds of energy which can be transformed into one another — just as mechanical motion can be transformed into heat and *vice versa*. The flesh (*i.e.* the animal soul as such) is strong only in the weakness of the spirit and lives only by its death. Therefore, for the spirit to preserve itself and to increase in power, the flesh must be subdued and transferred from the actual to the potential state. This is the real meaning of the moral law that flesh must be subordinate to the spirit, and the true basis of all moral asceticism.

---

4. [See 1 Corinthians 6:19; 15:40, 44, 50. — *Editor's note.*] Sometimes in the Scriptures the word 'flesh' is used in the wide sense of material being in general: *e.g.* 'The Word was made flesh' (John 1:14), *i.e.* became a physical event, which did not prevent the incarnate word from being a purely spiritual and sinless God-man. But usually the terms 'flesh' and 'fleshly' are used in the Scriptures in the bad sense of material nature which violates its due relation to the spirit, is opposed to and exclusive of it. Such terminology is found both in the New and in the Old Testament; *e.g.* "My spirit shall not dwell in these men for they are flesh" [Gen. 6:3; this phrase is translated directly from the Russian Bible. — *Editor's note*].

IV

The moral demand to subordinate the flesh to the spirit conflicts with the actual striving of the flesh to subject the spirit to itself. Consequently the ascetic principle has a double aspect. It requires in the first place that the spiritual life should be safeguarded from the encroachments of the flesh, and secondly, that the animal life should be made merely the potentiality or the matter of the spirit. Owing to the intimate inner connection and constant interaction between the spiritual and the carnal aspects of the human being as a whole, these two demands — the preservation of the spirit from the flesh and the realisation of the spirit in the flesh — cannot be fulfilled separately, but inevitably pass into one another. In actual life spirit can defend itself against the encroachments of the flesh only at the expense of the latter, that is, by being partially realised in it; at the same time the realisation of the spirit is only possible on the condition of its constantly defending itself against the continued attempts of the flesh to destroy its independence.

The three chief moments in this process are: (1) the *distinction* which the spirit inwardly draws between itself and the flesh; (2) the struggle of the spirit for its *independence;* (3) the *supremacy* achieved by the spirit over nature or the annihilation of the evil carnal principle as such. The first moment, which is characteristic of man in contradistinction to animals, is directly given in the feeling of shame. The third, being the consequence of the moral perfection already attained, cannot at the present stage be the direct object of the moral demand or rule. It is useless to confront even a moral man, while he is still imperfect, with the categorical imperative "become at once immortal and incorruptible!" Thus only the second moment is left for ethics, and our moral principle may be more closely defined as follows: *subordinate the flesh to the spirit, in so far as this is necessary for the dignity and the independence of the latter. Hoping finally for a complete mastery over the physical forces in yourself and in nature as a whole, take for your immediate and binding purpose not to be, at any rate, the bondman of rebellious matter or chaos.*

Flesh is existence that is not self-contained, that is wholly directed outwards; it is emptiness, hunger, and insatiability; it is lost in externality and ends in actual disintegration. In contradistinction to it, spirit is existence determined inwardly, self-contained and self-possessed. Its outward expression is due to its own spontaneity, and does not cause it to become external or to be lost and dissolved in externality. Hence self-preservation of the spirit is, above all things, the preservation of its *self-control*. This is the main point of all asceticism.

The human body, in its anatomic structure and physiological functions, has no moral significance of its own. It may be the expression and the instrument both of the flesh and of the spirit. Hence the moral struggle between these two aspects of our being takes place in the domain of the bodily or the organic life as well, and assumes the form of a struggle for the mastery over the body.

V

With regard to the corporeal life our moral task consists in not being passively determined by fleshly desires, especially in reference to the two most important functions of our organism — nutrition and reproduction.

By way of preliminary exercise, which in itself, however, has no moral value, it is important for the spirit to acquire power over such functions of our animal organism as are not directly related to the 'lusts of the flesh' — namely, over *breathing* and *sleep*.[5]

Breathing is the fundamental condition of life and the constant means of communication between our body and its environment. For the power of the spirit over the body it is desirable that this fundamental function should be under the control of the human will. Consequently there arose long ago and everywhere different ascetic practices with regard to breathing. The practice and theory of breathing exercises is found among the Indian hermits, among the sorcerers of ancient and more recent times, among the monks of Mount Athos and similar monasteries, in Swedenborg, and, in our own day, in Thomas Lake-Harris and Laurence Oliphant.[6] The mystical details of the matter have nothing to do with moral philosophy. I will therefore content myself with a few general remarks. A certain control of the will over breathing is required by ordinary good manners. For ascetic purposes one merely goes further in this direction. By constant exercise it is easy to learn not to breathe through the mouth either when awake or when asleep; the next stage is to learn to suppress breathing altogether for a longer or shorter time.[7] The power acquired over this organic function undoubtedly increases the strength of the spirit and gives it a secure foundation for further ascetic achievements.

5. I mean normal sleep; abnormal will be dealt with further on.

6. Thomas Lake-Harris (1823-1903) was an American poet and spiritualist; Laurence Oliphant (1829-1888) was a British-born spiritualist and author. — *Editor's note.*

7. The so-called 'nostril breathing,' and also complete stoppage of breathing, used to be, and in places still is, zealously practised by Orthodox ascetics, as one of the conditions of the contemplation of divine things.

Sleep is a temporary break in the activity of the brain and of the nervous system — the direct physiological instruments of the spirit — and it therefore weakens the tie between the spiritual and the bodily life. It is important that the spirit should not in this case play a purely passive part. If sleep is caused by physical causes, the spirit must be able, for motives of its own, to ward it off, or to interrupt sleep that has already begun. The very difficulty of this task, which is undoubtedly a possible one, shows its importance. The power to overcome sleep and to wake at will is a necessary demand of spiritual hygiene. Moreover, sleep has another aspect, which distinguishes it from breathing and other organic functions that are in the moral sense indifferent, and connects it with nutrition and reproduction. Like the two latter functions sleep may be misused to the advantage of the carnal and to the detriment of the spiritual life. The inclination to excessive sleep in itself shows the predominance of the material or the passive principle; a surrender to this inclination and actual abuse of sleep undoubtedly weaken the spirit and strengthen the lusts of the flesh. This is the reason why in the history of ascetic practices — for instance in Christian monasticism — struggle with sleep plays so important a part. Of course, the loosening of the bond between the spiritual and the corporeal life (or more exactly between the conscious and the instinctive life) may be of two kinds: sleepers must be distinguished from dreamers. But as a general rule a special faculty to dream significant and prophetic dreams indicates a degree of spiritual power that has been already developed by ascetic practices — struggle with the pleasure of carnal sleep among them.

VI

In animals the predominance of matter over form is due to excess of food, as can be clearly seen in caterpillars among the lower, and fattened pigs among the higher, animals.[8] In man the same cause (excess of food) leads to a predominance of the animal life, or the flesh, over the spirit. This is why abstinence in food and drink — fasting — has always and everywhere been one of the fundamental demands of ethics. Abstinence has reference, in the first place, to the quantity — with regard to which there can be no general rule — and secondly, to the quality of food. In this last respect the rule has always and everywhere been abstinence from animal food and especially from meat (*i.e.* from the flesh of warm-blooded animals). The reason is that meat is more easily and completely converted into blood, and increases the energy of the

8. See the essay "Beauty in Nature" by the present author.

carnal life more powerfully and rapidly than other foods do.[9] Abstinence from flesh food can unquestionably be affirmed as a universal rule. Objections to it cannot stand the test of criticism, and have long ago been disposed of both by ethics and by natural science. There was a time when eating raw or cooked *human* flesh was regarded as normal.[10] From the ascetic point of view abstinence from meat (and animal food in general) is doubly useful, first, because it weakens the force of the carnal life, and secondly, because the hereditary habit has developed a natural craving for such food, and abstinence from it exercises the will at the expense of material inclinations and thus heightens the spiritual energy.

As to drinking, the simplest good sense forbids excessive use of strong drinks that leads to the loss of reason. The ascetic principle requires, of course, more than this. Speaking generally, wine heightens the energy of the nervous system, and, through it, of the psychical life. At our stage of spiritual development the soul is still dominated by carnal motives, and all that excites and increases the nervous energy in the service of the soul goes to strengthen this predominant carnal element, and is therefore highly injurious to the spirit; so that here complete abstinence from wine and strong drink is necessary. But at the higher stages of moral life which were sometimes attained even in the pagan world — for instance by Socrates (see Plato's *Symposium*) — the energy of the organism serves the spiritual rather than the carnal purposes. In that case the increase of nervous energy (of course within the limits compatible with bodily health) heightens the activity of the spirit and therefore, in a certain measure, may be harmless or even directly useful. There can be here only one absolute and universal rule: *to preserve spiritual sobriety and a clear mind.*[11]

The most important and decisive significance in the struggle of the spirit

---

9. Another moral motive for abstaining from meat food is not ascetic but altruistic, namely, the extension to animals of the law of love or pity. This motive is predominant in the ethics of Buddhism, and the ascetic one is predominant in the Christian Church.

10. According to the Biblical teaching the food of the normal human being before the Fall consisted solely of raw fruits and herbs. This is still the rule for the strictest monastic fast, both in the East and in the West (the Trappists). Between this extreme and the light Roman Catholic fast for the laity there are many degrees which have a natural foundation (*e.g.* the distinction between the warm- and the cold-blooded animals, owing to which fish is regarded as a food to be taken during fasts) but involve no question of principle and have no universal significance.

11. At the present moral level of humanity the mastery of the carnal desires is the rule, and the predominance of spiritual motives the exception, and one not to be depended upon; so that total abstinence from strong drinks and all other stimulants may well be preached without any practical disadvantage. But this is a pedagogical and prophylactic question involving no moral principle.

with the flesh in the physiological sphere belongs to the sexual function. The element of moral wrong (the sin of the flesh) is not to be found of course in the physical fact of childbirth (and conception) which is, on the contrary, a certain redemption of the sin — but only in the unlimited and blind desire (lust of the flesh, *concupiscentia*) for an external, animal, and material union with another person (in reality or imagination), a union taken to be an end in itself, an independent object of enjoyment. The predominance of flesh over spirit expresses itself most strongly, clearly, and permanently in the carnal union of two persons. It is not for nothing that the immediate feeling of shame is connected precisely with this act. To stifle or to pervert its testimony; after many thousands of years of inward and outward development, and from the heights of a refined intelligence to pronounce good that which even the simple feeling of the savage acknowledges to be wrong — this is, indeed, a disgrace to humanity and a clear proof of our demoralisation. The actual or the supposed necessity of a certain act for other purposes cannot be a sufficient reason for judging of its essential quality as such. In some diseases it may be necessary to take poison, but that necessity is itself an anomaly from the hygienic point of view.

The moral question with regard to the sexual function is in the first place the question of one's *inner* relation to it, of passing judgment upon it as such. How are we inwardly to regard this fact from the point of view of the final norm, of the absolute good — are we to approve of it or to condemn it? *Which path* must we choose and follow in respect to it: to affirm and develop or to deny, limit, and finally to abolish it? The feeling of shame and the voice of conscience in each concrete case definitely and clearly give the second answer, and all that is left for moral philosophy to do is to give it the form of a universal rational principle. The carnal means of reproduction is for man an evil; it expresses the predominance of the senseless material process over the self-control of the spirit; it is contrary to the dignity of man, destructive of human love and life. Our moral relation to this fact must be absolutely negative. We must adopt the path that leads to its limitation and abolition; how and when it will be abolished in humanity as a whole or even in ourselves is a question that has nothing to do with ethics. The entire transformation of our carnal life into spiritual life does not *as an event* lie within our power, for it is connected with the general conditions of the historical and cosmical process. It cannot therefore be the object of moral duty, rule, or law. What is binding upon us, and what has moral significance, is our inner relation to this fundamental expression of the carnal life. We must regard it as an evil, be determined not to submit to that evil, and, so far as in us lies, conscientiously carry out this determination. From this point of view we may of course judge our external actions, but we may do so only because we know their connection with their inner moral conditions; other people's actions in this sphere we may not judge — we may judge only their *principles*. As a principle the affirmation of the carnal relation of the sexes is in any case an evil. Man's final acceptance of the kingdom of death which is maintained and perpetuated by carnal reproduction deserves absolute condemnation. Such is the positive Christian point of view which decides this all-important question according to the spirit and not according to the letter, and consequently without any *external* exclusiveness. "He that is able to receive it, let him receive it."[12] Marriage is approved and sanctified, child-bearing is blessed, and celibacy is praised as 'the condition of the angels.' But this very designation of it as *angelic* seems to suggest a third and higher path — the *divine*. For man in his ultimate destiny is higher than the angels.[13]

If the Divine Wisdom, according to its wont, brings forth out of evil a greater good and uses our carnal sins for the sake of perfecting humanity by means of new generations, this, of course, tends to its glory and to our comfort, but not to our justification. It treats in exactly the same way all other evils, but this fact cancels neither the distinction between good and evil nor the obligatoriness of the former for us. Besides, the idea that the preaching of sexual abstinence, however energetic and successful, may *prematurely* stop the propagation of the human race and lead to its annihilation is so absurd that one may justly doubt the sincerity of those who profess to hold it. It is not likely that any one can seriously fear this particular danger for humanity. So long as the change of generations is necessary for the development of the human kind, the taste for bringing that change about will certainly not disappear in men. But in any case, the moment when all men will finally overcome the fleshly lust and become entirely chaste — even if that moment, *per impossibile,* came tomorrow — will be the end of the historical process and the beginning of 'the life to come' for all humanity; so that the very idea of child-bearing coming to an end 'too soon' is absolute nonsense, invented by hypocrites. As if any one, in surrendering to the desire of the flesh, had ever thought of safeguarding thereby the future of humanity![14]

---

12. Matthew 19:12. — *Editor's note.*

13. See *The Meaning of Love* and "The Drama of Plato's Life" by the present author.

14. I am not speaking here of the marriage union in its highest spiritual sense, which has nothing to do either with the sin of the flesh or with child-bearing, but is the pattern of the most perfect union between beings: "This is a great mystery; but I speak concerning Christ and the church" (Eph. 5:32). Concerning this mystical meaning of marriage see *The Meaning of Love.*

VII

All the rules of ascetic morality in the sphere of the bodily life — to acquire power over breathing and sleep, to be temperate in food and to abstain from fleshly lust — have essentially an inward and morally psychological character, as rules for the will; but owing to the difference in their objects they do not stand in the same relation to the psychological side of the carnal life. The first and partly the second rule (with regard to breathing and sleep) have for their object purely physiological functions which are not, as such, hostile to the spirit, nor a source of danger to it. The spirit simply wants to control them for the sake of increasing its own power for the more important struggle before it. Nutrition and reproduction — and consequently the ascetic rules with regard to them — have a different character. The positive feeling of pleasure which accompanies these functions may become an end for the will, bind the spiritual forces and draw them into the stream of the carnal life. The latter of the two functions is particularly incompatible (under ordinary conditions) with the preservation of spiritual self-control. On the other hand, breathing and sleep are merely processes in our own organism, while nutrition and reproduction are connected with external objects which, apart from their actual existence and relation to us, may, as subjective *representations,* dominate the imagination and the will and encroach on the domain of the spirit; hence the necessity of ascetic struggle with the inward sins of the flesh, still more shameful than the outward. An epicure whose mouth waters at the very idea of *recherché* dishes, no doubt falls away from human dignity more than a person who indulges himself at the table without particularly thinking about the matter.

In this sense the ascetic attitude to the nutritive and the sexual functions belongs to the psychological and not to the physiological side of the struggle between the flesh and the spirit. The struggle in this case is not against the functions of the organism as such, but against the states of the soul — gluttony, drunkenness, sensuality. These sinful propensities, which may become passions and vices, are on a level with evil emotions such as anger, envy, cupidity, etc. The latter passions, which are *evil* and not merely *shameful,* fall within the province of altruistic and not of ascetic morality, for they involve a certain relation to one's neighbours. But there are some general rules for the inner, morally-psychological struggle with sinful inclinations as such, whether they refer to other men or to our own material nature.

The inner process in and through which an evil desire takes possession of the self has three main stages. To begin with, there arises in the mind the idea of some object or some action which corresponds to one of the bad propensities of our nature. This idea causes the spirit to reflect upon it. At that first stage a simple act of will *rejecting* such reflection is sufficient. The spirit must simply show its firmness or impermeability to foreign elements.[15] If this is not done, the reflection develops into an imaginary picture of this or that nature — sensual, vindictive, vain, and so on.[16] This picture forces the mind to attend to it, and cannot be got rid of by a mere negative act of will; it is necessary to *draw the mind away* by thinking in the opposite direction (for instance, by thinking about death). But if at this second stage the mind, instead of being drawn away from the picture of sin, dwells upon it and identifies itself with it, then the third moment inevitably comes when not only the mind, secretly impelled by the evil desire, but the whole spirit *gives itself up* to the sinful thought and enjoys it. Neither a rejecting act of will nor a distracting reflection of the mind can then save the spirit from bondage — practical moral work is necessary to *re-establish* the inner equilibrium in the whole man. Otherwise the victory of the sinful emotion over the spirit will become a passion and a vice. Man will lose his rational freedom, and moral rules will lose their power over him.

Ethics is the hygiene and not the therapeutics of the spiritual life.

VIII

The supremacy of the spirit over the flesh is necessary in order to preserve the moral dignity of man. The principle of true asceticism is the principle of spiritual self-preservation. But the inner self-preservation of a *separate* man, of a

15. Ecclesiastical writers describe this rule as "dashing the babes of Babylon against the stones," following the allegorical line in the Psalms: "O daughter of Babylon, who art to be destroyed . . . happy shall he be that taketh and dasheth thy little ones against the stones" (Ps. 137:8-9; Babylon = the kingdom of sin; a babe of Babylon = a sin conceived in thought and as yet undeveloped; stone = the firmness of faith).

16. When one is young and has a lively imagination and little spiritual experience, the evil thought develops very rapidly, and, reaching absurd proportions, calls forth a strong moral reaction. Thus you think of a person you dislike, and experience a slight emotion of injury, indignation, and anger. If you do not immediately dash this 'babe of Babylon' against the stones, your imagination, obedient to the evil passion, will immediately draw a vivid picture before you. You meet your enemy and put him into an awkward position. All his worthlessness is exposed. You experience the *velleitas* of magnanimity, but the passion is roused and overwhelms you. At first you keep within the limits of good breeding. You make subtly stinging remarks which, however, soon become more stinging than subtle; then you 'insult him verbally,' and then you 'assault him.' Your devilishly strong fist deals victorious blows. The scoundrel is felled to the ground, the scoundrel is killed, and you dance on his corpse like a cannibal. One can go no further — nothing is left but to cross oneself and renounce it all in disgust.

being who, though spiritual (*i.e.* possessing reason and will), is nevertheless *limited* or relative in his separateness, cannot be the *absolute good* or the supreme and final end of life. The slavery of man to fleshly desires in the wide sense of the term, *i.e.* to all that is senseless and contrary to reason, transforms him into the worst species of animal, and is, no doubt, evil. In this sense no one can honestly argue against asceticism, that is, against self-restraint as a principle. Every one agrees that incapacity to resist animal instincts is a weakness of the spirit, *shameful* for a human being, and therefore bad. The capacity for such resistance or self-restraint is then a good, and must be accepted as a norm from which definite rules of conduct may be deduced. On this point, as on others, moral philosophy merely explains and elaborates the testimony of ordinary human consciousness. Apart from any principles, gluttony, drunkenness, lewdness immediately call forth disgust and contempt, and abstinence from these vices meets with instinctive respect, *i.e.* is acknowledged as a good. This good, however, taken by itself, is *not* absolute. The power of the spirit over the flesh, or the strength of will acquired by rightful abstinence, may be used for immoral purposes. *A strong will may be evil.* A man may suppress his lower nature in order to boast or to pride himself on his superior power; such a victory of the spirit is not a good. It is still worse if the self-control of the spirit and the concentration of the will are used to the detriment of other people, even apart from the purposes of low gain. Asceticism has been, and is, successfully practised by men given to spiritual pride, hypocrisy, and vanity, and even by vindictive, cruel, and selfish men. According to the general verdict, such an ascetic is in the moral sense far inferior to a simple-hearted drunkard or glutton or to a kind profligate. Asceticism in itself is not necessarily a good, and cannot therefore be the supreme or the absolute principle of morality. The true (the moral) ascetic acquires control over the flesh, not simply for the sake of increasing the powers of the spirit, but for furthering the realisation of the Good. Asceticism which liberates the spirit from shameful (carnal) passions only to attach it more closely to evil (spiritual) passions is obviously a false or immoral asceticism.[17] Its true pro-

---

17. If the suppression of the flesh is taken not as a means for good or evil but as an end in itself, we get a peculiar kind of false asceticism which identifies flesh with the physical body, and considers every bodily torment a virtue. Although this false asceticism of self-laceration has no evil purpose to begin with, in its further development it easily becomes an evil: it either proves to be a slow suicide or becomes a peculiar kind of sensuality. It would be unwise, however, thus to condemn all cases of self-laceration. Natures that have a particularly strong material life may require heroic means for its suppression. One must not therefore indiscriminately condemn Stylitism, fetters, and other similar means of mortifying the flesh that were in use in the heroic times of asceticism.

totype, according to the Christian idea, is the devil, who does not eat or drink and remains in celibacy. If, then, from the moral point of view we cannot approve of a wicked or a pitiless ascetic, it follows that the principle of asceticism has only a relative moral significance, namely, that it is *conditioned* by its connection with the principle of altruism, the root of which is pity. I now pass to consider this second moral principle.

CHAPTER III

Pity and Altruism

I

It has for a long time been thought — and many are beginning to think so again — that the highest virtue or holiness is to be found in asceticism and 'mortification of the flesh,' in suppressing natural inclinations and affections, in abstinence and freedom from passions. We have seen that this ideal undoubtedly contains some truth, for it is clear that the higher or the spiritual side of man must dominate the lower or the material. The efforts of will in this direction are acts of spiritual self-preservation and are the first condition of all morality. The *first condition,* however, cannot be taken to be *the ultimate end.* Man must strengthen his spirit and subordinate his flesh, not because this is the purpose of his life, but because it is only when he is free from the bondage to blind and evil material desires that he can serve truth and goodness in the right way and attain real perfection.

The rules of abstinence strengthen the spiritual power of the man who practises them. But in order that the strong spirit may have moral worth — *i.e.* that it may be good and not evil — it must unite the power over its own flesh with a rightful and charitable attitude to other beings. History has shown that, apart from this condition, the supremacy of the ascetic principle, even when combined with a true religion, leads to terrible consequences. The ministers of the Mediaeval Church, who used to torture and burn heretics, Jews, sorcerers and witches, were for the most part men irreproachable from the ascetic point of view. But the one-sided force of the spirit and the absence of pity made them devils incarnate. The bitter fruits of mediaeval asceticism sufficiently justify the reaction against it, which, in the sphere of moral philosophy, has led to the supremacy of the *altruistic* principle in morality.

This principle is deeply rooted in our being in the form of the feeling of pity which man has in common with other living creatures. If the feeling of shame differentiates man from the rest of nature and distinguishes him from other animals, the feeling of pity, on the contrary, unites him with the whole world of the living. It does so in a double sense: in the first place because man shares it with all other living creatures, and secondly because all living creatures can and must be the *objects* of that feeling to man.

II

That the natural basis of our moral relation to others is the feeling of pity or compassion, and not the feeling of unity or solidarity in general, is a truth which is independent of any system of metaphysics[1] and in no way involves a pessimistic view of the world and of life. As is well known, Schopenhauer maintains that the ultimate nature of the universe is Will, and will is essentially a state of dissatisfaction (for satisfaction implies that there is nothing to wish for). Hence dissatisfaction or suffering is the fundamental and positive determination of all existence in its inward aspect, and the inner moral bond between beings is compassion. But altogether apart from this doubtful theory — and the equally doubtful calculations of Hartmann,[2] who tries to prove that the amount of pain in humanity is incomparably greater than the amount of pleasure — we find that from the nature of the case the only basis of the moral relation to other beings is, *as a matter of principle,* to be found in pity or compassion, and certainly not in co-rejoicing or co-pleasure.

Human delight, pleasure, and joy may of course be innocent and even positively good — and in that case sharing in them has a positive moral character. But, on the other hand, human pleasures may be, and often are, immoral. A wicked and vindictive man finds pleasure in insulting and tormenting those near him, rejoices in their humiliation, delights in the harm he has done. A sensual man finds the chief joy of life in profligacy; a cruel man in killing animals or even human beings; a drunkard is happy when he is stupefying himself with drink, etc. In all these cases the feeling of pleasure cannot be separated from the bad actions which produce it, and sometimes, indeed, the pleasure gives an immoral character to actions which would in themselves be indifferent. Thus when a soldier in war kills an enemy at the word of command

1. Such as the doctrine of Buddhism or Schopenhauer's 'Philosophy of the Will.'

2. Solovyov is referring to the German philosopher Eduard von Hartmann (1842-1906), whose chief work was *The Philosophy of the Unconscious.* Solovyov discusses Hartmann at length in his early work *The Crisis of Western Philosophy* (1874). — *Editor's note.*

from no other motive than 'his duty as a soldier,' no one would accuse him of immoral cruelty, whatever our attitude to war might be. But it is a different thing if he finds *pleasure* in killing and bayonets a man with relish. In more simple cases the thing is clearer still; thus it is obvious that the immorality of drunkenness consists not in the external action of swallowing certain drinks but in the inner *pleasure* which a man finds in artificially stupefying himself.

But if a certain pleasure is in itself immoral, the participation in it by another person (co-rejoicing, co-pleasure) also receives an immoral character. The fact is that positive participation in a pleasure implies the *approval* of that pleasure. Thus in sharing the drunkard's delight in his favourite pleasure I approve of drunkenness; in sharing somebody's joy at successful revenge I approve of vindictiveness. And since these pleasures are bad pleasures, those who sympathise with them approve of what is evil, and consequently are themselves guilty of immorality. Just as participation in a crime is itself regarded as a crime, so sympathy with vicious pleasure or delight must itself be pronounced vicious. And indeed sympathy with an evil pleasure not only involves an approval of it, but also presupposes the same bad propensity in the sympathiser. Only a drunkard delights in another person's drunkenness, only a vindictive man rejoices in another's revenge. Participation in the pleasures or joys of others may then be good or bad *according to their object;* and if it may be immoral, it cannot *as such* be the *basis* of the moral relation.

The same thing cannot be said about suffering and compassion. According to the very idea of it, suffering is a state in which the will of the one who suffers has no direct and positive part. When we speak of 'voluntary suffering,' we mean, not that suffering is desired as such, but that the object of will is that which makes suffering necessary, in other words, that the object of will is the good which is attained by suffering. A martyr undergoes torments, not for their own sake, but because in the circumstances they are a necessary consequence of his faith and a means to higher glory and to the kingdom of heaven. On the other hand, suffering may be deserved, *i.e.* its cause may lie in bad actions; but the suffering as such is distinct from its cause and contains no moral guilt; on the contrary, it is regarded as its expiation and redemption. Though drunkenness is a sin, no moralist, however stern, would pronounce the headache that results from drinking to be a sin also. For this reason participation in the suffering of others (even when they deserve it) — *i.e.* pity or compassion — can never be immoral. In commiserating with one who suffers I do not in the least approve of the evil cause of his suffering.[3] Pity for the

---

3. An *apparent* instance to the contrary is the case of a person sympathising with another who is grieved at the failure of his crime. But, in truth, even in this case in so far as sympathy

criminal's suffering does not mean approval or justification of his crime. On the contrary, the greater my pity for the sad consequences of a man's sin, the greater my *condemnation* of the sin.

Participation in the pleasures of others may always have an element of self-interest. Even in the case of an old man sharing the joy of a child doubt may be felt with regard to the altruistic nature of his sentiment; for in any case it is pleasant for the old man to refresh the memory of his own happy childhood. On the contrary, all genuine feeling of regret at the suffering of others, whether moral or physical, is painful for the person who experiences that feeling, and is therefore opposed to his egoism. This is clear from the fact that sincere grief about others disturbs our personal joy, damps our mirth, that is, proves to be incompatible with the state of selfish satisfaction. Genuine compassion or pity can have no selfish motives and is purely *altruistic*, while the feeling of co-rejoicing or co-pleasure is, from the moral point of view, a mixed and indefinite feeling.

III

There is another reason why participation in the joys or pleasures of others cannot in itself have the same fundamental importance for ethics as the feeling of pity or compassion. The demand of reason is that morality should be *based* only upon such feelings as always contain an impulse for definite action and, being generalised, give rise to a definite moral principle or principles. But pleasure or joy is the *end* of action; in it the purpose of the activity is reached, and participation in the pleasure of others as well as the experience of one's own pleasure contains no impulse and no ground for further action. Pity, on the contrary, directly urges us to act in order to help a fellow-being and to save him from suffering. The action may be purely inward — thus pity for my enemy may prevent me from insulting or injuring him — but in any case it is an action, and not a passive state like joy or pleasure. Of course, I may find inward satisfaction in the fact that I did not hurt my neighbour, but this can only happen after the act of will has taken place. Similarly in the case of rendering help to a fellow-being who is in pain or in need, the pleasure or

---

arises solely out of pity it does not in the least refer to the bad cause of the grief, in no way presupposes an approval of it, and therefore is good and innocent. But if, in being sorry for the murderer who missed his aim, I also deplore his failure, the immorality will lie not in my pity for the criminal, but in my *lack of pity* for his victim. Speaking generally, when several persons prove to be at one in some wrong, the moral condemnation refers not to the fact of their solidarity, but only to the bad object of it.

joy resulting therefrom, both for him and for the person who helps him, is only the final consequence and the culmination of the altruistic act, and not its source or its ground. If I see or hear that some one is suffering, one of two things happens. Either that other person's suffering calls forth in me also a certain degree of pain and I experience pity — in which case *that* feeling is a direct and sufficient reason for me to render active help. Or, if another's suffering does not rouse pity in me, or does not rouse it sufficiently to incite me to act, the idea of the pleasure which would ensue from my action would obviously be still less likely to do so. It is clear that an abstract and conditioned thought of a future mental state cannot possibly have more effect than the immediate contemplation or concrete representation of actual physical and mental states which call for direct action. Therefore the true ground or the producing cause *(causa efficiens)* of every altruistic action is the perception or the idea of another person's suffering as it actually exists at the moment, and not the thought of the pleasure which may arise in the future as the result of the benevolent act. Of course, if a person decides out of pity to help a fellow-being in distress, he may, if he have time to do so, imagine — especially on the ground of the remembered experiences in the past — the joy he will thereby give to himself and to that other person. But to take this concomitant and accidental thought for the true motive of action is contrary both to logic and to psychological experience.

On the one hand, then, participation in the actual joys and pleasures of others cannot from the very nature of the case contain either a stimulus for action or a rule of conduct, for in these states satisfaction is already attained. On the other hand, a conditional representation of future pleasures, which are supposed to follow upon the removal of the suffering, can only be a secondary and an indirect addition to the actual feeling of compassion or pity which moves us to do active good. Consequently it is this feeling alone which must be pronounced to be the true ground of altruistic conduct.

Those who pity the sufferings of others will certainly participate in their joys and pleasures when the latter are harmless and innocent. But this natural consequence of the moral relation to others cannot be taken as the *basis* of morality. That alone is truly good which is good in itself, and therefore *always* preserves its good character, never becoming evil. Therefore the morality (or the good) in any given sphere of relations can be based only upon such data from which a *general* and absolute rule of conduct may be deduced. Such precisely is the nature of pity towards our fellow-beings. To pity all that suffers is *always* and *unconditionally good;* it is a rule that requires no reservations. But participation in the joys and pleasures of others may be approved conditionally only, and even when it is laudable it contains, as we have seen, no rule of conduct.

IV

The unquestionable and familiar fact that a distinct individual being may, as it were, transcend in feeling the limits of his individuality, and respond painfully to the suffering of others, experiencing it as if it were his own pain, may appear to some minds mysterious and enigmatic. It was regarded as such by the philosopher who found in compassion the sole foundation of morality.

"How is it possible," he asks, "that suffering which is not mine should become an immediate motive of my action in the same way as my own suffering does?" "This presupposes," he goes on, "that I have to a certain extent identified myself with another, and that the barrier between *the self* and the *not self* has been for the moment removed. It is then only that the position of another, his want, his need, his suffering, immediately (?) becomes mine. I no longer see him then as he is given me in empirical perception — as something foreign and indifferent (?) to me, as something absolutely (?) separate from me. On the contrary, in compassion it is I who suffer in him, although his skin does not cover my nerves. Only through such identification can *his* suffering, *his* need, become a motive for *me* in a way in which ordinarily only my own suffering can. This is a highly mysterious phenomenon — it is a real mystery of Ethics, for it is something for which reason cannot directly account (?!) and the grounds of which cannot be discovered empirically. And yet it is of everyday occurrence. Each has experienced it himself and seen it in other people. It happens every day before our eyes on a small scale in individual cases every time that, moved by an immediate impulse, without any further reflection, a man helps another and defends him, sometimes risking his own life for the sake of a person whom he sees for the first time, thinking of nothing but the obvious distress and need of that person. It happens on a large scale when a whole nation sacrifices its blood and its property for the sake of defending or setting free another, oppressed, nation. For such actions to deserve unconditional moral approval, it is necessary that there should be present that mysterious act of compassion or of inner identification of oneself with another, without any ulterior motives."[4]

This discussion of the mysterious character of compassion is distinguished by literary eloquence more than by philosophic truth. The mystery is not to be found in the fact itself, but is due to a false description, which lays exaggerated emphasis on the extreme terms of the relation, and leaves the connecting links between them entirely out of account. In his sphere Schopenhauer abused the rhetorical method of contrast or antithesis quite as much as

---

4. Schopenhauer, *Die beiden Grundprobleme der Ethik,* 2nd ed., Leipzig, 1860, p. 230.

Victor Hugo did in his. The matter is described in such a way as if a given being, *absolutely separate* from another, all of a sudden *immediately identified* itself with that other in the feeling of compassion. This would, indeed, be highly mysterious. But, in truth, neither the absolute separateness nor the immediate identification of which Schopenhauer speaks exists at all. To understand any relation one must take first the earliest and most elementary instance of it. Take the maternal instinct of animals. When a dog defends her puppies or suffers at losing them, where does all the mystery of which Schopenhauer speaks come in? Are these puppies something 'foreign and indifferent' to their mother, and 'absolutely separate' from her? Between her and them there was from the first a real physical and organic connection, clear and obvious to the simplest observation and independent of all metaphysics. These creatures were for a time actually a part of her own body, her nerves and theirs had been covered by one and the same skin, and the very beginning of their existence involved a change in her organism, and was painfully reflected in her sensations.[5] At birth this real organic connection is weakened, becomes looser, so to speak, but it is not completely severed or replaced by 'absolute separateness.' Therefore the participation of a mother in the sufferings of her children is as much a natural fact as the pain we feel when we cut a finger or dislocate a leg. In a sense, of course, this, too, is mysterious — but not in the sense in which the philosopher of compassion takes it to be. Now all the other and more complex manifestations of the feeling of pity have a similar ground. All that exists, and, in particular, all living beings are connected by the fact of their compresence in one and the same world, and by the unity of origin; all spring from one common mother — nature, of which they are a part; nowhere do we find the 'absolute separateness' of which Schopenhauer speaks. The natural organic connection of all beings as parts of one whole is given in experience, and is not merely a speculative idea. Hence the psychological expression of that connection — the inner participation of one being in the suffering of others, compassion or pity — can be understood even from the empirical point of view as the expression of the natural and obvious *solidarity* of all that exists. This participation of beings in one another is in keeping with the general plan of the universe, is in harmony with reason or perfectly rational. What is senseless or irrational is the mutual estrangement of beings, their subjective separateness, contradictory of their objective unity. It is this inner egoism and not

---

5. Certain animals, like human mothers, have been observed to suffer from *nausea a conceptu* ["nausea of pregnancy" — *Editor's note*]. The maternal feeling established on the physical basis may afterwards, like all feelings, be diverted from its natural object and transferred to the young of *another* animal that have been substituted for her own.

the mutual sympathy between the different parts of one nature that really is mysterious and enigmatic. Reason can give no direct account of it, and its grounds are not to be found empirically.

Absolute separateness is merely affirmed but is not established by egoism; it neither does nor can exist as a fact. On the other hand, the mutual connection between beings which finds its psychological expression in sympathy or pity is certainly not of the nature of immediate identification as Schopenhauer takes it to be. When I am sorry for my friend who has a headache the feeling of sympathy does not as a rule become a headache. So far from my being identified with him even our states remain distinct, and I clearly distinguish my head, which does not ache, from his, which does. Also, so far as I am aware, it has never happened that a compassionate man, who jumps into the water to save another from drowning, should take that other person for himself or himself for that other. Even a hen — a creature more noted for her maternal instinct than for intelligence — clearly understands the distinction between herself and her chicks, and, therefore, behaves in relation to them in a certain way, which would be impossible if in her maternal compassion 'the barrier between the self and the not self were removed.' If this were the case, the hen might confuse herself with her chickens, and, when hungry, might ascribe that sensation to them and start feeding them, although in reality they were satisfied and she almost starving; or, another time, she might feed herself at their expense. In truth, in all these real cases of pity, the barriers between the being who pities and those whom it pities are not removed at all; they simply prove not to be so absolute and impermeable as the abstract reflection of scholastic philosophers would make them.

The removal of barriers between the *self* and the *not self* or immediate identification is merely a figure of speech and not an expression of real fact. Like the vibration of chords that sound in unison, so the bond of compassion between living beings is not simply identity but harmony of the similar. From this point of view, too, the fundamental moral fact of pity or compassion completely corresponds to the real nature of things or to the meaning of the universe. For the indissoluble oneness of the world is not a mere empty unity, but embraces the whole range of determinate variations.

V

As befits an ultimate moral principle, the feeling of pity has no external limits for its application. Starting with the narrow sphere of maternal love, strongly developed even in the higher animals, it may, in the case of man, as it gradually becomes wider, pass from the family to the clan and the tribe, to the civic community, the entire nation, to all humanity, and finally embrace all that lives. In individual cases, when confronted with actual pain or need, we may actively pity not only *every* man — though belonging to a different race or religion — but even every animal; this is beyond dispute and is, indeed, quite usual. Less usual is such a breadth of compassion which, without any obvious reason, at once embraces in a keen feeling of pity all the multitude of living beings in the universe. It is difficult to suspect of artificial rhetoric or exaggerated pathos the following description of *universal pity as an actual mental state* — very unlike the state of the so-called 'world-woe' *(Weltschmerz)*. "And I was asked what is a pitying heart? And I answered: the glow in a man's heart for all creation, for men, for birds, for animals, for *demons,* and for creatures of all kinds. When he thinks of them or looks upon them, his eyes gush with tears. Great and poignant pity possesses him and his heart is wrung with suffering, and he cannot bear either to hear or to see any harm or grief endured by any creature. And hence every hour he prays with tears even for the dumb beasts, and for the *enemies of truth* and those who do him wrong, that God may preserve them and have mercy on them; and for all of the crawling kind he prays with great *pity* which rises up in his heart beyond measure so that in that he is made like to God."[6]

In this description of the fundamental altruistic motive in its highest form we find neither 'immediate identification' nor removal of the barriers between the *self* and the *not self.* It differs from Schopenhauer's account like living truth from literary eloquence. These words of the Christian writer also prove that there is no need, as Schopenhauer mistakenly thought, to turn to the Indian dramas or to Buddhism in order to learn the prayer 'May all that lives be free from suffering.'

VI

The universal consciousness of humanity decidedly pronounces *pity to be a good thing.* A person who manifests this feeling is called *good;* the more deeply he experiences and the more he acts upon it, the more good he is considered to be. A pitiless man more than any other is called *wicked.* It does not follow, however, that *the whole* of morality or the essence of *all* good can be reduced, as it often is, to compassion or 'sympathetic feeling.'

"Boundless compassion for all living beings," observes Schopenhauer, "is

6. Isaac the Syrian, *Ascetic Orations,* Russian edition (Moscow, 1858), p. 299.

the surest guarantee of moral conduct and requires no casuistry. The man who is full of that feeling will be certain not to injure any one, not to cause suffering to any one; all his actions will be sure to bear the stamp of truth and mercy. Let any one say, 'This man is virtuous, but he knows no compassion,' or 'He is an unrighteous and wicked man, but he is very compassionate,' and the contradiction will be at once apparent."[7] These words are only true with considerable reservations. There is no doubt that pity or compassion is a real basis of morality, but Schopenhauer's obvious mistake is in regarding that feeling as the *only* foundation of *all* morality.[8]

In truth it is only one of the three ultimate principles of morality and it has a definite sphere of application, namely, it determines our rightful relation to other beings in our world. Pity is the only true foundation of *altruism,* but altruism and morality are not identical: the former is only a part of the latter. It is true that "boundless compassion for all living beings is the surest and most secure foundation," not of moral action in general, as Schopenhauer mistakenly affirms, but of moral action in relation to other beings who are the object of compassion. This relation however, important as it is, does not exhaust the whole of morality. Besides the relation to his fellow-men, man stands also in a certain relation to his own material nature and to the higher principles of all existence, and these relations, too, require to be morally determined so that the good in them may be distinguished from the evil. A man who is full of pity will certainly not injure or cause suffering to any one — that is, he will not injure *any one else,* but he may very well injure himself by indulging in carnal passions which lower his human dignity. In spite of a most compassionate heart one may be inclined to profligacy and other low vices, which, though not opposed to compassion, are opposed to morality — and this fact shows that the two ideas do not coincide. Schopenhauer rightly insists that one cannot say, "This man is malicious and unjust, but he is very compassionate"; curiously enough, however, he forgets that one may, and often has to say, "So and so is a sensual and dissolute man — a profligate, a glutton, a drunkard — but he is very kind-hearted"; equally familiar is the phrase, "Although so and so lives an exemplary ascetic life, he is pitiless to his neighbours." This means that on the one hand the *virtue* of abstinence is possible apart from pity, and on the other that although strongly developed sympathetic feelings — pity, kindness — exclude the possibility of

---

7. *Die beiden Grundprobleme der Ethik,* 2nd ed., p. 23.

8. It is all the more necessary for me to indicate this important error of the fashionable philosopher as I myself was guilty of it when I wrote my dissertation *The Critique of Abstract Principles.*

evil actions in the narrow sense of the term, *i.e.* cruel actions directly hurtful to others, they do not by any means prevent *shameful* actions. And yet such actions are not morally indifferent even from the altruistic point of view. A kind drunkard and profligate may be sorry for other people and never wish to hurt them, yet by his vice he certainly injures not only himself but his family, which he may finally ruin without the least intention of doing them harm. If then pity does not prevent such conduct, our inward opposition to it must be founded upon another aspect of our moral nature, namely, upon the feeling of shame. The rules of asceticism[9] spring from it in the same way as the rules of altruism develop out of the feeling of pity.

VII

The true essence of pity or compassion is certainly not the immediate identification of oneself with another, but the recognition of the inherent worth of that other — the recognition of his right to existence and to possible welfare. When I pity another man or animal, I do not confuse myself with him or take him for myself and myself for him. I merely see in him a creature that is akin and similar to me, with a consciousness like mine, and wishing, as I do, to live and to enjoy the good things of life. In admitting my own right to the fulfilment of such a desire, I admit it in the case of others; being painfully conscious of every violation of this right in relation to me, of every injury to myself, I respond in like manner to the violation of the rights of others, to the injury of others. Pitying myself, I pity others. When I see a suffering creature I do not identify or confuse it with myself, I merely imagine myself *in its place* and, admitting its likeness to myself compare its states to my own, and, as the phrase is, 'enter into its position.' This *equalisation* (but not identification) between myself and another which immediately and unconsciously takes place in the feeling of pity, is raised by reason to the level of a clear and distinct idea.

The intellectual content (the idea) of pity or compassion, taken in its universality, independently of the subjective mental states in which it is manifested — *i.e.* taken logically and not psychologically, — is truth and justice. It is true that other creatures are similar to me, and it is just that I should feel about them as I do about myself. This position, clear in itself, becomes still

9. It is curious that Schopenhauer admitted and even greatly exaggerated the importance of asceticism, but for some reason he completely excluded it from his moral teaching. It is one of the instances of the incoherent thinking of the famous writer.

more clear when tested negatively. When I am pitiless or indifferent to others, consider myself at liberty to injure them and do not think it my duty to help them, they appear to me not what they really are. A being appears as merely a thing, something living appears as dead, something animate as inanimate, something akin to me as foreign, something like me as absolutely different. The relation in which an object is taken to be not what it really is is a direct denial of truth; and actions that follow from it will be unjust. Therefore the opposite relation which is subjectively expressed as the inner feeling of sympathy, pity, or compassion is, from the objective point of view, *expressive of truth*, and actions following from it will be *just*. To measure by a different measure is acknowledged by all to be an elementary instance of injustice; but when I am pitiless to others, *i.e.* treat them as soulless and rightless things, and affirm myself as a conscious being fully possessed of rights, I evidently measure with different measures and crudely contradict truth and justice. On the contrary, when I pity others as I do myself, I measure with one measure and consequently act in accordance with truth and justice.

In so far as it is a constant quality and a practical principle, pitilessness is called *egoism*. In its pure and unmixed form consistent egoism does not exist, at any rate not among human beings. But in order to understand the general nature of egoism as such, it is necessary to characterise it as a pure and unconditional principle. Its essence consists in this: an absolute opposition, an impassable gulf is fixed between one's own self and other beings. I am everything to myself and must be everything to others, but others are nothing in themselves and become something only as a means for me. My life and well-being are an end in itself, the life and welfare of others are only a means for my ends, the necessary environment for my self-assertion. I am the centre and the world only a circumference. Such a point of view is seldom put forward, but with some reservations it undoubtedly lies at the root of our natural life. Absolute egoists are not to be found on earth: every human being appears to feel pity at least for some one, every human being sees a fellow-creature in some one person at least. But restricted within certain limits — usually very narrow ones — egoism manifests itself all the more clearly in other, wider spheres. A person who does not take up the egoistic attitude towards his own relatives, *i.e.* who includes his family within his self, all the more mercilessly opposes this widened self to all that is external to it. A person who extends his self — quite superficially as a rule — to include his whole nation, adopts the egoistic point of view, with all the greater fierceness, both for himself and for his nation, in relation to other nations and races, etc. The fact that the circle of inner solidarity is widened and the egoism is transferred from the individual to the family, the nation, and the state is unquestionably of great moral significance to the life of humanity, for within a given circle selfishness is restricted, outweighed, or even completely replaced by humane and moral relations. But this does not destroy *the principle* of egoism in humanity, which consists in the absolute inner opposition of oneself and one's own to what is other than it — in fixing a gulf between the two. This principle is essentially false, for in reality there is not, and there cannot be, any such gulf, any absolute opposition. It is clear that exclusiveness, egoism, pitilessness is essentially the same thing as untruth. Egoism is in the first place fantastic and *unreal,* it affirms what does not and cannot exist. To consider oneself (in the narrow or in the wide sense) as the exclusive centre of the universe is at bottom as absurd as to believe oneself to be a glass seat or the constellation of Ursa Major.[10]

If, then, egoism is condemned by reason as a senseless affirmation of what is non-existent and impossible, the opposite principle of altruism, psychologically based upon the feeling of pity, is entirely justified both by reason and by conscience. In virtue of this principle the individual person admits that other beings are, just like himself, relative centres of being and of living force. This is an affirmation of truth, an admission of what truly is. From this truth, to which the feeling of pity, roused by other beings akin and alike to us, inwardly bears witness in every soul, reason deduces a principle or a law with regard to all other beings: *Do unto others as you would they should do unto you.*

VIII

The general rule or principle of altruism[11] naturally falls into two more particular ones. The beginning of this division may be seen already in the funda-

---

10. Theoretical proof of the reality of the external world and of the inner conscious life of beings is offered in metaphysics. Moral philosophy is concerned only with a general consciousness of this truth, which even the extreme egoist involuntarily accepts. When for his selfish purposes he wants the help of other people not dependent on him, he treats them, contrary to his fundamental principle, as actual, independent persons fully possessed of rights; he tries to persuade them to side with him, takes their own interests into consideration. Thus egoism contradicts itself, and is in any case a *false* point of view.

11. This term, introduced by the founder of Positivism, Auguste Comte, is the exact expression of the logical antithesis to egoism and therefore answers to a real need of philosophical language (altruism, from *alter,* other, like egoism, from *ego,* self). Our violent opponents of foreign words ought to be consistent, and if they object to altruism, they should also renounce the word egoism. Instead of these terms they may use the words *'yachestvo'* ('selfness') and *'druzhachestvo'* ('otherism'); the former term, I believe, has already been used. If it were a question of merely *psychological* definitions, the words *self-love* and *love of others* could be substituted, but including as they do the idea of love, they are unsuitable for the designation of ethical *principles* which

mental altruistic feeling of pity. If I am genuinely sorry for a person, in the first place I would not myself cause him harm or suffering, would not *injure* him, and secondly, when, independently of me, he suffers pain or injury, I would *help* him. Hence follow two rules of altruism, the negative and the positive: (1) *Do not to others what you do not wish others to do to you.* (2) *Do to others what you would wish others to do to you.* More briefly and simply, these two rules, which are usually joined together, are expressed as follows: *Do not injure any one, and help every one so far as you are able (Neminem laede, imo omnes, quantum potes, juva).*[12]

The first, negative, rule is, more particularly, called the rule of justice, and the second the rule of mercy. But this distinction is not quite correct, for the second rule, too, is founded upon justice: if I want others to help me when in need, it is just that I, too, should help them. On the other hand, if I do not wish to injure any one, it is because I recognise others to be living and sentient beings like myself; and in that case I will, of course, as much as in me lies, save them from suffering. I do not injure them because I pity them, and if I pity them, I will also help them. Mercy presupposes justice, and justice demands mercy — they are merely different aspects or different manifestations of one and the same thing.[13]

There is a real distinction between these two sides or degrees of altruism, but there is not, and there cannot be, any opposition or contradiction. Not to help others means to injure them; a consistently just man will inevitably do works of mercy, and the truly merciful man cannot at the same time be unjust. The fact that the two altruistic rules, in spite of all the difference between them, are *inseparable,* is very important as providing the foundation for the inner connection between legal justice and morality, and between the political and the spiritual life of the community.

The general rule of altruism — "do unto others as you would they should do unto you" — by no means presupposes the material or the qualitative equality of all the individuals. There exists no such equality in nature, and it would be meaningless to demand it. It is not a question of equality, but simply of the equal right to exist and to develop the good potentialities of one's

---

are concerned not with feelings but with rules of action. One may love oneself far more than others, and yet, on principle, work for the good of others as much as for one's own. Such a person would undoubtedly be an altruist, but it would be equally absurd to speak of him as 'a lover of self' or 'a lover of others.'

12. Solovyov takes this maxim from Schopenhauer, who claimed that it constitutes the essence of all morality. — *Editor's note.*

13. In Hebrew ṣedeq means 'just,' and the noun derived from it, ṣĕdāqâ, means 'benevolence.'

nature. A wild man of the Bush has as much right to exist and to develop in his way, as St. Francis of Assisi or Goethe had in theirs. And we must respect *this* right equally in all cases. The murder of a savage is as much a sin as the murder of a genius or a saint. But this does not imply that they are, therefore, of the same value in other respects, and must be treated equally outside the scope of this universal human right. Material equality, and therefore equality of rights, does not exist either between different beings or in one and the same being whose particular and definite rights and duties change with changes in age and position; they are not the same in children and in adults, in mental disease or in health. And yet a person's fundamental or universally human rights and his moral value as an individual remain the same. Nor is it nullified by the infinite variety and inequality of separate persons, tribes, and classes. In all these differences there must be preserved something identical and absolute, namely, *the significance of each person as an end in himself,* that is to say, his significance as something that cannot be *merely a means* for the ends of others.

The logical demands of altruism are all-embracing, reason shows no favours, knows no barriers; in this respect it coincides with the feeling upon which altruism is psychologically based. Pity, as we have seen, is also universal and impartial, and through it man may be 'made like to God,' for his compassion equally embraces all, without distinction — the good and 'the enemies of truth,' men and demons, and even 'all of the crawling kind.'[14]

---

14. Regarding compassion for the "crawling kind," see Isaac the Syrian, *op. cit.* — *Editor's note.*

CHAPTER IV

The Religious Principle in Morality

I

Although the moral rules of justice and mercy, psychologically based upon the feeling of pity, include in their *scope* the whole realm of living creatures, their *content* does not exhaust the moral relations that hold even between human beings. Take, in the first place, the moral relation of children — young, but already able to understand the demands of morality — to their parents. It undoubtedly contains a peculiar, specific element, irreducible either to justice or to kindness and underivable from pity. A child immediately recognises his parents' *superiority* over himself, his *dependence* upon them; he feels *reverence* for them, and there follows from it the practical duty of obedience. All this lies outside the boundaries of simple altruism, the logical essence of which consists in my recognising another as my equal, as a being like myself and in attaching the same significance to him as I do to myself. The moral relation of children to their parents, so far from being determined by equality, has quite the opposite character — it is based upon the recognition of that in which the two are *unequal*. And the ultimate psychological basis of the moral relation in this case cannot be the participation in the sufferings of others (pity), for the parents immediately appear to the child not as needing the help of others, but as being able to help it in its needs.

This relation is not, of course, opposed to justice, but it contains something in addition to it. The general principle of justice requires that our relation to others should be what we wish their relation to be to us. It may logically include the moral relation of children to parents: in loving its mother or father, the child, of course, wants them to love it. But there is an essential difference between these two forms of love — that which the child feels for its parents, and that which it wants them to feel for it — and the difference does not spring from the general principle itself. The first relation is characterised by the feeling of admiration for the higher and by the duty of obedience to it, while no such reverence and submission are required by the child from the parents. Of course, formal reflection may be pursued further, and it may be affirmed that children (when they reach the years of discretion, of course), in revering their parents and obeying them, wish to be treated in the same way by their own children in the future. This circumstance, however, merely establishes the abstract relation between the general idea of justice and filial love; it certainly does not account for the peculiar nature of that love. Apart from all problematic thought of future children, the moral feeling of a real child for its parents has *a sufficient basis* in the actual relationship between this child and its parents — namely, in its *entire dependence* upon them as its Providence. This fact inevitably involves the admission of their essential superiority, and from it logically follows the duty of obedience. Thus filial love acquires quite a peculiar character of respect or reverence (*pietas erga parentes*), which carries it beyond the general limits of simple altruism.

It may be observed that parental (especially maternal) love, or pity, which is the first and the most fundamental expression of the altruistic attitude, presupposes the same inequality, but in the opposite direction. Here, however, the inequality is not essential. When parents pity their helpless children and take care of them, they *know* from their own experience the pain of hunger, cold, etc., which rouse their pity, so that this is really a case of comparing or equalising the states of another person with one's own states of the same kind. A child, on the contrary, has never experienced for itself the advantages of mature age, which call forth in it a feeling of respect or reverence for its parents, and make it see *higher beings* in them. Parents pity their children because of their *likeness* to themselves, because of their being the same, though, as a matter of fact, unequal. Inequality, in this case, is purely accidental. But the specific feeling of children for their parents is essentially determined by the superiority of the latter, and is therefore directly based upon inequality.

If one carefully observes a child who tries to defend its mother from an actual or imaginary insult, it will be easily seen that its dominant feelings are anger and indignation at the blasphemer. It is not so much sorry for the offended as angry with the offender. The child's feelings are essentially similar to those that animate the crowd defending its idol. "Great is Diana of the Ephesians! death to the ungodly!"[1]

All manifestations of pity and of altruism that follow from it are essen-

1. See Acts 19:28, 34. — *Editor's note.*

tially conditioned by *equality*. Inequality is merely an accidental and transitory element in them. In pitying another, I assimilate myself to him, imagine myself in his place, get, so to speak, into his skin — and this in itself presupposes my equality with him as a fellow-creature. In recognising another as equal to himself, the person who experiences pity compares the state of that other to similar states of himself, and from the likeness between them deduces the moral duty of sympathy and help.

Non ignara mali miseris succurrere disco.[2] To pity another, I must compare myself to him or him to me. The assumption of essential inequality or heterogeneity, excluding as it does the thought of *similar* states, destroys the very root of pity and of all altruistic relation. 'The twice born' Hindu is pitiless to the Sûdras and Pariahs. His relation to them is based on inequality, *i.e.* precisely on the impossibility of comparing himself with them. He cannot put himself in their place, assimilate their states to his, and cannot, therefore, sympathise with them. In this case, just as in the case of the white planters' attitude to the negroes, or of our old serf-owners to 'the brood of Ham,' it was sought to justify the cruel relation which existed as a fact by the conception of a fundamental inequality or heterogeneity.

Such recognition of inequality is purely negative; it severs the bond of union between beings and generates or justifies all kinds of immoral relations. A different character attaches to that positive inequality which we find in filial love or piety. The inequality between a Brahmin and a Pariah, or between a planter and a negro, destroys the unity of feeling and of interests between them; but the superiority of parents over children is, on the contrary, the condition of their unity and the basis of a particular kind of moral relation. This is the natural root of *religious morality,* which forms a distinct and important part in the spiritual life of man, independently of all particular religions and systems of metaphysics.

II

Since the appearance of de Brosses's book in the last century[3] the theory of the 'gods-fetishes' began to gain ground, and of late has become extremely

---

2. "Having known trouble myself, I learn to help those who suffer" (the words of Dido in Virgil's *Aeneid*).

3. Charles de Brosses, *Du culte des dieux fétiches ou parallèle de l'ancienne religion de l'Egypte avec la religion actuelle de la Nigritie* (The cult of the fetish gods or comparison of the religion of ancient Egypt with the religion of contemporary Africa) (Paris, 1860). — *Editor's note.*

popular under the influence of Auguste Comte's positive philosophy. According to this view, the primitive form of religion is *fetishism, i.e.* the deification of material objects, partly natural (stones, trees) and partly artificial, which have accidentally drawn attention to themselves or have been arbitrarily chosen. The beginnings or the remains of such a material cult are undoubtedly found in all religions; but to regard fetishism as the fundamental and primitive religion of humanity is contrary both to the evidence of history and sociology and to the demands of logic. (Fetishism may, however, have a deeper meaning, as the founder of positivism himself began to suspect in the second half of his career.)

In order to recognise a stone, a bit of tree, or a shell as a god, *i.e.* as a being of superior power and importance, one must already possess the idea of a higher being. I could not mistake a rope for a snake did I not already possess the idea of the snake. But what could the idea of the deity be derived from? The material objects which are made into fetishes and idols have in themselves, in their actual sensuous reality, no attributes of a higher being. The idea, therefore, cannot be derived from them. To call it innate is not to give an answer to the question. All that takes place in man is in a sense innate in him. There is no doubt that man is by nature capable of forming an idea of a higher being, for otherwise he would not have formed it. The question is asked not about the existence of this capacity but about its original *application,* which must have some immediate sufficient reason. In order to pass into *actual* consciousness every idea, even when potentially present in the human intellect, and in this sense innate, requires that certain sensuous impressions or perceptions should call it forth and give it a living concrete form, which subsequently undergoes a further process of intellectual modification, and is made wider and deeper, more complex and more exact. But the actual impressions from a chunk of wood or a rudely fashioned figure are not a sufficient ground for calling forth for the first time in the mind the idea of a higher being, or for helping to fashion that idea. More suitable in this respect are the impressions from the sun and the moon, the starry heaven, thunderstorms, sea, rivers, etc. But long before the mind becomes capable of dwelling on these events and of judging their significance, it has been given impressions of another kind — more familiar and more powerful — for generating in it the idea of a higher being. When dealing with the origin of some fundamental idea in human consciousness, we must think of the child and not of the adult. Now it is perfectly certain that the child is far more conscious of its dependence upon its mother, who feeds and takes care of it (and later on, on its father), than of its dependence upon the sun, the thunderstorm, or the river that irrigates the fields of its native land. The impressions it has from the first of its parents contain sufficient ground for evoking in it the idea of a higher being as well as the feelings of reverential love and fear of an immeasurable power. These feelings are associated with the idea of a higher being and form the basis of the religious attitude. It is an unquestionable fact, and a perfectly natural one, that until they reach a certain age children *pay no attention at all* to the most important natural phenomena. The sun appears no more remarkable to them than a simple lamp, and the thunder produces no more impression upon them than the rattle of crockery. In my own case the first impression of the starry sky that I remember refers to my sixth year, and even then it was due to a special reason (the comet of 1859), while the series of clear and connected family memories begins in my fourth year. Neither in life nor in literature have I seen any indications to the reverse order of development in children; and if we saw a baby of three years old suddenly develop an interest in astronomical phenomena, I think we should feel distinctly alarmed.

Not in accidental fetishes and hand-made idols, not in majestic or terrible phenomena of nature, but in the living image of *parents* is the idea of Godhead for the first time embodied for humanity in its childhood. For this reason the moral element — contrary to current opinion — has from the first an important though not an exclusive significance for religion. According to the elementary conception of it the deity has pre-eminently the character of *Providence.*

At first Providence is embodied in the *mother.* At the lower stages of social development, so long as the marriage relation is not yet organised, the importance of the mother and the cult of motherhood predominate. Different peoples, like individual men, have lived through an epoch of *matriarchy* or mother-right, the traces of which are still preserved in history, in ancient customs, and also in the present life of certain savages.[4] But when the patriarchal type of family comes to be established, the mother retains the part of Providence only while the children are materially dependent upon her for food and their first education. At that period the mother is the only higher being for the child; but as he reaches the age of reflection he sees that his mother is herself dependent upon another higher being — his father, who provides food for and protects all his family; he is the true Providence, and the religious worship is naturally transferred to him.

---

4. There is a special literature on the subject which first arose in connection with classical archeology (Bachofen, *Das Mutterrecht*), and subsequently passed into the domain of comparative ethnography and sociology. [J. J. Bachofen, *Das Mutterrecht* (Berlin, 1861). — *Editor's note.*]

III

The religious attitude of children toward their parents as toward their living Providence, arising naturally in primitive humanity, expresses itself most clearly and fully when the children are grown up and the parents are *dead*. Worship of dead fathers and ancestors unquestionably occupies the foremost place in the development of the religious, moral, and social relations of humanity. The immense population of China still lives by the religion of ancestor-worship, upon which all the social, political, and family structure of the Middle Kingdom is founded. And among other peoples of the globe — savage, barbarous, or civilised, including modern Parisians — there is not one which does not do homage to the memory of the dead in one form or another. The relation to living parents, although it is the first basis of religion, cannot have a purely religious character owing to the intimacy and constant interaction in everyday life. As a child grows up he hears from his father about his ancestors who died and are the object of an already established religious cult; thus the religion of parents who are still living is naturally merged into the religion of parents who have gone, and who, clothed in mysterious majesty, are raised above all that surrounds us. The father in his lifetime is merely a candidate for deity, and is only the mediator and the priest of the real god — the dead ancestor. *It is not fear but death that gives humanity its first gods.* The feeling of dependence and the conception of Providence, transferred from the mother to the father, become associated with the idea of the forefathers when the child learns that the parents upon whom he depends are in a far greater dependence upon the dead, whose power is not limited by any conditions of the material and corporeal existence. The idea of Providence and the moral duties of respect, service, and obedience that follow from it for man are thus transferred to them. To obey the will of the dead, one must know it. Sometimes they announce it directly, appearing in a vision or a dream; in other cases it must be learnt through divination. The mediators between this higher divine power and ordinary men are, first, the living fathers or the elders of the tribe, but afterwards, as the social relations become more complex, there arises a separate class of priests, diviners, sorcerers, and prophets.

It is only a subjective misanthropic mood that can reduce filial sentiments even in the primitive races to fear alone, to the exclusion of gratitude and of a disinterested recognition of superiority. If these moral elements are unquestionably present in the relation of a dog to its master in whom it sees its living Providence, they must *a fortiori* form part of the feelings of man to his Providence, originally embodied for him in his parents. When this interpretation is transferred to the dead ancestors, their cult also carries with it the moral element of filial love, which is in this case clearly differentiated from simple altruism and acquires a predominantly religious character.

According to a well-known theory, whose chief representative is Herbert Spencer, the whole of religion can be traced to ancestor-worship. Although this view does not express the complete truth, it is far more correct and suggestive than the theory of primitive fetishism or the theories which reduce all religion to the deification of the sun, the thunder, and other natural phenomena. The objects of religious worship were always active beings or spirits in the likeness of man. There can hardly be a doubt that the prototype of the spirits was the souls of the departed ancestors. In Lithuania and Poland the general name for all spirits is *forefathers — dziady;* with us the elementary spirits are spoken of as *grandfather* water-sprite, *grandfather* wood-demon, the *master* house-spirit. Ovid's *Metamorphoses,* chiefly borrowed from the popular beliefs of the Greeks and Romans, are full of stories of dead or dying men passing into the elementary, the zoomorphic, and the phytomorphic (vegetative) deities and spirits. The most widespread form of fetishism — *stone* worship — is undoubtedly connected with the cult of the dead. Among the Laps, Buriates, and other peoples, the names of the ancestors or the sorcerers who were transformed into sacred stones are remembered after death.[5] This transformation cannot be understood in the sense that the spirit of the dead becomes a stone, *i.e.* a soulless thing; on the contrary, it retains the power that it had in its lifetime, and is indeed more powerful than it was then. Thus among the Laps the petrified sorcerers foretell and cause storms and bad weather in all the region. The stone in this case is merely the visible abode of the spirit, the instrument of its action. Among the Semites sacred stones were called *beth-el,* that is, 'house of god.' The same thing must be said about sacred trees.

It is a well-known fact that among the Africans and other peoples the sorcerers are supposed to have for their chief characteristic the power of controlling atmospheric events, of producing good and bad weather. This power is ascribed in a still greater degree and more directly to the *spirits* of the dead sorcerers, whose living successors serve merely as their mediators and messengers. Now such a powerful spirit of a dead sorcerer, who produces at his will thunder and storm, differs in no way from a thunder god. There is no rational necessity to seek for a different explanation of *father* Zeus or of *grandfather* Percunas.[6]

---

5. See, among other things, Kharuzin's book on Laplanders, and my article *Ostatki pervobitnago yazichestva (The Remains of Primitive Paganism).* [N. Kharuzin's work *Russkie lopari* (Russian Laplanders) was published in Moscow in 1890. Solovyov's article appeared in 1890 in the periodical *Russkoe Obozrenie. — Editor's note.*]

6. Percunas, a god of thunder, is the chief god in Lithuanian mythology. — *Editor's note.*

It is not my object here to expound and explain the history of religious development, and I will not attempt to solve the question as to how far a genetic tie may be established between the cult of the dead and the solar, lunar, and stellar mythology. I will only mention some suggestive facts. In Egypt the solar deity Osiris reigned over the unseen world of the dead. In classical mythology Hecate was one of the deities of Hades. According to an ancient belief preserved in Manicheism the moon is an intermediate resting-place for the souls of the departed. I would also like to observe that the end of the theogonic process is true to its beginning — that the religious consciousness at its highest stage merely deepens and widens the content we find at the primitive stages. The religion of a primitive human family centres round the idea of the father or the nearest ancestor, first as living, then as dead. Their *own* particular parent is the highest principle for the family, the source of its life and welfare, the object of respect, gratitude, and obedience — in a word, its Providence. Through a natural historical process there arise the communal and the tribal gods, until at last the religious consciousness of humanity, united in thought if not in fact, rises to the idea of the universal Heavenly Father with His all-embracing Providence.

IV

The development of a religious idea involves a change in its extension, and also in the nature of the intellectual concepts and practical rules contained in it. But it does not affect the moral content of religion, *i.e.* man's fundamental relation to what he admits as higher than himself — to what he recognises as his Providence. That relation remains unchanged in all the forms and at all the stages of religious development. The *ideas* of the child about its parents, of the members of a tribe about the spirit of their first ancestor, the ideas of entire peoples about their national gods, and finally, the general human idea of the one all-good Father of all that is, *differ* essentially from one another, and there is also great difference in the *forms of worship*. The real tie between father and children needs no special institutions and no mediation; but the relation with the *invisible* spirit of the ancestor must be maintained by special means. The spirit cannot partake of ordinary human food. It feeds on the vapors of blood, and has therefore to be fed by sacrifices. Family sacrifices to the spirit of the tribe naturally differ from communal sacrifices to the national gods; the 'god of war' has greater and different requirements than the patron-spirit of the home, and the all-embracing and all-pervading Father of the universe requires no material sacrifices at all, but only worship in spirit and in truth. But in spite of all these differences, the filial relation to the higher being remains essentially the same at all these different stages. The crudest cannibal and the most perfect saint in so far as they are religious agree in that they both equally desire to do not their own will but the *will of the Father*. This permanent and self-identical filial relation to the higher (whatever this higher may be supposed to be) forms that principle of true *pietism* which connects religion with morality, and may equally well be described as the religious element in morality or the moral element in religion.[7]

Can this principle be affirmed as a generally binding moral rule, side by side with the principles of asceticism and altruism? Apparently the filial relation to the supreme will depends upon the faith in that will, and one cannot require such faith from those who have not got it; when there is nothing to be had, it is no use making demands. But there is a misunderstanding here. The recognition of what is higher than us is independent of any definite intellectual ideas, and therefore of any positive beliefs, and in its *general* character it is undoubtedly binding upon every moral and rational being. Every such being, in trying to attain the purpose of its life, is necessarily convinced that the attainment of it, or the final satisfaction of will, is beyond the power of man — that is, every rational being comes to recognise its *dependence* upon something invisible and unknown. Such dependence cannot be denied. The only question is whether that upon which I am dependent has a meaning. If it has not, my existence, dependent upon what is meaningless, is meaningless also. In that case there is no point in speaking of any rational and moral principles and purposes. They can have significance only on condition that there is a meaning in my existence, that the world is a rational system, that meaning predominates over what is meaningless in the universe. If there is no rational purpose in the world as a whole, there cannot be any in that *part* of it which is composed of human actions determined by moral rules. But in that case these rules too fall to the ground, for they do not lead to anything and cannot in any way be justified. If my higher spiritual nature is merely an accident, ascetic struggle with the flesh may destroy my spiritual being instead of strengthening it; and in that case why should I observe the rules of abstinence and deprive myself of real pleasures for the sake of an empty dream? In the same way, if there is no rational and moral order in the universe, and our work for the benefit of our neighbours may bring them harm instead of the intended help, the moral principle of altruism is destroyed by inner self-

---

7. I am speaking here of pietism in the direct and general sense of the term as designating the feeling of piety *(pietas)* raised to the rank of a moral principle. Usually the term 'pietism' in a special historical sense is applied to a certain religious movement among the Protestants.

contradiction. If, for instance, I suppose, with Schopenhauer, that the ultimate reality is blind and senseless Will, and that all existence is essentially pain, why should I try to help others to support their existence? On such a supposition it would be far more logical to use every effort to put to death the largest possible number of living creatures.

I can do good consciously and rationally only if I believe in the good and in its objective independent significance in the world, *i.e.* in other words, if I believe in the moral order, in Providence, in God. This faith is logically prior to all particular religious beliefs and institutions, as well as to all systems of metaphysics, and in this sense it forms the so-called natural religion.

V

Natural religion gives rational sanction to all the demands of morality. Suppose reason directly tells us that it is good to subordinate the flesh to the spirit, that it is good to help others and to recognise the rights of other people like our own. Now in order to obey these demands of reason, one must believe in reason — believe that the good it requires from us is not a subjective illusion, but has real grounds and expresses the truth, and that "Great is Truth, and mighty above all things."[8] Not to have this faith is to disbelieve that one's own existence has a meaning — it is to renounce the dignity of a rational being.

The absence of a natural religion is often fictitious. A negative relation to this or that form or degree of religious consciousness, predominant at a given time and at a given place, is easily taken for denial of religion as such. Thus the Pagans of the Roman Empire thought the Christians godless (ἄθεοι), and from their point of view they were right, for the Christians did reject all their gods. Apart from this, however, there exist cases of real godlessness or unbelief, *i.e.* of denying on principle anything higher than oneself — of denying good, reason, truth. But the fact of such denial, which coincides with the denial of morality in general, can be no more an argument against the generally binding character of the religiously-moral principle than the existence of shameless and carnal, or of pitiless and cruel men is an argument against the moral duty of abstinence and charity.

Religious morality, as all morality in general, is not a confirmation of everything that is, but an affirmation of the one thing that ought to be. Independently of all positive beliefs or of any unbelief, every man as a *rational* being *must* admit that the life of the world as a whole and his own life in

8. 1 Esdras 4:41. — *Editor's note.*

particular *have a meaning,* and that therefore everything depends upon a supreme rational principle, in virtue of which this meaning is preserved and realised. And in admitting this, he must put himself into a filial position in relation to the supreme principle of life, that is, gratefully surrender himself to its providence, and subordinate all his actions to the 'will of the Father,' which speaks through reason and conscience.

Just as the intellectual ideas about the parents and the external practical relations to them alter according to the age of the children, while the filial love must remain unchanged, so the theological conceptions and the forms of worship of the Heavenly Father assume many forms and undergo many changes with the spiritual growth of humanity; but the religiously-moral attitude of free subordination of one's will to the demands of a higher principle must always and everywhere remain the same.

VI

Speaking generally, in morality the higher demands do not cancel the lower, but presuppose and include them. This might seem to be a matter of course; and yet many have failed, and still fail, to understand this simple and obvious truth. Thus, according to the teaching of some Christian sects, both ancient and modern, the higher rule of celibacy cancels the seventh commandment as inferior, and therefore, in rejecting marriage, these sectarians readily allow all kinds of fornication. It is obvious that they are in error. Similarly, it is thought by many that the higher rule of pitying all living creatures absolves them from the lower duty of pitying their family and relatives, although, one would think, there could be no doubt about the latter also belonging to the class of living creatures.

Still more often such mistakes are made in the domain of religious morality. The higher stages of spiritual consciousness once reached, subordinate to themselves and consequently change, but by no means cancel, the demands which had force at the lower stages. A man who has a conception of the Heavenly Father cannot, of course, regard his earthly father in the same way as does a babe for whom the latter is the only higher being, but it does not follow that the first and the second commandments cancel the fifth. We cannot now render our dead ancestors the religious worship which they had in the patriarchal times; but this does not mean that we have no duties to the departed. We may well be conscious of our dependence upon the One Father of the universe, but this dependence is not immediate; our existence is, without a doubt, closely determined by heredity and environment. Heredity means the forefathers, and it is by them that our environment has been made. The supreme Will has determined our existence through our ancestors, and, bowing down before Its action, we cannot be indifferent to Its instruments. I know that if I were born among cannibals I should be a cannibal myself, and I cannot help feeling gratitude and reverence to men who by their labour and exploits have raised my people from the savage state and brought them to the level of culture upon which they are standing now. This has been done by Providence through men who have been specially called and who cannot be separated from their providential work. If I praise and value the fact that it has been given to my native land, with which my existence is so closely interwoven, to be a Christian and a European country, I am bound to hold in pious remembrance the Kiev prince who christened Russia, and that northern giant who with powerful blows shattered the Muscovo-Mongolian exclusiveness and brought Russia within the circle of educated nations,[9] as well as all those men who in the different spheres of life moved us forward along the path opened by those two historical forefathers of Russia. It is sometimes maintained that individuals count for nothing in history, and that what has been done by certain men would have been done just as well by others. Speaking in the abstract, we might of course have been born of other parents and not of our actual father and mother; but this idle thought about possible parents does not cancel our duties to the actual ones.

The providential men who gave us a share in the higher religion and in human enlightenment did not themselves create these in the first instance. What they gave us they had themselves received from the geniuses, heroes, and saints of the former ages, and our grateful memory must include them too. We must reconstruct as completely as possible the whole line of our spiritual ancestors — men through whom Providence has led humanity on the path to perfection. The pious memory of our ancestors compels us to do service to them actively. The nature of that service is conditioned by the ultimate character of the world as a whole, and cannot be understood apart from theoretical philosophy and æsthetics. Here one can only point to the moral principle involved, namely, the pious and grateful reverence due to the forefathers.

Such a cult of human ancestors in spirit and in truth does not belittle the religion of the one Heavenly Father. On the contrary, it makes it definite and real. It is what He put into these 'chosen vessels'[10] that we revere in them; in these visible images of the unseen, the Deity Itself is revealed and glorified. A person in whose mind the concrete images of providential action incarnate in

9. References to Prince Vladimir of Kiev and Peter the Great. — *Editor's note.*
10. Acts 9:15. — *Editor's note.*

history fail to evoke gratitude, reverence, and homage will be still less likely to respond to the pure idea of Providence. A truly religious attitude toward the higher is impossible for one who has never experienced the feelings to which the poet gives expression:

> When, in the drunkenness of crime,
> The crowd goes forth in violent rage,
> And evil genius through the mire
> Drags name of prophet and of sage,
> My knees are bent in one desire,
> My head is bowed towards the page
> Where clear and open for all time
> They wrote the message for their age.
> I call up their majestic shades
> In the dim church where tumult fades,
> In clouds of incense learn and glean,
> And forgetting the mob and its vulgar noise,
> I give my ears to the noble voice
> And take full breath of all they mean.[11]

11. Sonnet (1883) by the celebrated poet Afanasy Fet, a close friend of Solovyov. — *Editor's note.*

CHAPTER V

Virtues

I

Each of the moral foundations I have laid down — shame, pity, and the religious feeling — may be considered from three points of view: as a *virtue*, as a *rule* of action, and as the condition of a certain *good*.

Thus, in relation to shame, we distinguish, first of all, persons modest or shameless by nature, approving of the former and condemning the latter; *modesty*, therefore, is recognised as a good natural quality or as a virtue. But by that very fact it is abstracted from particular cases and is made *the norm* or the general rule of action (and, through this, a basis for passing *judgment* on actions) independently of the presence or absence of this virtue in this or in that individual. If modesty is not sometimes good and sometimes bad (in the way in which a loud voice is good at a public meeting and bad in the room of a sleeping invalid); if modesty is a good in itself, reason requires us in all cases to act in accordance with it, namely, to *abstain* from actions that are shameful — *i.e.* that express the predominance of the lower nature over the higher — and to *practise* actions of the opposite character. Behaviour in conformity with this rule leads in the end to permanent self-control, to freedom of the spirit, and its power over material existence; that is, it leads to a state which affords us a certain higher *satisfaction* and is a moral good.

In the same way, the capacity for feeling pity or compassion (in opposition to selfishness, cruelty, and malice) is, in the first place, a good personal quality or virtue. In so far as it is recognised as such, or is approved, it provides the norm for altruistic actions in accordance with the rules of justice and mercy. And such activity leads to the moral good of true community or oneness with other men, and, finally, with all living creatures.

In a similar manner, a grateful recognition of that which is higher than us, and upon which we depend, is the natural foundation of the virtue of piety, and at the same time provides a rational rule of religious conduct. It also leads to the moral good of unity with the first causes and bearers of existence: with our forefathers, with the departed in general, and with the whole of the invisible world which conditions our life from this point of view.

Since there is an indissoluble inner connection between any given virtue, the rules of action corresponding to it, and the moral good ensuing therefrom, there is no need, in inquiring into the subject more closely, to adopt every time all the three points of view. It will be sufficient to take one only, viz, the point of view of virtue, for it logically contains the other two, and no sharp line of demarcation can be drawn between them. It would be impossible to deny that the man who invariably acted in accordance with the rules of virtue was virtuous, even though he happened to possess but a small degree of the corresponding natural faculty, or was distinguished, indeed, by the presence of the opposite characteristic. On the other hand, that which, in contradistinction to virtue, I call a moral good, is also a virtue, though not as originally given but as acquired — it is *the norm of activity which has become second nature.*

II

A virtuous man is man *as he ought to be.* In other words, virtue is man's normal or *due relation* to everything (for unrelated qualities or properties are unthinkable). The due relation does not mean the same relation. In drawing the distinction between the self and the not self, we necessarily posit or determine the not self in three ways: either as the *lower* (by nature), or as *similar* to us (of the same kind), or as *higher* than we. It is obvious that there cannot be a fourth alternative. Hence it *logically* follows that the right or the moral relation must have a threefold character. It is clear that we ought not to regard the lower (say, an inclination of the material nature) as if it were the higher (*e.g.* a decree of the divine will); it would be equally opposed to what is right to regard a being like ourselves — say, a human being — either as lower than we (*i.e.* regard it as a soulless thing), or as higher (look upon it as a deity).

Thus, instead of one, we have three right or moral relations, or three kinds of virtue, corresponding to the three divisions into which the totality of objects correlated with us necessarily falls. I say *necessarily,* because man finds himself to be neither the absolutely supreme or highest being, nor the absolutely subordinate or lowest, nor, finally, alone of his kind. He is conscious of himself as an intermediate being and, moreover, *one of the many* intermediate beings. The direct logical consequence of this fact is the three-fold character of his moral relations. In virtue of it, one and the same quality or action may have quite a different and even opposite significance, according to the kind of object to which it refers. Thus, belittling oneself or recognising one's worthlessness is called *humility,* and is a virtue when it refers to objects of superior dignity; but in relation to unworthy objects it is considered base and is immoral.[1] In the same way, *enthusiasm,* when roused by high principles and ideals, is no doubt a virtue; in relation to indifferent objects it is an amusing weakness; and directed upon objects of the lower order it becomes a shameful mania. Virtues in the proper sense are always and in every one the same, for they express a quality determined in the right way, and correspond to the very meaning of one or another of the three possible spheres of relation. But from these definite and determining virtues must be distinguished qualities of will and ways of action which are not in themselves morally determined, and do not permanently correspond to a definite sphere of duty. These may sometimes be virtues, sometimes indifferent states, and sometimes even vices; but the change in the moral significance is not always accompanied by a corresponding change in the name of the psychological quality in question.

It is clear, then, that even if we did not find in our psychical experience the three fundamental moral feelings of shame, pity, and reverence, it would be necessary on logical grounds alone to divide the totality of moral relations into three parts, or to accept three fundamental types of virtue, expressing man's relation to what is lower than himself, to what is like him, and to what is above him.

III

If in addition to the foundations of morality recognised by us — shame, pity, and reverence for the higher — we go over all the other qualities which have, in ancient and modern times, been considered as virtues, not a single one of them will be found to deserve that name of itself. Each of these various qualities can be regarded as a virtue only when it accords with the objective norms of right, expressed in the three fundamental moral data indicated above. Thus *abstinence* or *temperance* has the dignity of virtue only when it refers to

1. In English the word humility has possibly a less conditional sense, as a state of mind or an attitude towards life. From a Christian point of view one can never be too humble. — *Translator's note.*

shameful states or actions. Virtue does not require that we should be abstinent or temperate *in general* or in everything, but only that we should abstain from that which is *below* our human dignity, and from the things in which it would be a shame to indulge ourselves unchecked. But if a person is moderate in seeking after truth, or abstains from goodwill to his neighbours, no one would consider or call him virtuous on that account; he would, on the contrary, be condemned as lacking in generous impulses. It follows from this that temperance is not in itself or essentially a virtue, but becomes or does not become one according to its right or wrong application to objects. In the same way, *courage* or *fortitude* is a virtue only in so far as it expresses the right relation of the rational human being to his lower material nature, the relation, namely, of mastery and power, the supremacy of the spirit over the animal instinct of self-preservation.[2] Praiseworthy courage is shown by the man who does not tremble at accidental misfortunes, who keeps his self-control in the midst of external dangers, and bravely risks his life and material goods for the sake of things that are higher and more worthy. But the *bravest* unruliness, the most *daring* aggressiveness, and the most *fearless* blaspheming are not praised as virtues; nor is the horror of sin or the fear of God reckoned as shameful cowardice. In this case then, again, the quality of being virtuous or vicious depends upon a certain relation to the object and not on the psychological nature of the emotional and volitional states.

The third of the so-called cardinal virtues,[3] *wisdom, i.e.* the knowledge of the best ways and means for attaining the purpose before us, and the capacity to apply these means aright, owes its significance as a virtue not to this formal capacity for the most expedient action as such, but necessarily depends upon the moral worth of the purpose itself. Wisdom as a virtue is the faculty of attaining the *best* purposes in the *best* possible way, or the knowledge of applying in the most expedient way one's intellectual forces to objects of the greatest worth. There may be wisdom apart from this condition, but such wisdom would not be a virtue. The Biblical 'serpent' had certainly justified its reputation as the wisest of earthly creatures by the understanding he showed of human nature, and the skill with which he used this understanding for the attainment of his purpose. Since however the purpose was an evil one, the serpent's admirable wisdom was not recognised as a virtue, but was cursed as

---

2. Concerning this virtue, see above, Chap. I.

3. From the early days of the scholastics the name of cardinal or *philosophic* virtues (in contradistinction to the three theological virtues of faith, hope, and charity) has been reserved to the four virtues which Plato defined in the *Republic,* namely, temperance, courage, wisdom, and justice. I take the names of these four virtues in their general sense, independently of the meaning they may bear in Plato's philosophy.

the source of evil; and the wisest creature has remained the symbol of an immoral creeping mind, absorbed in what is low and unworthy. Even in everyday life we do not recognise as virtue that worldly wisdom which goes no further than understanding human weaknesses and arranging its own affairs in accordance with selfish ends.

The conception of *justice* (the fourth cardinal virtue) has four different meanings. In the widest sense 'just' is synonymous with due, correct, normal, or generally right — not only in the moral sphere (with regard to will and action) but also in the intellectual (with regard to knowledge and thinking); for instance, 'you reason *justly*' or '*cette solution (d'un problème mathématique ou métaphysique) est juste.*'[4] Taken in this sense the conception of justice, approaching that of truth, is wider than the conception of virtue and belongs to theoretical rather than to moral philosophy. In the second, more definite sense, justice *(aequitas)* corresponds to the fundamental principle of altruism, which requires that we should recognise everybody's equal right to life and well-being which each recognises for himself. In this sense justice is not a *special* virtue, but merely a logical objective expression of the moral principle, which finds its subjective psychological expression in the fundamental feeling of pity (compassion or sympathy). The idea of justice is used in the third sense when a distinction is made between degrees of altruism (or of moral relation to our fellow-creatures) and when the first, negative stage ('not to injure any one') is described as justice proper *(justitia)*, while the second, positive stage ('to help every one') is designated as charity *(caritas, charité)*. As already pointed out (in Chapter III) this distinction is purely relative, and is certainly insufficient for making justice into a special virtue. No one would call just a man who decidedly refused to help any one or to alleviate anybody's suffering, even though he did not injure his neighbours by direct acts of violence. The *moral* motive both for abstaining from inflicting injury and for rendering help, is one and the same — namely, a recognition of the right of others to live and to enjoy life. No moral motive could be found to make any one halt *half-way* and be content with the negative side of the moral demand. It is clear, then, that such pause or such limitation cannot possibly correspond to any special virtue, and merely expresses a *lesser degree* of the general altruistic virtue — the sympathetic feeling. And there is no universally binding or constant measure for the lesser and the greater, so that each case must be judged upon its own merits. When moral consciousness in the community reaches a certain level of development, the refusal to *help* even a stranger or an enemy is condemned by the conscience as a direct wrong. This is perfectly

4. "This solution (of a mathematical or metaphysical problem) is correct." — *Editor's note.*

logical, for if, speaking generally, I *ought* to help my neighbour, I wrong him by not helping him. Even on the lower stages of moral consciousness a refusal to help is, within certain limits, regarded as a wrong and a crime — for instance within the limits of the family, the tribe, the army. Among barbarous people everything is permissible so far as enemies are concerned, so that the idea of wrong does not even apply with respect to them; but a peaceful traveller or guest has a *right* to the most active help and generous gifts. If, however, justice demands charity and mercy (among the barbarians in relation to some men only, and with the progress of morality, in relation to all) it clearly cannot be a virtue by itself, distinct from charity. It is simply an expression of the general moral principle of altruism which has different degrees and forms of application, but always contains an idea of justice.

Finally, there is a fourth sense in which the term may be used. On the supposition that the objective expression of what is right is to be found in *laws* (the laws of the state or of the Church), it may be maintained that an unswerving obedience to laws is an absolute moral duty, and that a corresponding disposition to be strictly law-abiding is a virtue identical with that of justice. This view is only valid within the limits of the supposition on which it is based — that is, it is wholly applicable to laws that proceed from the Divine perfection, and therefore express the supreme truth, but is applicable to other laws only on condition that they agree with that truth; for one ought to obey God more than men. Justice in this sense, then — that is, the striving to be *law-abiding* — is not in itself a virtue; it may or may not be that, according to the nature and the origin of the laws that claim obedience. For the source of human laws is a turbid source. The limpid stream of moral truth is hardly visible in it under the layer of other, purely historical elements, which express merely the actual correlation of forces and interests at this or that moment of time. Consequently justice as a virtue by no means always coincides with legality or judicial right, and is sometimes directly opposed to it, as the jurists themselves admit: *summum jus — summa injuria.*[5] But while fully admitting the difference and the possible conflict between the inner truth and the law, many people think that such conflicts should always be settled in favour of legality. They maintain, that is, that justice requires us in all cases to obey the law, even if the law be unjust. In support of their view they quote the authority and the example of a righteous man of antiquity, Socrates, who thought it wrong to run away from the lawful, though unjust, sentence of the Athenian judges against him. But in truth this famous example teaches something very different.

5. "Extreme justice is extreme injustice" (Cicero, *On Obligations*, I, 10, 33). — *Editor's note.*

So far as we know from Xenophon and Plato, Socrates was led to his decision by two different motives. In the first place, he thought that to save by flight the small remainder of life to which he, an old man of seventy, could look forward, would be shameful and cowardly, especially for him, who believed in the immortality of the soul, and taught that true wisdom was continual *dying* (to the material world). Secondly, Socrates thought that a citizen ought to sacrifice *his personal welfare* to the laws of his country, even if they were unjust, *for the sake of filial piety.* Socrates, then, was guided by the moral motives of asceticism and piety, and certainly not by the conception of the absolute value of legality, which he never admitted. Besides, in the case of Socrates, there was no conflict between two duties, but only a conflict between a personal *right* and a civic *duty,* and it may be accepted as a matter of general principle that right must give way to duty. No one is bound to defend *his own* material life: it is merely his right, which it is always permissible, and sometimes laudable, to sacrifice. It is a different matter when the civic duty of obedience to laws conflicts not with a personal right, but with a moral duty, as in the famous classical case of Antigone. She had to choose between the moral and religious duty of giving honourable burial to her brother, and the civic duty of obeying the prohibition to do so — a prohibition impious and inhuman, though legally just, for it proceeded from the lawful ruler of her native city. Here comes into force the rule that one ought to obey God more than men, and it is made abundantly clear that justice in the sense of legality, or of external conformity of actions to established laws, is not in itself a virtue, but may or may not be such according to circumstances. Therefore the heroism of Socrates, who submitted to an unjust law, and the heroism of Antigone, who violated such a law, are equally laudable — and not only because in both cases there was sacrifice of life, but from the nature of the case. Socrates renounced *his own* material right for the sake of the higher *ideas* of human dignity and patriotic duty. Antigone defended the right *of another,* and thereby fulfilled her duty — for the burial of her brother was *his* right and her duty, while it was in no sense Socrates' duty to escape from prison. Speaking generally, *pietas erga patriam,* like *pietas erga parentes,*[6] can compel us to sacrifice only our own right, but certainly not the right of others. Suppose, for instance, that filial piety developed to the point of heroism induced a man not to resist his father who intends to kill him. The moral worth of such heroism may be disputed, but it would certainly never even occur to any one to justify or to call heroic that same man if, out of obedience to his father, he thought it his duty to kill his own brother or sister. The same is applicable to unjust and in-

6. "Devotion to fatherland . . . devotion to parents." — *Editor's note.*

human laws, and from this it follows that justice, in the sense of obedience to laws as such, according to the rule *'fiat justitia, pereat mundus'*[7] is not in itself a virtue.

IV

The three so-called theological virtues recognised in the patristic and the scholastic ethics — faith, hope, and charity[8] — also have no unconditional moral worth in themselves, but are dependent upon other circumstances. Even for theologians, not every kind of faith is a virtue. The character of virtue does not attach to faith which has for its object something non-existent, or unworthy, or which unworthily regards that which is worthy. Thus, in the first case, if a person firmly believes in the philosopher's stone, *i.e.* a powder, liquid, or gas which transforms all metals to gold, such faith in an object which does not exist in the nature of things, is not regarded as a virtue, but as self-deceit. In the second case, if a person not merely admits — and rightly so — the existence of the power of evil as a fact, but makes that power an object of faith in the sense of confidence in and devotion to it, forms a compact with it, sells his soul to the devil, and so on, such faith is justly regarded as a terrible moral fall, for its object, though actual, is evil and unworthy. Finally, in the third case, the faith of the devils themselves, of whom the apostle writes that they believe (in God) and tremble,[9] is not recognised as a virtue, for although it refers to an object that exists, and is of absolute worth, it regards that object in an unworthy way (with horror instead of joy, with repulsion instead of attraction). Only that *faith in the higher being* may be regarded as a virtue, which regards it in *a worthy manner,* namely, with free filial piety. And such faith entirely coincides with the religious feeling which we found to be one of the three ultimate foundations of morality.

The second theological virtue — hope — comes really to the same thing. There can be no question of virtue when some one trusts in his own strength or wisdom, or indeed in God, but only in the sole expectation of material gain from Him. That hope alone is a virtue which looks to God as the source of true blessings to come; and this is, again, the same fundamental religious relation, to which are added an idea of the future and a feeling of expectation.

---

7. "Let justice be done though the world perish." — *Editor's note.*

8. According to the well-known text of St. Paul, in which, however, the term 'virtue' is not used. [1 Cor. 13:13. — *Editor's note.*]

9. James 2:19.

Finally, the moral significance of the third and greatest theological virtue — *love* — entirely depends upon the given objective determinations. Love in itself, or love in general, is not a virtue — if it were, all beings would alike be virtuous, for they all without exception love something and live by their love. But selfish love for oneself and one's property, passionate love of drink or of horse-racing, is not reckoned as a virtue.

"*Il faut en ce bas monde aimer beaucoup de choses,*"[10] teaches a neo-pagan poet. Such 'love' had been expressly rejected by the apostle of love:"*Love not the world, neither the things that are in the world.*"[11]

This is the first, negative part of the commandment of love, and it should not be overlooked as it usually is. It is simply the expression of the fundamental principle of asceticism: to guard ourselves from the lower nature and to struggle against its dominion. For it is clear from the context that by 'the world' which we must not love, the apostle means neither mankind as a whole, nor the totality of the creation which proclaims the glory of God, but precisely the dark and irrational basis of the material nature which ceases to be passive and potential, as it ought to be, and unlawfully invades the domain of the human spirit. Further on it is directly said that in the world there is *the lust of the flesh, i.e.* the desire of immoderate sensuality, *the lust of the eyes, i.e.* greed or love of money, and *the pride of life, i.e.* vainglory and ambition.

Biblical ethics adds to the negative '*love not the world*' two positive commands: *love God with all thy heart, and love thy neighbour as thyself.*[12] These two kinds of love are rightly distinguished, for the particular nature of the object necessarily conditions the particular moral relation to be adopted toward it. Love toward our neighbours has its source in pity, and love toward God in reverence. To love one's neighbour as oneself really means to feel for him as one does for oneself. Whole-hearted love for God means entire devotion to Him, full surrender of one's own will to His — *i.e.* the perfection of the filial or the religious feeling and relation.

Thus the commandment of love is not connected with any particular virtue, but is the culmination of all the fundamental demands of morality in the three necessary respects: in relation to the lower, to the higher, and to that which is on a level with us.

---

10. "It is necessary to love many things in this vile world." This is an imprecise quotation from Alfred de Musset's sonnet to Victor Hugo. The exact line is: "*Il faut, dans ce bas monde, aimer beaucoup de choses.*" — *Editor's note.*

11. 1 John 2:15.

12. See Matthew 22:37-39. — *Editor's note.*

V

I have shown that the four 'cardinal' as well as the three 'theological' virtues can be reduced, in one way or another, to the three ultimate foundations of morality, indicated above. It can now be left to the goodwill and the intelligence of the reader to continue the analysis of the other so-called virtues. There exists no generally recognised list of them, and, by means of scholastic distinctions, their number can be increased indefinitely. But for the sake of completing what has gone before, I should like to say a few words about five virtues which present a certain interest in one respect or another, namely, concerning *magnanimity, disinterestedness, generosity, patience,* and *truthfulness.*

We call *magnanimous* a man who is ashamed, or finds it *beneath his dignity,* to insist on his material rights to the detriment of other people, or to bind his will by *lower* worldly interests (such as vanity), which he therefore readily sacrifices for the sake of higher considerations. We also call magnanimous the man who is undisturbed by adversities and changes of fortune, because, again, he is *ashamed* of allowing his peace of mind to be dependent upon material and accidental things. The words italicised are sufficient to indicate that this virtue is simply a special expression or form of the first root of morality — viz, of the self-assertion of the human spirit against the lower, material side of our being. The essential thing here is the feeling of human dignity, which, in the first instance, manifests itself in the feeling of shame.

Disinterestedness is the freedom of the spirit from attachment to a certain kind of material goods, namely, to possessions. It is clearly a particular expression of that same feeling of human dignity. In a corresponding manner, vices opposed to this virtue — miserliness and cupidity — are felt to be *shameful.*

Generosity in its external manifestations coincides with magnanimity and disinterestedness, but it has a different inner basis, namely, an altruistic one. A virtuously generous man is one who shares his property with others out of *justice or benevolence* (for in so far as he does it out of vanity or pride, he is not virtuous). But at the same time such a man may be attached to the property he gives away to the degree of miserliness, and in that case he cannot, in strictness, be called disinterested. It must only be said that the altruistic virtue of generosity overcomes in him the vice of cupidity.

Patience (as a virtue) is only the passive aspect of that quality of the soul which, in its active manifestation, is called magnanimity or spiritual fortitude. The difference is almost entirely subjective, and no hard and fast line can be drawn between the two. A man who calmly endures torment or misfortune will be called magnanimous by some, patient by others, courageous by others, while yet others will see in him an example of a special virtue — serenity (ἀταραξία) and so on. The discussion of the comparative appropriateness of these definitions can have only a linguistic and not an ethical interest. On the other hand, the identity of the external expression may (as in the case of generosity) conceal important differences in the moral content. A man may patiently endure physical or mental suffering owing to a low degree of nervous sensitivity, dullness of mind and an apathetic temperament, and in that case patience is not a virtue at all. Or patience may be due to the inner force of the spirit, which does not give way to external influences — and then it is an ascetic virtue (reducible to our first basis of morality) or it may arise from meekness and love of one's neighbours *(caritas)*, which does not wish to pay back evil for evil and injury for injury — and in that case it is an altruistic virtue (reducible to the second principle — pity, which here extends even to enemies who inflict the injury). Finally, patience may spring from obedience to the higher will upon which all that happens depends — and then it is a religious virtue (reducible to the third principle).

A particuliar variety of patience is the quality which is designated in the Russian language by the grammatically incorrect term *'terpimost'* — tolerance *(passivum pro activo)*.[13] It means the admission of other people's freedom even when it seems to lead to error. This attitude is in itself neither a vice nor a virtue, but may, in different circumstances, become either. It depends on the object to which it refers (thus injury of the weak by the strong must not be tolerated, and 'tolerance' of it is immoral and not virtuous), and still more, on the inner motives from which it arises. It may spring from magnanimity or from cowardice, from respect for the rights of others and from contempt of the good of others, from profound faith in the conquering power of the higher truth and from indifference to that truth.[14]

VI

Among the derivative or secondary virtues *truthfulness* must be recognised as the most important, both owing to its specifically human character (for in the strict sense it is only possible for a being endowed with the power of speech[15])

---

13. "Receptivity to action." — *Editor's note.*

14. A more detailed discussion of it will be found at the beginning of my article "The Dispute about Justice" (in *Vestnik Evropy,* March 1894).

15. Animals may be naïve or cunning, but only man can be truthful or deceitful.

and to its significance for social morality. At the same time this virtue has been and still is the subject of much disagreement between different schools of moralists.

The word is the instrument of reason for expressing that which is, that which may be, and that which ought to be, *i.e.* for expressing the actual, the formal, and the ideal truth. The possession of such an instrument is part of the higher nature of man, and therefore when he misuses it, giving expression to untruth for the sake of lower material ends, he does something contrary to human dignity, something *shameful.* At the same time the word is the expression of human solidarity, the most important means of communication between men. But this applies only to true words. Therefore when an individual person uses speech to express untruth for his own selfish ends (not only individually selfish, but collectively selfish also, *e.g.* in the interests of his family, his class, his party, etc.) he violates the rights of others and injures the community. A lie is thus both shameful for the liar, and damaging and insulting to the deceived. The demand for truthfulness has then a twofold moral foundation. It is based, first, on the human *dignity* of the subject himself, and secondly upon *justice, i.e.* upon a recognition of the right of others not to be deceived by me, in as much as I myself cannot wish to be deceived by them.

All this is in direct conformity with the demands of reason and contains nothing dubious. But by abstracting the demand for truthfulness from its moral basis, and turning it into a *special* virtue possessed of absolute worth *in itself,* the scholastic philosophy has created difficulties and contradictions which do not follow from the nature of the case. If by a lie is meant the contrary of truth in the full sense of the word, *i.e.* not only of the real and formal, but also and chiefly of the ideal or purely moral truth (of that which *ought* to be), it would be perfectly correct and indisputable to ascribe absolute significance to the rule 'do not lie,' and to admit of no exception to it under any circumstances; for, clearly, truth ceases to be truth if there may be a single case in which it is permissible to depart from it. There could be no certainty here, at any rate not between people who understand that A = A and that 2 x 2 = 4. But the trouble is that the philosophers who particularly insist on the rule 'do not lie,' as allowing of no exception, are themselves guilty of a falsity by arbitrarily limiting the meaning of truth (in each given case) to the real, or more exactly, to the matter-of-fact aspect of it, *taken separately.* Adopting this point of view, they come to the following absurd dilemma (I give the usual instance as the clearest and simplest). When a person, having no other means at his command for frustrating a would-be murderer in pursuit of his innocent victim, hides the latter in his house, and to the pursuer's question whether that person is there, answers in the negative, or, for greater plausibility, 'puts him off the track' by mentioning quite a different place, — in lying thus he acts either in conformity with the moral law or in opposition to it. If the first, it is permissible to violate the moral command 'do not lie'; morality is thus deprived of its absolute value, and the way is open to justify every kind of evil. If the second — if the man has sinned by telling a lie — it appears that the moral duty of truthfulness actually compelled him to become a real accomplice of the murderer in his crime — which is equally opposed to reason and to the moral sense. There can be no middle course, for it is obvious that a refusal to answer or an evasive answer would simply confirm the pursuer's suspicion and would finally give away the victim.

It will be remembered that great moralists like Kant and Fichte, who insist on the absolute and formal character of the moral law, maintain that even in such circumstances a lie would be unjustifiable, and that, therefore, the person questioned ought to fulfil the duty of truthfulness without thinking of the consequences, for which (it is urged) he is not responsible. Other moralists, who reduce all morality to the feeling of pity or the principle of altruism, believe that lying is permissible and even obligatory when it can save the life or promote the welfare of others. This assertion, however, is too wide and indefinite and easily leads to all kinds of abuse.

How then are we to decide the question whether that unfortunate man ought to have told a lie or not? When both horns of a dilemma equally lead to an absurdity, there must be something wrong in the formulation of the dilemma itself. In the present case the 'something wrong' is to be found in the ambiguity of the words 'lie,' 'false,' and 'lying,' which are here taken to have one meaning only, or to combine both meanings in one, which is not really the case. Thus the main term is *falsely* understood at the very beginning of the argument, and this can lead to nothing but false conclusions.

I propose to consider it in detail, and let not the reader grudge a certain pedanticism of this examination. The question itself has arisen solely owing to the scholastic pedantry of the abstract moralists.

According to the formal definition of it a lie is a contradiction between somebody's assertion[16] concerning a given fact and the actual existence, or manner of existence, of that fact. But this formal conception of a lie has no direct bearing on morality. An assertion that contradicts reality may sometimes be simply *mistaken*, and in that case its actual falsity will be limited to the objective (or more exactly, to the phenomenal) sphere, without in the least

---

16. The general definition must include both affirmations and denials, and I therefore use the term 'assertion' to cover both. The words 'judgment' and 'proposition' involve a shade of meaning unsuitable in the present case.

touching upon the moral aspect of the subject; that is, it will contain no lie in the moral sense at all: a mistake is not a falsehood. Take an extreme case. It is no sin against truthfulness to talk nonsense through absent-mindedness, or through ignorance of language, like the German in the well-known anecdote who mixed up English and German words and affirmed that he 'became a cup of tea.' But apart from mistakes of speech, the same thing must be said of the mistakes of thought or errors. Many people have affirmed, and are still affirming, both in speech and in writing, things as *false* (in the objective sense) as the assertion that a man became a cup of tea, but do so consciously, intending to say precisely what they do say. If, however, they sincerely take falsity for truth, no one will call them liars or see anything immoral in their error. Thus neither the contradiction between speech and reality, nor the contradiction between thought and reality is a lie in the moral sense. Is it to be found in the contradiction between the will and reality as such, *i.e.* in the simple intention to lie? But there never is such simple intention. People — at any rate those who can be held morally responsible — lie for the sake of something, with some object. Some lie to satisfy their vanity, to make a show, to draw attention to themselves, to be noted; others for the sake of material gain, in order to deceive some one with profit to themselves. Both these kinds of lie, of which the first is called bragging, and the second cheating, fall within the moral sphere, and are to be condemned as shameful to the person who tells them, and as insulting and injurious to others. But in addition to the vainglorious lie or bragging, and the lie for the sake of gain or cheating, there exists a more subtle kind of lie, which has no immediately low purpose, but must nevertheless be condemned as insulting to one's neighbours. I mean the lie out of contempt for humanity, beginning with the usual 'I am not at home' and down to the most complex political, religious, and literary humbug. There is nothing shameful in the narrow sense of the word in this kind of lie (unless of course it is made for purposes of gain), but it is immoral from the altruistic point of view, as violating the rights of the deceived. The person who hoaxes others would obviously dislike to be deceived himself, and would regard an attempt to hoax him as a violation of his human rights. Consequently he ought to respect the same right in other people.

The case of a man who deceives the evil-doer for the sake of preventing murder obviously does not fall within the first two kinds of immoral lie, *i.e.* it is neither bragging nor cheating; could it possibly be classed with the last kind, that is, with hoaxing, which is immoral in the sense of being insulting to another person? Is it not a case of despising humanity in the person of the would-be murderer, who is, after all, a human being, and must not be deprived of any of his human rights? But the right of the criminal to have me for his accomplice in the perpetration of the murder can certainly not be reckoned among his human rights; and it is precisely the demand for an accomplice and *it alone* that is contained in his question as to the whereabouts of his victim. Is it permissible for a moralist to have recourse to what he knows to be fiction, especially when it is a question of a man's life? For it is sheer fiction to suppose that in asking his question the would-be murderer is thinking about the truth, wants to know the truth, and is, therefore, like any other human being, *entitled* to have a correct answer from those who know it. *In reality there is nothing of the kind.* The man's question does not exist as a separate and independent fact expressing his interest as to the place where his victim really is; the question is only an inseparable moment in a whole series of actions which, in their totality, form an attempt at murder. An affirmative answer would not be a fulfilment of the universal duty to speak the truth at all; it would simply be a criminal connivance which would convert the attempt into actual murder.

If we are to talk of truthfulness, truthfulness demands, in the first place, that we should take a case *as it really is,* in its actual completeness and its proper inner significance. Now the words and actions of the would-be murderer in the instance we are considering are held together by, and derive their actual meaning solely from, his intention to kill his victim; therefore it is only in connection with this intention that one can truly judge of his words and actions, and of the relation to them on the part of another person. Since we know the criminal intention, we have neither a theoretical ground nor a moral right to separate the man's question (and consequently our answer to it) from the object to which it *actually* refers. From this point of view, *which is the only true one,* the man's question means nothing but *'help me to accomplish the murder.'* A correct answer to it, overlooking the real meaning of the question, and, contrary to obvious fact, taking it to have some relation to truth — would be *false* from the theoretical point of view, and from the practical would simply mean *compliance with the criminal request.* The only possible means of *refusing* that request would be to put the would-be murderer off the track: such refusal is *morally binding* both in relation to the victim whose life it saves, and in relation to the criminal whom it gives time to think and to give up his criminal intention. Still less can there be question here of the violation of the man's right; it would be too crude an error to confuse a request for criminal assistance with the right of learning the truth from the person who knows it. It would be equally mistaken to insist that the man who, for motives of moral duty, prevented the murder by the only possible means, had nevertheless told a lie and therefore acted badly. This would mean a confusion between the two senses of the word 'lie' — the formal and the moral — the essential difference between which has been indicated above.

The upholders of pseudo-moral rigorism may still seek refuge on religious ground. Although no human right is violated by putting the murderer on the false track, perhaps the divine right is violated by it. If there existed a commandment from above 'do not lie,' we should be bound to obey it unconditionally, leaving the consequences to God. But the fact is that there exists in the word of God no abstract commandment[17] forbidding lying in general or lying in the formal sense, while the command to sacrifice our very souls — and not merely the formal correctness of our words — for our neighbours undoubtedly exists and must be fulfilled. It might however be thought that from the mystical point of view a means might be found to carry out the chief commandment with regard to love, and yet to avoid the formal lie. Thus we could, after surrendering the victim to his murderer, turn to God with a prayer to prevent the murder by some miracle. There certainly are cases on record of prayers producing the desired effect against all human probability. This however only happened in hopeless extremity, when there were no natural means left. But to require from God a miracle when you can yourself, by a simple and *harmless* means, prevent the disaster, would be extremely *impious.* It would be a different matter if the last human means available were immoral; but to fall back upon the immorality of the formal lie as such would mean to beg precisely that which is in question and which cannot be logically proved, for it is based on the confusion between two utterly distinct ideas of *falsity* and *falsehood.* In the instance we are considering, the answer to the murderer's question is undoubtedly *false,* but it is not to be condemned as *a lie.* The formal *falsity* of a person's words has *as such* no relation to morality, and cannot be condemned from the moral point of view. *Falsehood,* on the other hand, is subject to such condemnation as the expression of an intention which is in some way *immoral,* and it is in this alone that it differs from simple falsity. But in the present case it is impossible to find *any* such immoral intention, and consequently any falsehood.

Put briefly, our long argument may be expressed as follows. An assertion which is formally false, that is, which contradicts the fact to which it refers, is not always a lie in the moral sense. It becomes such only when it proceeds from the evil will which intentionally *misuses* words for its own ends; and the evil character of the will consists not in its contradicting any fact but in its contradicting *that which ought to be.* Now that which ought to be is of necessity determined in three ways — in relation, namely, to that which is be-

17. The commandment 'Thou shalt not bear false witness against thy neighbour' (Exod. 20:16), *i.e.* do not slander, has no bearing on this question, for it forbids not lying in general but only one definite kind of lie, which is always immoral.

low us, on a level with us, and above us — and amounts to three demands: to subordinate the lower nature to the spirit, to respect the rights of our fellow-creatures, and to be wholly devoted to the higher principle of the world. An expression of our will can be bad or immoral *only* if it violates one of these three duties, that is, when the will affirms or sanctions something shameful, or injurious, or impious. But the will of the man who puts the would-be murderer off his victim's track does not violate any of the three duties — there is nothing either shameful or injurious or impious about his will. Thus it is not a case of a lie in the moral sense at all, or of a breach of any commandment, and, in allowing such a means of preventing evil, we do not allow any exceptions to the moral law. For reasons indicated, the given case cannot be said to fall under the moral rule to which, in contradiction to fact, one is seeking to subordinate it.

One of the disputants maintains: *since* this is a lie, this *bad* means ought not to have been used *even* to save another person's life. The other side answers: *although* it is a lie, it is permissible to use this bad means to save the life of another, for the duty to save another person's life is more important than the duty to speak the truth. Both these false assertions are cancelled by the third, true one. *Since this is not a lie* (in the moral sense), the recourse to this *innocent* means, necessary for the prevention of murder, is *morally binding* on the person.[18]

VII

To make truthfulness into a separate formal virtue involves, then, an inner contradiction and is contrary to reason. Truthfulness, like all other 'virtues,' does not contain its moral quality in itself, but derives it from its conformity to the fundamental norms of morality. A pseudo-truthfulness divorced from them may be a source of falsehood, that is, of false valuations. It may stop at the request that our words should merely be an exact reflection of the external reality of isolated facts, and thus lead to obvious absurdities. From this point of view a priest who repeated exactly what he was told at a confession would satisfy the demands of truthfulness. Real truthfulness, however, re-

---

18. Although in this question Kant sides with the rigorists, in doing so he is really inconsistent with his own principle that an action, to be moral, must be capable of being made into a universal rule. It is clear that in putting the would-be murderer off the place where his victim is, I can, in reason and conscience, affirm my way of action as a universal rule: every one ought always thus to conceal the victim from the intending murderer; and if I put myself into the latter's place, I should wish that I might, in the same way, be prevented from committing the murder.

quires that our words should correspond to the inner *truth* or meaning of a given situation, to which our will applies the moral norms.

The analysis of the so-called virtues shows that they have moral significance only in so far as they are determined by the three norms of morality. And although these norms are *psychologically based* upon the corresponding primitive feelings of shame, pity, and reverence, they do not entirely rest upon this empirical basis, but are logically developed out of the idea of *right* or *truth* (in the wide sense). Truth demands that we should regard our lower nature as lower, that is, that we should subordinate it to rational ends; if, on the contrary, we surrender to it, we recognise it not for what it really is, but for something higher — and thus pervert the true order of things, violate the truth, regard that lower sphere in a wrong or immoral way. Likewise, truth demands that we should regard our fellow-creatures as such, should admit their rights as equal to ours, should put ourselves into their place; but if, whilst recognising ourselves as individuals possessed of full rights, we regard others as empty masks, we obviously depart from truth, and our relation to them is wrong. Finally, if we are conscious of a higher universal principle above us, truth demands that we should regard it as higher, that is, with religious devotion.

This moral conception of right or truth could certainly not have arisen were not the feelings of shame, pity, and reverence, which immediately determine man's rightful attitude to the three fundamental conditions of his life, present in his nature from the first. But once reason has deduced from these natural data their inner ethical content and affirmed it as a *duty,* it becomes an independent principle of moral activity, apart from its psychological basis.[19] One may imagine a man whose feeling of modesty is by nature little developed, but who is rationally convinced that it is his duty to oppose the encroachments of the lower nature, and conscientiously fulfils this duty. Such a man will prove in fact to be more moral in this particular respect than a man who is modest by nature, but whose reason is defenceless against the temptations of sense that overcome his modesty. The same is true of natural kindness (the point dwelt upon by Kant) and natural religious feeling. Without a consciousness of duty all these natural impulses to moral conduct are unstable, and can have no decisive significance in the conflict of opposing motives.

But does the consciousness of duty or of right possess such a decisive power? If righteousness from natural inclination is an *unstable* thing, righteousness from a sense of duty is an extremely *rare* thing. The idea of right as actually realised thus proves to be lacking in the characteristics of universality and necessity. The vital interests of moral philosophy and the formal de-

19. See *The Critique of Abstract Principles,* p. 70.

mands of reason cannot acquiesce in this and consequently there arises a new problem for reason: to find a practical principle which would not only be morally right, but also highly *desirable* in itself and for every one, possessing as such the power to determine human conduct with necessity, independently of the natural inclinations of the soul or of the degree of spiritual development — a principle equally inherent in, understandable to, and actual for all human beings.

When reason dwells exclusively or mainly on this aspect of the case, the moral end is understood as the highest good *(summum bonum)*, and the question assumes the following form: Does there exist, and what is the nature of, the highest good, to which all other goods are necessarily subordinate as to the absolute criterion of the *desirable in general?*

CHAPTER VI

The Spurious Basis of Practical Philosophy

(A Critique of Abstract Hedonism in Its Different Forms)

I

The moral good is determined by reason as truth (in the wide sense), or as the right relation to everything. This idea of the good, inwardly all-embracing and logically necessary, proves in fact to be lacking in universality and necessity. The good as the ideal norm of will does not, in point of fact, coincide with the good as the actual object of desire. The good is that which ought to be, but (1) not every one desires what he ought to desire; (2) not every one who desires the good is able to overcome, for its sake, the bad propensities of his nature; and finally (3) the few who have attained the victory of the good over the evil in themselves — the virtuous, righteous men or saints — are powerless to overcome by their good "the wickedness in which the whole world lieth." But in so far as the good is not desired by a person at all, *it is not a good* for him; in so far as it fails to affect the will, even though it may be affirmed as desirable by the rational consciousness, it is only an ideal and *not a real* good; finally, in so far as it fails to empower a given person to realise the moral order in the world as a whole, even though it may affect the will of that person by making him inwardly better, it is *not a sufficient good*.

This threefold discrepancy between the moral and the real good seems to render the idea of the good self-contradictory. The definition of the good as that which ought to be involves, in addition to its ideal content, a real demand that the moral content should not remain merely theoretical, but that it should be *realised* in practice. The very conception of that which ought to be implies that it *ought to be realised*. The powerlessness of the good is not a good. It cannot be right that only a *part* of humanity should desire what they ought to desire, that only a *few* should live as they ought, and that *none* should be able to make the world what it ought to be. All agree that the moral good and happiness ought to coincide; the latter ought to be the direct, universal, and necessary consequence of the former, and express the absolute desirability and actuality of the moral good. But in fact they do not coincide; the real good is distinct from the moral good, and, taken separately, is understood as *well-being.* The actual insufficiency of the idea of the good leads us to this conception of well-being, which, as a motive for action, apparently possesses the concrete universality and necessity which are lacking to the purely moral demands. For every end of action without exception is directly or indirectly characterised by the fact that the attainment of that end satisfies the agent or tends to his well-being, while by no means every end of action can be directly or even indirectly characterised as morally good. Every desire as such is apparently simply a desire for its satisfaction, *i.e.* for well-being; to desire calamity or dissatisfaction would be the same as to desire that which is known to be undesirable, and would, therefore, be manifestly absurd. And if, in order to be realised in practice, the moral good must become the object of desire, the ethical principle will be seen to depend upon the practical idea (practical in the narrow sense) of the real good or well-being, which is thus raised to the rank of the supreme principle of human action.

This eudaemonic principle (from the Greek εὐδαιμονία — the condition of blessedness, well-being) has the obvious advantage of not raising the question *Why?* One may ask why I should strive for the moral good when this striving is opposed to my natural inclinations and causes me nothing except suffering; but one cannot ask why I should desire my well-being, since I desire it naturally and necessarily. This desire is inseparably connected with my existence, and is a direct expression of it. I exist as desiring, and I desire only that, of course, which satisfies me or what is pleasant to me. Every one finds his well-being either in what immediately gives him pleasure or in what leads to it — that is, in what serves as a means for bringing about pleasurable states. Thus well-being is defined more closely through the idea of *pleasure* (Greek ἡδονή, hence the theory of Hedonism).

II

When that which ought to be is replaced by that which is desired, the end of life or the highest good is reduced to pleasure. This idea, clear, simple, and concrete as it appears to be, involves insuperable difficulties when applied in the concrete. It is impossible to deduce any general principle or rule of action from the general fact that every one desires that which is pleasing to him. The assertion that the final end of action is directly or indirectly pleasure, *i.e.* satisfaction of the subject desiring, is as indisputable and as pointless as the assertion, *e.g.,* that all actions end in something or lead to something. In concrete reality we do not find one universal pleasure, but an indefinite multitude of all kinds of pleasures, having nothing in common between them. One person finds the highest bliss in drinking vodka, and another seeks "a bliss for which there is no measure and no name"; but even the latter person, when extremely hungry or thirsty, forgets all transcendental joys, and desires above all things food and drink. On the other hand, under certain conditions, things which had given enjoyment or seemed pleasant in the past cease to be attractive, and, indeed, life itself loses all value.

In truth the idea of pleasure refers to a variety of accidental desires which differ according to the individual taste and character, the degree of mental development, age, external position, and momentary mood. No definite expression can be given to pleasure as a universal practical principle, unless it is to be "Let every one act so as to get for himself, as far as possible, what is pleasing to him at the given moment." This rule, on the whole firmly established and more or less successfully applied in the animal kingdom, is inconvenient in the human world for two reasons: (1) the presence in man of unnatural inclinations, the satisfaction of which, though yielding the desired pleasure, leads at the same time to clear and certain destruction, *i.e.* to what is highly undesirable for every one; (2) the presence in man of reason, which compares the various natural impulses and pleasures with one another, and passes judgment on them from the point of view of the consequences they involve. In a rudimentary form we find such judgment even among the animals who act or refrain from action, not from motives of immediate pleasant or unpleasant feeling only, but also from considerations of further, pleasant or unpleasant, consequences following upon certain behaviour. But with animals these considerations do not extend beyond simple associations of ideas. Thus, the idea of the piece of meat seized without permission is accompanied by the idea of the blows of the whip, etc. The more abstract character of the human reason allows us, in addition to such elementary considerations, to make a general comparison of the immediate motives of pleasure with their remote consequences. And it is in following this line of reflection that the most thorough-going hedonist of the ancient philosophy, Hegesias of Cyrenae, came to the conclusion that from the point of view of pleasure life is not worth living. The desire for pleasure is either fruitless and in this sense painful, or, in achieving its object, it proves to be deceptive, for a momentary feeling of pleasure is inevitably followed by tedium and a new painful search after illusion. Since it is impossible to reach true pleasure, we must strive to free ourselves from pain, and the surest means to do so is to die. Such was the outcome of Hegesias's philosophy, for which he was nicknamed *'the advocate of death'* (πεισιθάνατος). But even apart from such extreme conclusions, the analysis of the idea of pleasure makes it abundantly clear that 'pleasure' cannot furnish us with a satisfactory principle of conduct.

III

A simple striving for pleasure cannot be a principle of action because in itself it is indefinite and devoid of content. Its actual content is wholly unstable and is to be found solely in the accidental objects which call it forth. The only universal and necessary element in the infinite variety of pleasurable states is the fact that the moment of the attainment of any purpose or object of desire whatsoever is necessarily experienced and imagined beforehand as a pleasure, *i.e.* as satisfied or realised desire. But this elementary psychological truth does not contain the slightest indication either as to the nature of the object of desire or as to the means of obtaining it. Both remain empirically variable and accidental. The point of view of pleasure does not in itself give us any actual definition of *the highest good* to which all other goods must be subordinate, and consequently gives us no rule or principle of conduct. This becomes still more clear if, instead of taking pleasure in the general sense of satisfied desire, we take concrete instances of it — *i.e.* particular pleasurable states. These states are never desired as such, for they are simply the consequence of satisfied volition and not the object of desire. What is desired are certain definite realities and not the pleasant sensations that follow from them. For a person who is hungry and thirsty, bread and water are immediate objects of desire and not a means for obtaining pleasure of the sense of taste. We know, of course, from experience that it is very pleasant to eat when one is hungry; but a baby wants to suck previously to any experience whatever. And later, on reaching a certain age, the child has a very strong desire for objects about the actual pleasurableness of which it knows, as yet, nothing at all. It is useless to have recourse to 'heredity' in this case, for then we should have to go as far back as the chemical molecules, of which probably no one would say that they seek to enter into definite combinations simply because they remember the pleasure they had derived from it in the past.

There is another circumstance which does not permit of identifying the good with the fact of pleasure. Every one knows from experience that the degree of the desirability of an object or a state does not always correspond to the actual degree of pleasure to be derived from the attainment of it. Thus, in the case of strong erotic attraction to a person of the opposite sex, the fact of possessing this particular person is desired as the highest bliss, in comparison with which the possession of any other person is not desired at all; but the actual pleasure to be derived from this infinitely desirable fact has certainly nothing to do with infinity, and is approximately equal to the pleasure of any other satisfaction of the instinct in question. Speaking generally, the desirability of particular objects or their significance as goods is determined not by the subjective states of pleasure that follow the attainment of them, but by the objective relation of these objects to our bodily or mental nature. The source and the character of that relation are not as a rule sufficiently clear to us; they manifest themselves simply as a blind impulse.

But although pleasure is not the essence of the good or the desirable as such, it is certainly its constant attribute. Whatever the ultimate reasons of the desirability of the objects or states that appear to us as good may be, at any rate there can be no doubt that the achieved good or the fulfilled desire is always accompanied by a sensation of pleasure. This sensation, inseparably connected with the good as the necessary consequence of it, may then serve to determine the highest good as a practical principle.

The highest good is from this point of view a state which affords the greatest amount of satisfaction. This amount is determined both directly through the addition of pleasant states to one another, and indirectly through the subtraction of the unpleasant states. In other words, the highest good consists in the possession of goods which, in their totality, or as the final result, afford the maximum of pleasure and the minimum of pain.[1] The actions of the individual are no longer prompted by a mere desire for immediate pleasure, but by prudence which judges of the value of the different pleasures and selects those among them which are the most lasting and free from pain. The man who from this point of view is regarded as happy is not one who at the given moment is experiencing the most intense pleasure, but one in whose life as a whole pleasant sensations predominate over the painful — who in the long-run enjoys more than he suffers. "The wise man," writes Aristotle, "seeks freedom from pain, and not pleasure" (ὁ φρόνιμος τὸ ἄλυπον διώκει, οὐ τὸ ἡδύ).[2] This is the point of view of eudaemonism proper or of *prudent hedonism*. A follower of this doctrine will not 'wallow in the mire of

1. Apart from any pessimistic theories, freedom from pain is from the hedonistic point of view of more importance than the positive fact of pleasure. The pain of an unsatisfied and strongly individualised sexual passion, which not unfrequently drives people to suicide, is incomparably greater than the pleasure of the satisfaction. The latter can be pronounced to be a great good only in so far as it gives relief from the great pain of the unsatisfied desire.

2. *Nicomachean Ethics* 1152. — *Editor's note*.

sensuous pleasures,' which destroy both body and soul. He will find his greatest satisfaction in the higher intellectual and æsthetic pleasures, which, being the most durable, involve the least degree of pain.

IV

In spite of its apparent plausibility, prudent hedonism shares the fate of hedonism in general: it too proves to be an illusory principle. When the good is determined as happiness, the essential thing is the attainment and the secure possession of it. But neither can be secured by any amount of prudence.

Our life and destiny depend upon causes and factors beyond the control of our worldly wisdom; and in most cases the wise egoist simply loses the opportunities of actual, though fleeting pleasure, without thereby acquiring any lasting happiness. The insecurity of all pleasures is all the more fatal because man, in contradistinction to animals, knows it beforehand: the inevitable failure of all happiness in the future throws its shadow even over moments of actual enjoyment. But even in the rare cases in which a wise enjoyment of life does actually lead to a quantitative surplus of the painless over the painful states, the triumph of hedonism is merely illusory. It is based upon an arbitrary exclusion of the *qualitative* character of our mental states (taking quality not in the moral sense, which may be disputed, but simply in the psychological or, rather, in the psychophysical sense of the intensity of the pleasurable states). There is no doubt that the strongest, the most overwhelming delights are not those recommended by prudence but those to be found in wild passions. Granted that in the case of passions also the pleasure of satisfaction is out of proportion to the strength of desire, it is at any rate incomparably more intense than the sensations which a well-regulated and carefully ordered life can yield. When prudence tells us that passions lead to ruin, we need not in the least dispute this truth, but may recall another:

All, all that holds the threat of fate
Is for the heart of mortal wight
Full of inscrutable delight.[3]

No objection can be brought against this from the hedonistic point of view. Why should I renounce the 'inscrutable delight' for the sake of dull well-being? Passions lead to destruction, but prudence does not save from de-

3. From Pushkin's verse-drama *Feast in the Time of Plague. — Editor's note.*

struction. No one by means of prudent behaviour alone has ever conquered death.

It is only in the presence of something higher that the voice of passions may prove to be wrong. It is silenced by the thunder of heaven, but the tame speeches of good sense are powerless to drown it.

The satisfaction of passions which lead to destruction cannot of course be the highest good; but from the hedonistic point of view it may have a distinct advantage over the innocent pleasures of good behaviour *which do not save from destruction*. It is true that intellectual and æsthetic pleasures are not only innocent but noble; they involve limitations, however, which preclude them from being the highest good.

(1) These 'spiritual' pleasures are from the nature of the case accessible only to persons of a high degree of æsthetic and intellectual development, that is, only to a few, while the highest good must necessarily be universal. No progress of democratic institutions would give an ass the capacity of enjoying Beethoven's symphonies, or enable a pig, which cannot appreciate even the taste of oranges, to enjoy the sonnets of Dante or Petrarch or the poems of Shelley.

(2) Even for those to whom æsthetic and intellectual pleasures are accessible, they are insufficient. They cannot fill the whole of one's life, for they have relation to only some of our mental faculties, without affecting the others. It is the theoretic, contemplative side of human nature that is alone more or less satisfied by them, while the active, practical life is left without any definite guidance. The intellectual and æsthetic goods, as objects of pure contemplation, do not affect the practical will.

Whilst we admire the heavenly stars
We do not want them for our own.[4]

When from the hedonistic point of view a person puts the pleasures of science and of art above everything, his practical will remains without any definite determination, and falls easy prey to blind passions. And this shows that prudent hedonism is unsatisfactory as a guiding principle of life.

(3) Its unsatisfactoriness is also proved by the fact that hedonism is powerless against theoretical scepticism, which undermines the value of the actual objects of intellectual and æsthetic activity. Suppose I find a real enjoyment in the contemplation of beauty and in the pursuit of truth. But my reason — the highest authority for 'prudent' hedonism — tells me that beauty is a subjective mirage and that truth is unattainable by the human

4. From a poem by Goethe. — *Editor's note.*

mind. My pleasure is thus poisoned, and, in the case of a logical mind, is altogether destroyed. Even apart from real consistency, however, it is clear that the delight in what is known to be a deception cannot be the highest good.

(4) Now, suppose that our epicurean is free from such scepticism, and unreflectively gives himself up to the delights of thought and of creative art, without questioning the ultimate significance of these objects. To him these 'spiritual goods' may appear eternal; but his own capacity for enjoying them is certainly far from being so; it can at best survive for a brief period his capacity for sensuous pleasures.

And yet it is precisely the *security* or the continuity of pleasures that is the chief claim of *prudent* hedonism and the main advantage it is supposed to possess over the simple striving for immediate pleasure. Of course if our pleasures were abiding realities that could be hoarded like property, a prudent hedonist in his decrepit old age might still consider himself richer than a reckless profligate who had come to premature death. But since, in truth, *past* pleasures are mere memories, the wise epicurean — if he remains till his death true to the hedonistic point of view — will be sure to regret that for the sake of faint memories of the innocent intellectual and æsthetic pleasures he sacrificed opportunities of pleasures far more intense. Just *because* he never experienced them, they will now evoke in him painful and fruitless desire. The supposed superiority of prudent hedonism to a reckless pursuit of pleasure is based upon an illegitimate confusion between two points of view. It must be one or the other. Either we mean the *present* moment of enjoyment, and in that case we must give up prudence which is exhibited even in animal behaviour, or we are thinking of the *future* consequences of our actions, and in that case the question must be asked: What precise moment of the future is to be put at the basis of our reckoning? It would be obviously irrational to take any moment except the *last,* which expresses the *total* result of the whole life. But at that last moment before death all hedonistic calculus is reduced to naught, and every possible advantage of the prudent over the reckless pleasures disappears completely. All pleasures when they are over cease to be pleasures, and *we know this beforehand.* Hence the idea of *the sum of pleasures* is meaningless: the sum of zeros is not any larger than a simple zero.

V

The possession of *external* goods — whether they be pleasures of the moment or the more lasting happiness supposed to be secured by prudence — proves to be deceptive and impossible. Is, then, true welfare or the highest good to be found in *freedom* from external desires and affections which deceive and enslave man and thus make him miserable? All external goods either prove to be not worth seeking, or, depending as they do upon external causes beyond the control of man, they are taken away from him before their essential unsatisfactoriness has even been discovered; and man is thus made doubly miserable. No one can escape misfortune, and therefore no one can be happy so long as his will is attracted to objects the possession of which is accidental. If true welfare is the state of abiding satisfaction, then that man alone can be truly blessed who finds satisfaction in that of which he cannot be deprived, namely, in himself.

Let man be inwardly free from attachment to external and accidental objects, and he will be permanently satisfied and happy. Not submitting to anything foreign to him, fully possessing himself, he will possess all things and even more than all things. If I am free from the desire for a certain thing, I am more master of it than the person who possesses it and desires it; if I am indifferent to power, I am more than the ruler who cares for it; if I am indifferent to everything in the world, I am higher than the lord of all the world.

This principle of self-sufficiency (αὐτάρκεια), though expressing an unconditional demand, is in truth purely negative and conditional. In the first place, its force depends upon those very external goods which it rejects. So long as man is attached to them, freedom from such attachment is *desirable* for his higher consciousness and gives a meaning to his activity. Similarly, so long as man is sensitive to the accidental pains of the external life, triumph over them, steadfastness in adversity, can give him supreme satisfaction. But once he has risen above the attachment to external goods and the fear of external misfortune, what is to be the positive content of his life? Can it consist simply in the enjoyment of that victory? In that case the principle of self-sufficiency becomes vain self-satisfaction and acquires a comical instead of a majestic character. The unsatisfactoriness of the final result renders it superfluous to insist upon the fact that the force of spirit necessary for the attainment of it is not given to every one, and even when it is given, it is not always preserved to the end. The principle of self-sufficiency thus proves to be lacking in power of realisation, and shows itself in this respect also to be only a pseudo-principle. Freedom from slavery to the lower accidental goods can only be a *condition* of attaining the highest good, but not itself be that good. A temple cleared of idols which had once filled it, does not thereby become God's holy tabernacle. It simply remains an empty place.[5]

---

5. The principle of self-sufficiency in its practical application partly coincides with the moral principle of asceticism; but the essential difference between the two is in their starting-

VI

The individual finds no final satisfaction or happiness either in the outer worldly goods or in himself (*i.e.* in the empty form of self-consciousness). The only way out seems to be afforded by the consideration that man is not merely a separate individual entity but also part of a collective whole, and that his true welfare, the positive interest of his life, is to be found in serving the common good or universal happiness.

This is the principle of *utilitarianism*, obviously corresponding to the moral principle of altruism, which demands that we should live for others, help all so far as we are able, and serve the good of others as if it were our own. In the opinion of the utilitarian thinkers their teaching must coincide in practice with the altruistic morality or with the commandments of justice and mercy. "I must again repeat," writes J. S. Mill, *e.g.*, "what the assailants of utilitarianism seldom have the justice to acknowledge, that the happiness which forms the utilitarian standard of what is right in conduct, is not the agent's own happiness, but that of all concerned. As between his own happiness and that of others, utilitarianism requires him to be as strictly impartial as a disinterested and benevolent spectator. In the golden rule of Jesus of Nazareth we read the complete spirit of the ethics of utility. To do as one would be done by, and to love one's neighbour as oneself, constitutes the ideal perfection of utilitarian morality."[6]

But Mill does not see that the distinction between these two principles, the utilitarian and the altruistic, consists in the fact that the command to live for others is enjoined by altruism as the expression of the *right* relation of man to his fellow-creatures, or as a moral duty which follows from the pure idea of the good; while, according to the utilitarian doctrine, man ought to serve the common good and to decide impartially between his own interests and those of others simply because, in the last resort, this course of action (so it is contended) is more advantageous or useful to himself. Moral conduct thus appears to stand in no need of any special independent principle opposed to egoism, but to be a consequence of egoism rightly understood. And since egoism is a quality possessed by every one, utilitarian morality is suited to all without exception, which, in the opinion of its followers, is an advantage over the morality of pure altruism, whether based upon the simple feel-

---

point and their ultimate motive. Asceticism seeks to attain the mastery of the spirit over the flesh, or the *right* attitude of man to what is lower than he. The demand for self-sufficiency springs from a desire for happiness, so that the principle of αὐτάρκεια may be rightly described as *hedonistic asceticism*.

6. J. S. Mill, *Utilitarianism*, 2nd ed., London, 1864, pp. 24-25.

ing of sympathy or upon the abstract conception of duty. Another advantage of utilitarianism is, it is contended, to be found in the fact that the utilitarian principle is the expression of the actual historical origin of the moral feelings and ideas. All of these are supposed to be the result of the gradual extension and development of self-interested motives, so that the highest system of morality is simply the most complex modification of primitive egoism. Even if this contention were true, the advantage that would follow therefrom to the utilitarian theory would be illusory. From the fact that the oak tree grows out of the acorn and that acorns are food for pigs, it does not follow that oak trees are also food for pigs. In a similar manner, the supposition that the highest moral doctrine is *genetically* related to selfishness, that is, that it has developed from it through a series of changes in the past, does not warrant the conclusion that therefore this highest morality in its present perfect form can also be based upon self-interest or put at the service of egoism. Experience obviously contradicts this conclusion: the majority of people — now as always — find it *more profitable to separate their own interests from the common good.* On the other hand, the assumption that selfishness is the *only* and the ultimate basis of conduct is contrary to truth.

The view that morality develops out of individual selfishness is sufficiently disproved by the simple fact that at the early stages of the organic life, the chief part is played not by the individual but by the *generic* self-assertion, which, for separate entities, is *self-denial.* A bird giving up its life for its young, or a working bee dying for the queen bee, can derive no personal advantage and no gratification to its individual egoism from its act.[7] A decisive predominance of the personal over the generic motives, and at the same time the possibility of theoretical and consistent selfishness, arises in humanity only when a certain stage in the development of the individual consciousness has been reached. In so far, then, as utilitarianism requires that the individual should limit and sacrifice himself, not for the sake of any higher principles, but for the sake of his own selfishness rightly understood, it can have practical significance only as addressed to human individuals at a definite stage of development. It is from this point of view alone that utilitarianism ought to be considered here, especially because the questions as to the empirical origin of any given ideas and feelings have no direct bearing upon the subject of moral philosophy.

---

7. Concerning the primitive character of self-surrender or 'struggle for the life of others,' see, in particular, Henry Drummond, *Ascent of Man.* The fact that self-sacrifice of the individual for the species is based upon real genetic solidarity does not in the least prove that such sacrifice is the same thing as self-interest. [*The Lowell Lectures on the Ascent of Man* of Henry Drummond, a Scottish religious philosopher, were published in London in 1894. — *Editor's note.*]

VII

"Every one desires his own good; but the good of each consists in serving the good of all; therefore every one ought to serve the common good." The only thing that is true in this formula of pure utilitarianism is its conclusion. But its real grounds are not in the least contained in the two premises from which it is here deduced. The premises are false in themselves and placed in a false relation with one another.

It is not true that every one desires his own good, for a great many persons desire simply what affords them immediate pleasure, and find that pleasure in things which are not in the least good for them, or, indeed, in things that are positively harmful — in drinking, gambling, pornography, etc. Of course the doctrine of the common good may be preached to such people also, but it must rest upon some other basis than their own desires.

Further, even persons who admit the advantages of happiness or of lasting satisfaction over momentary pleasures, find their good in something very different from what utilitarianism affirms it to be. A miser is very well aware that all fleeting pleasures are dust and ashes in comparison with the real lasting goods which he locks up in a strong safe; and utilitarians have no arguments at their command whereby they could induce him to empty his safe for philanthropic purposes. They may say to him that it is in his own interests to bring his advantage into harmony with the advantage of others. But he has fulfilled this condition already. Suppose, indeed, that he obtained his riches by lending money at interest; this means that he has done service to his neighbours and helped them, when they were in need, by giving them loans of money. He risked his capital and received a certain profit for it, and they lost that profit but used his capital when they had none of their own. Everything was arranged to mutual advantage, and both sides judged impartially between their own and the other person's interests. But why is it that neither Mill nor any of his followers will agree to pronounce the behaviour of this sagacious money-lender to be a true pattern of utilitarian morality? Is it because he made no use of the money he hoarded? He made the utmost use of it, finding the highest satisfaction in the possession of his treasures and in the consciousness of his power (see Pushkin's poem *The Avaricious Knight*); besides, the greater the wealth hoarded, the more useful it will be to other people afterwards, so that on this side, too, self-interest and the interest of others are well balanced.

The reason that utilitarians will not admit the conduct of a prudent money-lender to be normal human conduct is simply that they really demand far more than mere *harmony* between self-interest and the interest of others. They demand that man should *sacrifice* his personal advantage for the sake of the common good, and that he should find in this his true interest. But this demand, directly contradicting as it does the idea of 'self-interest,' is based upon metaphysical assumptions that are completely foreign to the doctrine of pure utilitarianism, and is, apart from them, absolutely arbitrary.

Actual cases of self-sacrifice are due either (1) to an immediate impulse of sympathetic feeling — when, for instance, a person saves another from death at the risk of his own life without any reflections on the subject; (2) or to compassion as the dominating trait of character, as in the case of persons who from personal inclination devote their life to serving those who suffer; (3) or to a highly developed consciousness of moral *duty;* (4) or, finally, it may arise from inspiration with some religious idea. All these motives in no way depend upon considerations of self-interest. Persons whose will can be sufficiently influenced by these motives, taken separately or together, will sacrifice themselves for the good of others, without feeling the slightest necessity for motives of a different kind.[8]

But a number of people are unkind by nature, incapable of being carried away by moral or religious ideas, lacking in a clear sense of duty, and not sensitive to the voice of conscience. It is precisely over this type of person that utilitarianism ought to show its power, by persuading them that their true advantage consists in serving the common good, even to the point of self-sacrifice. This, however, is clearly impossible, for the chief characteristic of these people is that they find their good not in the good of others, but exclusively in their own selfish well-being.

By *happiness* as distinct from pleasure is meant *secure* or lasting satisfaction; and it would be utterly absurd to try to prove to a practical materialist that in laying down his life for others or for an idea he would be securing for himself an abiding satisfaction of *his own,* that is, of his material interests.

It is clear that the supposed connection between the good which each desires *for himself* and the true or real good, as the utilitarians understand it, is simply a crude sophism based upon the ambiguity of the word 'good.' First we have the axiom that each desires that which satisfies him; then all the actual multiplicity of the objects and the means of satisfaction is designated by one and the same term 'good.' This term is then applied to quite a different conception of *general* happiness or of the *common good.* Upon this identity of

---

8. A fifth possible motive is the thought of the life beyond the grave, the desire to obtain the eternal blessings of paradise. Although this motive is a utilitarian one in the broad sense, it is connected with ideas of a different order, which the modern utilitarian doctrine rejects on principle.

the term which covers two distinct and even opposed conceptions the argument is based that since each person desires his own good and the good consists in general happiness, each person ought to desire and to work for the happiness of all. But in truth the good which *each* desires for himself is *not necessarily* related to general happiness, and the good which consists in general happiness is not that which each desires for himself. A simple substitution of one term for another is not enough to make a person desire something different from what he really does desire or to find his good somewhere other than where he actually finds it.

The various modifications of the utilitarian formula do not make it more convincing. Thus, starting with the idea of happiness as *abiding* satisfaction, it might be argued that personal happiness gives no abiding satisfaction, for it is connected with objects that are transitory and accidental, while the general happiness of humanity, in so far as it includes future generations, is lasting and permanent, and may, therefore, give permanent satisfaction. If this argument is addressed to 'each person,' each can reply to it as follows: "To work for my personal happiness may give me no *abiding* satisfaction; but to work for the future happiness of humanity gives me no satisfaction *whatever*. I cannot possibly be satisfied with a good which, if realised at all, would certainly not be *my* good, for in any case I should not then exist. Therefore, if personal happiness does not profit me, general happiness does so still less. For how can I find my good in that which will never be of any good to me?"

The true thought involved in utilitarianism as worked out by its best representatives is the idea of human *solidarity*, in virtue of which the happiness of each is connected with the happiness of all. This idea, however, has no organic connection with utilitarianism, and, as a practical principle, is incompatible with the utilitarian, or, speaking generally, with the hedonistic range of ideas. One may quite well admit the fact of the oneness of the human race, universal solidarity and the consequences that follow from it in the natural order of things, and yet not deduce from it any moral rule of conduct. Thus, for instance, a rich profligate, who lives solely for his own pleasure and never makes the good of others the purpose of his actions, may nevertheless justly point out that, owing to the natural connection between things, his refined luxury furthers the development of commerce and industry, of science and arts, and gives employment to numbers of poor people.

Universal solidarity is a natural law, which exists and acts through separate individuals independently of their will and conduct; and if in thinking of my own good only, I involuntarily contribute to the good of all, nothing further can be required from me from the utilitarian point of view. On the other hand, universal solidarity is a very different thing from universal happiness.

From the fact that humanity is essentially one, it by no means follows that it must necessarily be happy: it may be one in misery and destruction. Suppose I make the idea of universal solidarity the practical rule of my own conduct, and, in accordance with it, sacrifice my personal advantage to the common good. But if humanity is doomed to perdition and its 'good' is a deception, of what *use* will my self-sacrifice be either to me or to humanity? Thus, even if the idea of universal solidarity could, as a practical rule of conduct, be inwardly connected with the principle of utilitarianism, this would be of *no use* at all for the latter.

In utilitarianism the hedonistic view finds its highest expression; if, therefore, utilitarianism be invalid the whole of the practical philosophy which finds the highest good in happiness or self-interested satisfaction stands condemned also. The apparent universality and necessity of the hedonistic principle, consisting in the fact that all necessarily desire happiness, prove to be purely illusory. For, in the first place, the general term 'happiness' covers an infinite multiplicity of different objects, irreducible to any inner unity, and secondly, the universal desire for one's own happiness (whatever meaning might be ascribed to this word) certainly contains no guarantee that the object desired can be attained, nor does it indicate the means for its attainment. Thus the principle of happiness remains simply a *demand,* and therefore has no advantage whatever over the principle of duty or of the moral good, the only defect of which is precisely that it may remain a demand, not having in itself the power necessary for its realisation. This defect is common to both principles, but the moral principle as compared with the hedonistic has the enormous advantage of *inner* dignity and of *ideal* universality and necessity. The moral good is determined by the universal reason and conscience and not by arbitrary personal choice, and is therefore necessarily one and the same for all. By happiness, on the other hand, every one has a right to understand what he likes.

So far then we are left with two *demands* — the rational demand of duty and the natural demand for happiness — (1) *all men must be virtuous* and (2) *all men want to be happy.* Both these demands have a natural basis in human nature, but neither contains in itself sufficient grounds or conditions for its realisation. Moreover, in point of fact the two demands are disconnected; very often they are opposed to one another, and the attempt to establish a harmony of principle between them (utilitarianism) does not stand the test of criticism.

These demands are not of equal value, and if practical philosophy compelled us to choose between the clear, definite, and lofty — though not sufficiently powerful — idea of the moral good and the equally powerless but also confused, indefinite, and low idea of well-being, certainly all rational arguments would be in favour of the first.

Before insisting, however, upon the sad necessity of such a choice, we must consider more closely the moral basis of human nature as a whole. So far we have only considered it with reference to the particular development of its three partial manifestations.

PART II

The Good Is from God

CHAPTER I

The Unity of Moral Principles

I

When a man does wrong by injuring his neighbour actively or by refusing to assist him, he afterwards feels *ashamed*. This is the true spiritual root of all human good and the distinctive characteristic of man as a moral being.

What precisely is here experienced? To begin with, there is a feeling of pity for the injured person which was absent at the actual moment of injury. This proves among other things that our mental nature may be stirred by impulses more profound and more powerful than the presence of sensuous motives. A purely ideal train of reflection is able to arouse a feeling which external impressions could not awake; the invisible distress of another proves to be more effective than the visible.

Secondly, to this simple feeling of pity, already refined by the absence of the visible object, there is added a new and still more spiritualised variation of it. We both pity those whom we did not pity before, and regret that we did not pity them at the time. We are sorry for having been pitiless — to the regret for the person injured there is added regret for oneself as the injurer.

But the experience is not by any means exhausted by these two psychological moments. The feeling in question derives all its spiritual poignancy and moral significance from the third factor. The thought of our pitiless action awakens in us, in addition to the reaction of the corresponding feeling of pity, a still more powerful reaction of a feeling which apparently has nothing to do with the case — namely, the feeling of shame. We not only regret our cruel action, but are ashamed of it, though there might be nothing specifically *shameful* in it. This third moment is so important that it colours the whole mental state in question. Instead of saying, 'My conscience reproaches me,' we

119

simply say, 'I am ashamed,' *j'ai honte, ich schäme.* In the classical languages the words corresponding to our term 'conscience' were not used in common parlance, and were replaced by words corresponding to 'shame' — a clear indication that the ultimate root of conscience is to be found in the feeling of shame. We must now consider what this implies.

II

The thought of having violated any moral demand arouses shame, in addition to the reaction of the particular moral element concerned. This happens even when the demands of shame in its own specific sphere (man's relation to his lower or carnal nature) have not been violated. The action in question may not in any way have been opposed to modesty or to the feeling of human superiority over material nature. Now this fact clearly shows that, although we may *distinguish* the three roots of human morality, we must not *separate* them. If we go deep enough they will be seen to spring from one common root; the moral order in the totality of its norms is essentially a development of one and the same principle which assumes now this and now that form. The feeling of shame most vitally connected with the facts of the sexual life transcends the boundaries of material existence, and, as the expression of moral disapproval, accompanies the violation of every moral norm to whatever sphere of relations it might belong. In all languages, so far as I am aware, the words corresponding to our *'stid'* (shame) are invariably characterised by two peculiarities: (1) by their connection with the sexual life (αἰδώς — αἰδοῖα, *pudor — pudenda, honte — parties honteuses, Scham — Schamteile*), and (2) by the fact that these words are used to express disapproval of the violation of any moral demands *whatsoever.* To deny the specific sexual meaning of shame (that is, the special shamefulness of the carnal relation between the sexes), or to limit shame to this significance *alone,* one must reject human language and acknowledge it to be senseless and accidental.

The general moral significance of shame is simply a further development of what is already contained in its specific and original manifestation with regard to the facts of the sexual life.

III

The essence and the chief purpose of the animal life undoubtedly consist in perpetuating, through reproduction, the particular form of organic being represented by this or by that animal. It is the essence of life *for* the animal and not merely in him, for the primal and unique importance of the genital instinct is inwardly experienced and sensed by him, though, of course, involuntarily and unconsciously. When a dog is waiting for a savoury piece, its attitude, the expression of its eyes, and its whole being seem to indicate that the chief nerve of its subjective existence is in the stomach. But the greediest dog will altogether forget about food when its sexual instinct is aroused — and a bitch will readily give up its food and even its life for its young. The individual animal seems in this case to recognise, as it were, conscientiously that what matters is not its own particular life as such, but the preservation of the given type of the organic life transmitted through an infinite series of fleeting entities. It is the only image of infinity that can be grasped by the animal. We can understand, then, the enormous, the fundamental significance of the sexual impulse in the life of man. If man is essentially more than an animal, his differentiation out of the animal kingdom, his inner self-determination as a human being must begin precisely in this centre and source of organic life. Every other point would be comparatively superficial. It is only *in this* that the individual animal becomes conscious of the infinity of the generic life, and, recognising itself as *merely a finite event,* as merely a means or an instrument of the generic process, surrenders itself without any struggle or holding back to the infinity of the genus which absorbs its separate existence. And it is *here,* in this vital sphere, that man recognises the insufficiency of the generic infinity in which the animal finds its supreme goal. Man, too, is claimed by his generic essence; through him, too, it seeks to perpetuate itself — but his inner being resists this demand. It protests "I am not what thou art, I am above thee, I am *not* the genus, though I am *of* it — I am not *'genus'* but *'genius.'* I want to be and I can be immortal and infinite, not in thee only, but in myself. Thou wouldst entice me into the abyss of thy bad, empty infinity in order to absorb and destroy me — but I seek for myself the true and perfect infinity which I could share with thee also. That which I have from thee wants to be mingled with thee and to drag me down into the abyss above which I have risen. But my own being, which is not of thee, is ashamed of this mingling and opposed to it; it desires the union which alone is worthy of it — the true union which is for all eternity."

The enormous significance of sexual shame as the foundation of both material and formal morality is due to the fact that in that feeling man acknowledges as shameful, and therefore bad and wrong, not any particular or accidental deviation from some moral norm but the very essence of that law of nature which the whole of the organic world obeys. That which man is ashamed *of* is more important than the general fact of his *being* ashamed.

Since man possesses the faculty of shame, which other animals do not possess, he might be defined as the animal *capable of shame*. This definition, though better than many others, would not make it clear, however, that man is the citizen of a different world, the bearer of a new order of being. But the fact of his being ashamed above all and first of all of the very essence of animal life, of the main and the supreme expression of natural existence, directly proves him to be a super-natural and super-animal being. It is in *this* shame that man becomes in the full sense human.

IV

The sexual act expresses the infinity of the natural process, and in being ashamed of the act man rejects that infinity as unworthy of himself. It is unworthy of man to be merely a means or an instrument of the natural process by which the blind life-force perpetuates itself at the expense of separate entities that are born and perish and *replace* one another in turn. Man as a moral being does not want to obey this natural law of *replacement* of generations, the law of *eternal death*. He does not want to be that which replaces and is replaced. He is conscious — dimly at first — both of the desire and the power to *include* in himself all the fulness of the *infinite life*. Ideally he possesses it already in that very act of human consciousness, but this is not enough; he wants to express the ideal in the real — for otherwise the idea is only a fancy and the highest self-consciousness is but self-conceit. The *power* of eternal life exists as a fact; nature lives eternally and is resplendent with eternal beauty; but it is 'an indifferent nature' — indifferent to the individual entities which by their change preserve its eternity. Among these beings, however, there is one who refuses to play this passive part. He finds that his involuntary service to nature is a thing to be ashamed of, and that the reward for it, in the form of personal death and generic immortality, is not enough. He wants to be not the instrument but the bearer of eternal life. To achieve this he need not create any new vital force out of nothing; he has only to gain possession of the force which exists in nature and to make better use of it.

We call man a genius when his vital creative force is not wholly spent on the external activity of physical reproduction, but is also utilised in the service of his inner creative activity in this or that sphere. A man of genius is one who perpetuates himself apart from the life of the genus and lives in the general posterity, even though he has none of his own. But if such perpetuation be taken as final, it obviously proves to be illusory. It is built upon the same basis of changing generations which replace one another and disappear, so that neither he who is remembered nor those who remember him have true life. The popular meaning of the word 'genius' gives only a *hint* of the truth. The true 'genius' inherent in us and speaking most clearly in sexual shame does not require that we should have a gift for art or science and win a glorious name in posterity. It demands far more than this. Like the true *'genius,' i.e.* as connected with the entire genus though standing above it, it speaks not to the elect only but to all and each, warning them against the process of bad infinity by means of which earthly nature builds up life upon dead bones — for ever, but in vain.

V

The object of sexual shame is not the external fact of the animal union of two human beings, but the profound and universal significance of this fact. This significance lies primarily, though not entirely, in the circumstance that in such union man surrenders himself to the blind impetus of an elementary force. If the path on to which it draws him were good in itself, one ought to accept the blind character of the desire in the hope of grasping, in time, its rational meaning and of following freely that which at first commanded our involuntary submission. But the true force of sexual shame lies in the fact that in it we are not ashamed simply of submitting to nature but of submitting to it in a *bad* thing, *wholly* bad. For the path to which the carnal instinct calls us, and against which we are warned by the feeling of shame, is a path which is to begin with shameful, and proves in the end to be both pitiless and impious. This clearly shows the inner connection between the three roots of morality, all of which are thus seen to be involved in the first. Sexual continence is not only an ascetic, but also an altruistic and a religious demand.

The law of animal reproduction of which we are ashamed is the law of the replacement or the driving out of one generation by another — a law directly opposed to the principle of human solidarity. In turning our life-force to the procreation of children we turn away from the fathers, to whom nothing is left but to die. We cannot create anything out of ourselves — that which we give to the future we take away from the past, and through us our descendants live at the expense of our ancestors, live by their death. This is the way of nature; she is indifferent and pitiless, and for that we are not responsible. But our participation in the indifferent and pitiless work of nature is our own fault, though an involuntary one — and we are dimly aware of that fault beforehand, in the feeling of sexual shame. And we are all the more guilty because our participation in the pitiless work of nature, which replaces the old generations by the new, immediately affects those to whom we owe the greatest and special duty — our own fathers and forefathers. Thus our conduct proves to be impious as well as pitiless.

VI

There is a great contradiction here; a fatal antinomy, which must be recognised even if there is no hope of solving it. *Child-bearing is a good thing;*[1] it is good for the mother, who, in the words of the Apostle, is saved by child-bearing, and is of course also good for those who receive the gift of life. But at the same time it is equally certain that there is evil in physical reproduction — not the external and accidental evil of any particular calamities which the newly born inherit with their very life, but the essential and moral evil of the carnal physical act itself, in and through which we sanction the dark way of nature *shameful* to us because of its blindness, *pitiless* to the departing generation, and *impious* because it is to our own fathers that we are pitiless. But the evil of the natural way for man can be put right only by man himself, and what has not been done by the man of the present may be done by the man of the future, who, being born in the same way of animal nature, may renounce it and change the law of life. This is the solution of the fatal antinomy: the evil of child-bearing may be abolished by child-bearing itself, which through this becomes a good. This saving character of child-bearing will, however, prove illusory if those who are born will do the same thing as those who bore them, if they sin and die in the same way. The whole charm of children, their peculiar human charm, is inevitably connected with the thought and the hope that they will not be what we are, that they will be better than we — not quantitatively better by one or two degrees, but essentially, — that they will be men of a different life, that in them indeed is our salvation — for us and for our forefathers. The *human* love for children must contain something over and above the hen's love; it must have a rational meaning. But what rational meaning can there be in regarding a future scoundrel as the purpose of one's life, and in feeling delight and tenderness for him, while condemning the present scoundrels? If the future for which children stand differs from the present only in the order of time, in what does the special charm of children lie? If a poisonous plant or a weed will grow out of the seed, what is there in the seed to admire? But the fact is that the possibility of a better, a different way of life, of a different and higher law which would lift us above nature with

1. See 1 Timothy 2:15. — *Editor's note.*

its vague and impotent striving for the fulness of light and power — this *possibility*, present both in us and in the children, is *greater* in them than in us, for in them it is still complete and has not yet been wasted, as in our case, in the stream of bad and empty reality. These beings have not yet sold their soul and their spiritual birthright to the evil powers. Every one is agreed that the special charm of children is in their innocence. But this actual innocence could not be a source of joy and delight to us were we certain that it is bound to be lost. There would be nothing comforting or instructive in the thought that their angels behold the face of the heavenly Father were it accompanied by the conviction that these angels will be sure to become immediately blind.

If the special moral charm of children upon which their æsthetic attractiveness is based depends upon a greater possibility open to them of a different way of life, ought we not, before bearing children for the sake of that *possibility, actually* to alter our own bad way? In so far as we are unable to do this, child-bearing *may be* a good and a salvation for us; but what ground have we for deciding beforehand that we are unable? And is the certitude of our own impotence a guarantee for the future strength of those to whom we shall pass on our life?

VII

Sexual shame refers not to the physiological fact taken in itself and as such morally indifferent, nor to sexual love as such which may be unashamed and be the greatest good. The warning and, later, the condemning voice of sexual shame refer solely to the way of the animal nature, which is essentially bad for man, though it may, at the present stage of human development, be a lesser and a necessary evil — that is, a relative good.

But the true, the absolute good is not to be found on this path, which begins, for human beings at any rate, with abuse. Sexual human love has a positive side, which, for the sake of brevity and clearness, I will describe as 'being in love.' This fact is of course analogous to the sexual desire of animals and develops on the basis of it, but clearly it cannot be reduced to such desire — unless man is to be altogether reduced to an animal. Being in love *essentially* differs from the sexual passion of animals by its individual, super-generic character: the object for the lover is *this* definite person, and he strives to preserve for all eternity not the genus but that person and himself with it. Being in love differs from other kinds of *individual* human love — parental, filial, brotherly, etc. — chiefly by the indissoluble unity there is in it between the spiritual and the physical side. More than any other love it embraces the whole being of man. To the lover both the mental and the physical nature of the beloved are *equally* interesting, significant, and dear; he is attached to them with an equal intensity of feeling, though in a different way.[2] What is the meaning of this from the moral point of view? At the time when all the faculties of man are in their first blossom there springs in him a new, spiritually-physical force which fills him with enthusiasm and heroic aspirations. A higher voice tells him that this force has not been given him in vain, that he may use it for great things; that the true and eternal union with another being, which the ecstasy of his love demands, may restore in both of them the image of the perfect man and be the beginning of the same process in all humanity. The ecstasy of love does not of course say the same words to all lovers, but the meaning is the same. It represents the other, or the positive, side of what is meant by sexual shame. Shame restrains man from the wrong, animal, way; the exultation of love points to the right way and the supreme goal for the positive overflowing force contained in love. But when man turns this higher force to the same old purpose — to the animal work of reproduction — he wastes it. It is not in the least necessary for the procreation of children whether in the human or in the animal kingdom. Procreation is carried on quite successfully by means of the ordinary organic functions, without any lofty ecstasy of personal love. If a simple action b is sufficient to produce result c, and a complex action $a + b$ is used instead, it is clear that the whole force of a is wasted.

VIII

The feeling of shame is the natural basis of the principle of asceticism, but the content of that feeling is not exhausted by the negative rules of abstinence. In addition to the formal principle of duty, which forbids shameful and unworthy actions and condemns us for committing them, shame contains a positive side (in the sexual sphere connected with 'being in love'), which points to the vital good that is preserved through our continence and is endangered or even lost through yielding to the 'works of the flesh.' In the fact of shame it is not the formal element of human dignity or of the rational super-animal power of infinite understanding and aspiration which alone resists the lure of the animal way of the flesh. The essential vital *wholeness* of man, concealed but not destroyed by his present condition, resists it also.

We are touching here upon the domain of metaphysics; but without entering it or forsaking the ground of moral philosophy, we can and must indi-

2. See *The Meaning of Love.*

cate this positive aspect of the fundamental moral feeling of shame, indubitable both from the logical and from the real point of view.

Shame in its primary manifestation would not have its peculiar vital character, would not be a *localised* spiritually-*organic* feeling, if it expressed merely the formal superiority of human reason over the irrational desires of the animal nature. *This* superiority of intellectual faculties is *not lost* by man on the path against which shame warns him. It is something else that is lost — something really and essentially connected with the direct object of shame; and it is not for nothing that *sexual* modesty is also called *continence*.[3]

Man has lost the *wholeness* of his being and his life, and in the true, continent love for the other sex he seeks, hopes, and dreams to re-establish this wholeness. These aspirations, hopes, and dreams are destroyed by the act of the momentary, external, and illusory union which nature, stifling the voice of shame, substitutes for the wholeness that we seek. Instead of the spiritually-corporeal interpenetration and communion of two human beings there is simply a contact of organic tissues and a mingling of organic secretions; and this superficial, though secret, union confirms, strengthens, and perpetuates the profound actual division of the human being. The fundamental division into two sexes or in half is followed by the division, conditioned by the external union of the sexes, into successive series of generations that replace and expel one another, and into a multitude of coexisting entities which are external, foreign, and hostile to one another. The wholeness or unity of man is broken in depth, in breadth, and in length. But this striving for division, this centrifugal force of life, though everywhere realised to some extent, can never be realised wholly. In man it assumes the inward character of wrong or sin, and is opposed to and in conflict with the wholeness of the human being, which is also an inward condition. The opposition expresses itself, to begin with, in the fundamental feeling of shame or modesty, which, in the sphere of sensuous life, resists nature's striving for mingling and division. It expresses itself also in the positive manifestation of shame — in the exultation of chaste love, which cannot reconcile itself either to the division of the sexes or to the external and illusory union. In the social life of man as already broken up into many, the centrifugal force of nature manifests itself as the *egoism of each* and the *antagonism of all,* and it is once more opposed by the wholeness which now expresses itself as the inner unity of externally separated entities, psychologically experienced in the feeling of pity.

---

3. The word translated by 'continence' is in the Russian *tselomudrie,* which, by derivation, means 'the wisdom of wholeness' (from *tselost'* — wholeness, and *mudrost'* — wisdom). — *Translator's note.*

IX

The centrifugal and disruptive force of nature which strives to break up the unity of man both in his psychophysical and in his social life, is also directed against the bond which unites him to the absolute source of his being. Just as there exists in man a natural materialism — the desire to surrender slavishly, with grovelling delight, to the blind forces of animality; just as there exists in him a natural egoism — the desire inwardly to separate himself from everything else and to put all that is his own unconditionally above all that appertains to others — so there exists in man a natural atheism or a proud desire to renounce the absolute perfection, to make himself the unconditional and independent principle of his life. (I am referring to practical atheism, for the theoretical often has a purely intellectual character and is merely an error of the mind, innocent in the moral sense.) This is the most important and far-reaching aspect of the centrifugal force, for it brings about a separation from the *absolute* centre of the universe, and deprives man not only of the possibility, but even of the desire for the all-complete existence. For man can become all only through being inwardly united to that which is the essence of all things. This atheistic impulse calls forth a powerful opposition from the inmost wholeness of man which in this case finds expression in the religious feeling of piety. This feeling directly and undoubtedly testifies to our dependence, both individual and collective, upon the supreme principle in its different manifestations, beginning with our own parents and ending with the universal Providence of the heavenly Father. To the exceptional importance of this relation (the religiously moral one) corresponds the peculiar form which the consciousness of wrong assumes when it is due to the violation of a specifically religious duty. We are no longer 'ashamed' or 'conscience-stricken,' but 'afraid.' The spiritual being of man reacts with special concentration and intensity in the feeling of the 'fear of God,' which may, when the divine law has been even involuntarily violated, become panic terror *(horror sacrilegii)*, familiar to the ancients.

Horror sacrilegii (in the classical sense) disappears as man grows up spiritually, but the fear of God remains as the necessary negative aspect of piety — as 'religious shame.' To have fear of God, or to be God-fearing, does not of course mean to be *afraid* of the Deity, but to be afraid of one's opposition to the Deity, or of one's wrong relation to Him. It is the feeling of being out of harmony with the absolute good or perfection, and it is the counterpart of the feeling of reverence or piety in and through which man affirms his right or due relation to the higher principle — namely, his striving to participate in its perfection, and to realise the wholeness of his own being.

X

If we understand shame rooted in the sexual life as the manifestation of the wholeness of the human being, we shall not be surprised to find that feeling overflowing into other moral spheres.

Speaking generally, it is necessary to distinguish the inner essence of morality both from its formal principle, or the moral law, and from its concrete expressions. The essence of morality is in itself *one* — the *wholeness* of man, inherent in his nature as an abiding *norm*, and realised in life and history as moral *doing*, as the struggle with the centrifugal and the disruptive forces of existence. The formal principle, or the law of that doing, is in its purely rational expression as *duty* also one: thou oughtest in all things to preserve the norm of human existence, to guard the wholeness of the human being, or, negatively, thou oughtest not to allow anything that is opposed to the norm, any violation of the wholeness. But the one essence and the one law of morality are manifested in various ways, according to the concrete actual relations of human life. Such relations are indefinitely numerous, though both logical necessity and facts of experience equally compel us, as we have seen, to distinguish three main kinds of relation that fall within the range of morality — the relations to the world below us, to the world of beings like us, and to the higher.

The roots of all that is real are hidden in darkest earth, and morality is no exception. It does not belong to a kingdom where trees grow with their roots uppermost. Its roots too are hidden in the lower sphere. The whole of morality grows out of the feeling of shame. The inner essence, the concrete expression, and the formal principle or law of morality are contained in that feeling like a plant in a seed, and are distinguished only by reflective thought. The feeling of shame involves at one and the same time a consciousness of the moral nature of man which strives to maintain its wholeness, a special expression of that wholeness — continence, — and a moral imperative which forbids man to yield to the powerful call of the lower nature, and reproaches him for yielding to it. The commands and the reproaches of shame are not merely negative and preventive in meaning. They have a positive *end* in view. We must preserve our inner potential wholeness in order to be able to realise it as a fact, and actually to create the whole man in a better and more lasting way than the one which nature offers us. 'That's not it, that's not it!' says the feeling of shame, thus promising us *the true, the right thing*, for the sake of which it is worth while to renounce the way of the flesh. This way, condemned by shame, is the way of psychophysical disruption — spiritual as well as corporeal, — and to such disruption is opposed not only the spiritual, but also the physical wholeness of man.

But realisation of *complete* wholeness, of which continence is merely the beginning, requires the fulness of conditions embracing the whole of human life. This realisation is complicated and delayed, though not prevented by the fact that man has already multiplied, and that his single being has been divided into a number of separate entities. Owing to this new condition which creates *man as a social being,* the abiding wholeness of his nature expresses itself no longer in continence alone that safeguards him from natural disruption but also in social solidarity which, through the feeling of pity, re-establishes the moral unity of the physically divided man. At this stage the difference between the moral elements, merged into one in the primary feeling of shame, becomes more clear. The feeling of pity expresses the inner solidarity of living beings, but is not identical with it, and it preserves its own psychological distinctness as compared with the instinctive shame. The formally-moral element of shame which at first was indistinguishable from its psychophysical basis, now develops into the more subtle and abstract feeling of *conscience* (in the narrow sense). Corresponding to the transformation of the carnal instinct into egoism, we have the transformation of shame into conscience. But the ultimate and fundamental significance of shame shows itself here also, for, as already pointed out, the words 'conscience' and 'shame' are interchangeable even in the case of actions that are purely egoistic and have nothing to do with sex. Morality is one, and being fully expressed in shame, it reacts both against the works of the flesh and *(implicite)* against the bad consequences of these works — among them, against the egoism of the divided man. The specific moral reaction against this new evil finds its psychological expression in pity, and its formally-moral expression in conscience — this 'social shame.'

But neither the moral purity of continence preserved by shame, nor the perfect moral solidarity which inspires our heart with equal pity for all living beings, empowers us to realise that which chaste love and all-embracing pity demand. And yet conscience clearly tells us 'you must, therefore you can.'

Man is ashamed of the carnal way because it is the way of the breaking up and scattering of the life-force, and the end of it is death and corruption. If he is really ashamed of it and feels it to be wrong, he must follow the opposite path of wholeness and concentration leading to eternal life and incorruptibility. If further, he really pities all his fellow-creatures, his *aim* must be to make *all* immortal and incorruptible. His conscience tells him that he must do it, and that therefore he can.

And yet it is obvious that the task of gaining immortal and incorruptible life for all is above man. But he is not divided by any impermeable barrier from that which is above him. In the religious feeling the hidden normal being of man reacts against human impotence as clearly as in the feeling of shame it reacts against carnal desires, and in pity against egoism. And conscience, assuming the new form of the fear of God, tells him: all that you ought to be and have the power to be is in God; you ought and therefore you can surrender yourself to Him completely, and through Him fulfil your wholeness — gaining the abiding satisfaction of your chaste love and your pity, and obtaining for yourself and for all immortal and incorruptible life. Your *impotence* is really as anomalous as shamelessness and pitilessness; this anomaly is due to your separation from the absolute principle of right and power. Through your reunion with Him, you must and can correct it.[4]

The supreme principle to which we are united through the religious feeling is not merely an *ideal* perfection. Perfection as an idea is possible for man. But man is powerless to make his perfection actual, to make his good the concrete good. Herein is the deepest foundation of his dependence upon the Being in whom perfection is given as an eternal reality, and who is the indivisible and unchangeable identity of Good, Happiness, and Bliss. In so far as we are united to It by the purity and the whole-heartedness of our aspirations, we receive the corresponding power to fulfil them, the force to render actual the potential wholeness of all humanity.

This is the reason why we are so ashamed or conscience-stricken at every bad action or even a bad thought. It is not an abstract principle or any arbitrary rule that is violated thereby. But a false step is taken, a delay is caused on the only true path to the one goal that is worth reaching — the restoration of immortal and incorruptible life for all.

Shame and conscience and fear of God are merely the negative expressions of the conditions that are indispensable to the real and great work of manifesting God in man.

XI

The moral good then is by its very nature a way of actually attaining true blessedness or happiness — such happiness, that is, as can give man complete and abiding satisfaction. *Happiness* (and blessedness) in this sense is simply another aspect of the good, or another way of looking at it — there are as much inner connection and as little possibility of contradiction between

---

4. In the church prayer human impotence is put side by side with sins and transgressions: "Lord, cleanse our sins; God, forgive our transgressions; Holy One, visit and heal our frailties." *Frailties* is here used especially in opposition to *holiness*.

these two ideas as between cause and effect, purpose and means, etc. One *ought* to desire the good *for its own sake,* but the purity of the will is not in the least marred by the consciousness that the good must *itself* necessarily mean happiness for the one who fulfils its demands. On the other hand, the circumstance that it is *natural* to desire happiness does not in any way prevent us from understanding and bearing in mind the empirical fact that all happiness which is not fictitious or illusory must be conditioned by the good, *i.e.* by the fulfilment of the moral demands.

If the law of blessedness or of true εὐδαιμονία is determined by the moral good, there can be no opposition between the morality of pure duty and eudaemonism in general. The good will must be autonomous; but the admission that right conduct leads to true happiness does not involve the heteronomy of the will. Such an admission bases happiness upon the moral good, subordinates it to the latter, and is therefore in perfect agreement with the autonomy of the will. Heteronomy consists, on the contrary, in separating happiness from what is morally right, in subordinating the desirable not to the moral law, but to a law *foreign* to morality. Thus the fundamental opposition is not between morality and eudaemonism as such, but between morality and eudaemonism which is abstract or, more exactly, which *abstracts* happiness from its true and purely moral conditions, thus rendering it fictitious and illusory.

Why then does the fulfilment of duty so often fail to give *complete* satisfaction? I so little wish to avoid this objection that I would make it stronger, and urge that human virtue *never* gives complete satisfaction. But is this virtue itself ever *complete,* and is there any one born 'ἐκ θελήματος σαρκός' . . . 'ἐκ θελήματος ἀνδρός' who has ever perfectly fulfilled his duty?[5] It is clear that the perfect good has never been realised by any individual human being; and it is just as clear that a superhuman being capable of realising the perfect good will find complete or perfect satisfaction in doing so. It follows also that the autonomy of the will, that is, the power to desire the pure good for its own sake *alone,* apart from any extraneous considerations, and to desire the *complete* good — is merely a formal and subjective characteristic of man. Before it can become real and objective, man must acquire the power actually to fulfil *the whole* good, and thus obtain perfect satisfaction. Apart from this condition, virtue has a negative and insufficient character, which is not due to the nature of the moral principle itself. Thus when, in the first place, the moral principle demands that the spirit should have power over the flesh, this demand involves no external limitations. The norm is the perfect and absolute power of the

---

5. "Of the will of the flesh . . . of the will of man" (John 1:13). — *Editor's note.*

spirit over the flesh, its complete and actual autonomy, in virtue of which it must not submit to the extraneous law of carnal existence — the law of death and corruption. In this respect, then, immortal and incorruptible life is alone a perfect good, and it also is perfect happiness. Morality which does not lead to a really immortal and incorruptible life, cannot in strictness be called autonomous, for it obviously submits to the law of material life that is foreign to it. Similarly, with reference to altruism the moral demand to help every one puts no limit to that help, and obviously the *complete* good here requires that we should obtain for all our fellow-beings perfect blessedness or absolute happiness. Our altruism does not fulfil this demand; but the insufficiency of our good is due not to the moral law, whose requirements are unlimited, but to the law of limited material being that is alien to it. Consequently, altruism which obeys this foreign law cannot in the strict sense be called an expression of autonomous morality, but proves to be heteronomous.

XII

The good then is accompanied by dissatisfaction or absence of happiness only when and in so far as it is incomplete and imperfect, only in so far as the moral law is not fulfilled to the end and still gives way before another law, extraneous to it. But the perfect or the purely autonomous good gives also perfect satisfaction. In other words, the good is separated from happiness not by the nature of its demands, but by the external obstacles in the way of their realisation. Moral principle consistently carried out to the end, duty perfectly fulfilled inevitably leads to the highest good or happiness. The opposition, therefore, between the theory of general happiness and pure morality is merely accidental, due to the empirical imperfection of the human good or to a wrong conception both of good and of happiness. In the first case, the discrepancy between good and happiness ("the afflictions of the righteous")[6] proves merely the insufficiency or the incompleteness — the *unfinished* character — of the given moral condition. In the second case, that of a wrong conception, the moral interest is absent altogether, both when the wrongly conceived good coincides or when it does not coincide with the wrongly conceived happiness. Thus, for instance, if a person zealously prays that he might pick up in the street a purse full of money, or win in a lottery, the *failure* of such prayer has no bearing whatever upon the question as to the disharmony between virtue (in this case religious virtue) and well-being, or

6. Psalm 34:19. — *Editor's note.*

good and happiness. For in this case both are wrongly understood. Prayer as a means to a low and selfish end is opposed to the Divine and the human dignity, and is not a real good; nor is the acquisition of money which one has not deserved a blessing or real happiness. On the other hand, when a man does philanthropic work not out of pity or altruistic motives, but only for the sake of obtaining an order of merit, and actually receives such an order, such *coincidence* between the wrongly conceived good and the wrongly conceived happiness is of as little interest to ethics as the discrepancy between the two in the first case. There is no need to prove that although such philanthropy may be useful from the social and practical point of view, it is not a virtue, nor that an order of merit is but an illusory blessing. It is clear that true welfare can only be born of feelings and actions that are themselves well conceived, *i.e.* that possess moral dignity and are in harmony with the good; and that real good in its turn cannot in the long run lead to misfortune, *i.e.* to evil. It is very significant indeed that the same conception of 'evil' equally expresses the opposition both to virtue and to happiness. Evil actions and evil fortune are equally called evil, which clearly indicates the inner kinship between the good and blessedness, and indeed these two ideas are often identified in ordinary speech, one term being substituted for the other. The separation between moral good and happiness is then merely conditional: the absolute good involves also the fulness of happiness.

The ultimate question as to the meaning of life is not then finally solved either by the existence of good feelings inherent in human nature, or by the principles of right conduct which reason deduces from the moral consciousness of these feelings. Moral sentiments and principles are a relative good, and they fail to give complete satisfaction. We are compelled both by reason and by feeling to pass from them to the good in its absolute essence, unconditioned by anything accidental or by any external limitations, and consequently giving real satisfaction, and true and complete meaning to life as a whole.

XIII

That the pure moral good must finally be experienced as blessedness, that is, as perfect satisfaction or bliss, was admitted by the stern preacher of the categoric imperative himself. But the method whereby he sought to reconcile these two ultimate conceptions can certainly not be pronounced satisfactory.

The great German philosopher[7] admirably defined the formal essence of

---

7. Immanuel Kant. — *Editor's note.*

morality as the absolutely free or autonomous activity of pure will. But he was unable to avoid in the domain of ethics the one-sided subjective idealism which is characteristic of his philosophy as a whole. On this basis there can only be a fictitious synthesis of good and happiness, only an illusory realisation of the perfect moral order.

Subjectivism, in the crude and elementary sense, is of course excluded by the very conception of the *pure will,* of a will, that is, free from any empirical and accidental motives, and determined only by the idea of absolute duty *(das Sollen), i.e.* by the universal and necessary norm of practical reason. In virtue of this norm the moral principle of our conduct (and of our every action) must, without inner contradiction, be capable of being affirmed as a universal and necessary law, applicable to ourselves in exactly the same way as to everybody else.

This formula is in itself (*i.e.* logically) perfectly objective; but wherein does its real power lie? Insisting upon the unconditional character of the moral demand, Kant answers only for the *possibility* of fulfilling it: you must, therefore you can. But the possibility by no means warrants the actuality, and the perfect moral order may remain altogether unrealised. Nor is it clear from the Kantian point of view what is the ultimate inner foundation of the moral demand itself. In order that our will should be pure or (formally) autonomous it must be determined solely by respect for the moral law — this is as clear as A = A. But why should this A be necessary at all? Why demand a 'pure' will? If I want to get pure hydrogen out of water, I must of course take away the oxygen. If, however, I want to wash or to drink I do not need pure hydrogen, but require a definite combination of it with oxygen, H_2O, called water.

Kant must undoubtedly be recognised as the Lavoisier of moral philosophy. His analysis of morality into the autonomous and the heteronomous elements, and his formulation of the moral law, is one of the greatest achievements of the human mind. But we cannot rest satisfied with the theoretical intellectual interest alone. Kant speaks of practical reason as the unconditional principle of actual human conduct, and in doing so he resembles a scientist who would demand or think it possible that men should use pure hydrogen instead of water.

Kant finds in conscience the actual foundation of his moral point of view. Conscience is certainly more than a demand — it is a fact. But in spite of the philosopher's sincere reverence for this testimony of our higher nature, it lends him no help. In the first place, the voice of conscience says not exactly what according to Kant it ought to say, and secondly, the objective significance of that voice remains, in spite of all, problematic from the point of view of our philosopher.

Kant, it will be remembered, pronounces all motives other than pure reverence for the moral law to be foreign to true morality. This is unquestionably true of motives of selfish gain, which induce us to do good for our own advantage. According to Kant, however, a man who helps his neighbour in distress out of a simple feeling of pity does not manifest a 'pure' will either, and his action, too, is devoid of moral worth. In this case Kant is again right from the point of view of his moral chemistry; but the supreme court of appeal to which he himself refers — conscience — does not adopt this point of view. It is only as a joke that one can imagine — as Schiller does in his well-known epigram — a man whose conscience reproaches him for pitying his neighbours and helping them with heartfelt compassion:

"Willingly serve I my friends, but I do it, alas, with affection,
Hence I am plagued with the doubt, virtue I have not attained."

"This is your only resource, you must stubbornly seek to abhor them,
Then you can do with disgust that which the law may enjoin."

In truth, conscience simply demands that we should stand in the right relation to everything, but it says nothing as to whether this right relation should take the form of an abstract consciousness of general principles, or directly express itself as an immediate feeling, or — what is best — should unite both these aspects. This is the question as to the degrees and forms of moral development and, though very important in itself, it has no decisive significance for the general valuation of the moral character of human conduct.

Apart, however, from the circumstance that Kant's ethical demands are at variance with the testimony of conscience to which he appeals, it may well be asked what significance can attach to the very fact of conscience from the point of view of 'transcendental idealism.' The voice of conscience bearing witness to the moral order of the universe filled Kant's soul with awe. He was inspired with the same awe, he tells us, at the sight of the starry heaven. But what is the starry heaven from Kant's point of view? It may have had some reality for the author of *The Natural History and Theory of the Heavens*,[8] but the author of the *Critique of Pure Reason* has dispelled the delusions of simple-hearted realism. The starry heaven, like the rest of the universe, is merely a representation, an appearance in our consciousness. Though due to an unknown action upon us of something independent of us, the phenomenon as actually presented has nothing to do with those utterly mysterious entities,

---

8. The chief work of Kant's pre-critical period.

and does not in any way express the true nature of things: it entirely depends upon the forms of our sensuous intuition and the power of our imagination acting in accordance with the categories of our understanding. And if Kant felt awestruck at the grandeur of the starry heaven, the true object of that feeling could only be the grandeur of human intellect, or, rather, of intellectual activity, which creates the order of the universe in order to cognise it.

Kant's 'idealism' deprives the mental as well as the visible world of its reality. In his criticism of rational psychology he proves that the soul has no existence on its own account, that in truth all that exists is the complex combination of the phenomena and the series of phenomena of the inner sense, which are no more real than the phenomena of the so-called external world. The connectedness between the inner (as well as between the 'outer') phenomena is not due to the fact that they are experienced by one and the same being, who suffers and acts in and through them. The connectedness or the unity of the mental life depends entirely upon certain laws or general correlations which form the definite order or the working mechanism of psychical events.

If we do happen to find in this mechanism an important spring called conscience, this phenomenon, however peculiar it may be, takes us as little beyond the range of subjective ideas as does the ring of Saturn, unique of its kind, which we observe through the telescope.

XIV

Kant suffered from his subjectivism in moral philosophy quite as much as he prided himself on it in theoretical philosophy; and he was well aware that the fact of conscience is not in itself a way of escape. If conscience is merely a psychological phenomenon, it can have no compelling force. And if it is something more, then the moral law has its foundation not in us only, but also independently of us. In other words, this unconditional law presupposes an absolute lawgiver.

At the same time Kant, who in spite of the influence of Rousseau had none of the moral optimism of the latter, clearly saw the gulf between what ought to be according to the unconditional moral law and what is in reality. He well understood that the gulf cannot be bridged, the good cannot completely triumph, the ideal cannot be perfectly realised in the conditions of the given empirical existence or of the mortal life. And so he 'postulated' the immortality of the soul — of that very soul the existence of which he disproved in the *Critique of Pure Reason*.

Thus, notwithstanding his critical philosophy, Kant wanted to find God behind the starry heaven above us, — and behind the voice of conscience in us an immortal soul in the image and likeness of God.

He called these ideas *postulates of practical reason* and objects of *rational faith*.[9] But there is no faith about it, for faith cannot be a deduction, and there is not much rationality either, for the whole argument moves in a vicious circle: God and immortality of the soul are deduced from morality, while morality itself depends upon God and the immortal soul.

No certainty can attach, from Kant's point of view, to these two metaphysical ideas themselves, but they must be admitted as valid truths, since the reality of the moral law demands the reality of God and immortality. Every sceptic or 'critical philosopher' has, however, a perfect right to turn this argument against Kant. Since pure morality can be based only upon the existence of God and of an immortal soul, and the certainty of these ideas cannot be proved, pure morality dependent upon these ideas cannot be proved either, and must remain a mere supposition.

If the moral law has absolute significance, it must rest upon itself and stand in no need of these 'postulates,' the object of which has been so systematically put to shame in the *Critique of Pure Reason*. But if in order to have real force, the moral law must be based upon something other than itself, its foundations must be independent of it and possess certainty on their own account. The moral law cannot possibly be based upon things which have their ground in it.

Kant rightly insisted that morality is autonomous. This great discovery, connected with his name, will not be lost for humanity. Morality is autonomous precisely because its essence is not an abstract formula hanging in the air, but *contains in itself all the conditions of its realisation*. The necessary presupposition of morality, namely, the existence of God and of an immortal soul, is not a demand for something extraneous to morality and additional to it, but is its own inner basis. God and the soul are not the postulates of the moral law, but the direct creative forces of the moral reality.

The fact that the good is not finally and universally realised for us, that virtue is not always effective and *never*, in our empirical life, *wholly* effective, does not disprove the fact that the good exists and that the measure of good in humanity is, on the whole, *on the increase*. It is not increasing in the sense that individual persons are becoming more virtuous or that there is a greater number of virtuous people, but in the sense that the average level of *the universally binding* moral demands *that are fulfilled* is gradually raised. This is a

---

9. I confine myself here to these two postulates only, for the question of the freedom of will belongs to a different order of ideas.

historical fact, against which one cannot honestly argue. What then is the source of this increase of good in humanity as a collective whole, independently of the moral state of human units *taken separately?* We know that the growth of a physical organism is due to the superabundance of nourishment which it receives from its actual physico-organic environment, the existence of which *precedes* its own. In a similar way, moral growth, which cannot logically be explained by the physical (for such explanation would in the long run mean deducing the greater from the lesser, or something from nothing, which is absurd), can also be explained only by a superabundance of nourishment, that is, by the general positive effect of the actual moral or spiritual environment. In addition to the inconstant and, for the most part, doubtful moral growth of separate human beings, traceable to the educative effect of the social environment, there is a constant and indubitable spiritual growth of humanity, or of the social environment itself — and this is the whole meaning of history. To account for this fact we must recognise the reality of a superhuman environment which spiritually nourishes the collective life of humanity and, by the superabundance of this nourishment, conditions its moral progress. And if the reality of the superhuman good must be admitted, there is no reason to deny its effect upon the individual moral life of man. It is clear that this higher influence extends to everything capable of receiving it. The effect of the social environment must not, however, be regarded as the source, but only as one of the necessary conditions of the moral life of the individual. If moral life, both collective and personal, be understood as the interaction between man (and humanity) and the perfect, superhuman good, it cannot belong to the sphere of transitory material events. In other words, both the individual and the collective soul must be immortal. Immortality does not necessarily presuppose the soul as an independent substance. Each soul can be conceived as one of a number of inseparably connected, constant and therefore immortal *relations* of the Deity to some *universal* substratum of the life of the world, a closer definition of which does not directly belong to the scope of moral philosophy. We know nothing *as yet — i.e.* before a theoretical inquiry into metaphysical questions — about the substantiality of the soul or the substantiality of God; but one thing we know with certainty: *As God lives, my soul lives.* If we give up this fundamental truth we cease to understand and to affirm ourselves as moral beings, that is, we give up the very meaning of our life.

CHAPTER II

The Unconditional Principle of Morality

I

Neither the natural inclination to the good in individual men, nor the rational consciousness of duty, is in itself sufficient for the realisation of the good. But our moral nature contains an element of something greater than itself.

Even the first two foundations of morality — shame and pity — cannot be reduced either to a certain *mental condition* of this or that person, or to a universal rational *demand* of duty. When a man is ashamed of desires and actions that spring from his material nature, he does more than express thereby his personal opinion or the state of his mind at the given moment. He *actually apprehends* a certain *reality* independent of his opinions or accidental moods — the reality, namely, of the spiritual, supermaterial essence of man. In the feeling of shame the fundamental material inclinations are *rejected* by us as foreign and hostile to us. It is clear that the person who rejects and the thing which is rejected cannot be identical. The man who is ashamed of a material fact cannot himself be a *mere* material fact. A material fact that is ashamed of and rejects itself, that judges itself and acknowledges itself unworthy, is an absurdity and is logically impossible.

The feeling of shame which is the basis of our right relation to material nature is something more than a simple psychical fact. It is a self-evident revelation of a certain universal truth, — of the truth, namely, that man has a spiritual supermaterial nature. In shame, and in ascetic morality founded upon it, this spiritual essence of man manifests itself not only as a possibility but also as an *actuality,* not as a demand only but also as a certain reality. Men whose spirit dominates their material nature have actually existed in the past and exist now. The fact that they are comparatively few in number simply proves that the moral demand has not yet been fully and finally realised; it does not prove that it is not realised at all and remains a mere demand. It cannot be said that the moral principle of shame is lacking in actuality, or, what is the same thing, in actual perfection.

In a similar manner, the feeling of pity or compassion which is the basis of man's right relation to his fellow-beings expresses not merely the mental condition of a given person, but also a certain universal objective truth, namely, the unity of nature or the real solidarity of all beings. If they were alien and external to one another, one being could not put himself into the place of another, could not transfer the sufferings of others to himself or feel together with others; for compassion is an actual and not an imagined state, not an abstract idea. The bond of sympathy between separate beings, which finds expression in the fundamental feeling of pity and is developed in the morality of altruism, is not merely a demand, but a beginning of realisation. This is proved by the solidarity of human beings, which exists as a fact, and increases throughout the historical development of society. The defect of social morality is not that it is not realised at all, but that it is not fully and perfectly realised. The feeling of shame gives us no *theoretical conception* of the spiritual principle in man, but indubitably proves the *existence* of that principle. The feeling of pity tells us nothing definite about the metaphysical nature of the universal unity, but *concretely* indicates the existence of a certain fundamental connection between distinct entities, *prior to all experience*. And although these entities are empirically separate from one another, they become more and more united in the empirical reality itself.

II

In the two moral spheres indicated by shame and pity, the good is already known as truth, and is realised in fact, but as yet imperfectly. In the third sphere of moral relations, determined by the religious feeling or reverence, the true object of that feeling reveals itself as the highest or perfect good, wholly and absolutely realised from all eternity. The inner basis of religion involves more than a mere recognition of our dependence upon a power immeasurably greater than we. Religious consciousness in its pure form is a joyous *feeling* that there *is* a Being infinitely better than ourselves, and that our life and destiny, like everything that exists, are dependent upon It — not upon an irrational fate, but upon the actual and perfect Good, *the One which embraces all.*

In true religious experience the reality of that which is experienced is immediately given; we are directly conscious of the real presence of the Deity, and feel Its effect upon us. Abstract arguments can have no force against actual experience. When a man is ashamed of his animal desires, it is impossible to prove to him that he is a mere animal. *In the very fact* of shame he is aware of himself as being, and proves himself to be, more and higher than an animal. When in the feeling of pity we are affected by the sufferings of another person, and are conscious of him as of a fellow-being, no force can attach to the theoretical argument that perhaps that other, for whom my heart aches, is only my representation, devoid of all independent reality. If I am conscious of the inner connection between myself and another, that consciousness testifies to the actual existence of the other no less than to my own. This conclusion holds good of the religious feeling as well as of pity and compassion. The only difference is that the object of the former is experienced not as equal to us but as absolutely superior, all-embracing, and perfect. It is impossible that a creature which excites in me a living feeling of compassion should not actually live and suffer. It is still more impossible that the highest, that which inspires us with reverence and fills our soul with unutterable bliss, should not exist at all. We cannot doubt the reality of that which perceptibly affects us, and whose effect upon us is given in the very fact of the experience. The circumstance that I do not always have the experience, and that other people do not have it at all, no more disproves its reality and the reality of its object than the fact of my not seeing the sun at night, and of persons born blind never seeing it at all, disproves the existence of the sun and of vision. Moreover, many people have a wrong conception of the sun, taking it to be small and to move round the earth, and this, indeed, was the universal belief in former days. But neither the existence of the sun nor my certainty of its existence is in the least affected by this fact. In the same way, theological errors and contradictions do not in any way touch upon the real object of religion. Theological systems, like the astronomical ones, are the work of human intellect, and depend upon the degree of its development and the amount of positive knowledge. Correct theology, like correct astronomy, is important and necessary; but it is not a thing of the *first* importance. The epicycles of the Alexandrian astronomers and the division of the solar system according to the theory of Tycho Brahe did not prevent any one from enjoying the light and the warmth of the sun; and when these astronomers were proved to be in error, no one was led thereby to doubt the actual existence of the sun and the planets. In the same way the most false and absurd theological doctrine cannot prevent any one from experiencing the Deity, nor cause any doubt as to the reality of what is given in experience.

Abstract theoretical doubts had arisen in the past and still arise, not only with regard to the existence of God, but to all other existence. No one at all familiar with philosophical speculation can imagine that the existence of the physical world, or even of our neighbours, is self-evident *to the intellect.* A doubt of that existence is the first foundation of all speculative philosophy worthy of the name. These theoretical doubts are disposed of in one way or another by means of various epistemological and metaphysical theories. But however interesting and important these theories may be, they have no direct bearing upon life and practice. Such direct significance attaches to moral philosophy, which is concerned with the actual data of our spiritual nature and the guiding practical truths which logically follow from them.

The parallelism between spiritual and physical blindness is also borne out by the following consideration. It is well known that people blind from birth are perfectly sound in other respects, and have indeed an advantage over persons with normal sight in that their other senses — hearing, touch — are better developed. In a similar way persons lacking in receptivity to the divine light are perfectly normal in all other respects, both practical and theoretical, and, indeed, they generally prove superior to others in their capacity for business and for learning. It is natural that a person who is particularly drawn to the absolute centre of the universe cannot pay equal attention to objects that are relative. It is not to be wondered at, therefore, that in the special, worldly tasks of humanity, a great share of work and of success falls to the men for whom the higher world is closed. Such 'division of labour' is natural, and it provides a certain teleological explanation of atheism which must serve some positive good purpose on the whole, whatever its negative causes in each particular case may be. If the work of history is necessary, if the union of mankind is to become a fact, if it is necessary that at a given epoch men should invent and make all sorts of machines, dig the Suez Canal, discover unknown lands, etc., then it is also necessary for the successful performance of all these tasks that some men should not be mystics, or even earnest believers. It is clear, of course, that the supreme will does not make any one an atheist for the sake of its historical purposes; but once the complex chain of causes, finally confirmed by this or that voluntary decision of the man himself, has produced in a given case spiritual blindness, it is the business of Providence to give such a direction to this 'ill' that it too should be not wholly devoid of 'good' — that a subjective wrong should have an objective justification.

III

The reality of the Deity is not a *deduction* from religious experience but the *content* of it — *that which is experienced.* If this immediate reality of the higher principle be taken away, there would be nothing left of religious experience. It would no longer exist. But it *does* exist, and therefore that which is given and experienced in it exists also. *God is in us, therefore He is.*

However complete the feeling of our inner unity with God may be, it never becomes a consciousness of mere identity, of simple merging into one. The feeling of unity is inseparably connected with the consciousness that the Deity with which we are united, and which acts and reveals itself in us, is something distinct and independent of us — that it is prior to us, higher and greater than we. God exists on His own account. That which is experienced is logically prior to any given experience. The actuality of an object does not depend upon the particular way in which it acts. When one has to say to a person '*there is no God in you,*' every one understands that this is not a denial of the Deity, but merely a recognition of the moral worthlessness of the person in whom there is no room for God, *i.e.* no inner receptivity to the action of God. And this conclusion would stand even if we had to admit that all men were thus impenetrable to the Deity.

My compassion for another person does not in the least imply that I am identical with that other. It simply means that I am of the same nature as he is and that there is a bond of union between us. In the same way, the religious experience of God in us or of ourselves in God by no means implies that He is identical with us, but simply proves our inner relationship to Him — "for we are also His offspring."[1] The relation is not brotherly, as with our fellow-beings, but filial — it is not the bond of equality, but the bond of dependence. The dependence is not external or accidental, but inward and essential. True religious feeling regards the Deity as the fulness of all the conditions of our life — as that without which life would be senseless and impossible for us, as the *first beginning,* as the true *medium,* and as the *final end* of existence. Since everything is already contained in God we can add nothing to Him from ourselves, no new content; we cannot make the absolute perfection more perfect. But we can partake of it more and more, be united with it more and more closely. Thus our relation to the Deity is that of *form* to *content.*

A further analysis of what in religious feeling is given as a living experience of the reality of Godhead shows that we stand in a threefold relation to this perfect reality, this absolute or supreme good. (1) We are conscious of our

---

1. Acts 17:28. — *Editor's note.*

difference from it; and since it contains the fulness of perfection, we can differ from it only by negative qualities or determinations — by our imperfection, impotence, wickedness, suffering. In this respect we are the opposite of the Deity, its *negative other;* this is the lower earthly principle *out of which* man is created (his ὕλη or *causa materialis*), that which is called in the Bible 'the dust of the ground' *('āphār hā'ădām)*. (2) But although we are nothing but a complex of all possible imperfections, we are conscious of the absolute perfection as of that which truly is, and in this consciousness are ideally united to it, reflect it in ourselves. This idea of the all-embracing perfection as the informing principle of our life (εἶδος, *causa formalis*) is, in the words of the Bible, 'the image of God' in us (or, more exactly, 'the reflection': ṣelem from ṣēl, 'shadow'). (3) In God the ideal perfection is fully realised; hence we are not content with being conscious of Him as an idea, or in reflecting Him in ourselves, but want, like God, to be *actually* perfect. And since our empirical existence is opposed to this, we seek to transform, to perfect our bad reality, and to assimilate it to the absolute ideal. Thus although in our given (or inherited) condition we are opposed to the Deity, we are likened to It in that towards which we aspire. The end of our life, that for the sake of which we exist (οὗ ἕνεκα, *causa finalis*), is this 'likeness of God' *(dĕmût)*.

The religious attitude necessarily involves discriminating and comparing. We can stand in a religious relation to the higher only if we are aware of it as such, only if we are conscious of its superiority to us, and consequently of our own unworthiness. But we cannot be conscious of our unworthiness or imperfection unless we have an idea of its opposite — *i.e.* an idea of perfection. Further, the consciousness of our own imperfection and of the divine perfection cannot, if it be genuine, stop at this opposition. It necessarily results in a desire to banish it by making our reality conform to the highest ideal, that is, to the image and likeness of God. Thus the religious attitude as a whole logically involves three moral categories: (1) *imperfection* (in us); (2) *perfection* (in God); and (3) the process of *becoming perfect* or of establishing a harmony between the first and the second as the task of our life.

IV

The logical analysis of the religious attitude into its three component elements finds confirmation both from the psychological and the formally moral point of view.

Psychologically, *i.e.* as a subjective state, the typical religious attitude finds expression in the feeling of reverence, or, more exactly, of reverent love.[2] This feeling necessarily involves (1) self-depreciation on the part of the person who experiences it, or his disapproval of himself as he actually is at the present moment; (2) positive awareness of the higher ideal as of a reality of a different order, as of that which truly is — since to feel reverence for what one knows to be an invention or an image of fancy is psychologically impossible; (3) a striving to work a real change in oneself, and to draw nearer to the highest perfection. Apart from this striving the religious feeling becomes an abstract idea. On the contrary, real striving towards God is the beginning of union with Him. By experiencing His reality in ourselves we become united to this supreme reality, and make a beginning — an inner and subjective one — of the future complete union of all the world with God. This is the reason why the true religious attitude is characterised by the feeling of bliss and enthusiasm, which the Apostle calls "the earnest of the Spirit in our hearts" and "joy of the Holy Ghost."[3] It is the prophetic spirit anticipating our complete and final union with the Deity: the union is not yet attained but it has begun, and we have a foretaste of the joy of fulfilment.

From the formally moral point of view, the consciousness (involved in the religious feeling) that the supreme ideal actually exists and that we are out of harmony with it *compels* us to become more perfect. That which excites our reverence, affirms thereby its *right* to our devotion. And if we are conscious of the actual and absolute superiority of the Deity over ourselves, our devotion to it must be real and unlimited, *i.e.* it must be the unconditional rule of our life.

The religious feeling expressed in the form of the categorical imperative commands us not merely *to desire perfection* but to *be perfect*. And this means that, in addition to having a good will, being honest, well-behaved and virtuous, we must be free from pain, immortal and incorruptible, and must, moreover, make all our fellow-beings morally perfect and free from pain, deathless, and incorruptible in their bodies. For, indeed, true perfection must embrace the whole of man, must include all his reality — and of that reality other beings, too, form part. If *we do not want* that, in addition to moral perfection, they should be free from pain, immortal and incorruptible, we have no pity for them, that is, we are inwardly imperfect. And if we want it, but *cannot* do it, we are impotent, that is, our inner perfection is not sufficient to manifest

2. This subjective basis of religion is best rendered by the German *Ehrfurcht, ehrfurchtsvolle Liebe* [reverence, reverent love]. It may also be called an ascending love, *amor ascendens*. See the conclusion of this book.

3. 2 Corinthians 1:22; 1 Thessalonians 1:6. — *Editor's note.*

itself objectively; it is merely a subjective, incomplete perfection, or, in other words, it is imperfection. In either case we have not fulfilled the demand, "Be ye perfect."

But what can the demand mean? It is clear that by willing alone, however pure and intense the will may be, we cannot even — contrary to the claim of 'mental healing' — save ourselves or our neighbours from toothache or gout, let alone raise the dead.

The imperative 'be ye perfect' does not refer, then, to separate acts of will, but puts before us a *life-long task*. A simple act of pure will is necessary for *accepting* the task, but is not in itself sufficient for fulfilling it. The *process of becoming perfect* is a necessary means to perfection. Thus the unconditional demand 'be perfect' means, in fact, '*become perfect*.'[4]

V

Perfection, *i.e.* the completeness of good, or the unity of good and happiness, expresses itself in three ways: (1) as the absolutely real, eternally actual perfection in God; (2) as potential perfection in human consciousness which contains the absolute fulness of being in the form of an idea, and in human will which makes that fulness of being its ideal and its norm; (3) as the actual realisation of perfection or as the historical process of *becoming perfect*.

The adherents of *abstract morality* put at this point a question, the answer to which they prejudge from the first. They ask what need is there for this third aspect — for perfection as concretely realised, for historical *doing* with its political problems and its work of civilisation. If the light of truth and a pure will is within us, why trouble about anything further?

But the purpose of historical doing is precisely the final *justification* of the good given in our true consciousness and our good will. The historical process as a whole creates the concrete conditions under which the good may really become common property, and apart from which it cannot be realised. The whole of historical development, both of the human and of the physical world, is the necessary means to perfection. No one will argue that a mollusc or a sponge can know the truth, or bring their will into harmony with the absolute good. It was necessary for more and more complex and refined organic forms to be evolved until a form was produced in which the consciousness of perfection and the desire for it could be manifested. This consciousness and desire contain, however, only the *possibility* of perfection; and if man is con-

---

4. See Matthew 5:48. — *Editor's note.*

scious of and desires that which he does not possess, it is clear that the consciousness and the will cannot be the *completion,* but are only the *beginning* of his life and activity. A speck of living protoplasm, the production of which also demanded much creative energy, contains the possibility of the human organism. But that possibility could be realised only through a long and complex biological process. A formless bit of organic matter, or an insufficiently formed living being like a sponge, a polypus, a cuttle-fish, cannot of themselves produce man, though they contain him potentially. In the same way a formless horde of savages, or an insufficiently formed barbarian state, cannot directly give birth to the Kingdom of God, that is, to the image of the perfect unity of the human and the universal life — even though the remote possibility of such unity may be contained in the thoughts and feelings of the savages and barbarians.

Just as the spirit of man in nature requires for its concrete expression the most perfect of physical organisms, so the spirit of God in humanity or the Kingdom of God requires for its actual manifestation the most perfect social body which is being slowly evolved through history. In so far as the ultimate constituents of this historical process — human individuals — are more capable of conscious and free action than the ultimate constituents of the biological process — organic cells — the process of evolving the collective universal body is more conscious and voluntary in character than the organic processes which determine the evolution of our corporeal being. But there is no absolute opposition between the two. On the one hand, rudiments of consciousness and will are undoubtedly present in all living beings, though they are not a decisive factor in the general process of perfecting the organic forms. On the other hand, the course and the final outcome of universal history are not exhausted by the conscious and purposive activity of historical persons. But in any case, at a certain level of intellectual and moral development the human individual must inevitably determine his own attitude with regard to the problems of history.

The significance of the historical, as distinct from the cosmical, process lies in the fact that the part played in it by individual agents is always increasing in importance. And it is strange that at the present day, when this characteristic fact of history has become sufficiently clear, the assertion should be made that man must renounce all historical doing, and that the state of perfection for humanity and for all the universe will be attained *of itself.* 'Of itself' does not, of course, in this connection mean through the play of blind physical forces which have neither the desire nor the power to create the Kingdom of God out of themselves. 'Of itself' here means by the immediate action of God. But how are we to explain from this point of view the fact that hitherto God has never acted immediately? If for the realisation of the perfect life two principles only are necessary — God and the human soul, potentially receptive of Him — then the Kingdom of God might have been established with the advent of the first man. What was the need for all these centuries and millenniums of human history? And if this process was necessary because the Kingdom of God can as little be revealed among wild cannibals as among wild beasts, if it was necessary for humanity to work up from the brutal and formless condition of separateness to definite organisation and unity, it is as clear as day that this process is not yet completed. Historical doing is as necessary today as it was yesterday, and will be as necessary tomorrow, until the conditions are ripe for the actual and perfect realisation of the Kingdom of God.

VI

The historical process is a long and difficult *transition* from the bestial man to the divine man. No one can seriously maintain that the last step has already been taken, that the image and likeness of the beast has been inwardly abolished in humanity and replaced by the image and likeness of God, that there is no longer any historical task left demanding the organised activity of social groups, and that all we have to do is to bear witness to this fact and trouble no further. This view when expressed simply and directly is absurd, and yet it sums up the doctrine so often preached nowadays of social disintegration and individual quietism — a doctrine which claims to be the expression of the unconditional principle of morality.[5]

The unconditional principle of morality cannot be a deception. But it is obvious deception for a separate individual to pretend that his own impotence to realise the ideal of universal perfection proves such realisation to be *unnecessary*. The truth which, on the basis of genuine religious feeling, our reason and our conscience tell us is this: —

I cannot alone carry out in practice all that ought to be; I cannot do anything alone. But, thank God, there is no such thing as 'I alone'; my impotence and isolation are only a subjective state which depends upon myself. Although in my thoughts and my will I can separate myself from everything, it is mere self-deception. Apart from these false thoughts and this bad will nothing exists separately; everything is inwardly and externally connected.

5. Solovyov is referring here to the religious views of Tolstoy and his followers. — *Editor's note.*

I am not alone. With me is God Almighty and the world — that is, all that is contained in God. And if both these exist, there is positive interaction between them. The very idea of Godhead implies that things to which God stands in a purely negative relation, or things to which He is unconditionally opposed, cannot exist at all. But the world does exist, therefore there must be the positive activity of God in it. The world cannot, however, be the end of that activity, for it is imperfect. And if it cannot be the end, it must be the means. It is the system of conditions for realising the kingdom of ends. That in it which is capable of perfection will enter that kingdom with full rights; all the rest is the material and the means for bringing it about. All that exists, exists only in virtue of being approved by God. But God approves in two ways: some things are good as a means and others as a purpose and an end (*shabbath*). Each stage in the world creation is approved of from above, but the Scripture distinguishes between simple and enhanced praise. Of all things created in the first six days of the world it says that they are *good* (ṭôb, καλά), but only the last creature — man — is said to be *very good* (ṭôb mĕ'od, καλὰ λίαν). In another holy book it is said that the Divine Wisdom[6] looks after all creatures, but that her joy is in the sons of man. In man's consciousness and his freedom lies the inner possibility for each human being to stand in an independent relation to God, and therefore to be His direct purpose, to be a citizen possessed of full rights in the kingdom of ends. Universal history is the realisation of this possibility for every one. Man who takes part in it attains to actual perfection through his own experience, through his interaction with other men. This perfection attained by himself, this full, conscious, and free union with the Godhead, is that which God definitively desires — the unconditional good. Inner freedom, *i.e.* voluntary and conscious preference of good to evil in everything, is, from the point of view of principle, the chief condition of this perfection or of the absolute good (*ṭôb mĕ'od*).

Man is dear to God, not as a passive instrument of His will — there are enough of such instruments to be found in the physical world — but as a voluntary ally and coparticipant in His work in the universe. This participation of man must necessarily be included in the very purpose of God's activity in the world. Were this purpose thinkable apart from human activity, it would have been attained from all eternity, for in God Himself there can be no process of becoming perfect, but only an eternal and unchangeable fulness of all that is good. Just as it is unthinkable for an absolute being to increase in goodness or perfection, so it is unthinkable for man to attain perfection at once, apart from the process of becoming perfect. Perfection is not a thing which one person

6. See Proverbs 8. — *Editor's note.*

can make a gift of to another; it is an inner condition attainable through one's own experience alone. No doubt perfection, like every positive content of life, is received by man from God. But in order to be capable of receiving it, in order to become a receptive form for the divine content (and it is in this alone that human perfection consists), it is necessary that man should through actual experience get rid of and be purged of all that is incompatible with this perfect state. For mankind as a whole this is attained through the historical process, by means of which God's will is realised in the world.

This will reveals itself to the individual — not of course as he is in his false separateness, but as he truly is. And man's true nature consists not in separating himself from all else, but in being together with all that is.

VII

The moral duty of religion demands that we should unite our will with the will of God. The will of God is all-embracing, and in being united to it, or in entering into true harmony with it, we obtain an absolute and universal rule of action. The idea of God that reason deduces from what is given in true religious experience is so clear and definite that we always can know, if we want to, what God demands of us. In the first place, God wants us to be conformable to and like Him. We must manifest our inner kinship with the Deity, our power and determination to attain free perfection. This idea can be expressed in the form of the following rule: *Have God in you.*

A man who has God in him regards everything in accordance with God's thought or 'from the point of view of the absolute.' The second rule, then, is *Regard everything in God's way.*

God's relation to everything is not indifference. Inanimate objects are indifferent to good and evil, but this lower state cannot be attributed to the Deity. Although, according to the words of the Gospel, God lets the sun shine on the just and the unjust, it is precisely this single light which, in illuminating different persons and actions, shows the difference between them. Although, according to the same words, God sends His rain to the righteous and to the sinners, yet this one and the same moisture of God's grace brings forth from the different soil and different seed fruits that are not identical.[7] God cannot be said either to affirm evil or to deny it unconditionally. The first is impossible, because in that case evil would be good, and the second is impossible, because in that case evil could not exist at all — and yet it does exist. God denies

---

7. See Matthew 5:45. — *Editor's note.*

evil as final or abiding, and in virtue of this denial it perishes. But He permits it *as a transitory condition of freedom, i.e. of a greater good.* On the one hand, God permits evil inasmuch as a direct denial or annihilation of it would violate human freedom and be a greater evil, for it would render perfect (*i.e.* free) good *impossible* in the world; on the other hand, God permits evil inasmuch as it is *possible* for His Wisdom to extract from evil a greater good or the greatest possible perfection, and this is the cause of the existence of evil.[8] Evil, then, is something subservient, and an unconditional rejection of it would be wrong. We must regard evil also in God's way, *i.e.* without being indifferent to it, we must rise above absolute opposition to it and allow it — when it does not proceed from us — as a means of perfection, in so far as a greater good can be derived from it. We must recognise the *possibility, i.e.* the potentiality, of good in all that is, and must work for that possibility to become an actuality. The direct possibility of perfect good is given in rational and free beings like ourselves. Recognising our own unconditional significance as bearers of the *consciousness* of the absolute ideal (the image of God), and of the *striving* to realise it completely (the likeness of God), we must in justice recognise the same thing of all other persons. Our duty of attaining perfection we must regard not merely as the task of the individual life, but as an inseparable part of the world-wide work of history.

The unconditional principle of morality can therefore be expressed as follows: —

In complete inner harmony with the higher will and recognising the absolute worth or significance of all other persons, since they too are in the image and likeness of God, participate, as fully as in thee lies, in the work of making thyself and every one more perfect, so that the Kingdom of God may be finally revealed in the world.

VIII

It will be easily seen that the unconditional principle of morality includes and gives expression to all positive moral principles, and that at the same time it completely satisfies the natural demand for happiness in the sense of possessing the highest good.

In demanding that man should be a friend and helper of God, the uncon-

---

8. I must content myself here with a general logical reflection. A real solution of the question must be based upon a metaphysical inquiry into the nature of God and the origin of evil in the world.

ditional principle of morality does not cancel the particular moral demands. On the contrary, it confirms them; it puts them in a higher light and gives them a supreme sanction.

In the first place, it refers to the religious basis of morality, of which it is the direct development and the final expression. The higher demand presupposes the lower. A babe at the breast naturally cannot be his father's friend and helper. In the same way, a man spiritually under age is inwardly precluded from standing in the relation of free and immediate harmony with God. In both cases authoritative guidance and education are necessary. This is the justification of external religious institutions — of sacrifices, hierarchy, etc. Apart from their profound mystical significance, which makes them an abiding link between heaven and earth, they are undoubtedly of the first importance to humanity from the pedagogical point of view. There never was, and never could be, a time when all men would be spiritually equal to one another. Making use of this inevitable inequality, Providence has from the first elected the best to be the spiritual teachers of the crowd. Of course the inequality was merely relative — the teachers of savages were half-savage themselves. Therefore the character of religious institutions changes and becomes more perfect in conformity with the general course of history. But so long as the historical process is not yet completed, no one could in all conscience consider unnecessary for himself and for others the mediation of religious institutions which connect us with the work of God that has already found concrete embodiment in history. And even if such a man could be found, he would certainly not reject the 'external' side of religion. Indeed for him it would not be *merely external,* for he would understand the fulness of the inner meaning inherent in it and its connection with the future realisation of that meaning. A person who is above school age and has reached the heights of learning has certainly no reason to go to school. But he has still less reason to reject schools and to persuade the schoolboys that their teachers are a pack of idle swindlers, and that they themselves are perfect men or that educational institutions are the root of all evil and ought to be wiped off the face of the earth.

The true 'friend of God' understands and cares for all manifestations of the divine both in the physical world and, still more so, in human history. And if he stands on one of the upper rungs of the ladder that leads from man to God, he will certainly not cut down the lower rungs on which his brethren are standing and which are still supporting him too.

Religious feeling raised to the level of an absolute and all-embracing principle of life lifts to the same height the other two fundamental moral feelings, as well as the duties that follow from them — namely, the feeling of pity which determines our right relation to our fellow-creatures, and the feeling of shame upon which our right attitude to the lower material nature is based.

IX

Pity which we feel towards a fellow-being acquires another significance when we see in that being the image and likeness of God. We then recognise the *unconditional* worth of that person; we recognise that he is an end in himself for God, and still more must be so for us. We realise that God Himself does not treat him *merely* as a means. *We respect that being since God respects him, or, more exactly, we consider him since God considers him.* This higher point of view does not exclude pity in cases when it would naturally be felt — on the contrary, pity becomes more poignant and profound. I pity in that being not merely his sufferings but also the cause of them — I regret that his actual reality falls so short of his true dignity and possible perfection. The *duty* that follows from the altruistic sentiment also acquires a higher meaning. We can no longer be content with refraining from injuries to our neighbour or even with assisting him in his troubles. We must help him to become more perfect, so that the image and likeness of God which we recognise in him might be actually realised. But no human being can alone realise either in himself or in any one else that absolute fulness of perfection in seeking which we are likened to God. Altruism at its highest religious stage compels us, therefore, actively to participate in the universal historical process which brings about the conditions necessary for the revelation of the Kingdom of God. Consequently it demands that we should take part in the collective organisations — especially in that of the state as inclusive of all the others — by means of which the historical process is, by the will of Providence, carried on. Not every one is called to political activity or to the service of the state in the narrow sense of the term. But it is the duty of every one to serve, in his own place, that same purpose — the common good — which the state ought to serve also.

In the domain of religion the unconditional principle of morality leads us to accept ecclesiastical institutions and traditions as educational means whereby humanity is led in the end to ultimate perfection. In a similar way in the domain of purely human relations inspired by pity and altruism the unconditional moral principle demands that we should give active service to the collective organisations, such as the state, by means of which Providence prevents humanity from material disruption, holds it together, and enables it to become more perfect. We know that only in virtue of that which has been and is being given to humanity by the historical forms of religion can we truly attain to that free and perfect union with the Divine, the possibility and the promise of which are contained in our inner religious feeling. Similarly, we know that apart from the concentrated and organised social force which is found in the state we cannot give all our neighbours that help which we are bidden to give both by the simple moral feeling of pity for their sufferings and by the religious principle of respect for their unconditional dignity which demands to be realised.

In both cases we connect our allegiance to the ecclesiastical and the political forms of social life with the unconditional principle of morality, and in doing so we recognise that allegiance as *conditional,* as determined by this higher truth and dependent upon it. Institutions which ought to serve the good in humanity may more or less deviate from their purpose or even be wholly false to it. In that case the duty of man true to the good consists neither in entirely rejecting the institutions in question on the ground of the abuses connected with them — which would be unjust — nor in blindly submitting to them both in good and in evil, which would be impious and unworthy. His duty would be to try to actively reform the institutions, insisting on what their function ought to be. If we know why and for what sake we ought to submit to a certain institution, we also know the form and the measure of such submission. It will never become unlimited, blind, and slavish. We shall never be passive and senseless instruments of external forces; we shall never put the Church in the place of God, or the state in the place of humanity. We shall not take the transitory forms and instruments of the providential work in history for the essence and the purpose of that work. We subordinate our personal impotence and insufficiency to the historical forces, but in our higher consciousness we regard them in God's way, using them as the means or the conditions of the perfect good. In doing so we do not renounce our human dignity — rather we affirm it and realise it as unconditional.

When I make use of physical force and move my arms in order to save a drowning man or to give food to the hungry, I do not in any way detract from my moral dignity; on the contrary, I increase it. Why then should it be a detriment, rather than a gain, to our morality to take advantage of the spiritually-material forces of the state and use them for the good of nations and of humanity as a whole? To submit to material powers is shameful, but to deny their right to existence is perilous and unjust. In any case the *unconditional* principle of morality extends to the domain of matter also.

X

The natural feeling of shame bears witness to the autonomy of our being, and safeguards its wholeness from the destructive intrusion of foreign elements. At the lower stages of development, when sensuous life predominates, special significance attaches to bodily chastity, and the feeling of shame is originally connected with this side of life. But as moral feelings and relations are developed further, man begins to form a wider conception of his dignity. He is ashamed not only of yielding to the lower material nature, but also of all violations of *duty* in relation to gods and men. The unconscious instinct of shame becomes now, as we have seen, the clear voice of *conscience* which reproaches man not for carnal sins alone but also for all wrong-doing — for all unjust and pitiless actions and feelings. At the same time there is developed a special feeling of the fear of God, which restrains us from coming into conflict with anything that expresses for us the holiness of God. When the relation between man and God is raised to the level of absolute consciousness, the feeling which protects the wholeness of man is also raised to a new and final stage. What is now being safeguarded is not the relative but the absolute dignity of man, that is, his ideal perfection which is to be realised. The negative voice of shame, conscience, and the fear of God becomes at this stage a direct and positive consciousness in man of his own divinity or a consciousness of God in him. This consciousness no longer reproaches him for doing what is bad and injurious, but for feeling and acting as an imperfect being, while perfection is his duty and his goal. Instead of the demon which restrained Socrates from wrong actions, we hear the Divine voice: "Be ye perfect even as your Father in heaven is perfect."[9]

If perfection is to be perfectly realised it must include the material life. The unconditional principle gives a new meaning to the ascetic morality. We refrain from carnal sins no longer out of the instinct of spiritual self-preservation or for the sake of increasing our inner power, but for the sake of our body itself, as the uttermost limit of the manifestation of God in man, as the predestined abode of the Holy Spirit.

9. Matthew 5:48. — *Editor's note.*

CHAPTER III

The Reality of the Moral Order

I

The unconditional principle of morality, logically evolving from the religious sense, contains the complete good (or the right relation of all to everything) not merely as a demand or an idea, but as an actual power that can fulfil this demand and create the perfect moral order or the Kingdom of God in which the absolute significance of every being is realised. It is by virtue of this supreme principle alone that the moral good can give us final and complete satisfaction, can be for us a true blessing and a source of infinite bliss.

We experience the reality of God not as something indefinitely divine — δαιμόνιόν τι, but we are conscious of Him as He really is, all-perfect or absolute. And our soul too is revealed to us in our inner experience not merely as something distinct from material facts, but as a positive force which struggles with the material processes and overcomes them. The experience of physiological asceticism does more than support the truth that the soul is immortal — a postulate beyond which Kant would not go; it also justifies the hope of the resurrection of the body. For in the triumph of the spirit over matter, as we know from our own preliminary and rudimentary experience, matter is not destroyed but is made eternal as the image of a spiritual quality and an instrument of the activity of the spirit.

We do not know from experience what matter is in itself; this is a subject for metaphysical investigation. Psychical and physical phenomena are qualitatively distinct so far as knowledge is concerned: the first are known by direct introspection and the second by means of the outer senses. But experience — both immediate individual and universal, scientific, and historical experience — undoubtedly proves that in spite of this there is no gulf between the real essence of spiritual and material nature, that the two are most intimately connected and constantly interact. Since the process whereby the universe attains perfection is the process of manifesting God in man, it must also be the process of manifesting God in matter.

The chief concrete stages of this process, given in our experience, bear the traditional and significant name of *kingdoms*. It is significant because it really is applicable only to the last and highest stage, which is usually not taken into account at all. Counting this highest stage there are five kingdoms altogether: the *mineral* (or, more generally, the inorganic) kingdom, the *vegetable* kingdom, the *animal* kingdom, the *human* kingdom, and *God's kingdom*. Minerals, plants, animals, natural humanity and spiritual humanity — such are the typical forms of existence from the point of view of the ascending process of universal perfection. From other points of view the number of these forms and stages might be increased, or, on the contrary, be reduced to four, three, and two. Plants and animals may be grouped together into one organic world. Or the whole realm of physical existence, both organic and inorganic, may be united in the one conception of nature. In that case there would be a threefold division only, into the Divine, the human, and the natural kingdoms. Finally, one may stop at the simple opposition between the Kingdom of God and the kingdom of this world.

Without in the least rejecting these and all other divisions, it must be admitted that the five kingdoms indicated above represent the most characteristic and clearly defined *grades of existence* from the point of view of the moral meaning realised in the process of manifesting God in matter.

Stones and metals are distinguished from all else by their extreme self-sufficiency and conservatism; had it rested with them, nature would never have wakened from her dreamless slumber. But, on the other hand, without them her further growth would have been deprived of a firm basis or ground. Plants in unconscious, unbroken dreams *draw towards* warmth, light, and moisture. Animals by means of *sensations* and free *movements seek* the fulness of sensuous being: repletion, sexual satisfaction, and the joy of existence (their games and singing). Natural humanity, in addition to all these things, rationally strives to *improve* its life by means of sciences, arts, and social institutions, actually improves it in various respects, and finally rises to the *idea* of absolute perfection. Spiritual humanity or humanity born of God not only understands this absolute perfection with the intellect but accepts it in its heart and its conduct as *the true beginning of that which must be fulfilled in all things*. It seeks to realise it to the end and to embody it in the life of the universe.

Each preceding kingdom serves as the immediate basis of the one that follows. Plants derive their nourishment from inorganic substances, animals exist at the expense of the vegetable kingdom, men live at the expense of animals, and the Kingdom of God is composed of men. If we consider an organism from the point of view of its material constituents we shall find in it nothing but elements of inorganic matter. That matter, however, ceases to be mere matter in so far as it enters into the special *plan* of organic life, which *makes use* of the chemical and physical properties of matter but is not reducible to them. In a similar way, human life on its material side consists of animal processes, which, however, have in it no significance on their own account as they do in the animal world. They serve as a means or an instrument for new purposes and new objects which follow from the new, higher plan of rational or human life. The sole purpose of the typical animal is satisfaction of hunger and of the sexual instinct. But when a human being desires nothing further he is rightly called bestial, not only as a term of abuse, but precisely in the sense of sinking to a lower level of existence. Just as a living organism consists of chemical substances which cease to be mere substances, so humanity consists of animals which cease to be *merely* animal. Similarly, the Kingdom of God consists of men who have ceased to be *merely* human and form part of a new and higher plane of existence in which their purely-human ends become the means and instruments for another final purpose.

II

The stone exists; the plant exists and is living; the animal lives and is conscious of its life in its concrete states; man understands the meaning of life according to ideas; the sons of God actively realise this meaning or the perfect moral order in all things to the end.

The stone exists, this is clear from its sensible effect upon us. Anyone who denies this truth can easily convince himself of his error, as has been observed long ago, by knocking his head against the stone.[1] Stone is the most typical embodiment of the category of being as such, and, in contradistinction to Hegel's abstract idea of being, it shows no inclination whatever to pass into its opposite:[2] a stone is what it is and has always been the symbol of changeless

1. Kant rightly points out that this argument is insufficient for theoretical philosophy; and when dealing with the theory of knowledge I propose to discuss the question as to the being of things. But in moral philosophy the above argument is sufficient, for *in all conscience* it is convincing.

2. It will be remembered that in Hegel's Dialectic pure being passes into pure nothing. In

being. It merely exists — *it does not live* and it does not die, for the parts into which it is broken up do not qualitatively differ from the whole.[3] The plant not merely exists but lives, which is proved by the fact that it dies. Life does not presuppose death, but death obviously presupposes life. There is a clear and essential difference between a growing tree and logs of wood, between a fresh and a faded flower — a difference to which there is nothing corresponding in the mineral kingdom.

It is as impossible to deny life to plants as to deny consciousness to animals. It can only be done with the help of an arbitrary and artificial terminology, which is not binding upon any one. According to the natural meaning of the word, consciousness in general is a definite and regular correspondence or interrelation between the inner psychical life of a given being and its external environment. Such correlation is undoubtedly present in animals. The presence of life in the vegetable kingdom is clearly seen in the distinction between a living and a dead plant; the presence of consciousness in animals is, at any rate in the case of the higher and typical animals, clearly seen in the distinction between a sleeping and a waking animal. For the distinction consists precisely in the fact that a waking animal consciously takes part in the life that surrounds it, while the psychical world of a sleeping animal is cut off from direct communication with that life.[4] An animal not merely has sensations and images; it connects them by means of correct associations. And although it is the interests and the impressions of the present moment that predominate in its life, it *remem-*

---

answer to a learned critic, I would like to observe that although I regard the stone as the most typical embodiment and symbol of unchanging being, I do not in the least *identify* the stone with the category of being and do not deny the mechanical and physical properties of the concrete stone. Every one, for instance, takes the pig to be the most typical embodiment and symbol of the moral category of unrestrained carnality, which is on that account called 'piggishness.' But in doing so no one denies that a real pig has in addition to its piggishness four legs, two eyes, etc.

3. I am speaking here of the stone as the most characteristic and concrete instance of inorganic bodies in general. Such a body *taken in isolation* has no real life of its own. But this in no way prejudges the metaphysical question as to the life of nature in general or of the more or less complex natural wholes such as the sea, rivers, mountains, forests. And indeed, separate inorganic bodies too, such as stones, though devoid of life on their own account, may serve as constant mediums for the localised living activity of spiritual beings. Of this nature were the sacred stones — the so-called *bethels* or *bethils* (houses of God) which were associated with the presence and activity of angels or Divine powers that seemed to inhabit these stones.

4. The usual ways in which an animal becomes conscious of his environment are closed in sleep. But this does not by any means exclude the possibility of a different environment and of other means of mental correlation, *i.e.* of another sphere of consciousness. In that case, however, the periodical transition of a given mental life from one sphere of consciousness into another would prove still more clearly the general conscious character of that life.

bers its past states and *foresees* the future ones. If this were not the case, the education or training of animals would be impossible, yet such training is a fact. No one will deny *memory* to a horse or a dog. But to remember a thing or to be conscious of it is one and the same. To deny consciousness to animals is merely an aberration of the human consciousness in some philosophers.

One fact of comparative anatomy ought alone to be sufficient to disprove this crude error. To deny consciousness to animals means to reduce the whole of their life to the blind promptings of instinct. But how are we to explain in that case the gradual development in the higher animals of the organ of conscious mental activity — the brain? How could this organ have appeared and developed if the animals in question had no corresponding functions? Unconscious, instinctive life does not need the brain. This is shown by the fact that the development of instinct is prior to the appearance of that organ, and that it reaches its highest development in creatures that have no brain. The excellence of ants' and bees' social, hunting, and constructive instincts depends of course not on the brain, which, strictly speaking, they have not got, but upon their well-developed sympathetic nervous system.

Man differs from animals not by being conscious, since the same is true of them also, but by possessing reason or the faculty of forming general concepts and ideas. The presence of consciousness in animals is proved by their purposive movements, mimicry, and their language of various sounds. The fundamental evidence of the rationality of man is the *word*, which expresses not only the states of a particular consciousness, but the general meaning of all things. The ancient wisdom rightly defined man not as a conscious being — which is not enough — but as a being endowed with language or a rational being.

The power inherent in the very nature of reason and of language to grasp the all-embracing and all-uniting truth has acted in many different ways in various and separate peoples, gradually building up the human kingdom upon the basis of the animal life. The ultimate essence of this human kingdom is the ideal *demand* for the perfect moral order, *i.e.* a demand for the Kingdom of God. By two paths — of prophetic inspiration among the Jews, and of philosophic thought among the Greeks — has the human spirit approached the *idea* of the Kingdom of God, and the *ideal* of the God-man.[5] Parallel to this double inner process, but naturally more slow than it, was the external process of bringing about political unity and unity of culture among the chief historical peoples of East and West, completed by the Roman Em-

---

5. Both these paths — the Biblical and the philosophical — coincided in the mind of the Alexandrian Jew Philo, who is, from this point of view, the last and the most significant thinker of antiquity.

pire. In Greece and Rome natural or pagan humanity reached its limit. In the beautiful sensuous form and speculative idea among the Greeks, and in the practical reason, will, or power among the Romans, it affirmed its absolute divine significance. There arose the idea of the absolute man or *man-god*. This idea cannot, from its very nature, remain abstract or purely speculative. It demands *embodiment*. But it is as impossible for man to make himself a god as it is impossible for animals by their own efforts to attain human dignity, rationality, and power of speech. Remaining upon its own level of development, animal nature could only produce the ape, and human nature — the Roman Caesar. Just as the ape is the forerunner of man, so the deified Caesar is the forerunner of the God-man.

III

At the period when the pagan world contemplated its spiritual failure in the person of the supposed man-god — the Caesar impotently aping the deity, individual philosophers and earnest believers were awaiting the incarnation of the Divine Word or the coming of the Messiah, the Son of God and the King of Truth. The man-god, even if he were lord of all the world, is but an empty dream; the God-man can reveal His true nature even in the guise of a wandering rabbi.

The historical existence of Christ, as well as the reality of His character recorded in the Gospels, is not open to serious doubt. It was impossible to invent Him, and no one could have done it. And this perfectly historical image is the image of the perfect man — not of a man, however, who says, 'I have become god,' but of one who says, 'I am born of God and am sent by Him, I was one with God before the world was made.' We are compelled by reason to believe this testimony, for the historical coming of Christ as God made manifest in man is inseparably connected with the whole of the world-process. If the reality of this event is denied, there can be no meaning or purpose in the universe.

When the first vegetable forms appeared in the inorganic world, developing subsequently into the luxurious kingdom of trees and flowers, they could not have appeared of themselves, out of nothing. It would be equally absurd to suppose that they had sprung from the accidental combinations of inorganic elements. Life is a new positive content, something *more* than lifeless matter; and to reduce the greater to the lesser is to assert that something can come out of nothing, which is obviously absurd. The phenomena of vegetable life are continuous with the phenomena of the inorganic world; but that *of which* they are the phenomena is essentially distinct in the two kingdoms, and the heterogeneity becomes more and more apparent as the new kingdom develops further. In the same way, the world of plants and the world of animals spring, as it were, from one root; the elementary forms of both are so similar that biology recognises a whole class of animal-plants (the Zoophites). But under this apparent or phenomenal homogeneity there is undoubtedly concealed a fundamental and essential difference of type, which evinces itself later in the two divergent directions or planes of being — the vegetable and the animal. In this case, again, that which is new and greater in the animal, as compared with the vegetable type, cannot, without obvious absurdity, be reduced to the lesser, *i.e.* to the qualities they have in common. This would mean identifying $a + b$ with a, or recognising something as equal to nothing. In exactly the same way there is close proximity and intimate material connection, in the phenomenal order, between the human and the animal world. But the essential peculiarity of the latter — which is certainly more apparent in a Plato or a Goethe than in a Papuan or an Eskimo — is a new positive content, a certain *plus* of existence, which cannot be deduced from the old animal type. A cannibal may not in himself be much above the ape; but then he is not a final type of humanity. An uninterrupted series of *more perfect* generations lead from the cannibal to Plato and Goethe, while an ape, so long as it is an ape, does not become essentially *more perfect*. We are connected with our half-savage ancestors by the bond of historical memory, or the unity of collective consciousness — which animals do not possess. Their memory is individual only, and the physiological bond between generations that finds expression in heredity does not enter their consciousness. Therefore, though animals participate to a certain extent in the process of making the animal form more perfect (in accordance with the evolutionary theory), the results and the purpose of this process remain external and foreign to them. But the process whereby humanity is made more perfect is conditioned by the faculties of reason and will which are found in the lowest savage, though in a rudimentary degree only. Just as these higher faculties cannot be deduced from the animal nature and form a separate human kingdom, so the qualities of the spiritual man — of man made perfect or of the God-man — cannot be deduced from the states and qualities of the natural man. Consequently, the Kingdom of God cannot be taken to be the result of the unbroken development of the purely-human world. The *God-man is not the same as the man-god,* even though distinct individuals among natural humanity may have anticipated the higher life which was to come. As the 'sea lily' appears at first sight to be a plant, while it undoubtedly is an animal, so, at the beginning, the bearers of the Kingdom of God apparently do not seem in any way to differ from men of this world, though there lives and acts within them the principle of a new order of being.

The fact that the higher forms or types of being appear, or are revealed, after the lower does not by any means prove that they are a product or a creation of the lower. The order of reality is not the same as the order of appearance. The higher, the richer, and the more positive types and states of being are metaphysically prior to the lower, although they are revealed or manifested subsequently to them. This is not a denial of evolution; evolution cannot be denied, it is a fact. But to maintain that evolution creates the higher forms out of the lower, or, in the long-run, out of nothing, is to substitute a logical absurdity for the fact. Evolution of the lower types of being cannot of itself create the higher. It simply produces the material conditions or brings about the environment necessary for the manifestation or the revelation of the higher type. Thus, every appearance of a new type of being is in a certain sense a *new creation*. But it is not created out of nothing. The material basis for the appearance of the new is the old type. The special positive content of the higher type does not arise *de novo*, but exists from all eternity. It simply enters, at a certain moment in the process, into a different order of being — the phenomenal world. The conditions of the appearance are due to the natural evolution of the material world; that which appears comes from God.[6]

IV

The interrelation between the fundamental types of being — which are the chief stages in the world-process — is not exhausted by the negative fact that these types, each having its own peculiar nature, are not reducible to one another. There is a direct connection between them which gives positive unity to the process as a whole. This unity, into the essential nature of which we cannot here inquire, is revealed in three ways. In the first place, each new type is a *new condition* necessary for the realisation of the supreme and final end, namely, for the actual manifestation in the world of the perfect moral order, the Kingdom of God, or for 'the revelation of the freedom and glory of the sons of God.'[7] In order to attain its highest end or manifest its absolute worth, a being must in the first place *be*, then it must be *living*, then be *conscious*, then be *rational*, and finally be *perfect*. The defective notions of not being,

6. The primordial relation of God to nature lies outside the boundaries of the world-process and is a subject for pure metaphysics, which I will not touch upon here.

7. See Romans 8:19-21. — *Editor's note.*

lifelessness, unconsciousness, and irrationality are *logically* incompatible with the idea of perfection. The concrete embodiment of each of the positive states of existence forms the actual kingdoms of the world, so that even the lower enter into the moral order as the necessary conditions of its realisation. This instrumental relation, however, does not exhaust the unity of the world as given in experience. The lower types are inwardly drawn to the higher, strive to attain to them, having in them, as it were, their purpose and their end. This fact also indicates the purposive character of the process as a whole (the most obvious instance of the striving is the likeness, already indicated, of the ape to man). Finally, the positive connection of the graduated kingdoms shows itself in the fact that each type includes or embraces the lower types within itself — and the higher it is, the more fully it does so. The world-process may thus be said to be the process of *gathering the universe together,* as well as of developing and perfecting it. Plants physiologically absorb their environment (the inorganic substances and physical phenomena which nourish them and promote their growth). Animals, in addition to feeding on plants, psychologically absorb, *i.e.* take into their consciousness, a wider circle of events correlated with them through sensation. Man, in addition to this, grasps, by means of reason, remote spheres of being which are not immediately sensed; at a high stage of development he can embrace all in one or understand the meaning of all things. Finally the God-man or the Living Reason (Logos) not only abstractly understands but actively realises the meaning of everything, or the perfect moral order, as he embraces and connects together all things by the living personal power of love. The highest end of man as such (pure man) and of the human world is to *gather the universe together in thought.* The end of the God-man and of the Kingdom of God is to gather the universe together *in reality.*

The vegetable world does not abolish the inorganic world, but merely relegates it to a lower, subordinate place. The same thing happens at the further stages of the world-process. At the end of it, the Kingdom of God does not, when it appears, abolish the lower types of existence, but puts them all into their right place, no longer as separate spheres of existence but as the spiritually-physical organs of a *collected* universe, bound together by an absolute inner unity and interaction. This is the reason why the Kingdom of God is identical with the reality of the absolute moral order, or, what is the same thing, with universal resurrection and ἀποκατάστασις τῶν πάντων.[8]

---

8. "The restitution of all things" (see Acts 3:21). The "Apocatastasis" is the idea, usually associated with Origen and Gregory of Nyssa, that all beings will inevitably be saved and united with God. — *Editor's note.*

V

When the God-man who begins the Kingdom of God is described as 'an ideal,' this does not mean that he is thinkable only and not real. He can be called ideal only in the sense in which a man may be said to be an ideal for the animal, or a plant an ideal for the earth out of which it grows. The plant is more ideal in the sense of possessing greater worth, but it has a greater and not a lesser *reality* or fulness of existence as compared with a clod of earth. The same must be said of the animal as compared with the plant, of the natural man as compared with the animal, and of the God-man as compared with the natural man. On the whole, the greater worth of the ideal content is in *direct proportion* to the increase in real power: the plant has concrete powers (such as the power to transmute inorganic substances for its own purposes) which the clod of earth has not; man is far more powerful than the ape, and Christ has infinitely more power than the Roman Caesar.

The natural man differs from the spiritual not by being utterly devoid of the spiritual element, but by not having the power to realise that element completely. To obtain this power the spiritual being of man must be fertilised by a new creative act or by the effect of what in theology is called *grace,* which gives the sons of men 'the power to become the children of God.' Even according to orthodox theologians grace does not abolish nature in general, and the moral nature of man in particular, but *perfects* it. The moral nature of man is the necessary condition and presupposition of the manifestation of God in man. Not every inorganic substance but only certain chemical combinations can be affected by the vital force and form part of vegetable and animal organisms. Similarly, not all living beings but only those endowed with a moral nature can receive the effects of grace and enter into the Kingdom of God. The beginnings of spiritual life are inherent in the very nature of man and are to be found in the feelings of shame, pity, and reverence, as well as in the rules of conduct that follow from these feelings and are safeguarded by conscience or the consciousness of duty. This natural good in man is an imperfect good, and it is logically inevitable that it should, as such, remain for ever imperfect. Otherwise we should have to admit that the infinite can be the result of the addition of finite magnitudes, that the unconditional can arise out of the conditioned, and, finally, that something can come out of nothing. Human nature does not contain and therefore cannot of itself give rise to the real infinity or fulness of perfection. But by virtue of reason or universal meaning inherent in it, it contains the possibility of this moral infinity and a striving for its realisation, *i.e.* for the apprehension of the Divine. A dumb creature striving towards reason is a mere animal, but a being actually possessed of reason ceases to be an animal and becomes man, forming a new kingdom not to be deduced by a simple continuous evolution from the lower types. Similarly, this new being, rational, though not wholly rational, imperfect and only striving towards perfection, is a mere man, while a being *possessing* perfection cannot be *merely* human. He is a revelation of a new and final Kingdom of God, in which not the relative but the absolute Good or worth is realised, not to be deduced from the relative; for the distinction is one of quality and not of quantity or degree.

The God-man differs from the ordinary man not by being an imagined ideal but by being a *realised* ideal. The false idealism which takes the ideal to be non-existent, and thinks its realisation unnecessary, is not worth criticising. But there is another question involved here which must be reckoned with. While admitting that the divine or perfect man must have reality, and not merely significance for thought, one may deny the historical fact of His appearance in the past. Such denial, however, has no rational grounds, and, moreover, it robs the process of universal history of all meaning. If the historical person known to us from the books of the New Testament was not the God-man or, in Kant's terminology, the realised 'ideal,' He could only be the natural product of historical evolution. But in that case why did not this evolution go further in the same direction and produce other persons still more perfect? Why is it that after Christ there is progress in all spheres of life except in the fundamental sphere of personal spiritual power? Every one who does not deliberately shut his eyes must admit the gulf there is between the noblest type of natural, searching wisdom immortalised by Xenophon in his notes and by Plato in his dialogues, and the radiant manifestation of triumphant spirituality which is preserved in the Gospels and had blinded Saul in order to regenerate him. And yet, less than four centuries elapsed between Socrates and Christ. If during this short period historical evolution could produce such an increase of spiritual force in human personality, how is it that during a far longer time, and in a period of rapid historical progress, evolution has proved utterly powerless not only to bring about a corresponding advance in personal spiritual perfection, but even to keep it on the same level? Spinoza and Kant, who lived sixteen and seventeen centuries after Christ, and were very noble types of natural wisdom, may well be compared with Socrates, but it would not occur to any one to compare them with Christ. It is not because they had a different sphere of activity. Take men celebrated in the religious sphere — Muhammad, Savonarola, Luther, Calvin, Ignatius Loyola,[9]

9. It will be remembered that Auguste Comte, in some letters he wrote shortly before his death, declared Ignatius Loyola to be higher than Christ. But this judgment, as well as other

Fox, Swedenborg. All these were men of powerful personality; but try honestly to compare them with Christ! And historical characters, such as St. Francis, who come nearest to the moral ideal, definitely acknowledge their direct dependence upon Christ as a higher being.

VI

If Christ represents only a relative stage of moral perfection, the absence of any further stages during almost two thousand years of the spiritual growth of humanity is utterly incomprehensible. If He is the absolutely highest type produced by the process of natural evolution, He ought to have appeared *at the end* and not in the middle of history. But indeed He could not in any case be a simple product of historical evolution, for the difference between absolute and relative perfection is not one of quantity or degree, but is qualitative and essential, and it is logically impossible to deduce the first from the second.

The meaning of history in its concrete development compels us to recognise in Jesus Christ not the last word of the human kingdom, but the first and all-embracing Word of the Kingdom of God — not the man-god, but the God-man, or the absolute individual. From this point of view it can be well understood why He first appeared in the *middle* of history and not at the end of it. The purpose of the world-process is the revelation of the Kingdom of God or of the perfect moral order realised by a new humanity *which spiritually grows out of the God-man.* It is clear, then, that this universal event must be preceded by the individual appearance of the God-man Himself. As the first half of history up to Christ was preparing the environment or the external conditions for His individual birth, so the second half prepares the external conditions for His universal revelation or for the coming of the Kingdom of God. Here once more the general and logically certain law of the universe finds application: the higher type of being is *not created* by the preceding process but is phenomenally conditioned by it. The Kingdom of God is not a *product* of Christian history any more than Christ was a product of the Jewish and the Pagan history. History merely worked out in the past and is working out now the necessary natural and moral *conditions* for the revelation of the God-man and the divine humanity.

---

similar opinions and actions of the founder of the Positivist philosophy, prove to all unprejudiced critics that the thinker in question, who had in his youth suffered for two years with brain disease, was in the last years of his life once more on the verge of insanity. See my article on Comte in the *Brockhaus-Efron Encyclopaedia.*

VII

By His word and the work of His whole life, beginning with the victory over all the temptations of *moral* evil and ending with the resurrection, *i.e.* the victory over *physical* evil or the law of death and corruption, the true God-man revealed to men the Kingdom of God. But, according to the very meaning and law of this new Kingdom, revelation cannot in this case coincide with attainment. In making real the absolute significance of each person the perfect moral order presupposes the moral freedom of each. But true freedom is acquired by the finite spirit through experience only. Free choice is possible only for the person who knows or has experienced that which he is choosing as well as its opposite. And although Christ finally conquered evil in the true centre of the universe, *i.e.* in Himself, the victory over evil on the circumference of the world, *i.e.* in the collective whole of humanity, has to be accomplished through humanity's own experience. This necessitates a new process of development in the Christian world which has been baptized into Christ but has not yet put on Christ.[10]

The true foundation of the perfect moral order is the *universality* of the spirit of Christ capable of embracing and regenerating *all* things. The essential task of humanity, then, is to accept Christ and regard *all* things in His spirit, thus enabling His spirit to become incarnate in *all* things. For this incarnation cannot be a physical event only. The individual incarnation of the Word of God required the consent of a personal feminine will: "Be it unto Me according to Thy word."[11] The universal incarnation of the Spirit of Christ or the manifestation of the Kingdom of God requires the consent of the collective will of humanity, that all things should be united to God. In order that this consent should be fully conscious, Christ must be understood not only as the absolute *principle* of the good, but as the *fulness* of the good. In other words, there must be established a Christian (and an antichristian) relation to all aspects and spheres of human life. In order that this consent should be perfectly free, that it should be a true moral act or a fulfilment of the inner truth and not the effect of an overwhelming superior force, it was necessary for Christ to withdraw into the transcendental sphere of the invisible reality and to withhold His active influence from human history. It will become

10. The least attention on the part of the reader will convince him that I have not given any ground for serious critics to reproach me with the absurd identification of the Kingdom of God with historical Christianity or the visible Church (which one?). I reject such identification both implicitly and explicitly; nor do I recognise every scoundrel who has been baptized as a 'spiritual' man or 'a son of God.'

11. Luke 1:38. — *Editor's note.*

manifest when human society as a whole, and not merely separate individuals, is ready for a conscious and free choice between the absolute good and its opposite. The unconditional moral demand, "Be ye perfect even as your Father in heaven is perfect,"[12] is addressed to each man, not as a separate entity but as together with others ('be *ye*,' not 'be *thou*'). And if this demand is understood and accepted as an actual problem of life, it inevitably transports us into the realm of conditions which determine the concrete *historical* existence of *society* or the collective man.

12. Matthew 5:48. — *Editor's note.*

PART III

The Good through Human History

CHAPTER I

The Individual and Society

I

We know that the good in its full sense, including the idea of happiness or satisfaction, is ultimately defined as the true moral order which expresses the absolutely right and the absolutely desirable relation of each to all and of all to each. It is called the Kingdom of God. From the moral point of view it is quite clear that the realisation of the Kingdom of God is the only final end of life and activity, being the supreme good, happiness, and bliss. It is equally clear, if one thinks of the subject carefully and concretely, that the true moral order or the Kingdom of God is both perfectly universal and perfectly individual. *Each* wants it for himself and for every one, and is able to attain it only *together with every one.* Therefore there can be no essential opposition between the individual and society; the question which of the two is an end and which is merely a means cannot be asked. Such a question would presuppose the real existence of the individual as a self-sufficient and self-contained entity. In truth, however, each individual is only the meeting-point of an infinite number of relations with the other and with others. To abstract him from these relations means to deprive his life of all its concrete content and to transform a personality into an empty possibility of existence. To imagine that the personal centre of our being is really cut off from our environment and from the general life which connects us with other minds is simply a morbid illusion of self-consciousness.

When a line is chalked before the eyes of a cock, he takes that line to be a fatal obstacle which he cannot possibly overstep. He is evidently incapable of understanding that the fatal, overwhelming significance of the chalk line is due simply to the fact that he is exclusively *occupied* with this unusual and unexpected fact, and is therefore *not free* with regard to it. The delusion is quite natural for a cock, but is less natural for a rational thinking human being. Nevertheless human beings fail but too frequently to grasp that the given limitations of our personality are insuperable and impermeable solely because our attention is exclusively concentrated on them. The fatal separateness of our 'self' from all else is due simply to the fact that we imagine it to be fatal. We too are victims of auto-suggestion, which, though it has certain objective grounds, is as fictitious and as easily got over as the chalked line.

The self-deception in virtue of which a human individual regards himself as real in his separateness from all things, and presupposes this fictitious isolation to be the true ground and the only possible starting-point for all his relations — this self-deception of abstract subjectivism plays terrible havoc not only in the domain of metaphysics — which, indeed, it abolishes altogether — but also in the domain of the moral and political life. It is the source of many convoluted theories, irreconcilable contradictions, and insoluble questions. But all of them would disappear of themselves if, without being afraid of authoritative names, we would grasp the simple fact that the theories and the insoluble problems in question could only have arisen from the point of view of the hypnotised cock.

II

Human personality, and therefore every individual human being, is *capable of realising infinite fulness of being,* or, in other words, *it is a particular form with infinite content.* The reason of man contains an infinite possibility of a truer and truer knowledge of the meaning of all things. The will of man contains an equally infinite possibility of a more and more perfect realisation of this universal meaning in the particular life and environment. Human personality is infinite: this is an axiom of moral philosophy. But the moment that abstract subjectivism draws its chalk line before the eyes of the unwary thinker the most fruitful of axioms becomes a hopeless absurdity. Human personality as containing infinite possibilities is abstracted from all the concrete conditions and results of its realisation in and through society — and is indeed opposed to them. There ensues insoluble contradiction between the individual and society, and the 'fatal question' arises as to which of the two must be sacrificed to the other. Persons hypnotised by the individualistic view affirm the independence of separate personality which determines all its relations from within, and regard social ties and collective order as merely an external limit and an arbitrary restriction which must at any cost be removed. On the other hand, thinkers who are under the spell of collectivism take the life of humanity to be simply an interplay of human masses, and regard the individual as an insignificant and transient element of society, who has no rights of his own, and may be left out of account for the sake of the so-called common good. But what are we to make of society consisting of moral zeros, of rightless and non-individual creatures? Would it be *human* society? Where would its dignity and the inner value of its existence spring from, and wherein would it lie? And how could such a society hold together? It is clear that this is nothing but a sad and empty dream, which neither could nor ought to be realised. The opposite ideal of self-sufficient personality is equally chimeric. Deprive a *concrete* human personality of all that is in any way due to its relations with social and collective wholes, and the only thing left will be an animal entity containing only a pure possibility or an empty form of man — that is, something that does not really exist at all. Those who had occasion to go down to hell or to rise up to heaven, as, for instance, Dante and Swedenborg, did not find even there any isolated individuals, but saw only social groups and circles.[1]

Social life is not a condition superadded to the individual life, but is contained in the very definition of personality which is essentially a rationally-knowing and a morally-active force — both knowing and acting being possible only in the life of a community. Rational knowledge on its *formal* side is conditioned by *general notions* which express a unity of meaning in an endless multiplicity of events; the real and objective universality (the general meaning) of notions manifests itself in language as a means of communication, without which rational activity cannot develop, and, for lack of realisation, gradually disappears altogether or becomes merely potential. Language — this concrete reason — could not have been the work of an isolated individual, and consequently such an individual could not be rational, could not be human. On its *material* side knowledge of truth is based upon experience — hereditary, collective experience which is being gradually stored up. The experience of an absolutely isolated being, even if such a being could exist, would obviously be quite insufficient for the knowledge of truth. As to the *moral* determination of personality, it is clear that, although the idea of the good or of moral value is not wholly due to social relations as is often maintained, concrete development of human morality or the *realisation* of the idea of the good is possible for the individual only in a social environment and through interaction with it. In this all-important respect society is nothing but the objective realisation of what is contained in the individual.

1. Solovyov is referring to Dante's *Divine Comedy* and to Swedenborg's *Coelestia Arcana* . — *Editor's note.*

Instead of an insoluble contradiction between two mutually exclusive principles — between two abstract *isms,* — we really find two correlative terms each of which logically and historically requires and presupposes the other. In its essential signification society is not the external limit of the individual but his inner fulfilment. It is not an arithmetical sum or a mechanical aggregate of the individuals that compose it, but the indivisible whole of the communal life. This life has been partly realised in the past and is preserved in the abiding social *tradition,* is being partly realised in the present by means of social *service,* and finally, it anticipates in the form of a social *ideal,* present in the best minds, its perfect realisation in the future.

Corresponding to these three fundamental and abiding moments of the individually-social life — the religious, the political, and the prophetic — there are three main concrete stages through which human life and consciousness pass in the course of the historical development, namely, (1) the stage of organisation based upon kinship, which belongs to the past though it is still preserved in a changed form in the family; (2) the *national state,* prevalent at the present time; and finally (3) the *universal* communion of life, as the ideal of the future.

At all these stages society is essentially the moral *fulfilment* or the *realisation* of the individual in a given environment. But the environment is not always the same. At the first stage it is limited for each to his own tribe; at the second, to his own fatherland; and it is only at the third that the human personality, having attained a clear consciousness of its inner infinity, endeavours to realise it in a *perfect* society, abolishing all limitations both in the nature and in the extent of concrete interaction.

III

Each single individual possesses as such the potentiality of perfection or of positive infinity, namely, the capacity to understand all things with his intellect and to embrace all things with his heart, or to enter into a living communion with everything. This double infinity — the power of representation and the power of striving and activity, called in the Bible, according to the interpretation of the Fathers of the Church, the image and likeness of God — necessarily belongs to every person. It is in this that the absolute significance, dignity, and worth of human personality consist, and this is the basis of its inalienable rights.[2] It is

---

2. This meaning of the image and likeness of God is essentially the same as that indicated in Part II. It is clear, indeed, that an infinite power of representation and understanding can only

clear that the realisation of this infinity, or the actuality of the perfection, demands that all should participate in it. It cannot be the private possession of each *taken separately,* but becomes his through his relation to all. In other words, by remaining isolated and limited an individual deprives himself of the real fulness of life, *i.e.* deprives himself of perfection and of infinity. A consistent affirmation of his own separateness or isolation would indeed be physically impossible for the individual person. All that the life of the community contains is bound in one way or another to affect individual persons; it becomes a part of them and in and through them alone attains its final actuality or completion. Or if we look at the same thing from another point of view — all the *real* content of the personal life is obtained from the social environment and, in one way or another, is conditioned by its state at the given time. In this sense it may be said that *society is the completed or magnified individual, and the individual is compressed or concentrated society.*

The world purpose is not to create a solidarity between each and all, for it already exists in the nature of things, but to make each and all aware of this solidarity and spiritually alive to it; to transform it from a merely metaphysical and physical solidarity into a morally-metaphysical and a morally-physical one. The life of man already is, both at its lower and its upper limit, an involuntary participation in the developing life of humanity and of the whole world. But the *dignity* of human life and the meaning of the universe as a whole demand that this involuntary participation of each in everything should become voluntary and be more and more conscious and free, *i.e.* really *personal* — that each should more and more understand and fulfil the *common work* as if it were *his own.* It is clear that in this way alone can the infinite significance of personality be realised or, in other words, pass from possibility to actuality.

But this transition itself — this spiritualisation or moralisation of the natural fact of solidarity — is also an inseparable part of the common work. The fulfilment of this supreme task depends not upon personal efforts alone, but is also necessarily conditioned by the general course of the world's history, or by the actual state of the social environment at a given moment in history. Thus the individual improvement in each man cannot be severed from the universal, nor the personal morality from the social.

---

give us the *image* ('the schema') of perfection, while an infinite striving, having for its purpose the *actual* realisation of perfection, is the beginning of our *likeness* to God, who is the real and not only the ideal perfection.

IV

True morality is the rightful interaction between the individual and his environment — taking the term 'environment' in the wide sense to embrace all spheres of reality — the higher as well as the lower — with which man stands in the practical relation. The true personal dignity of each undoubtedly finds expression and embodiment in his relations to his surroundings. The infinite possibilities inherent in the very nature of man gradually become realised in this *individually-social* reality. Historical experience finds man as already having his completion in a certain social milieu, and the subsequent course of history is nothing but a refinement and enlargement of this double-sided individually-social life. The three main stages or strata in this process that have been indicated above — the patriarchal, the national, and the universal — are of course connected by a number of intermediate links. A higher form does not replace or entirely cancel the lower, but, absorbing it into itself, makes it a subordinate part instead of an independent whole. Thus with the appearance of the state the tribal union becomes a subordinate part of it in the form of the family. But the relation of kinship, so far from being abolished, acquires a greater moral depth. It merely changes its sociological and juridical significance, ceasing to be a seat of independent authority or of proper jurisdiction.

As the lower forms of the collective life pass into the higher, the individual, in virtue of the infinite potentiality of understanding and of striving for the better latent in him, appears as the principle of progress and of movement (the dynamic element in history), while the social environment, being a reality already achieved, a completed objectification of the moral content in a certain sphere and at a certain stage, naturally represents the stable, conservative principle (the static element of history). When individuals who are more gifted or more developed than others begin to be conscious that their social environment is no longer a realisation or a completion of their life, but is simply an external barrier and obstacle to their positive moral aspirations, they become the bearers of a higher social consciousness which seeks embodiment in new forms and in a new order of life that would correspond to it.

All social environment is the objective expression or embodiment of morality (of right relations) at a certain stage of human development. But the moral individual, in virtue of his striving towards the absolute good, outgrows a given limited form of morality embodied in the social structure and takes up a negative attitude towards it — not towards it as such, but towards the given lower stage of its embodiment. It is obvious that such a conflict is not an opposition of principle between the individual and the social element, but is simply an opposition between the earlier and the later stages of the individually-social development.

V

The moral worth and dignity of man finds its first expression in *social life as determined by kinship.*[3] We find in it a rudimentary embodiment or organisation of morality as a whole — religious, altruistic, and ascetic. In other words, a group held together by the tie of kinship is the realisation of personal human dignity in the narrowest and most fundamental sphere of society. The first condition of the true dignity of man — reverence for that which is higher than himself, for the super-material powers that rule his life — here finds expression in the worship of the ancestors or of the founders of the clan. The second condition of personal dignity — the recognition of the dignity of others — is found in the solidarity of the members of the group, their mutual affection and consideration. The third, or, from another point of view, the first condition of human dignity — freedom from the predominance of carnal desires — is here to some extent attained by means of certain compulsory limitation or regulation of the sexual relations through the different forms of marriage and also by means of other restraining rules of the communal life, all of which demand the *shame* to which the ancient chronicler refers.

Thus in this primitive circle of human life the moral dignity of the person is in all respects realised by the community and in the community. How can there be any contradiction and conflict here between the individual and the collective principle and what expression can it assume? The relation between the two is direct and positive. The social law is not extraneous to the individual, it is not imposed upon him from without contrary to his nature; it merely gives a definite, objective, and constant form to the inward motives of personal morality. Thus the person's inner religious feeling (rudiments of which are already found in certain animals) impels him to hold in reverence the secret causes and conditions of his existence — and the cult of ancestor worship merely gives an objective expression to this desire. The feeling of pity, equally inherent in man, inclines him to treat his relatives with fairness — the social law merely confirms this personal altruism by giving it a fixed and definite form and making it capable of realisation; thus the defence of the weak

3. I am speaking of kinship in the wide sense and have in mind a group of persons forming one self-contained community, united by the blood-tie and intermarriage, whether the connection between them takes the form of mother-right or of father-right.

members of the social group from injury is impossible for a single individual to undertake, but is organised by the clan as a whole or by a union of clans. Finally, man's inherent modesty finds realisation in definite social rules of abstinence. Personal morality cannot be separated from the social, for the first is the inner beginning of the second, and the second the objective realisation of the first. The rules of social life at the patriarchal stage — worship of common ancestors, mutual help between the individual members of the clan, limitation of sensuality by marriage — have a moral source and character, and it is clear that to carry out these social rules is a gain and not a loss to the individual. The more an individual member of a clan enters into the spirit of its social structure, which demands reverence for the unseen, solidarity with his neighbours, and control of carnal passions, obviously the more moral he becomes; and the more moral he is, the higher is his inner worth or personal dignity; thus *subordination to society uplifts the individual.* On the other hand, the more free this subordination, the more independently does the individual follow the inner promptings of his own moral nature which accord with the demands of social morality, the greater support does the society find in such a person; therefore *the independence of the individual lends strength to the social order.* In other words, the relation between the true significance of the individual and the true force of society is a direct and not an inverse one.

What concrete form, then, could the principle of the opposition of the individual to society and of his superiority to it take at this early stage? Perhaps the supposed champion of the rights of the individual would desecrate the tombs of his ancestors, insult his father, outrage his mother, kill his brothers, and marry his own sisters? It is clear that such actions are below the very lowest social level, and it is equally clear that true realisation of absolute human dignity cannot be based upon a simple rejection of a given social structure.

VI

The moral content of social life as determined by kinship is permanent; its external and limited form is inevitably outgrown by the historical process, with the active help of individuals. The first expansion of the primitive life is, of course, due to the natural increase of population. Within the limits of one and the same family the more intimate degrees of kinship are followed by the more remote, although the moral duties extend to the latter also. Similarly to the progressive division of a living organic cell, the social cell — the group united by kinship — divides into many groups, which preserve, however, their connection and the memory of their common descent. Thus a new social unit is formed — the tribe — which embraces several contiguous clans. For instance, the North American Red Indian tribe Seneca, described by the well-known sociologist Morgan,[4] consisted of eight independent clans, evidently formed by the subdivision of one original clan, and standing in definite relation to one another. Each clan was based on kinship, and marriages within the clan were strictly forbidden as incestuous. Each clan was autonomous, though in certain respects subordinate to the common authority of the whole tribe, namely, to the tribal council, which consisted of the representatives of all the eight clans. In addition to this political and military institution, the unity of the tribe found expression in a common language and common religious celebrations. The transition stage between the clan and the tribe was the groups which Morgan designates by the classical name of *fratrias*. Thus the tribe of Seneca was divided into two *fratrias*, each consisting of an equal number of clans. The first contained the clans of Wolf, Bear, Tortoise, Beaver; the second, Deer, Woodcock, Heron, Falcon. The clans in each group were regarded as *brother* clans, and in relation to the clans of the other group as cousins. It is clear that the original clan from which the Seneca tribe was descended was first divided into two new clans, each of which became subdivided into four, and this succession has been preserved in the common memory.

There is no reason why the consciousness of social solidarity, extended to a group of clans, should stop at the limits of the tribe. The widening of the moral outlook on the one hand, and the recognised advantages of common action on the other, induce many tribes to form first temporary and, later, permanent alliances with one another. Thus the tribe of Seneca, together with many others, entered into the union of tribes bearing the common name of Iroquois. The tribes forming such unions are generally, though not necessarily, supposed to have a common ancestor. It often happens that when several tribes whose ancestors had parted in times immemorial, and which have grown and developed independently of one another, come together again under new conditions, they form a union by means of *treaties* for the sake of mutual defence and common enterprise. The treaty in this case is certainly regarded as of far greater significance than the blood-tie, which need not be presupposed at all.

The union of tribes, especially of those that have reached a certain degree of culture and occupy a definite territory, is the transition to a state, the embryo of a nation. The Iroquois, like most Red Indian tribes who remained in the wild forests and prairies of North America, did not advance further than

---

4. Solovyov is referring to L. H. Morgan's *League of the Ho-de-no-sau-nee, or Iroquois* (Rochester, NY, 1851). — *Editor's note.*

such an embryo of a nation and state. But other representatives of the same race, moving southwards, fairly rapidly passed from the military union of tribes to a permanent political organisation. The Aztecs of Mexico, the Incas of Peru founded real national states of the same type as the great theocratical monarchies of the Old World. The essential inner connection between the original social cell — the group united by kinship — and the wide political organisation is clearly expressed in the word *fatherland,* which almost in all languages designates the national state. The term fatherland, implying as it does a relation of kinship (*patria, Vaterland,* etc.), indicates not that the state is an expansion of the family — which is not true — but that the moral principle of this new great union must be essentially the same as the principle of the narrower union based upon kinship. In truth, states have arisen out of wars and treaties, but this does not alter the fact that the purpose or meaning for which they came into being was to establish in the wide circle of national, and even international, relations the same solidarity and peaceable life as had existed of old within the limits of the family.

The process of the formation of states and the external changes in human life connected with it do not concern us here. What is of interest to ethics is the moral position of the individual with regard to his new social environment. So long as the only higher forms of social life, in contradistinction to the clan, were found in the tribe and the union of tribes, the position of the individual was not essentially altered. It only changed, so to speak, quantitatively: moral consciousness received greater satisfaction and was more completely realised as the sphere of practical interaction became wider; and that was all. The divine ancestor of a given clan found brothers in the ancestors of other clans, each other's deities were mutually recognised, the religions of separate peoples were amalgamated and to a certain extent received a universal meaning (at the periods of tribal festivities), but the character of worship remained the same. The expression of human solidarity — the defence of one's kinsmen and the duty of avenging their wrongs — also remained intact when the tribe and the union of tribes came to be formed. Essential change took place only with the appearance of the fatherland and the state. The national religion may have developed out of ancestor worship, but the people have themselves forgotten its origin; similarly, the dispassionate justice of the state is essentially different from blood-vengeance. Here we have not simply an expansion of the old order based upon kinship, but the appearance of a new one. And in connection with this new order of the national state there may have arisen, and there did arise, a conflict of principle between the constituent forces of society — a conflict which might, to a superficial observer, appear as the conflict between the individual and the society as such.

VII

Neither the tribe, nor the union of tribes, nor the national state — the fatherland — destroys the original social cell; it only alters its signification. The change may be expressed in the following short but perfectly correct formula: *the state order transforms the clan into the family.* Indeed, until the state is formed, family life, strictly speaking, does not exist. The group of individuals held together by a more or less intimate blood-tie, which in primitive times forms the social unit, differs from the real family in one essential respect. The distinguishing characteristic of the family is that it is a form of private, in contradistinction to public, life: 'a public family' is a contradiction in terms. But the difference between public and private could only have arisen with the formation and the development of the state, which essentially stands for the public aspect of common life. Until then, so long as the legal and political functions of the social life were still undifferentiated — when judgment and execution, war and peace were still the private concerns of the primitive groups connected by the blood-tie — such groups, even the smallest of them, obviously could not possess the distinguishing characteristic of the family or home. They acquired this new character only when the functions in question were taken over by the state as a public or national organisation.

Now this transformation of the clan, *i.e.* of the political and social union, into the family, *i.e.* into an exclusively social, private, or domestic union, could be looked upon in two ways. It might be regarded as involving the purification of the tie of kinship which thus acquires greater inward dignity, or as involving its external lessening and degradation.[5] Since the duties of the individual to his clan were for a long time the sole expression of individual morality, conservative and passive natures might regard the submission of the clan to a new and higher unity of the state or fatherland as immoral. The personal consciousness was for the first time confronted with the question as to which of the two social unions it was to side with — with the more narrow and intimate, or with the wider and more remote. But whichever way this question might be settled by this or that individual, it is in any case clear that this is not a question of conflict between the individual and society, nor even between two kinds of social relation — the relation of kinship and of nation-

---

5. This double point of view may be brought out by an analogous example from quite a different sphere of relations. The loss by the Pope of his political power, or the abolition of the Church-state, may be regarded even by good and genuine Roman Catholics in two different and, indeed, opposite ways. It may be taken to be either a favourable condition for the *increase* of the inward moral authority of the Pope, or a lamentable detraction and *decrease* in the scope of his political activity.

ality. It is simply a question whether human life should stop at the stage of kinship or be further developed by means of the organisation of the state.

In the social group determined by kinship with its moral conditions and institutions, the human individual can realise his inner dignity better than in the state of brutal isolation. History has proved that the further development or improvement of the individual demands the more complex conditions of life which are to be found in civilised states only. The immature fancy of the young poet may glorify the half-savage life of nomadic gypsies; the unanswerable criticism of his view is contained in the simple fact that Pushkin, a member of a civilised community, could create his *Gypsies,* while the gypsies, in spite of all their alleged advantages, could not create a Pushkin.[6]

All the things whereby our spiritual nature is nurtured, all that lends beauty and dignity to our life in the sphere of religion, science and art, has sprung from the foundation of ordinary civilised life, conditioned by the order of the state. It has all been created not by the clan but by the fatherland. When the clan life still predominated, the men who took their stand with the fatherland, which till then was non-existent or only just dawning on their own inner vision, were bearers of a higher consciousness, of a better individually-social morality. They were benefactors of humanity and saints of history, and it is not for nothing that the grateful city-states of Greece and other countries did homage to them as their heroes — the eponyms.

Social progress is not an impersonal work. The conflict of individual initiative with its immediate social environment led to the foundation of a wider and more important social whole — the fatherland. The bearers of the *supertribal* consciousness, or, more exactly, of the half-conscious striving towards a wider moral and social life, felt cramped in the narrow sphere of the clan life, broke away from it, gathered a band of *free followers* round themselves, and founded states and cities. The pseudo-scientific criticism has arbitrarily converted into a myth the fugitive Dido who founded Carthage, and the outlaw brothers, founders of Rome. In quite historical times, however, we find a sufficient number of instances to inspire us with legitimate confidence in those legends of antiquity. Personal exploit breaking down the given social limits for the sake of creating new and higher forms of political and social life, is a fact so fundamental that it is bound to be met with at all periods of human development.[7]

6. The same poet, however, 'with reverence' dedicates one of his more mature works to the *historian of the Russian Empire.* [Pushkin dedicated his drama *Boris Godunov* to the historian Nikolai Karamzin. — *Editor's note.*]

7. The absurdity of the point of view generally assumed by the negative historical criticism escapes general ridicule simply owing to the 'darkness of time,' which conceals the objects upon

Historical as well as natural-scientific experience shows that it is impossible for a given organised group to break up or undergo any substantial transformation (for instance, to enter into another and a greater whole) apart from the activity of the finite units which compose it. The ultimate unit of human society is the individual who has always been the active principle of historical progress, *i.e.* of the transition from the narrow and limited forms of life to social organisations that are wider and richer in content.

VIII

A given narrow social group (say, a clan) has a claim upon the individual, for it is only in and through it that he can begin to realise his own inner dignity. But the rights of the community over the individual cannot be *absolute*, for a given group in its isolation is only one relative stage of the historical development, while human personality may pass through all the stages in its striving for infinite perfection, which is obviously not exhausted or finally satisfied by any limited social organisation. In other words, *in virtue of his inner infinity the individual can be absolutely and entirely at one with the social environment not in its given limitations, but only in its infinite completeness, which becomes gradually manifest as the forms of social life, in their interaction with individual persons, become wider, higher, and more perfect.* It is only in a community that personal achievement is fruitful, but in a community which develops. Unconditional surrender to any limited and immovable form of social life, rather than being the duty of the individual, is positively wrong, for it could only be to the detriment of his human dignity.

An enterprising member of the clan is, then, morally right in rebelling against the conservatism of the clan, and in helping to create the state which transforms the once independent social groups into elementary cells of a new and greater whole. But this implies that the new social organisation has no *absolute* rights over the old, tribal, or, henceforth, *family* relations. The order of the state is a *relatively* higher but by no means a perfect form of social life,

---

which it is exercised. If its favourite methods and considerations were applied, *e.g.,* to Muhammad or Peter the Great, there would be as little left of these historical heroes as of Dido or Romulus. Every one who has read Whateley's admirable pamphlet on Napoleon will agree that the solar significance of this mythological hero is proved in it, in accordance with the strict rules of the critical school, and is worked out with a consistency, clearness, and completeness not often to be found in the more or less famous works of the negative critics, although the latter wrote without the least irony but with the most serious intentions. [Solovyov is referring to R. Whateley's *Historical Doubts Relative to Napoleon Buonaparte* (London, 1819). — *Editor's note.*]

and it therefore has only a *relative* advantage over the organisation based upon kinship. And although the latter is merely a transitory stage in the social development, it contains a moral element of absolute value, which retains its force in the state and must be sacred to it. Indeed, two aspects are clearly apparent in primitive morality. In the first place, certain moral conceptions are connected with the idea of the clan as an independent or autonomous form of common life — which, in fact, it had been once, but ceased to be when the state was formed. This is the transitory and supersedable element of the clan morality. In the second place, certain natural duties arise from the intimate tie of kinship and common life, and these obviously retain all their significance in the transition to the state, or in the transformation of the clan into the family. The hard shell of the clan organisation has burst and fallen apart, but the moral kernel of the family has remained, and will remain to the end of history. Now when the transition from one organisation to another has just been effected, the representatives of the newly-formed state-power, conscious of its advantages over the clan structure, might easily ascribe to the new order an absolute significance which does not belong to it, and place the law of the state above the law of nature. In conflicts which arise on this ground, moral right is no longer on the side of these representatives of the *relatively* higher social order, but on the side of the champions of what is *absolute* in the old, and of what must remain equally sacred under any social order. Conservatism now ceases to be a blind or selfish inertness, and becomes a pure consciousness of supreme duty. Woman, the incarnation of the conservative principle, the bulwark of humble routine, now becomes the embodiment of moral heroism. Sophocles's Antigone impersonates the element of absolute value contained in the old order of life — the element which retains its permanent significance as the clan becomes the family within the new organisation of the state. She has no thought of the political autonomy of the clan, of the right of blood-vengeance, etc.; she simply stands up for her unconditional right to fulfil her unconditional duty of piety and sisterly love — to give honourable burial to her nearest kinsman who can receive it from no one but her. She has no enmity towards the moral foundations of the state; she simply feels — and quite rightly — that apart from these foundations the demands of the positive law are not absolute but are limited by the natural law which is sanctified by religion and safeguards family duties against the state itself if need be, when it appropriates what does not belong to it. The conflict between Creon and Antigone is not a conflict between two moral forces — the social and the individual; it is a conflict of the moral and the anti-moral force. It is impossible to agree with the usual view of Antigone as the bearer and champion of personal feeling against a universal law, embodied in the representative of the state — Creon. The true meaning of the tragedy is entirely different. A religious attitude to the dead is a moral duty, the fulfilment of which lies at the basis of all social life; personal feeling expresses merely the subjective aspect of the matter. In our own day, the burial of dead relatives and the homage paid to them are not due to personal feeling only; and this was still more the case in ancient times. The feeling may not be there, but the duty remains. Antigone had heartfelt affection for both her brothers, but sacred duty bound her to the one who needed her religious help. Being the pattern of a moral individual, Antigone at the same time is the representative of true social order, which is preserved only by the fulfilment of duty. She does not in the least conceal her feelings, and yet as the motive of her action she refers not to her feelings but to a sacred obligation which has to be fulfilled to the end (φίλη μετ' αὐτοῦ κείσομαι, φίλου μέτα — ὅσια πανουργήσασα). This obligation is not of course an abstract duty, but an expression of the eternal order of reality: "I owe a longer allegiance to the dead than to the living; in that world *I shall abide for ever*. But if thou wilt be guilty of dishonouring laws which *the gods* have stablished in honour. . . ."

To Creon's question, "And thou didst dare to transgress the law?" she answers not by referring to her personal feeling but to the absolute supremacy of the eternal moral order which cannot be cancelled by civil laws: "For it was not Zeus that had published me that edict: not such are the laws set among men by the Justice who dwells with the gods below; nor deemed I that thy decrees were of such force, that a mortal could override the unwritten and unfailing statutes of heaven."

As for Creon, he certainly does not represent the principle of the state, the moral basis of which is the same as that of the family, though with the advantage of a fuller realisation. He is the representative of the state that has become perverted or has put itself into a false position — of the state that has *forgotten its place*. But since such perversion does not form part of the essence or the purpose of the state, it can arise only from the evil passions of its representatives — in this case, of Creon. It would then be right to say, in direct opposition to the popular view, that Antigone stands for the universal and Creon for the individual element. Both statements, however, would be incorrect and inexact. It is clear that the opposition between the individual and society, the particular and the general, does not as such ever correspond to reality. The true opposition and conflict is not sociological but purely moral; it is the conflict between good and evil, each of which finds expression both in the individual and in the social life. Cain killed Abel not because he represented the principle of individuality as against the family union — for in that case all developed 'personalities' would have to kill their brothers; he killed him because he stood for the principle of *evil*, which may manifest itself both individually and collectively, privately or publicly. Creon in his turn forbade the citizens to fulfil certain religiously-moral duties, not because he was the head of the state, but because he was wicked and followed the same principle which was active in Cain previously to any state. Every law is of course a state enactment, but Creon's position is determined not by the fact that he enacted a law, but that he enacted an *impious* law. This is not the fault of the state-power but of Creon's own moral worthlessness; for it could hardly be maintained that the function of the state consists precisely in enacting impious and inhuman laws.

Creon then does not stand for the principle of the state but for the principle of evil which is rooted in the personal will, though it also finds expression and embodiment in the life of the community — in the present case in the form of a bad law of the state. On the other hand, Antigone, who lays down her life for the fulfilment of a religious and moral duty that lies at the basis of social life, is simply the representative of the principle of good, which is also rooted in the personal will, but is realised in the true communal life.

All human conflict is *in the last resort* reducible not to the relative sociological oppositions but to the absolute opposition of the good and self-asserting evil. The inmost essence of the question is always one and the same; but it does not follow that the various historical situations in which it is revealed again and again are therefore devoid of interest and importance of their own even from the ethical point of view. The inner essence of good and evil can be clearly known only through their typical manifestations. Thus, the evil which expresses itself as the perversion of the idea of the state, or as putting the law of the state above the law of morality, is quite a specific form of evil. It is a higher grade of evil than, for instance, a simple murder or even fratricide; but precisely because it is more complex and subtle, it is more excusable from the subjective point of view and is less blameworthy than the cruder crimes. Therefore Creon, for instance, though socially he is more pernicious, is personally less guilty than Cain.

There is another important shade of meaning in this profound tragedy. Speaking generally, the state is a higher stage of historical development than the clan. This higher stage had just been attained in Greece. The memory of how it came to be established, of the struggle and the triumph, is still fresh in the minds of its representatives. This recent victory of the new over the old, of the higher over the lower, is not merely accidental. In view of the obvious advantages of the state union over the feuds of the clans, its triumph is recognised as something necessary, rightful, and progressive. Hence Creon's self-confidence at the beginning of the play. The bad law proclaimed by him, putting as it does the loyalty to the new state above the original religious duties, is not merely an abuse of the power of the state, but an abuse of *victory* — not of the local victory of the Thebans over the Argives, but of the general victory of the state order — of the city state — over the clan. Creon cannot therefore be looked upon simply as a tyrant, or as a representative of personal arbitrariness and material power — and this is not the way in which the ancients regarded him.[8] The law he enacted was supposed to be the expression of the common will of the citizens. The short preface by Aristophanes the grammarian, usually placed at the beginning of the tragedy, begins thus: "Antigone who buried Polyneices *against the order of the city* (or the state) — παρὰ τὴν πρόσταξιν τῆς πόλεως." In the play itself, Ismene justifies her refusal to help Antigone by saying that she cannot do violence to the will of her fellow-citizens. Creon, too, bases his argument not upon the principle of autocracy but upon the unconditional significance of patriotism: "If any makes a friend of more account than his fatherland, that man has no place in my regard."

The ethico-psychological basis of the bad law lies of course in Creon's bad will. This will, however, is not merely senseless and arbitrary but is connected with a general although a false idea according to which the power of the state and the laws of the state are higher than the moral law. Creon formulates this false idea with perfect clearness: "Whomsoever the city may appoint, that man must be obeyed, in little things and great, in just things and *unjust.*"

This idea, outrageously false as it is, has been and still is the inspiration of men who have not even Creon's excuse, namely, intoxication with the recent victory of the state order over the tribal anarchy. In those half-historical times no clear protest — such as Sophocles puts into the mouth of his Antigone — may have been raised by the better consciousness against this idea, but, at the epoch of Sophocles himself, the best minds were well aware that historical progress in bringing about new forms of society cannot possibly supersede the essential foundations of all social life. They understood that although such progress is both important and necessary, it is relative and subordinate to a higher purpose, and that it loses all justification when it is turned against the unconditional moral good, the realisation of which is the sole object of the historical development. And however highly we might value those who

---

8. It will be remembered that the Greek word τύραννος did not originally have a bad meaning, but designated every monarch. In the same trilogy of Sophocles, the first play is called Οἰδίπους τύραννος, which is rightly translated *Oedipus rex;* and the word ought to be translated in the same way in the *Antigone* in reference to Creon.

further the triumphant march of progress, the highest dignity of man, worthy of whole-hearted sympathy and approval, consists not in winning temporal victories, but in observing *eternal limits* equally sacred both for the past and for the future.

The Chief Moments in the Historical Development of the Individual-Social Consciousness

I

With the establishment of the national state the moral outlook of the individual is no doubt considerably widened and a greater field is opened for the exercise of his good feelings and of his active will in moral conduct. The conception of the deity becomes higher and more general, a certain religious development takes place. Altruism, or moral solidarity with other human beings, increases quantitatively or in extension and becomes qualitatively higher, losing its dominant character of natural instinct and being directed upon invisible and ideal objects — the state, the fatherland. These ideal objects are concretely realised in the unity of language, customs, in the actual representatives of authority, etc., but, as is clear to every one, they are not exhausted by these concrete facts. The nation does not disappear with the change of its customs, the state does not cease to exist when its particular rulers pass away. The spiritual nature and the ideal significance of objects such as the nation and the state are preserved in any case, and the individual's moral relation to them, expressing itself as true patriotism or civic virtue, is in this sense, other conditions being equal, a higher stage of morality than the simple feeling of kinship or of the blood-tie. On the other hand, however, it is often pointed out that as the range of moral relations or the social environment becomes wider, the inner personal basis of morality loses its living force and reality. It is urged that the intensity of moral motives is in inverse ratio to their objective extension; that it is impossible to love one's country as sincerely and immediately as one's friends or relatives, and that the living interest in one's private welfare can never be compared with the abstract interest in the welfare of the state, not to speak of the general welfare of humanity. The interest in the latter is indeed often denied as fictitious.

Leaving aside for the moment the question of humanity, it must be admitted that the argument concerning the inverse relation between the intensity and the extension of moral feelings has a foundation in fact. But to be correctly understood it requires the following three reservations:

(1) Independently of the relation of individual persons, taken separately, to the more or less wide social whole, there exists *collective* morality, which embraces these persons in their totality — as a crowd or as a people. There is such a thing as the criminal crowd, upon which the criminologists have now turned their attention; still more prominent is the senseless crowd, the human herd; but there is also the splendid, the heroic crowd. The crowd excited by brutal or bestial instincts lowers the spiritual level of individuals that are drawn into it. But the human mass animated by collectively-moral motives lifts up to its level individuals in whom these motives are, as such, devoid of genuine force. At the kinship-group stage, the striving of the best men for a wider collective morality conditions the appearance of the state or the nation, but once this new social whole, real and powerful in spite of its ideal nature, has been created, *it begins to exert direct influence not only upon the best, but also upon the average and even the bad men that form part of it.*

(2) Apart from collective morality, the quantitative fact that most men taken separately are bad patriots and poor citizens, is qualitatively counterbalanced by the few high instances of true patriotism and civic virtue which could not have arisen in the primitive conditions of life, and only became possible when the state, the nation, the fatherland had come into being.

(3) Finally, whether the moral gain obtained by the widening of the social environment in the national state be great or small, it is in any case a *gain*. The good contained in the tribal morality is not annulled by this extension but is merely modified and made more pure as it assumes the form of family ties and virtues, which are supplemented and not replaced by patriotism. Thus, even from the individual point of view, our love for millions of our fellow-citizens, even though it cannot be as great as our love for some dozens of our friends, is a direct gain, for the wider love that is less intense does not destroy the more intense one. Consequently, from whatever point of view we look at it, the extension of the sphere of life from the limits of the clan to the state unquestionably means moral progress. This progress is apparent both in man's relation to the gods and to his neighbours, and also, as will be presently shown, in man's relation to his lower material nature.

II

The moral principle which demands from man subordination to the higher and solidarity with his neighbours, requires him to dominate physical nature as the basis upon which reason works. This domination has for its immediate object the body of the individual himself — hence ascetic morality in the narrow sense of the term. But the material life of the single individual is only a portion of the general material life that surrounds him, and to separate this portion from the whole is neither logically legitimate nor practically possible. So long as the outer nature completely overwhelms man, who, helpless and lost in virginal forests among wild beasts, is compelled to think of nothing but the preservation and maintenance of his existence, the thought of the mastery of the spirit over the flesh can hardly even arise, let alone the attempt to carry it out. Man who starves from need is not given to fasting for ascetic purposes. Suffering all kinds of privations from his birth onwards, living under the constant menace of violent death, man in the savage state is an unconscious and involuntary ascetic, and his marvellous endurance has as little moral worth as the sufferings of small fish pursued by pikes or sharks.

The manifestation of the inner moral power of the spirit over the flesh presupposes that man is to a certain extent secure from the destructive powers of external nature. Now such security cannot be attained by a single individual — it requires social union. Although ascetic morality in some of its aspects seeks to sever the social ties, it is clear that such a striving could only have arisen on the basis of an already existing society. Both in India of the Brahmins and in Christian Egypt ascetic hermits were the product of a civilised social environment. They had spiritually outgrown it, but without it they themselves would have been historically and physically impossible. Solitary hermits who had voluntarily forsaken society for the desert by their very presence subdued wild beasts, which had no reason whatever for being subdued by the enforced solitude of vagrant savages, inferior to them in physical strength, but inwardly very much on their level. For the victory both over evil beasts without and over evil passions within a certain amount of civilisation was necessary, which could be attained only through the development of social life. Consequently ascetic morality is not the work of the individual taken in the abstract; it can only be manifested by man as a social being. The inner foundations of the good in man do not depend upon the forms of social life, but the actual realisation of them does presuppose such forms.

At the early beginnings of social life — at the kinship-group stage — ascetic morality is purely negative in character. In addition to the regulation of the sexual life by marriage, we find prohibitions of certain kinds of food (*e.g.*

of the 'totemic' animals, connected with a given social group as its protecting spirits or as the incarnation of its ancestors), and also the restriction of meat foods to sacrificial feasts (thus, among the Semitic peoples especially, the flesh of domestic animals was originally for religious uses only.[1])

But in the conditions of the tribal life asceticism could not from the very nature of the case go beyond such elementary restrictions. So long as personal dignity finds its realisation in a social organisation determined by kinship, or, at any rate, is conditioned by it, there can be no question of the ideal of complete continence or of the moral duty to struggle with such passions upon which the very existence of the tribe depends. The virtuous tribesman must be distinguished by vindictiveness and acquisitiveness, and has no right to dream of perfect purity. The ideal representative of tribal morality is the Biblical Jacob, who had two wives and several concubines, who begat twelve sons, and increased the family property without troubling about the means whereby he did it.

The formation of the state had an enormous, though indirect, influence upon ascetic morality in the wide sense of the term, *i.e.* upon that aspect of morality which is concerned with the material nature of man and of the world, and aims at the complete mastery of the rational spirit over the blind material forces. Power over nature is utterly impossible for a lonely savage or for the bestial man, and only a rudimentary degree of it is acquired at the barbarous stage of the tribal life. Under the conditions of civilised existence in strong and extensive political unions it becomes considerable and lasting, and is continually on the increase. The means of spiritual development for the individual, the school of practical asceticism for the masses of the people, and the beginning of subjugating the earth for humanity, are to be found in the military and theocratic empires which united men into large groups for carrying on the work of civilisation in four different quarters of the globe — between the Blue and the Yellow rivers, between the Indus and the Ganges, between the Tigris and Euphrates, and, finally, in the valley of the Nile. These military and theocratic monarchies — which Arakcheev's 'military settlements'[2] recalled to us in miniature — were, of course, very far from the

---

1. See W. Robertson Smith, *Lectures on the Religion of the Semites,* first series, *The Fundamental Institution* (London, 1889).

2. The so-called 'military settlements' were villages in which every peasant was compelled to be a soldier and to live under military discipline. Minute regulations with regard to domestic life, work, dress, etc., were enforced with ruthless severity and made the life of the settlers intolerable. The idea of establishing military settlements belonged to Alexander I and was carried out by Arakcheev, his favourite, who founded the first settlement in 1810. Military settlements were finally abolished by Alexander II in 1857. — *Editor's note.*

ideal of human society. But their great historical importance as a necessary moral school for primitive humanity is recognised even by the champions of absolute anarchism.[3]

Speaking generally, *in order to rise above the compulsory form of social morality, savage humanity had to pass through it — in order to outgrow despotism it had to experience it.* More particularly, three considerations are undoubtedly involved here. (1) The harder the original struggle with primitive nature was, the more necessary it was for men to be united into wide but closely-connected communities. And the wide extension of a social group could be combined with an intimate and strong tie between its members only by means of the strictest *discipline,* supported by the most powerful of all sanctions, namely, the religious sanction. Therefore political unions which had for the first time subdued wild nature and laid the corner-stone of human culture were bound to have the character of a religious and military monarchy, or of compulsory theocracy. This work of civilisation done under the pressure of the moral and the material needs — this 'Egyptian labour' — was by its very nature a school of human solidarity for the masses and, from the point of view of its objective purpose and result, it was the first achievement of collective asceticism in humanity, the first historical triumph of reason over the blind forces of matter.

(2) The compulsory character of this collective achievement prevents us from ascribing ideal worth to it, but does not altogether deprive it of moral significance. For compulsion was not merely material. It rested in the last resort upon the faith of the masses themselves in the divine character of the power which compelled them to work. However imperfect in its form and content that faith might be, to subordinate one's life to it, to endure at its behest all kinds of privation and hardship, is in any case a moral course of action. Both its general historical result and its inner psychological effect upon each individual composing the mass of the people had the character of true, though imperfect, asceticism — that is, of victory of the spiritual principle over the carnal. If the innumerable Chinese genuinely believe that their Emperor is the son of the sky; if the Hindus were seriously convinced that the priests sprang from the head of Brahma and the kings and princes from his arms; if the Assyrian king really was in the eyes of his people the incarnation

---

3. I would like especially to mention the interesting book by Leon Metchnikov, *La Civilisation et les grands fleuves* (Civilization and the great rivers) (Paris, 1889). See my article about it, "Iz istorii philosophii" (Concerning the philosophy of history), in the *Voprosi Philosophii* (1891), and also Professor Vinogradov's article in the same magazine. One worthy critic imagined that in speaking of the military theocracy as the historical school of asceticism I was referring to the *personal intentions* of the Egyptian Pharaohs and Chaldean kings!

of the national deity Assur, and the Pharaoh truly was for the Egyptians the manifestation of the solar deity — then absolute submission to such rulers was for these peoples a religiously-moral duty, and compulsory work at their command an ascetic practice. This, however, did not apply to slaves in the strict sense — prisoners of war to whom their masters' gods were *strange gods*. And even apart from this national limitation the whole structure of these primitive religiously-political unions was essentially imperfect because the gods who received the voluntary and involuntary human sacrifices (both in the figurative and in the literal sense) did not possess absolute inner worth. They stood merely for the infinity of force, not for the infinity of goodness. Man is morally superior to such gods by his power of renunciation; and therefore in sacrificing himself for these gods and their earthly representatives he does not find the higher for the sake of which it is worth while to sacrifice the lower. If the meaning of the sacrifice is to be found in the progress of civilisation, this meaning is purely relative, for progress itself is obviously only a means, a way, a direction, and not the absolute and final goal. But human personality contains an element of intrinsic value, which can never be merely a means — the possibility, namely, inherent in it, of infinite perfection through the contemplation of and union with the absolute fulness of being. A society in which this significance of personality is not recognised and in which the individual is regarded as having only a relative value, as a means for political and cultural ends — even the most lofty ones, — cannot be the ideal human society but is merely a transient stage of the historical development. This is particularly true of the military and theocratic monarchies with which universal history begins.

(3) The primitive forms of the religiously-political union were so imperfect that they made further progress inevitable, and at the same time they naturally produced the external conditions necessary for that progress. Within the limits of the tribal life each member of a given social group was both physically and morally compelled to prey, plunder, and kill, to fight wild beasts, breed cattle, and produce numerous offspring. Obviously there was no room there for the higher spiritual development of the human personality. It only became possible when, with the compulsory division of labour in the great religiously-political organisations of the past, there arose, in addition to the masses doomed to hard physical work, the leisurely, propertied class of free men. By the side of warriors there appeared professional priests, scribes, diviners, etc., among whom the higher consciousness was first awakened. This great historical moment is recorded in the Bible in the significant and majestic story of the best representative of the patriarchal order, Abraham, with the crowd of his armed dependants, bowing down before the priest of

the Most High, Melchizedek, who was *without descent* and came before him with the gifts of the new higher culture — bread and wine and the spiritual blessing of Truth and Peace.[4]

While by the sword of the great conquerors the hard collective work of the masses was gradually made to extend over a wider and wider area, securing the external material success of human culture, the inner work of thought among the leisured and peaceful representatives of the nationally-theocratic states was leading human consciousness to a more perfect ideal of individual and social *universalism*.

III

In the course of world-history the first awakening of human self-consciousness took place in the land where its sleep had most abounded with fantastic and wild dreams — in India. To the overwhelming variety of Indian mythology corresponded a confusing variety of religious, political, and customary forms and conditions of life. Nowhere else had the theocratic order been so complex and burdensome, so full of national and class exclusiveness. Not from Egypt or China, not from the Chaldeans, Phoenicians, or the Greco-Roman world, but from India have we borrowed conceptions expressive of the extreme degree of separation between the classes of men[5] and of the denial of human dignity. The 'pariahs' were deprived of human dignity as standing outside the law; men belonging to castes within the law and even to the highest of them were deprived of all freedom owing to a most complex system of religious and customary rites and regulations. But the more narrow and artificial the fetters fashioned by the spirit for itself and out of itself the more they testify to its inner strength and to the fact that nothing external can finally bind and conquer it. The spirit awakes from the nightmare of sacrificial rites, compulsory actions, and ascetic tortures, and says to itself: All this is my own invention which in my sleep I took to be reality; if only I can keep awake, the fear and the pain will vanish. But what will then remain? A subtle and significant, though not at first sight a clear, answer is given to this question by *the religion of awakening*. It perpetuates the moment when human personality turns from external objects into itself and comes to know its purely negative or for-

---

4. I am referring here, of course, simply to the historical meaning of the fact, and not to its mystical significance. [See Genesis 14:17-20. — *Editor's note.*]

5. Although the word *caste* is Portuguese and not Indian, it had arisen (in the sense in question) precisely for the designation of the social relations of India.

mal infinity devoid of all definite content. The individual is aware of his infinitude, freedom, and universality simply because he transcends all given determination, relation, and character, because he is conscious of something within himself which is more and higher than this caste, this nationality, this cult, this manner of life — of something that is higher than *all this*. Whatever objective determination a self-conscious person might put before himself, he does not stop there; he knows that he had himself posited it and that his own creation is not worthy of him and therefore he forsakes it: *'all is empty.'* All that belongs to the external world is rejected, nothing is found to be worthy of existence, but man's spiritual power of rejecting remains; and it is very significant that Buddhism recognises this power not as belonging to the solitary individual, but as having an individually-social form of the so-called *Triratna, i.e.* 'three jewels' or 'three treasures,' in which every Buddhist must believe: "I take my refuge in the Buddha; I take my refuge in the doctrine or the law *(Dharma);* I take my refuge in the order of the disciples *(Sangha).*" Thus even in the consciousness of its negative infinity human personality cannot remain separate and isolated, but by means of a universal doctrine is inevitably led to a social organisation.

All is deception except three things that are worthy of belief: (1) the spiritually-awakened man; (2) the word of awakening; (3) the brotherhood of those who are awake. This is the true essence of Buddhism which still nurtures millions of souls in distant Asia.[6] This is the first lasting stage of human universalism that rose above the national and political exclusiveness of the religious and social life.

Born in the country of caste, Buddhism did not in the least reject the division of society into castes, or seek to destroy it; its followers simply ceased to believe in the principle of that organisation, in the absolute hereditary inequality of the classes. Appearing in the midst of a nation with a distinct character of its own, it did not reject nationality, but simply transferred human consciousness into the domain of other, universal and super-national

---

6. It should be noted, by the way, that after the fashion set by Schopenhauer, who was prejudiced in favour of Buddhism, the number of Buddhists is usually exaggerated beyond all measure; one hears of 400, 600, 700 million followers of this religion. These figures would be probable were China and Japan wholly populated by Buddhists. In truth, however, the teaching of Buddha in its various modifications is the religion of the masses only in Ceylon, Indo-China, Nepal, Tibet, Mongolia, and among the Bouriats and Kalmucks; this amounts at most to 75 or 80 millions. In China and Japan Buddhism is simply one of the permitted religions which is more or less closely followed by the educated people, who do not, however, give up their national cult; in a similar manner in Russia, for instance, under Alexander I many Orthodox people used to frequent the meetings of the Freemasons.

ideas. In consequence of this, this Indian religion, the outcome of Hindu philosophy, was able, when finally rejected in India, to take root among many various peoples of different race and different historic education.

The negative infinity of human personality had been apparent to individual philosophers before the time of Buddhism.[7] But it was in Buddhism that this view found its first historical expression in the collective life of humanity. Owing to his morally-practical universalism which proceeded from the heart even more than from the mind, Buddha Sakya-muni created a form of common life hitherto unknown in humanity — the brotherhood of beggar-monks from every caste and nation, — the 'listeners' (Shravaki) of the true doctrine, the followers of the true way. Here for the first time the worth of the individual and his relation to society were finally determined not by the *fact* of being born into a certain class or a definite national and political organisation, but by the inner *act* of choosing a certain moral ideal. The theoretical conceptions of the first Buddha and the conditions of life of his monastic brotherhood have undergone a number of changes in the course of history, but the moral essence of his teaching and work has remained in a clear-cut, crystallised form in the Lamaian monasteries of Mongolia and Tibet.

The moral essence of Buddhism as an individually-social system has, during the two and a half thousand years of its historical existence, evinced itself as the feeling of religious reverence for the blessed master, who was the first to awake to the true meaning of reality, and is the spiritual progenitor of all who subsequently became awake; as the demand for holiness or perfect *absence of will* (inner asceticism in contradistinction to the external mortification of the flesh which had been and still is practised by the 'Gymnosophists,' and which did not satisfy Buddha Sakya-muni); and, finally, as the commandment of universal benevolence or kindly compassion for all beings. It is

7. Many fantastic ideas used to prevail with regard to the antiquity of the Hindu philosophy, but they are beginning to disappear in the light of the more scientific inquiry. Most of their philosophic wealth the Hindus acquired in later times, partly under the direct influence of Greeks after Alexander the Great, and partly later still with the help of the Arabs who brought Aristotle to the East no less than to the West. But, on the other hand, there is no doubt that even the Greeks — not to speak of Arabs — on their first acquaintance with India found there a peculiar local philosophy of the 'naked wise men' *(Gymnosophists)* as a typical and traditional institution of ancient standing. From their outward appearance these Indian adamites cannot be identified with the followers of Buddhism; most probably they were adepts of ascetic mysticism — Yoga, which existed before the time of Buddha. Still more ancient was the pantheism of the Upanishads. There is ground to believe that the immediate forerunner of Sakya-muni was the author of the system of spiritualistic dualism (expounded in Sankya-Karika), although the person and even the name of this sage — Kapila — are somewhat doubtful.

this latter, the simplest and most attractive aspect of Buddhism, that brings to light the defects of the whole doctrine.

IV

What, from the Buddhistic point of view, is the difference between the man who is spiritually awake and the man who is not? The latter, influenced by the delusions of sense, takes apparent and transitory distinctions to be real and final, and therefore desires some things and fears others, is attracted and repelled, feels love and hate. The one who has awakened from these dream emotions understands that their objects are illusory and is therefore at rest. Finding nothing upon which it would be worth his while to concentrate his will, he becomes free from all willing, preference, and fear, and therefore loses all cause for dissension, anger, enmity and hatred, and, free from these passions, he experiences for everything, without exception, the same feeling of benevolence or compassion. But why should he experience precisely *this* feeling? Having convinced himself that *all is empty,* that the objective conditions of existence are vain and illusory, the awakened sage ought to enter a state of perfect *impassibility,* equally free both from malice and from pity. For both these opposed feelings equally presuppose to begin with a conviction of the reality of living beings; secondly, their distinction from one another (*e.g.* the distinction between the man who suffers in his ignorance and appeals to my pity, and the perfectly blessed Buddha who stands in no need of it); and, thirdly, pity, no less than malice, prompts us to perform definite actions, determined by the objective qualities and conditions of the given facts. Now all this is absolutely incompatible with the fundamental principle of universal emptiness and indifference. The moral teaching of Buddhism demands active self-sacrifice, which is involved in the very conception of a Buddha. The perfect Buddha — such as Gautama Sakya-muni — differs from the imperfect or solitary Buddha (Pratyeka Buddha) precisely by the fact that he is not satisfied by his own knowledge of the agonising emptiness of existence, but decides to free from this agony all living beings. This decision was preceded in his former incarnations by individual acts of extreme self-sacrifice, descriptions of which abound in Buddhist legends. Thus in one of his previous lives he gave himself up to be devoured by a tiger in order to save a poor woman and her children. Such holy exploits, in contradistinction to the aimless self-destruction of the ancient ascetics of India, are a direct means to the highest bliss for every one who is 'awake.' A well-known and typical story is told of one of the apostles of Buddhism — Arya-Deva. As he was approaching a city, he saw a wounded dog covered with worms. To save the dog without destroying the worms, Arya-Deva cut a piece off his own body and placed the worms upon it. At that moment both the city and the dog disappeared from his eyes, and he entered at once into Nirvana.

Active self-sacrifice out of pity for all living beings, so characteristic of Buddhist morality, cannot be logically reconciled with the fundamental principle of Buddhism — the doctrine that all things are empty and indifferent. To feel equal pity for every one, beginning with Brahma and Indra, and ending with a worm, is certainly not opposed to the principle of indifference but as soon as the feeling of universal compassion becomes the work of mercy, the indifference must be given up. If instead of a dog with worms, Arya-Deva had met a man suffering from vice and ignorance, pity for *this* living creature would require from him not a piece of his flesh, but words of true doctrine — while to address words of rational persuasion to a hungry worm would be no less absurd than to feed with his own flesh a man not hungry but erring. *Equal pity to all beings demands not the same, but quite a different active relation to each one of them.* Even for a Buddhist this difference proves to be not merely illusory, for he too would certainly admit that had Arya-Deva not distinguished a worm or a dog from a human being, and offered moral books to suffering animals, he would hardly be likely to have performed any holy exploit and deserved Nirvana. *All-embracing pity* necessarily involves *discriminating truth,* which gives each his due: a piece of meat to the animal, and words of spiritual awakening to the rational being. But we cannot stop at this. Pity for every one compels me to desire for all and each the supreme and final blessedness which consists not in satiety, but in complete freedom from the pain of limited existence and of the necessity of rebirth. This freedom, this only true blessedness, the worm — so long as it remains a worm — cannot attain; it is possible only to a self-conscious and rational being. Therefore if I am to extend my pity to the lower creatures, I cannot be content with simply alleviating their suffering at a given moment. I must help them to attain the final end through rebirth in higher forms. But the objective conditions of existence are rejected by Buddhism as an illusion and empty dream, and consequently the ascent of living beings up the ladder of rebirths depends exclusively on their own actions (the law of *Karma*). The form of the worm is the necessary outcome of former sins, and no help from without can lift that worm to the higher stage of dog or elephant. Buddha himself could directly act only upon rational self-conscious beings, and that only in the sense that his preaching enabled them to accept or to reject the truth, and, in the first case, to escape from the torture of rebirth, and, in the second, continue to endure it. The work of salvation that those who are 'awake' can accomplish amounts simply to pushing their sleeping neighbours, some of whom are awakened by it, while others merely exchange one series of bad dreams for another, still more agonising.

The principle of active pity for all living beings, however true it is in itself can, from the Buddhist point of view, have no real application. We are utterly incapable of bringing true salvation to the lower creatures, and our power of influencing rational creatures in this respect is extremely limited. Whatever their commandments and legends may be, the very formula of the faith[8] indicates that the true sphere of moral relations and activity is for the Buddhist limited to the brotherhood of those who, like himself, are 'awake,' and support one another in a peaceful life of contemplation — the last remainder of their former activities — before they finally pass into Nirvana.

V

The significance of Buddhism in world-history lies in the fact that in it the human individual was for the first time valued not as the member of a tribe, a caste, a state, but as the bearer of a higher consciousness, as a being capable of awakening from the deceptive dream of everyday existence, of becoming free from the chain of causality. This is true of man belonging to any caste or nationality, and in this sense the Buddhist religion signalises a new stage in the history of the world — the universal as opposed to the particular tribal or national stage. It is clear, however, that the universality of Buddhism is merely abstract or negative in character. It proclaims the principle of indifference, rejects the importance of caste or national distinctions, gathers into a new religious community men of all colours and classes — and then leaves everything as it was before. The problem of gathering together the *disjecta membra* of humanity and forming out of them a new and higher kingdom, is not even contemplated. Buddhism does not go beyond the universalism of a monastic order. When the transition is effected from the clan to the state, the former independent social wholes — the clans — enter as subordinate parts into the new and higher whole, the organised political union. Similarly, the third and highest stage of human development — the universal — demands that states and nations should enter as constituent parts into the all-embracing new organisation. Otherwise, however broad the theoretical principles might be, the positive significance in concrete life will entirely remain with the already existing national and political groups. 'All men' and, still more, 'all living beings'

8. See above.

will simply be an abstract idea symbolically expressed by the monastery that is severed from life. Buddhism remains perfectly strange to the task of truly uniting all living beings, or even the scattered parts of humanity, in a new, universal kingdom. It therefore proves to be merely the first rudimentary stage of the human understanding of life.

The personality manifests here its infinite worth in so far as the absolute self negates all limitation, in so far as it asserts, "I am not bound by anything, I have experienced all things, and know that all is an empty dream and I am above it all." *Negation of existence through the knowledge of it* — this is in what, from the Buddhist point of view, the absolute nature of the human spirit consists. It lifts man above all earthly creatures and even above all gods, for they are gods by nature only, while the awakened sage becomes god through his own act of consciousness and will: he is an *auto-god, a god self-made.* All creation is material for the exercise of will and of knowledge, by means of which the individual is to become divine. Single individuals who have entered upon the path that leads to this end form the normal society or brotherhood (the monastic order) which is included in the Buddhist confession of faith (I take my refuge . . . in the Sangha). But this society obviously has significance temporarily only, until its members attain perfection; in Nirvana communal life, like all other determinations, must disappear altogether. In so far as the absolute character of the personality is understood in Buddhism in the negative sense only, as freedom from all things, the individual stands in no need of completion. All his relations to other persons simply form a ladder which is pushed away as soon as the height of absolute indifference is attained. The negative character of the Buddhist ideal renders morality itself, as well as all social life, a thing of purely transitory and conditional significance.

The religiously-moral feeling of reverence *(pietas)* has in Buddhism no true and abiding object. The sage who knows all things and has become free from everything finds no longer anything to worship. When Buddha Sakyamuni attained to the supreme understanding, not only Indra with the host of all the Vedanta deities, but the supreme god of the all-powerful priests, Brahma, came like a humble listener to hear the new doctrine, and, becoming enlightened, worshipped the teacher. And yet Buddha was a man, who by his own power became god or reached the absolute state — and this is the supreme goal for every human being. Buddhists reverence the memory and the relics of their teacher to the point of idolatry, but this is possible only so long as the worshippers are still imperfect. The perfect Buddhist who has attained Nirvana no longer differs from Buddha himself, and loses any and all objects of religious feeling. Therefore, in principle, the Buddhist ideal destroys the possibility of the religious relation, and, in its inmost essence, Buddhism is not only a religion of negation, but a religion of self-negation.

The altruistic part of morality also disappears at the higher stages of the true way, for then all distinctions are seen to be illusory, including those which evoke in us a feeling of pity towards certain objects, events, and states. "Be merciful to all beings," proclaims the elementary moral teaching of the Sutras. "There are no beings, and all feeling is the fruit of ignorance," declares the higher metaphysics of Abhidhamma.[9] Not even the ascetic morality has positive justification in Buddhism, in spite of its monasteries. These monasteries are simply places of refuge for contemplative souls who have given up worldly vanity and are awaiting their entrance into Nirvana. But the positive moral asceticism — struggle with the flesh for strengthening the spirit and *spiritualising the body* — lies altogether outside the range of Buddhist thought. The spirit is for it only the knower, and the body a phantom known as such. Bodily death, the sight of which had so struck Prince Siddhartha, merely proves that life is illusion, from which we must become free; but no Buddhist would dream of resurrection. If, however, the supreme goal of asceticism is absent, the means towards it can have no significance. From the point of view of absolute indifference ascetic rules, like all other, lose their own inherent meaning. They are preserved in the external practice of Buddhism simply as pedagogical means for spiritual babes, or as the historical legacy of Brahmanism. The perfect Buddhist will certainly not refrain from plentiful food, or distinguish between meat and vegetable diet. It is very remarkable that according to the legend, the truth of which there is no reason to doubt, the founder of this religion, which is supposed to demand strict vegetarianism, died of having unwisely partaken of pig's flesh.

VI

Like every negative doctrine Buddhism is dependent upon what it denies — upon this material world, this sensuous and mortal life. "All this is illusion," it repeats — and it gets no further, for to it this illusion is everything. It knows with certainty only what it denies. Of what it affirms, of what it regards as not illusory, it has no positive idea at all, but determines it negatively only: Nirvana is inaction, immovability, stillness, non-existence. Buddhism knows

---

9. The Buddhist doctrine is divided into three sections of the Holy Law, called, therefore, 'The three baskets' (Tripitaka): Sutra contains the moral doctrine, Vinâya the monastic rules, and Abhidhamma the transcendental wisdom.

only the lower, the illusory; the higher and the perfect it does not know, but merely *demands* it. Nirvana is only a postulate, and not the idea of the absolute good. The *idea* came from the Greeks and not from the Hindus.

Human reason, having discovered its own universal and absolute nature by rejecting everything finite and particular, could not rest content with this first step. From the consciousness that material existence is illusory it was bound to pass to that which is not illusory, to that for the sake of which it rejected deceptive appearance. In Indian Buddhism the personality finds its absolute significance in the rejection of being that is unworthy of it. In Greek thought, which found its practical embodiment in Socrates, and was put into a theoretical form by his pupil, the absolute value of personality is justified by the affirmation of being that is worthy of it — of the world of ideas and ideal relations. Greek idealism no less than Buddhism realises that all transitory things are illusory, that the flux of material reality is only the phantom of being, is essentially non-being (τὸ μὴ ὄν). The practical pessimism of the Buddhist is entirely shared by the Greek consciousness.

"Whoso craves the ampler length of life, not content to desire a modest span, him will I judge with no uncertain voice: he cleaves to folly. For the long days lay up full many things nearer grief than joy; but as for thy delights, their place shall know them no more, when a man's life hath lapsed beyond the fitting term."[10]

Although there is here involved the conception of *measure* so characteristic of the Greek mind, reflection does not stop at this. Not only a disproportionately long life, but *all* life is nothing but pain.

"Not to be born is, past all prizing, best; but when a man hath seen the light, this is next best by far, that with all speed he should go thither, whence he hath come.

"For when he hath seen youth go by, with its light follies, what troublous affliction is strange to his lot, what suffering is not therein? — envy, frictions, strife, battles, and slaughters; and last of all, age claims him for her own — age, dispraised, infirm, unsociable, unfriended, with whom all woe of woe abides."[11]

It was as clear to the Greek higher consciousness as to the Hindu that human will blindly striving for material satisfaction cannot find it under any material conditions, and that therefore the real good from this point of view is not the enjoyment of life but the absence of life.

"The Deliverer comes at the last to all alike — when the doom of Hades is

10. The *Oedipus Coloneus.*
11. *Ibid.*

suddenly revealed, without marriage song, or lyre, or dance — even Death at the last."[12]

This pessimistic conception expressed by poetry was also confirmed by Greek philosophy in sentences which have become the alphabetic truths of all idealistic and spiritualistic morality: sensuous life is the prison of the spirit, body is the coffin of the soul, true philosophy is the practice of death, etc. But although the Greek genius appropriated this fundamental conception of Buddhism, it did not stop there. The non-sensuous aspect of reality revealed to it its ideal content. In the place of Nirvana the Greeks put the Cosmos of eternal intelligible essences (Platonic Ideas) or the organism of universal reason (in the philosophy of the Stoics). Human personality now affirms its absolute significance not by merely denying what is false, but by intellectually participating in what is true. The personal bearer of this higher universal consciousness is not the sage-monk who renounces the emptiness of real being, in accordance with the principle of indifference, but the sage-thinker who shares in the fulness of ideal being in the inner unity of its many forms. Neither the one nor the other wishes to live by the senses, but the second lives by his intellect in the world of pure Ideas, that is, of what is worthy of existence, and is therefore true and eternal. It is a dualistic point of view: all that exists has a true positive aspect, in addition to the false, material side. With regard to the latter the Greek philosophers adopt an attitude as negative as the Hindu 'Gymnosophists.' That which to the senses and sensibility is a deceptive appearance contains for reason 'a reflection of the Idea,' according to Plato, or 'the seed of Reason,' according to the Stoics (λόγοι σπερματικοί). Hence in human life there is an opposition between that which is conformable to Ideas and in harmony with Reason, and that which contradicts the ideal norm. The true sage is no longer a simple hermit or a wandering monk, who has renounced life and is mildly preaching the same renunciation to others; he is one who boldly denounces the wrong and irrational things of life. Hence the end is different in the two cases. Buddha Sakya-muni peacefully dies after a meal with his disciples, while Socrates, condemned and put to prison by his fellow-citizens, is sentenced by them to drink a poisoned cup. But in spite of this tragic ending, the attitude of the Greek idealist toward the reality unworthy of him is not one of decisive opposition. The highest representative of humanity at this stage — the philosopher — is conscious of his absolute worth in so far as he lives by pure thought in the truly-existent intelligible realm of Ideas or of the all-embracing rationality, and despises the false, the merely phenomenal being of the material and sensuous world. This

12. *Ibid.*

contempt, when bold and genuine, rouses the anger of the crowd which is wholly engrossed with the lower things, and the philosopher may have to pay for his idealism with his life — as was the case with Socrates. But in any case his attitude toward the unworthy reality is merely one of contempt. The contempt is certainly different in kind from that characteristic of Buddhism. Buddha despises the world because everything is illusion. The very indefiniteness of this judgment, however, takes away its sting. If all is equally worthless, no one in particular is hurt by it, and if nothing but Nirvana is opposed to the bad reality, the latter may sleep in peace. For Nirvana is an absolute state and not the norm for relative states. Now the idealist does possess such a norm and he despises and condemns the life that surrounds him not because it inevitably shares in the illusory character of everything, but because it is abnormal, irrational, opposed to the Idea. Such condemnation is no longer neutral, it has an element of defiance and demand. It is slighting to all who are bound by worldly irrationality and therefore leads to hostility, and sometimes to persecution and the cup with poison.

And yet there is something accidental about this conflict. Socrates condemned Athenian customs all his life long but he was not persecuted for it until he was an old man of seventy; the persecution was obviously due to a change in political circumstances. The irrationality of the Athenian political order was a local peculiarity; the customs of Sparta were better. The greatest of Socrates' pupils, Plato, went later on to Sicily in order to found there, with the help of Dionysius of Syracuse, an ideal state in which philosophers would receive the reins of government instead of a cup of poison. He did not succeed, but on returning to Athens he was able to teach in his academy without hindrance, and lived undisturbed to a profound old age. The disciples of Socrates, as well as other preachers of idealism, never suffered systematic persecution; they were disliked but tolerated. The fact is that idealism by the nature of the case has its centre of gravity in the intelligible world. The opposition it establishes between the normal and the abnormal, the right and the wrong, though comparatively definite, remains essentially intellectual and theoretical. It touches upon the reality it condemns but does not penetrate to the heart of it. We know how superficial were the practical ideals of Plato, the greatest of the idealists. They come much nearer to the bad reality than to what truly is. The realm of Ideas is an all-embracing, absolutely-universal unity; there are no limitations, dissensions, or hostility in it. But Plato's pseudo-ideal state, though involving some bold conceptions and a general beauty of form, is essentially connected with such limitations of which humanity soon freed itself not in idea only but in reality. His kingdom of philosophers is nothing more than a narrow, local, nationally Greek community based upon slavery, constant warfare, and such relations between the sexes as remind one of stables for mating. It is clear that the political problem is not in any inner connection with Plato's main interest and that he does not really care in what way men are going to live upon earth, where truth does not and will not dwell. He finds his own true satisfaction in the contemplation of eternal intelligible truth. The natural impulse to realise or embody truth in the environment is checked by two considerations, which idealism necessarily involves. The first is the conviction that though the ideal truth can be reflected from or impressed upon the surface of real existence, it cannot become substantially incarnate in it. The second is the belief that our own spirit is connected with this reality in a purely transitory and external fashion, and therefore can have no absolute task to fulfil in it.

The dying Socrates rejoiced at leaving this world of false appearance for the realm of what truly is. Such an attitude obviously excludes in the last resort all practical activity; there can in that case be neither any obligation nor any desire to devote oneself to the changing of this life, to the salvation of this world. Platonic idealism, like Buddhist nihilism, lifts up human personality to the level of the absolute, but does not create for it a social environment corresponding to its absolute significance. The brotherhood of monks, like the state of philosophers, is merely a temporal compromise of the sage with the false existence. His true satisfaction is in the pure indifference of Nirvana, or in the purely intelligible world of Ideas. Are we to say, then, that for idealism too the actual life is devoid of meaning? We discover at this point so great an inner contradiction in the idealistic line of thought that human consciousness is unable to stop at this stage and to accept it as the highest truth.

VII

If the world in which we live did not share in the ideal or the true being at all, idealism itself would be impossible. The direct representative of the ideal principle in this world is, of course, the philosopher himself, who contemplates that which truly is. But the philosopher did not drop down from heaven; his reason is only the highest expression of the universal human reason embodied in *the word* which is an essentially universal fact and is the real idea or the sensible reason. This was clearly perceived by Heraclitus, worked out and explained by Socrates, Plato, Aristotle, and Zeno the Stoic. But the presence of the higher principle is not limited to the human world. The purposive organisation and movements of living creatures and the general teleological connection of events provided Socrates himself with his favourite argument for proving the presence of reason in the world. The ideal principle, however, is found not only where there is evidence of purpose; it extends to all determinate being and excludes only the principle directly opposed to it — the unlimited, the chaos (τὸ ἄπειρον = τὸ μὴ ὄν).[13] Measure, limit, norm, necessarily involve Reason and Idea. But if so, the opposition, so essential for idealism, between the world of sensible appearances and the world of intelligible essences proves to be relative and changeable. Since all determinate existence participates in Ideas, the difference can only be in the degree of the participation. A plant or an animal exhibits a greater wealth of definitely-thought content, and stands in more complex and intimate relations to all other things than a simple stone or an isolated natural event. Therefore we must admit that animal and vegetable organisms have a greater share of the Idea or a greater degree of ideality than a stone or a pool of water. Further, every human being as possessing the power of speech or capable of rational thought, presents, as compared with an animal, a greater degree of ideality. The same relation holds between an ignorant man given to passions and vices and the philosopher whose word is an expression of reason not only in the formal sense but in its concrete application. Finally, even philosophers differ from one another in the degree to which they have mastered the higher truth. This difference in *the degree of rationality* in the world, ranging from a cobblestone to the 'divine' Plato, is not anything meaningless or opposed to the Idea. It would be that if reason demanded indifference and the 'Idea' designated uniformity. But reason is the universal connectedness of all things, and the Idea is the form of the inner union of the many in the one. (Take, *e.g.*, the idea of the organism which includes many parts and elements subservient to a common end; or the idea of the state combining a multitude of interests in one universal good; or the idea of science, in which many pieces of knowledge form a single truth.) Therefore our reality, in which innumerable things and events are combined and coexist in one universal order, must be recognised as essentially rational or conformable to the Idea. Condemnation of this reality on the part of the idealist can in justice refer not to the general nature of the world, or to the differences of degree that follow from it and are essential to the higher unity, but only to such mutual relation of degrees as does not correspond to their inner dignity. The Idea of man is not violated but completed by the fact that in addition to intellect man has active will and sensuous receptivity. But since intellect, which contemplates universal truth, is essentially higher than desires and sensations, which are limited to the particular, it ought to dominate them. If on the contrary, these lower aspects gain the up-

13. "The unlimited = non-being." — *Editor's note.*

per hand in the life of man, his Idea becomes distorted and what takes place in him is abnormal and meaningless. In the same way, the distinction of state or class is not opposed to the idea of civic community provided the interrelation between the classes is determined by their inner quality. But if a group of men who have more capacity for menial work than for knowledge and realisation of higher truth dominate the community and take into their hands the government and the education of the people, while men of true knowledge and wisdom are forced to devote their powers to physical labour, then the state contradicts its Idea and loses all its meaning. The supremacy of the lower faculties of the soul over reason in the individual, and the supremacy of the material class over the intellectual in society, are instances of one and the same kind of distortion and absurdity. This is how idealism regards it when it resolutely denounces the fundamental evil both in the mental and in the social life of man. It is for thus denouncing it that Socrates had to die, but, strange to say, not even this tragic fact made his disciples realise that in addition to the *moral* and *political* there exists in the world a third kind of *evil* — the *physical* evil, *death*. This illogical limitation to the first two anomalies — the bad soul and the bad society, — this artificial break between the morally-social and the naturally-organic life is characteristic of the idealist point of view as of an intermediary and transitional stage of thought, a half-hearted and half-expressed universalism.

And yet it is clear that the dominion of death in the world of the living is the same kind of *disorder*, the same distortion of degrees, as the mastery of blind passions in the rational soul or the mastery of the mob in human society. There is no doubt that the inwardly purposive structure and life of the organism realise the ideal principle in nature in a greater measure and a higher degree than do the elementary forces of inorganic substance. It is clear then that the triumph of these forces over life, their escape from its power and the final disruption of the organism by them, is contradictory to the normal, ideal order, is senseless or anomalous. Life does not destroy the lower forces of substance but subordinates them to itself and thereby vivifies them. It is clear that such subordination of the lower to the higher is the norm, and that therefore the reverse relation, involving, as it does, the destruction of the higher form of existence in its given reality, cannot be justified or pronounced legitimate from the point of view of reason and of the Idea. Death is not an Idea, but the rejection of the Idea, the rebellion of blind force against reason. Therefore Socrates' joy at his death was, strictly speaking, simply an excusable and touching weakness of an old man wearied by the troubles of life, and not an expression of the higher consciousness. In a mind occupied with the essence of things and not with personal feeling, this death ought to evoke, instead of joy, a double grief. Grievous was the sentence of death as a social wrong, as the triumph of the wicked and ignorant over the righteous and the wise; grievous was the process of death as a physical wrong, as the triumph of the blind and soulless power of a poisonous substance over a living and organised body, the abode of a rational spirit.

All the world — not merely the mental and political, but the physical world as well — suffers from the violated norm and stands in need of help. And it can be helped not by the will-lessness of the ascetic, renouncing all life and all social environment, not by the intellectual contemplation of the philosopher who lives by thought alone in the realm of Ideas, but by the living power of the entire human being possessing absolute significance not negatively or ideally only, but as a concrete reality. Such a being is the perfect man or the God-man, who does not forsake the world for Nirvana or the realm of Ideas, but comes into the world in order to save it and regenerate it and make it the Kingdom of God, so that the perfect individual could find his completion in the perfect society.

VIII

The absolute moral significance of human personality demands perfection or fulness of life. This demand is not satisfied either by the mere negation of imperfection (as in Buddhism) or by the merely ideal participation in perfection (as in Platonism and all idealism). It can only be satisfied by perfection being *actually present and realised in the whole man and in the whole of human life.* This is what true Christianity stands for and wherein it essentially differs from Buddhism and Platonism. Without going at present into the metaphysical aspect of Christianity, I am simply referring here to the fact that Christianity — and it alone — is based upon the idea of the really perfect man and perfect society, and therefore promises to fulfil the demand for true infinity, inherent in our consciousness. It is clear that in order to attain this purpose it is necessary first of all to cease to be satisfied with the limited and unworthy reality, and to renounce it. It is equally clear, however, that this is only the first step, and that if man goes no further he is left with a mere negation. This first step which the universal human consciousness had to take, but at which it ought not to stop, is represented by Buddhism. Having renounced the unworthy reality, I ought to replace it by what is worthy of existence. But to do so I must first understand or grasp the very idea of worthy existence — this is the second step, represented by idealism. And once more it is clear that we cannot stop at this. Truth which is thinkable only and not realisable — truth which does not embrace the whole of life — is not what is demanded, is not absolute perfection. The third and final step which Christianity enables us to take consists in a positive realisation of worthy existence in all things.

The Nirvana of the Buddhists *is external to everything* — it is *negative universalism*. The ideal cosmos of Plato represents only the intelligible or *the thinkable aspect of everything* — it is *incomplete* universalism. The Kingdom of God, revealed by Christianity, alone *actually* embraces *everything*, and is *positive, complete,* and *perfect* universalism. It is clear that at the first two stages of universalism the absolute element in man is not developed to the end, and therefore remains *fruitless*. Nirvana lies outside the boundaries of every horizon; the world of Ideas, like the starry heaven, envelops the earth but is not united to it; the absolute principle incarnate in the Sun of Truth alone penetrates to the inmost depths of earthly reality, brings forth a new life, and manifests itself as a new order of being — as the all-embracing Kingdom of God: *virtus ejus integra si versa fuerit in terram.*[14] And without the earth there can be no heaven for man.

We have seen that Buddhism, unable to satisfy the unconditional principle of morality and bring about the fulness of life or the perfect society, is destructive, when consistently worked out, of the chief foundations of morality as such. The same thing must be said with regard to Platonism. Where is a consistent idealist to find an object for his piety? The popular gods he regards sceptically, or at best with wise restraint. The ideal essences, which are for him the absolute truth, cannot be an object of religious worship either for his mortal 'body,' which knows nothing about them, or for his immortal spirit, which knows them too intimately and, in immediate contemplation, attains complete equality with them. Religion and religious morality are a bond between the higher and the lower — a bond which idealism, with its dual character, breaks up, leaving on the one side the divine incorporeal and sterile spirit, and on the other, the material body utterly lacking in what is divine. But the bond thus severed by idealism extends farther still. It is the basis of pity as well as of reverence. What can be an object of pity for a consistent idealist? He knows only two orders of being — the false, material, and the true, ideal being. The false being, as Anaximander of Miletus had taught before Plato, *ought* in justice to suffer and to perish, and it deserves no pity. The true, from its essence, *cannot* suffer, and therefore cannot excite pity — and this

14. "Its power is whole when it turns into earth" (from *Tabula smaragdina*). [The *Tabula smaragdina* or *Emerald Tablet* was a short hermetic text consisting in a series of obscure aphorisms, ascribed to the mythical Hermes Trismegistus, associated with the teachings of Apollonius of Tyana, and much beloved of alchemists and connoisseurs of esoterica. — *Editor's note.*]

was the reason why the dying Socrates did nothing but rejoice at leaving a world unworthy of pity for a realm where there is no object for it. Finally, idealism provides no real basis for the ascetic morality either. A consistent idealist is ashamed of the *general* fact of having a body, in the words of the greatest of Plato's followers — Plotinus, but such shame has no significance from the moral point of view. It is impossible for man so long as he lives on earth to be incorporeal, and, according to the indisputable rule *ad impossibilia nemo obligatur*,[15] the shame of one's corporeality either demands that we should commit suicide or demands nothing at all.

If instead of taking Buddhism and Platonism to be what they really were, viz, necessary stages of human consciousness, we regard either the one or the other as the last word of universal truth, the question is, what precisely had they given to humanity, what did they gain for it? Taken in and for themselves they have neither given nor promised anything. There had been from all eternity the opposition between Nirvana and Sansara — empty bliss for the spiritually awake, and empty pain for the spiritually asleep; there had been the inexorable law of causal actions and caused states — the law of Karma, which through a series of innumerable rebirths leads a being from painful emptiness to empty bliss. As it was before Buddha, so it remained after him, and so it will remain for all eternity. From the point of view of Buddhism itself, not one of its followers capable of critical reflection can affirm that Buddha had changed anything in the world order, had created anything new, had actually saved any one. Nor is there any room for promise in the future. The same thing must in the long-run be said of idealism. There are the eternal realm of intelligible essences which truly is and the phenomenal world of sensuous appearance. There is no bridge between the two; to be in the one means not to be in the other. Such duality has always been and will remain for ever. Idealism gives no reconciliation in the present and no promise of it in the future.[16]

Christianity has a different message. It both gives and promises to humanity something new. It gives the living image of a personality possessing not the merely negative perfection of indifference or the merely ideal perfection of intellectual contemplation, but perfection absolute and entire, fully realised, and therefore victorious over death. Christianity *reveals* to men the absolutely perfect and therefore physically immortal personality. It promises mankind a perfect society built upon the pattern of this personality. And

15. "No one is obliged to do the impossible." — *Editor's note.*

16. Plato's thought rose for a moment to the conception of Eros as the bridge between the world of true being and the material reality, but did not follow it out. In enigmatic expressions the philosopher indicated this bridge, but was incapable of crossing it himself or leading others across it.

since such a society cannot be created by an external force (for in that case it would be imperfect), the *promise* of it sets a *task* before humanity as a whole and each man individually, to co-operate with the perfect personal power revealed to the world in so transforming the universe that it might become the embodiment of the Kingdom of God. The final truth, the absolute and positive universalism obviously cannot be either exclusively individual or exclusively social: it must express the completeness and fulness of the individually-social life. True Christianity is a perfect synthesis of three inseparable elements: (1) the *absolute event* — the revelation of the perfect personality, the God-man — Christ, who had bodily risen from the dead; (2) the absolute *promise* — of a community conformable to the perfect personality, or, in other words, the promise of the Kingdom of God; (3) the absolute *task* — to further the fulfilment of that promise by regenerating all our individual and social environment in the spirit of Christ. If any one of these three foundations is forgotten or left out of account the whole thing becomes paralysed and distorted. This is the reason why the moral development and the external history of humanity have not stopped after the coming of Christ, in spite of the fact that Christianity is the absolute and final revelation of truth. That which has been fulfilled and that which has been promised stand firmly within the precincts of eternity and do not depend upon us. But the task of the present is in our hands; the moral regeneration of our life must be brought about by ourselves. It is with this general problem that the special task of moral philosophy is particularly concerned. It has to define and explain, within the limits of historical fact, what the relation between all the fundamental elements and aspects of the individually-social whole ought to be in accordance with the unconditional moral norm.

CHAPTER III

Abstract Subjectivism in Morality

I

At the historical stage reached by human consciousness in Christianity, moral life reveals itself as a universal and all-embracing *task*. Before going on to discuss its concrete historical setting, we must consider the view which, on principle, rejects morality as a historical problem or as the work of collective man, and entirely reduces it to the subjective moral impulses of individuals. This view arbitrarily puts such narrow limits to the human good as in reality it has never known. Strictly speaking, morality never has been solely the affair of personal feeling or the rule of private conduct. At the patriarchal stage the moral demands of reverence, pity, and shame were inseparably connected with the duties of the individual to his kinsmen. The 'moral' was not distinguished from the 'social,' or the individual from the collective. And if the result was a morality of rather a low and limited order, this was not due to the fact of its being a collective morality, but to the generally low level and narrow limits of the tribal life, which expressed merely the rudimentary stage of the historical development. It was low and limited, however, only by comparison with the further progress of morality, and certainly not by comparison with the morality of savages living in caves and in trees. When the state came into being, and the domestic life became to a certain extent a thing apart, morality in general was still determined by the relation between individuals and the collective whole to which they belonged — henceforth a wider and a more complex one. It was impossible to be moral apart from a definite and positive relation to the state; morality was in the first place a civic virtue. And the reason that this *virtus antiqua* no longer satisfies us, is not that it was a *civic* and not merely a *domestic* virtue, but that the civic life itself was too remote from

215

the true social ideal, and was merely a transition from the barbarous to the truly human culture. Morality was rightly taken to consist in honourably serving the social whole — the state, but the state itself was based upon slavery, constant wars, etc.; what is to be condemned is not the social character of morality, but the immoral character of the social whole. In a similar way we condemn the ecclesiastical morality of the Middle Ages, not of course because it was ecclesiastical, but because the Church itself was then far from being a truly moral organisation, and was responsible for evil as well as for good — the terrible evil of religious persecutions and torture — thus violating the unconditional principle of morality in its own inner domain.

Christianity as the 'Gospel of the Kingdom' proclaims an ideal that is unconditionally high, demands an absolute morality. Is this morality to be *subjective only*, limited to the inner states and individual actions of the subject? The question contains its own answer; but to make the matter quite clear, let us first grant all that is true in the exclusively-subjective interpretation of Christianity. There is no doubt that a perfect or absolute moral state must be inwardly fully experienced or felt by the subject — must become *his own* state, the content of his life. If perfect morality were recognised as subjective in this sense, the difference would be purely verbal. But something else is really meant. The question is, how is this moral perfection to be attained by the individual? Is it enough that each should strive to make himself inwardly better and act accordingly, or is it attained *with the help of* a certain social process the effects of which are collective as well as individual? The adherents of the former theory, which reduces everything to individual moral activity, do not reject, of course, either the social life or the moral improvement of its forms. They believe, however, that such improvement is simply the inevitable consequence of the personal moral progress: like individual, like society. As soon as each person understands and reveals to others his own true nature, and awakens good feelings in his soul, the earth will become paradise. Now it is indisputable that without good thoughts and feelings there can be neither individual nor social morality. It is equally indisputable that *if* all individual men were good, society would be good also. But to think that the actual virtue of the few best men is *sufficient* for the moral regeneration of all the others, is to pass into the world where babies are born out of rose-bushes, and where beggars, for lack of bread, eat cakes. The question we are mainly concerned with is not whether the individual's moral efforts are sufficient to make *him* perfect, but whether those unaided individual efforts can induce *other people,* who are making no moral efforts at all, to *begin* to make them.

II

The insufficiency of the subjective good and the necessity for a collective embodiment of it are unmistakably proved by the whole course of human history. I will give one concrete illustration.

At the end of Homer's *Odyssey* it is related, with obvious sympathy, how this typical hero of the Greeks re-established justice and order in his house, having overcome at last the enmity of gods and men and destroyed his rivals. With his son's help he executed those of his servants who, during his twenty years' absence, when everybody had given him up for dead, sided with Penelope's suitors and did not oppose the latter making themselves at home in Odysseus's house:

"Now when they had made an end of setting the hall in order, they led the maidens forth from the stablished hall, and drove them up in a narrow space between the vaulted room and the goodly fence of the court, whence none might avoid; and wise Telemachus began to speak to his fellows, saying: 'God forbid that I should take these women's lives by a clean death, these that have poured dishonour on my head and on my mother, and have lain with the wooers.' With that word he tied the cable of a dark-prowed ship to a great pillar and flung it round the vaulted room, and fastened it aloft, that none might touch the ground with her feet. And even as when thrushes, long of wing, or doves fall into a net that is set in a thicket, as they seek to their roosting-place, and a loathly bed harbours them, even so the women held their heads all in a row, and about all their necks nooses were cast, that they might die by the most pitiful death. And they writhed with their feet for a little space, but for no long while. Then they led out Melanthius through the doorway and the court and cut off his nostrils and his ears with the pitiless sword, and drew forth his vitals for the dogs to devour raw, and cut off his hands and feet in their cruel anger" (*Odyssey*, xxii. 457-477).

Odysseus and Telemachus were not monsters of inhumanity; on the contrary, they represented the highest ideal of the Homeric epoch. Their personal morality was irreproachable, they were full of piety, wisdom, justice, and all the family virtues. Odysseus had, into the bargain, an extremely sensitive heart, and in spite of his courage and firmness in misfortune, shed tears at every convenient opportunity. This very curious and characteristic feature attaches to him throughout the poem. As I have not in literature come across any special reference to this peculiar characteristic of the Homeric hero, I will allow myself to go into some detail.

At his first appearance in the *Odyssey* he is represented as weeping: —

"Odysseus . . . sat weeping on the shore even as aforetime, straining his soul with tears and groans and griefs, and as he wept he looked wistfully over the unharvested deep" (v. 82-84; also 151, 152, 156-158).

In his own words: "There I abode for seven years continually, and watered with my tears the imperishable raiment that Calypso gave me" (vii. 259-260).

He wept at the thought of his distant native land and family, and also at remembering his own exploits: —

". . . The Muse stirred the minstrel to sing the songs of famous men. . . . The quarrel between Odysseus and Achilles, son of Peleus. . . . This song it was that the famous minstrel sang; but Odysseus caught his great purple cloak with his stalwart hands, and drew it down over his head, and hid his comely face, for he was ashamed to shed tears beneath his brows in presence of the Phaeacians" (viii. 73-86).

Further: —

"This was the song that the famous minstrel sang. But the heart of Odysseus melted, and the tear wet his cheeks beneath the eyelids. And as a woman throws herself wailing about her dead lord, who hath fallen before his city and the host, warding from his town and his children the pitiless day . . . even so pitifully fell the tears beneath the brows of Odysseus" (viii. 521-525).

He weeps on being told by Circe of the journey — though a perfectly safe one — he has to make to Hades: —

"Thus spake she, but as for me, my heart was broken, and I wept as I sat upon the bed, and my soul had no more care to live and to see the sunlight" (x. 496-499).

It is no wonder that Odysseus weeps when he sees his mother's shadow (xi. 87), but he is affected just as much by the shadow of the worst and most worthless of his followers, of whom "an evil doom of some god was the bane and wine out of measure" (xi. 61).

"There was one, Elpenor, the youngest of us all, not very valiant in war, neither steadfast in mind. He was lying apart from the rest of my men on the housetop of Circe's sacred dwelling, very fain of the cool air, as one heavy with wine. Now when he heard the noise of the voices and of the feet of my fellows as they moved to and fro, he leaped up of a sudden and minded him not to descend again by the way of the tall ladder, but fell right down from the roof, and his neck was broken from the bones of the spine, and his spirit went down to the house of Hades" (x. 552-561).

"At the sight of him I wept and had compassion on him" (xi. 55).

He weeps, too, at the sight of Agamemnon: —

"Thus we twain stood sorrowing, holding sad discourse, while the big tears fell fast" (xi. 465-466).

He weeps bitterly at finding himself at last in his native Ithaca (xiii. 219-221), and still more so on beholding his son: —

". . . In both their hearts arose the desire of lamentation.

And they wailed aloud, more ceaselessly than birds, sea-eagles or vultures of crooked claws, whose younglings the country folk have taken from the nest, ere yet they are fledged. Even so pitifully fell the tears beneath their brows" (xvi. 215-220).

Odysseus shed tears, too, at the sight of his old dog Argus: —

"Odysseus looked aside and wiped away a tear that he easily hid from Eumaeus" (xvii. 304-305).

He weeps before assassinating the suitors, he weeps as he embraces the godlike swine-herd Eumaeus, and the goodly cow-herd Philoetius (xxi. 225-227), and also after the brutal murder of the twelve maid-servants and the goat-herd Melanthius: —

"A sweet longing came upon him to weep and to moan, for he remembered them every one" (xxii. 500-501).

The last two chapters of the *Odyssey* also have, of course, an abundant share of the hero's tears: —

". . . in his heart she stirred yet a greater longing to lament, and he wept as he embraced his beloved wife and true" (xxiii. 231-232).

And further: —

"Now when the steadfast goodly Odysseus saw his father thus wasted with age and in great grief of heart, he stood still beneath a tall pear tree and let fall a tear" (xxiv. 233-235).

So far as the personal, subjective feeling is concerned Odysseus was obviously quite equal to the most developed and highly-strung man of our own day. Speaking generally, Homeric heroes were capable of all the moral sentiments and emotions of the heart that we are capable of — and that not only in relation to their neighbours in the narrow sense of the term, *i.e.* to men immediately connected with them by common interests, but also in relation to people remote and distant from them. The Phaeacians were strangers to the shipwrecked Odysseus, and yet what kindly human relations were established between him and them! And if, in spite of all this, the heroes of antiquity performed with a clear conscience deeds which are now morally impossible for us, this was certainly not due to their lack of personal, subjective morality. These men were certainly as capable as we are of good human feelings towards both neighbours and strangers. What then is the difference and what is the ground of the change? Why is it that virtuous, wise, and *sentimental* men of the Homeric age thought it permissible and praiseworthy to hang frivolous maid-servants like thrushes and to chop unworthy servants as food for the dogs, while at the present day such actions can be done only by maniacs or born criminals? Reasoning in an abstract fashion one might suppose that although the men of that distant epoch had good mental feelings and impulses, they had no conscious good *principles* and rules. Owing to the absence of a formal criterion between right and wrong, or a clear consciousness of the distinction between good and evil, morality was purely empirical in character, and even the best of men, capable of the finest moral emotions, could indulge unchecked in wild outbursts of brutality. In truth, however, we find no such formal defect in the thought of the ancients.

Men of antiquity, just like ourselves, both had their good and bad qualities as a natural fact, and drew the distinction of principle between good and evil, recognising that the first was to be preferred unconditionally to the second. In those same poems of Homer which often strike us by their ethical barbarisms, the idea of moral duty appears with perfect clearness. Certainly Penelope's mode of thought and expression does not quite coincide with that of Kant; nevertheless the following words of the wife of Odysseus contain a definite affirmation of the moral good as an eternal, necessary, and universal principle: —

"Man's life is brief enough! And if any be a hard man and hard at heart, all men cry evil on him for the time to come, while yet he lives, and all men mock him when he is dead. But if any be a blameless man and blameless of heart, his guests spread abroad his fame over *the whole earth,* and many people call him noble" (xix. 328-334).

III

The *form* of moral consciousness, the idea, namely, of the good as absolutely binding and of evil as absolutely unpermissible, was present in the mind of the ancients as it is in our own. It might be thought, however, that the important difference between us and them in the moral valuation of the same actions is due to the change in the actual *content* of the moral ideal. There can be no doubt that the Gospel has raised our ideal of virtue and holiness and made it much higher and wider than the Homeric ideal. But it is equally certain that this perfect ideal of morality, when it has no objective embodiment and is accepted purely in the abstract, produces no change whatever either in the life or in the actual moral *consciousness* of men, and does not in any way raise their practical *standards* for judging their own and other people's actions.

It is sufficient to refer once more to the representatives of mediæval

Christianity, who treated the supposed enemies of their Church with greater cruelty than Odysseus treated the enemies of his family — and did so with a clear conscience, and even with the conviction of fulfilling a moral duty. At a time more enlightened and less remote the American planters who belonged to the Christian faith, and therefore stood under the sign of an unconditionally high moral ideal, treated their black slaves on the whole no better than the pagan Odysseus treated his faithless servants, and, like him, considered themselves *right* in doing so. So that not only their actions but even their practical consciousness remained unaffected by the higher truth which they theoretically professed in the abstract.

I. I. Dubasov's *Historical Sketches of the Tambov District* contain an account of the exploits of K., a landowner in the district of Yelatma, who flourished in the forties of the present century. The Commission of Inquiry established that many serfs (children especially) had been tortured by him to death, and that on his estate there was not a single peasant who had not been flogged, and not a single serf-girl who had not been outraged. But more significant than this 'misuse of power' was the relation of the public to it. When cross-examined, most of the gentry in the district spoke of K. as 'a true gentleman.' Some added, "K. is a true Christian and observes all the rites of the Church." The Marshal of Nobility wrote to the Governor of the province: "All the district is alarmed by the *troubles* of Mr. K." In the end the 'true Christian' was excused from legal responsibility, and the local gentry could set their hearts at rest.[1] The same sympathy from men of his own class was enjoyed by another and still more notorious Tambov landowner, Prince U. N. G—n, of whom it was written with good reason to the Chief of the Police: "Even animals on meeting U. N. instinctively seek to hide wherever they can."[2]

Some three thousand years elapsed between the heroes of Homer and the heroes of Mr. Dubasov, but no essential and stable change had taken place in the conduct and the moral consciousness of men with regard to the enslaved part of the population. The same inhuman relations that were approved of by the ancient Greeks in the Homeric age were regarded as permissible by the American and Russian slave-owners in the first half of the nineteenth century. These relations are revolting to us now, but our ethical standards have been raised not in the course of three thousand years, but only in the course of the last *thirty years* (in our case and that of the Americans, and a few dozens of years earlier in Western Europe). What, then, had happened so recently? What has produced in so short a period the change which long centuries of historical

---

1. *Ocherki iz istorii Tambovskago Kraia,* by I. I. Dubasov, vol. i (Tambov, 1890), pp. 162-67.
2. *Ibid.,* p. 92.

development were unable to accomplish? Has some new moral conception, some new and higher ideal of morality appeared in our day?

There has been and there could have been nothing of the kind. No ideal can be conceived higher than that revealed eighteen hundred years ago. That ideal was known to the 'true Christians' of the American States and the Russian provinces. They could learn no new idea in this respect; but they *experienced a new fact*. The idea restricted to the subjective sphere of personal morality could not during thousands of years bear the fruit which it bore in the course of the few years when it was embodied as a social force, and became the *common task*. Under very different historical conditions the organised social whole invested with power decided, both in America and in Russia, to put an end to the too glaring violation of Christian justice — both human and divine — in the life of the community. In America it was attained at the price of blood, through a terrible civil war; in Russia — by the authoritative action of the Government.[3] It is owing to this fact alone that the fundamental demands of justice and humanity, presupposed by the supreme ideal though not exhaustive of it, were transferred from the narrow and unstable limits of subjective feeling to the wide and firm ground of objective reality and transformed into a universally binding law. And we see that this external political act immediately raised the standard of our inner consciousness, that is, achieved a result which millenniums of moral preaching alone could not achieve. The social movement and the action of the Government were of course themselves conditioned by the previous moral preaching, but that preaching had effect upon the majority, upon the social environment as a whole, only when *embodied* in measures organised by the Government. Owing to external restraint, brutal instincts were no longer able to find expression; they had to pass into a state of inactivity, and were gradually *atrophied* from lack of exercise; in most people they disappeared altogether and were no longer passed on to the generations that followed. At present even men who openly sigh for serfdom make *sincere* reservations with regard to the *abuse* of the owners' power, while forty years ago that abuse was regarded as compatible with 'true nobility,' and even with 'true Christianity.' And yet there is no reason to believe that the fathers were intrinsically worse than the sons.

Let it be granted that the heroes of Mr. Dubasov's chronicle, whom the Tambov gentry defended simply from class interests, were really below the average of the society around them. But apart from them there was a multitude of perfectly decent men, free from all brutality, who *conscientiously* felt they had a right to make full use of the privileges of their class — for instance, to

3. The emancipation of the serfs in Russia in 1861. — *Editor's note.*

sell their serfs like cattle, retail or wholesale. And if such things are now impossible even for scoundrels, — however much they might wish for them, — this objective success of the good, this concrete improvement of life cannot possibly be ascribed to the progress of personal morality.

The moral nature of man is unchangeable in its inner subjective foundations. The relative number of good and bad men also, probably, remains unchanged. It would hardly be argued by any one that there are now more righteous men than there were some hundreds or thousands of years ago. Finally, there can be no doubt that the highest moral ideas and ideals, taken in the abstract, do not as such produce any stable improvement in life and in moral consciousness. I have referred to an indisputable and certain fact of history: the same and even worse atrocities which were committed by a virtuous pagan of the Homeric poem with the approval of the community were done thousands of years after him by the champions of Christian faith — the Spanish inquisitors, and by Christian slave-owners, also with the approval of the community, and this in spite of the fact that a higher ideal of individual morality has meanwhile been evolved. In our day such actions are possible only for lunatics and professional criminals. And this sudden progress is solely due to the fact that the organised social force was inspired by moral demands and transformed them into an objective law of life.

IV

The principle of the perfect good revealed in Christianity does not abolish the external structure of human society, but uses it as a form and an instrument for the embodiment of its own absolute moral content. It demands that human society should become morally *organised*. Experience unmistakably proves that when the social environment is not morally organised, the subjective demands of the good in oneself and in others are inevitably lowered. It is not, then, really a choice between personal or subjective and social morality, but between weak and strong, realised and unrealised morality. At every stage the moral consciousness inevitably strives to realise itself both in the individual and in the society. The final stage differs from the lower stages, not, of course, by the fact that morality at its highest remains for ever subjective, *i.e.* powerless and unrealised — this, indeed, would be a strange advantage! — but by the fact that the realisation must be full and *all-embracing*, and therefore requires a far more difficult, long, and complex process than was necessary in the case of the former collective embodiments of morality. In the patriarchal life the degree of the good of which it is capable becomes realised freely and easily

— without any *history*. The formation of extensive national-political groups, which is to realise a greater sum and a higher grade of the good, fills many centuries with its history. The moral task left us by Christianity — to form the environment for the actual realisation of *absolute* and *universal* good — is infinitely more complex. The positive conception of this good embraces the totality of human relations. Humanity morally regenerated cannot be poorer in content than natural humanity. The task then consists not in abolishing the already existing social distinctions, but in bringing them into right, good, or moral relation with one another. When the higher animal forms came to be evolved in the course of the cosmical process, the lower form — that of worm — was not excluded as intrinsically unworthy, but received a new and more fitting position. It ceased to be the sole and obvious foundation of life, but decently clothed it still exists within the body in the form of the alimentary canal — a subservient part of the organism. Other forms, predominant at the lower stages, were also preserved, both materially and formally, as subordinate constituent parts and organs of a higher whole. In a similar way, Christian humanity — the highest form of collective spiritual life — finds realisation not by destroying the different forms of the social life evolved in the course of history, but by bringing them into due relation to itself and to each other, in harmony with the unconditional principle of morality.

The demand for such harmony deprives moral subjectivism, based on the wrongly conceived view of the autonomy of the will, of all justification. The moral will must be determined to action solely through itself; any subordination of it to an *external* rule or command violates its autonomy and must therefore be recognised as unworthy — this is the *true* principle of moral autonomy. But the organisation of social environment in accordance with the principle of the *absolute good* is not a limitation but a *fulfilment* of the personal moral will — it is the very thing which it desires. As a moral being I *want* the good to reign upon earth, I *know* that alone I cannot bring this to pass, and I *find* a collective organisation intended for this purpose of mine. It is clear that such an organisation does not in any sense limit me but, on the contrary, removes my individual limitations, widens and strengthens my moral will. Every one, in so far as his will is moral, inwardly participates in this universal organisation of morality, and it is clear that relative external limitations, which may follow therefrom for individual persons, are sanctioned by their own higher consciousness and consequently cannot be opposed to moral freedom. For the moral individual one thing only is important in this connection, namely, that the collective organisation should be *really* dominated by the *unconditional principle of morality,* that the social life should *indeed* conform to moral standards — to the demands of justice and mercy in all human affairs and relations — that the individual-social environment should *really* become *the organised good.* It is clear that in subordinating himself to a social environment which is itself subordinate to the principle of the absolute good and conformable to it, the individual cannot lose anything. Such a social environment is from the nature of the case incompatible with any arbitrary limitation of personal rights and still less compatible with rude violence or persecution. *The degree of subordination of the individual to society must correspond to the degree of subordination of society to the moral good,* apart from which social environment has no claim whatever upon the individual. Its rights arise simply from the moral satisfaction which it gives to *every person.* This aspect of moral universalism will be further developed and explained in the next chapter.

As to the autonomy of the *bad will,* no organisation of the good can prevent conscious evil-doers from desiring evil for its own sake and from acting in that direction. The organisation of the good is concerned merely with external limitations of the evil reality — limitations that inevitably follow from the nature of man and the meaning of history. These objective limits to objective evil, necessarily presupposed by the organisation of the good but not by any means exhaustive of it, will be discussed later on in the chapters on punishment and on the relation between legal justice and morality.

CHAPTER IV

The Moral Norm of Social Life

I

The true definition of society as an *organised morality* disposes of the two false theories that are fashionable in our day — the view of *moral subjectivism* which prevents the moral will from being concretely realised in the life of the community, and the theory of *social realism,* according to which given social institutions and interests are of supreme significance in and for themselves, so that the highest moral principles prove at best to be simply the means or the instrument for safeguarding those interests. From this point of view, at present extremely prevalent, this or that *concrete form* of social life is essential *per se,* although attempts are made to give it a moral justification by connecting it with moral norms and principles. But the very fact of seeking a moral basis for human society proves that neither any concrete form of social life nor social life *as such* is the highest or the final expression of human nature. If man were defined as essentially a social animal (ζῷον πολιτικόν)[1] and *nothing more,* the *content* of the term 'man' would be very much narrowed and its *scope* would be considerably increased. Humanity would then include animals such as ants, of whom social life is as essential a characteristic as it is of man. Sir John Lubbock, the greatest authority on the subject, writes: "Their nests are no mere collections of independent individuals, nor even temporary associations like the flocks of migratory birds, but organised communities labouring with the utmost harmony for the common good."[2] These communities sometimes contain a population so numerous that, in the words of the same naturalist, of

---

1. Aristotle's definition in the *Nicomachean Ethics.* — *Editor's note.*
2. *Ants, Bees, and Wasps,* by Sir John Lubbock, 7th ed., p. 119.

human cities London and Pekin can alone be compared to them.[3] Far more important are the three following inner characteristics of the ants' community. They have a complex social organisation. There is a distinct difference between different communities in the degree of that organisation — a difference completely analogous to the gradual development in the forms of human culture from the hunting to the agricultural stage. This proves that the social life of ants did not arise in any accidental or exceptional fashion but developed according to certain general sociological laws. Finally, the social tie is remarkably strong and stable, and there is wonderful practical solidarity between the members of the ants' community, so far as the common good is concerned.

With regard to the first point, if division of labour be the characteristic feature of civilised life, it is impossible to deny civilisation to ants. Division of labour is in their case carried out very sharply. They have very brave soldiers armed with enormously developed pincer-like jaws by which they adroitly seize and snap off the heads of their enemies, but who are incapable of doing anything else. They have workmen remarkable for their skill and industry. They have gentlemen with opposite characteristics who go so far that they can neither feed themselves nor move about and only know how to use other ants' services. Finally, they have slaves (not to be confused with workmen[4]) who are obtained by conquest and belong to other species of ants, which fact does not, however, prevent them from being completely devoted to their masters. Apart from such division of labour, the high degree of civilisation possessed by ants is proved by their keeping a number of domestic animals (*i.e.* tamed insects belonging to other zoological groups), "So that we may truly say," Sir John Lubbock remarks, of course with some exaggeration, "that our English ants possess a much greater variety of domestic animals than we do ourselves."[5]

Some of these domestic insects carefully brought up by ants serve for food (in particular the plant-lice *aphidae*, which Linnaeus calls ants' cows *(Aphis formicarum vacca)*; others perform certain necessary work in the community, *e.g.* act as dustmen; the third, in Lubbock's opinion, are kept simply for amusement like our pug-dogs or canaries. The entomologist André has made a list of 584 species of insects which are usually found in ants' communities.

At the present time many large and well-populated communities of ants live chiefly on the large stores of vegetable products they collect. Crowds of working ants skilfully and systematically cut blades of grass and stems of

---

3. *Ibid.*
4. Working ants (like working bees) do not form a distinct species; they are descended from the common queen but are sexually under-developed.
5. *Ibid.*, p. 73.

leaves — *reap* them, as it were. But this semblance of agriculture is neither their only nor their original means of subsistence. "We find," writes Lubbock, "in the different species of ants different conditions of life, curiously answering to the earlier stages of human progress. For instance, some species, such as *Formica fusca,* live principally on the produce of the chase; for though they feed partly on the honey-dew of aphides, they have not domesticated those insects. These ants probably retain the habits once common to all ants. They resemble the lower races of men, who subsist mainly by hunting. Like them they frequent woods and wilds, live in comparatively small communities, and the instincts of collective action are but little developed among them. They hunt singly, and their battles are single combats, like those of the Homeric heroes. Such species as *Lassius fiavus* represent a distinctly higher type of social life; they show more skill in architecture, may literally be said to have domesticated certain species of aphides, and may be compared to the pastoral stage of human progress, to the races which live on the produce of their flocks and herds. Their communities are more numerous; they act much more in concert; their battles are not mere single combats, but they know how to act in combination. I am disposed to hazard the conjecture that they will gradually exterminate the mere hunting species, just as savages disappear before more advanced races. Lastly, the agricultural nations may be compared with the harvesting ants. Thus there seem to be three principal types, offering a curious analogy to the three great phases — the hunting, pastoral, and agricultural stages in the history of human development."[6]

In addition to the complexity of social structure and the graduated stages in the development of culture, ants' societies are also noted, as has been said above, for the remarkable stability of the social tie. Our author continually remarks on "the greatest harmony that reigns between members of one and the same community." This harmony is *exclusively* conditioned by the common good. On the ground of many observations and experiments, Sir John Lubbock proves that whenever an individual ant undertakes something useful for the community and exceeding its own powers, *e.g.* attempts to bring to the ant-heap a dead fly or beetle it has come across, it always calls and finds comrades to help it. When, on the contrary, an individual ant gets into trouble which concerns it alone, this does not as a rule excite any sympathy whatever and no help is rendered to it. The patient scientist had a number of times brought separate ants into a state of insensibility by chloroform or spirits and found that their fellow-citizens either did not take the slightest notice of the unfortunate ones or threw them out as dead. Tender sympathy with personal

6. *Ibid.,* p. 91.

grief is not connected with any social function and therefore does not form part of the idea of social life as such. But the feeling of civic duty or the devotion to general order is so great among ants that they never have any quarrels or civil wars. Their armies are intended solely for outside wars. And even in the highly developed communities, which have a special class of dustmen and a breed of domestic clowns, not a single observer could discover any trace of organised police or gendarmerie.

II

Social life is at least as essential a characteristic of these insects as it is of man. If, however, we do not admit that they are equal to ourselves — if we do not agree to bestow upon each of the innumerable ants living in our forests the rights of man and of citizen, it means that man has another and a more essential characteristic, one that is independent of social instincts and, on the contrary, conditions the distinctive character of *human* society. This characteristic consists in the fact that each man, as such, is a moral being — *i.e.* a being who, apart from his social utility, has absolute worth and an absolute right to live and freely develop his positive powers. It directly follows from this that *no man under any conditions or for any reason may be regarded as only a means* for ends extraneous to himself. We cannot be merely an *instrument either for the good of another person* or for the good of a *whole class* or even for the so-called *common good, i.e.* the good of the majority of men. This 'common good' or 'general utility' has a claim not upon man as a person, but upon his activity or work to the extent to which that work, being useful for the community, secures at the same time a worthy existence to the worker. The right of the person as such is based upon his human dignity inherent in him and inalienable, upon the formal infinity of reason in every human being, upon the fact that each person is unique and individual, and must therefore be an end in himself and not merely a means or an instrument. This right of the person is from its very nature *unconditional,* while the rights of the community with regard to the person are *conditioned* by the recognition of his individual rights. Society, therefore, can compel a person to do something only through an act of his own will, — otherwise it will not be a case of laying an obligation upon a person, but of making use of a thing. This does not mean, of course (as one of my critics imagined),[7] that in order to pass a legal or administrative measure, the

---

7. Solovyov is referring to B. N. Chicherin and his article "On the Principles of Ethics" (1897). — *Editor's note.*

central power must ask the individual consent of each person. The moral principle in its application to politics logically involves not an absurd *liberum veto* of this kind, but the right of each responsible person freely to change his allegiance as well as his religion. In other words, *no social group or institution has a right forcibly to detain any one among its members.*

The human dignity of each person or his nature as a moral being does not in any way depend upon his particular qualities or his social utility. Such qualities and utility may determine man's external position in society and the relative value set upon him by other people; they do not determine his own worth and his human rights. Many animals are by nature far more virtuous than many human beings. The conjugal virtue of pigeons and storks, the maternal love of hens, the gentleness of deer, the faithfulness and devotion of dogs, the good nature of seals and dolphins, the industry and civic virtues of ants and bees, etc., are characteristic qualities adorning our younger brothers, while they are by no means predominant in the majority of human beings. Why is it then that it has never occurred to any one to deprive the most worthless of men of his human rights in order to pass them to the most excellent of animals as a reward for its virtue? As to utility, not only one strong horse is more useful than a number of sick beggars, but even inanimate objects, such as the printing-press or the steam-boiler, have undoubtedly been of far more use to the historical process as a whole than entire tribes of savages or barbarians. And yet if *(per impossibile)* Gutenberg and Watt had, for the sake of their great inventions, intentionally and consciously to sacrifice the life even of a single savage or barbarian, the usefulness of their *work* would not prevent their *action* from being decidedly condemned as immoral — unless indeed the view be taken that the end justifies the means.

If the common good or the general happiness is to have the significance of a moral principle, they must be in the full sense general, *i.e.* they must refer not merely to many or to the majority of men but to *all without exception.* That which is truly the good of all is for that very reason the good of *each* — no one is excluded and, therefore, in serving *such* a social good as an end, the individual does *not* thereby become merely a means or an instrument of something extraneous and foreign to himself. True society which recognises the absolute right of each person is not the negative limit but the positive complement of the individual. In serving it with whole-hearted devotion, the individual does not lose but *realises* his absolute worth and significance. For when taken in isolation he is only *potentially* absolute and infinite, and becomes so actually only by being inwardly united to all.[8]

8. See above, Part III, Chapter 1, 'The Individual and Society.'

The only moral norm is the principle of human dignity or of the absolute worth of each individual, in virtue of which society is determined as the inward and free harmony of all.[9] It is just as impossible that there should be many moral norms in the strict sense of the term, as it is impossible that there should be many supreme goods or many moralities. It is not difficult to show that religion (as concretely given in history), family, and property do not as such contain a moral norm in the strict sense of the term. A thing which, taken by itself, may or may not be moral, must obviously be determined as one or the other by means of something else. It cannot, therefore, be a moral norm on its own account — that is, it cannot give to other things a character which it itself does not possess. Now there is no doubt that religion may or may not be moral. Such religions as, for instance, the cult of Moloch or Astarte (the survivals or analogies of which are to be met now and then to this day), cannot possibly serve as a moral norm of anything, since their very essence is directly opposed to all morality. When, therefore, we are told that religion is the norm and the moral foundation of society, we must first see whether religion itself has a moral character and agrees with the principle of morality; and this means that the ultimate criterion is that principle and not religion as such. The only reason why we regard Christianity as the true foundation and norm of all that is good in the world is that, being a perfect religion, Christianity contains the unconditional moral principle in itself. But if a separation be introduced between the demand for moral perfection and the actual life of Christian society, Christianity at once loses its absolute significance and becomes historically accidental.

If now we take the family, it cannot be denied that the family too may or may not be moral, both in individual cases and in the whole given structure of society. Thus the family of ancient Greece had no moral character. I refer not to the exceptional heroic families in which wives murdered their husbands and were killed by their sons, or sons killed their fathers and married their mothers, but to the usual normal family of a cultured Athenian, which required as its necessary complement the institution of hetæras and worse things than that. The Arabic family (before Islam), in which newborn girl babies, if there were more than one or two of them, were buried alive, had no moral character either, though it was stable in its way. The very stable family of the Romans in which the head of the house had the right of life and death over his wife and children, also cannot be said to have been moral. Thus the family, like religion, has no intrinsically moral char-

---

9. This position is logically established in moral philosophy in its elementary part, which, thanks to Kant, became as strictly scientific in its own sphere as pure mechanics is in another.

acter, and, before it can become the norm for anything else, must itself be put upon a moral basis.

As to property, to recognise it as the moral foundation of normal society, *i.e.* as something sacred and inviolable, is neither logically nor, in my own case (and I think in that of my contemporaries), psychologically possible. The first awakening of conscious life and thought in our generation was accompanied by the thunder of the destruction of property in its two fundamental historical forms of serfdom and slavery. And this abolition of property, both in America and in Russia, was demanded and accomplished *in the name of social morality.* The alleged inviolability was brilliantly disproved by the fact of so successful a violation, approved by the conscience of all. It is obvious that property is a thing which stands in need of justification, and so far from containing a moral norm, demands such a norm *for itself.*

All historical institutions — whether religious or social — are of a mixed character. But there is no doubt that the moral norm can only be found in a pure principle, and not in a mixed fact. A principle which unconditionally affirms that which *ought* to be is something essentially inviolable. It may be rejected and disobeyed, but this is detrimental not to the principle but to the person who rejects and disobeys it. The law which proclaims "you ought to respect the human dignity of each person, you ought to make no one a means or an instrument," does not depend upon any fact, does not affirm any fact, and therefore cannot be affected by any fact.

The principle of the absolute worth of human personality does not depend upon any one or anything; but the moral character of societies and institutions depends entirely upon it. We know in ancient and modern heathendom of highly civilised great national bodies in which the institutions of family, of religion, of property were extremely stable, but which nevertheless were devoid of the moral character of a human society. At best they resembled communities of wise insects in which the mechanism of the good order is present, but that which the mechanism is to subserve — the good itself — is absent, for the bearer of it, the free personality, is not there.

III

A vague and distorted consciousness of the essence of morality and of the true norm of human society exists even where the moral principle has apparently no application. Thus, in the despotic monarchies of the East, the real man or person was rightly regarded as possessed of full rights, but such dignity was ascribed to one man only. Thus transformed, however, into an exclusive and externally determined privilege, human right and worth loses its moral character. The sole bearer of it ceases to be a person, and since as a concrete real being it cannot become a pure ideal, it becomes an idol. The moral principle demands of the individual that he should respect human dignity as such — that is, should respect it in other people as in himself. It is only in treating others as persons that the individual is himself determined as a person. The Eastern despot, however, finds in his world no persons possessed of rights, but only rightless things. And since it is thus impossible for him to have personal moral relations to any one, he inevitably himself loses his personal moral character, and becomes a thing — the most important, sacred, divine, worshipped thing — in short, a fetish or an idol.

In the civic communities of the classical world the fulness of rights was the privilege not of one man but of a few (in the aristocracies) or of many (in the democracies). This extension was very important for it rendered possible, though within narrow limits only, independent moral interaction of individuals, and consequently personal self-consciousness, and realised, at any rate for the given social union, the idea of justice or equality of rights.[10] But the moral principle is in its essence universal, since it demands the recognition of the absolute inner worth of man as such, without any external limitations. The communities of the ancients, however, — the aristocracy of Sparta, the Athenian demos, and the peculiar combination of the two — *senatus populusque Romanus*[11] — recognised the true dignity of man only within the limits of their civic union. They were not therefore societies based upon the moral principle, but at best approached and anticipated such a society.

This structure of life has more than merely a historical interest for us: in truth, we have not outlived it yet. Consider, indeed, what it was that limited the moral principle and prevented its realisation in the world of antiquity. There were three classes of men who were not recognised as bearers of any rights or as objects of any duties. They were therefore in no sense an *end* of action, were not included in the idea of the *common good* at all, and were regarded merely as material *instruments* of, or material *obstacles* to, that good. Namely, these were (1) *enemies, i.e.* originally all strangers,[12] then (2) *slaves,*

10. In the despotic monarchies of the East there could be no question of any *equality of rights* — there was only the negative equality of general rightlessness. But equal distribution of an injustice does not render it just. The idea of equality taken in the abstract is mathematical only, not ethical.

11. "The senate and people of Rome." This is the official formula designating the bearer of supreme governmental power in the Roman republic. — *Editor's note.*

12. Hospitality to peaceful strangers is a fact of very ancient date, but can hardly be said to be primitive. In Greece its founder was supposed to be Zeus — the representative of the *third*

and, finally, (3) *criminals.* In spite of individual differences the legalised relation to these three categories of men was essentially the same, for it was
equally immoral. There is no need to represent the institution of slavery,
which replaced the simple slaughter of the prisoners of war, in an
exaggeratedly horrible form. Slaves had means of livelihood secured to them,
and on the whole were not badly treated. This, however, was an accident —
though one of frequent occurrence — and not a duty, and, therefore, had no
moral significance. Slaves were valued for their utility, but this had nothing to
do with the recognition of their worth as human beings. In contradistinction
to these useful things, which ought to be looked after for reasons of expedi-
ency, external and internal enemies, as *things* unquestionably *harmful,* were
to be mercilessly exterminated. With regard, however, to the enemy in war,
mercilessness might be tempered by the respect for his force or the fear of revenge; but with regard to defenceless criminals, real or supposed, cruelty
knew no limits. In cultured Athens, persons accused of ordinary crimes were
tortured as soon as they were taken into custody, previously to any trial.

All these facts — war, slavery, executions — were legitimate for the ancient world, in the sense that they logically followed from the view held by every one, and were conditioned by the general level of consciousness. If the
worth of man as an independent individual and the fulness of his rights and
dignity depend exclusively upon his belonging to a certain civic union, the
natural consequence is that men who do not belong to that union and are
strange and hostile to it, or men who, though they belong to it, violate its laws
and are a menace to common safety, are by that very fact deprived of human
rights and dignity, and that with regard to them all things are lawful.

This point of view, however, came to be changed. The development of
ethical thought first among the Sophists and in Socrates, then among the
Greco-Roman Stoics, the work of Roman lawyers and the very character of
the Roman Empire, which embraced many peoples and nations, and therefore inevitably widened the theoretical and practical outlook, — all this gradually effaced the old limits and established a consciousness of the moral prin-

---

generation of gods (after Chronos and Uranus). Before being a guest in the sense of simply a
friendly visitor, the stranger was a 'guest' in the sense of 'merchant,' and earlier still he was only
regarded in the sense of the Latin *hostis* (enemy). In times still more ancient, accounts of which
have been handed down in classical tradition, a good guest was met with still greater joy than in
the later, hospitable times, but only as a savoury dish at the family feast. Apart from such extremes, the prevalent attitude to strangers in primitive society was no doubt similar to that observed by Sir John Lubbock among ants. When a stranger ant belonging to a different community, though one of the same species, came to an ant heap, ants would drag it about for a while
by its antennae till it was half-dead, and then either finish it off or drive it away.

ciple in its formal universality and infinity. At the same time, in the East the religiously moral teaching of the Jewish prophets was evolving a living ideal of absolute human dignity. And while a Roman in the theatre of the eternal city proclaimed, by the mouth of the actor, the new word '*homo sum*' ("I am a man") as the expression of the highest personal dignity, instead of the old '*civis Romanus*' ("Roman citizen"), another Roman in a remote Eastern province and at a scene more tragic completed the statement of this new principle by simply pointing to the actual personal incarnation of it: *Ecce homo!*[13]

The inner change which took place in humanity as the result of the interaction of the events in Palestine and the Greco-Roman theories ought, it would seem, to have been the beginning of an entirely new order of things. Indeed, a complete regeneration of the physical world was expected; and yet the social and moral world of heathendom still stands essentially unchanged. This will not be an object for grief and wonder if the problem of the moral regeneration of humanity is considered in its full scope. It is clear from the nature of the case, and is foretold in the Gospels,[14] that this problem can only be solved by a gradual process before the final catastrophe comes. The process of such preparation is not yet completed, but is being carried on, and there is no doubt that from the fifteenth and especially from the end of the eighteenth century there has been a noticeable change in the rate of the historical progress. It is important from the practically moral point of view to make clear to ourselves what has been done already and what still remains to be done in certain definite directions.

IV

When men of different nationality and social position were spiritually united in worshipping a *foreigner and a beggar* — the Galilean who was executed as a *criminal* in the name of national and class interests — international wars, rightlessness of the masses, and executions of criminals were *inwardly* undermined. Granted that the inner change took eighteen centuries to manifest itself even to a small extent; granted that its manifestation is becoming noticeable just at the time when its first mover — the Christian faith — is weakened, and seems to disappear from the surface of consciousness — still, man's inner attitude towards the old heathen foundations of society is changing, and the change shows itself more and more in his life. Whatever the

13. "Behold the man!" See John 19:5. — *Editor's note.*
14. In the parables of the leaven, of wheat and tares, of the mustard seed, etc.

thoughts of individual men may be, advanced humanity as a collective whole has reached a degree of moral maturity, a state of feeling and consciousness, which is beginning to make impossible for it things which to the ancient world were natural. And even individual men, if they have not renounced reason altogether, hold, in the form of rational conviction if not in the form of religious faith, the moral principle which does not permit the legalisation of collective crimes. The very fact of the remotest parts of humanity coming into contact, of getting to know one another and becoming mutually connected, does much to abolish the barriers and estrangement between men, natural from the narrow point of view of the ancients, for whom the Straits of Gibraltar were the extreme limit of the universe, and the banks of the Dnieper or the Don were populated by men with dogs' heads.

International wars are not yet abolished, but the point of view with regard to them has changed in a striking degree, especially of late. The *fear* of war has become the predominant motive of international policy, and no Government would venture to confess to harbouring plans of conquest. Slavery in the proper sense has been finally and wholly abolished. Other crude forms of personal dependence which survived till the last century, and, in places, till the middle of the present century, have also been done away with. What remains is only indirect economic slavery, but this too is a question whose turn has come. Finally, the point of view with regard to criminals has since the eighteenth century been clearly tending to become more moral and Christian. And to think that this progress — belated, but quick and decisive — along the path mapped out nineteen centuries ago, should cause anxiety for the moral foundations of society! In truth, a false conception of these foundations is the chief obstacle to a thorough moral change in the social life and consciousness. Religion, family, property cannot as such, that is, simply as existent facts, be the norm or the moral foundation of society. The problem is not to preserve these institutions at any cost *in statu quo* but to make them conformable to the one and only moral standard, so that they might be wholly permeated by the one moral principle.

This principle is essentially universal, the same for all. Now, religion as such need not be universal, and all religions of antiquity were strictly national. Christianity, however, being the embodiment of the absolute moral ideal, is as universal as the moral principle itself, and at the beginning it had this character. But historical institutions, which in the course of history came to be connected with it, ceased to be universal and therefore lost their pure and all-embracing moral character. And so long as we affirm our religion, *first*, in its denominational peculiarity, and *then only* as universal Christianity, we deprive it both of a sound logical basis and of moral significance, and make it an obstacle in the way of the spiritual regeneration of humanity. Further, universality expresses itself not only by the absence of external, national, denominational and other limitations, but still more by freedom from inner limitations. To be truly universal, religion must not separate itself from intellectual enlightenment, from science, from social and political progress. A religion which fears all these things has obviously no faith in its own power and is inwardly permeated with unbelief. While claiming to be the sole moral norm of society, it fails to fulfil the most elementary moral condition of being genuine.

The positive significance of the *family*, in virtue of which it may, in a sense, be the moral norm of society, is apparent from the following consideration. It is physically impossible for a *single* individual concretely to realise in his everyday life his moral relation to *all*. However sincerely a man may recognise the absolute demands of the moral ideal, he cannot, in real life, apply these demands to *all* human beings, for the simple reason that the 'all' do not concretely exist for him. He cannot give *practical* proof of his respect for the human dignity of the millions of men about whom he knows nothing; he cannot make them *in concreto* the positive end of his activity. And yet, unless the moral demand is *completely* realised in *perceptible* personal relations, it remains an abstract principle which enlightens the mind, but does not regenerate the life of man. The solution of this contradiction is that moral relations ought to be fully realised within a certain limited environment in which each man is placed in his concrete everyday existence. This is precisely the true function of the family. Each member of it is not only intended and meant to be, but actually is, an end for all the others; each is perceptibly recognised to have absolute significance, each is irreplaceable. From this point of view the family is the pattern and the elementary constitutive cell of universal brotherhood or of human society as it ought to be. But in order to preserve such a significance, the family obviously must not become the embodiment of mutual egoism. It must be the first stage from which each of its members may be always able to ascend, as much as in him lies, to a greater realisation of the moral principle in the world. The family is either the *crowning stage* of egoism or the *beginning* of world-wide union. To uphold it in the first sense does not mean to uphold a 'moral foundation' of society.

Property as such has no moral significance. No one is morally bound either to be rich or to enrich other people. General equality of property is as impossible and unnecessary as sameness in the colouring or in the quantity of hair. There is one condition, however, which renders the question as to the distribution of property a moral question. It is inconsistent with human dignity and with the moral norm of society that a person should be unable to support his existence, or that in order to do so he should spend so much time and strength as to have none left for looking after his human, intellectual and moral improvement. In that case man ceases to be an end for himself and for others, and becomes merely a material instrument of economic production, on a level with soulless machines. And since the moral principle unconditionally demands that we should respect the human dignity of all and each, and regard every one as an end in himself and not only as a means, a society that desires to be morally normal cannot remain indifferent to such a position of any one of its members. It is its direct duty to secure to each and all a certain *minimum* of well-being, just as much as is necessary to support a worthy human existence. The way to attain this is a problem for economics and not for ethics. In any case it ought to be, and therefore it can be, done.

All human society, and especially society that professes to be Christian, must, if it is to go on existing and to attain to a higher dignity, conform to the moral standard. What matters is not the external preservation of certain institutions, which may be good or bad, but a sincere and consistent striving inwardly to improve *all* institutions and social relations which may be good by subordinating them more and more to the one unconditional moral ideal of the *free union of all in the perfect good.*

Christianity put forward this ideal as a practical task for all peoples and nations, answered for its being realisable — given a good will on our part — and promised help from above in the execution of it — help, of which there is sufficient evidence both in personal and in historical experience. But just because the task Christianity sets before us is a moral and therefore a free one, the supreme Good cannot help man by thwarting the evil will or externally removing the obstacles which that will puts in the way of the realisation of the kingdom of God. Humanity as represented by individuals and nations must itself outlive and overcome these obstacles, which are to be found both in the individual evil will and in the complex effects of the *collective evil will.* This is the reason why progress in the Christian world is so slow, and why Christianity *appears* to be lifeless and inactive.

CHAPTER V

The National Question
from the Moral Point of View

The work of embodying perfect morality in the collective whole of mankind is hindered, in addition to individual passions and vices, by the inveterate forms of collective evil which act like a contagion. In spite of the slow but sure progress in the life of humanity, that evil shows itself now, as it did of old, in a threefold hostility, a threefold immoral relation — between different nations, between society and the criminal, between the different classes of society. Listen to the way in which the French speak of the Germans, the Portuguese of the Dutch, the Chinese of the English, and Americans of the Chinese. Consider the thoughts and feelings of the audience at a criminal trial, the behaviour of a crowd using lynch law in America, or settling accounts with a witch or a horse-stealer in Russia. Hear or read the remarks exchanged between socialist workmen and representatives of the propertied classes at meetings, and in the newspapers. It will then become evident that apart from the anomalies of the personal will we must also take into account the power of superpersonal or collective hostility in its three aspects. The national, the penal and the socially economic questions have, independently of all considerations of internal and external policy, a special interest for the moral consciousness. To deal with them from this point of view is all the more essential, because a new and worse evil has been added of late to the calamity of the hereditary disease — namely, the rash attempt to cure it by preaching new forms of social violence on the one hand, and a passive disintegration of humanity into its individual units on the other.

I

Man's relation to nationality is in our day generally determined in two ways: as *nationalistic* or as *cosmopolitan*. There may be many shades and transition stages in the domain of feeling and of taste, but there are only two clear and definite points of view. The first may be formulated as follows: *We must love our own nation and serve it by all the means at our command, and to other nations we may be indifferent. If their interests conflict with ours, we must take up a hostile attitude to foreign nations.* The essence of the cosmopolitan view is this: *Nationality is merely a natural fact, devoid of all moral significance; we have no duties to the nation as such (neither to our own nor to any other); our duty is only to individual men without any distinction of nationality.*

It is at once apparent that neither view expresses the right attitude towards the fact of national difference. The first ascribes to this fact an absolute significance which it cannot possess, and the second deprives it of all significance. It will be easily seen also that each view finds its justification solely in the *negative* aspect of the *opposite* view.

No rational believer in cosmopolitanism would, of course, find fault with the adherents of nationalism for loving their own country. He would only blame them for thinking that it is permissible, and in some cases even obligatory, to hate and despise men of a different race and nationality. In the same way the most ardent nationalist will not, unless he is altogether devoid of reason, attack the champions of cosmopolitanism for demanding justice for other nations, but will accuse them of being indifferent to their own. So that in each of these views even its direct opponents cannot help distinguishing the good side from the bad, and the question naturally arises whether these two sides are necessarily connected. Does love for one's own people necessarily imply the view that all means of serving it are permissible, and justify an indifferent and hostile relation to other nations? Does the same *moral* relation to all human beings necessarily mean indifference to nationality in general, and to one's own in particular?

The first question is easily solved by analysing the content of the idea of true patriotism or love for one's country. The necessity for such an elementary analysis will be recognised by every one. For every one will agree that patriotism may be *irrational*, do harm instead of the intended good, and lead nations to disaster; that patriotism may be *vain*, and based on unfounded pretensions; and, finally, that it may be directly *false*, and serve merely as a cloak for low and selfish motives. In what, then, does true or real patriotism consist?

When we really love some one, we wish and strive to obtain for them both moral and material good, — the latter, however, only on condition of the former. To every one whom I love I wish, among other things, material prosperity, provided, of course, that it is attained by honourable means and made good use of. But if, when my friend is in need, I were to assist him in making his fortune by fraud, even supposing that he would be certain to escape punishment — or, if he were a writer, and I advised him to increase his literary fame by a successful plagiarism, I should be rightly considered by every one to be either a madman or a scoundrel, and certainly not a good friend.

It is clear then that the goods which love leads us to desire for our neighbours differ both in their external character and in their inner meaning for the will. Spiritual goods exclude, by their very conception, the possibility of being attained by bad means; one cannot steal moral dignity, or plunder justice, or appropriate benevolence. These goods are *unconditionally* desirable. Material goods, which, from the nature of the case, admit of bad means, are on the contrary desirable *on condition* that such means are not used, *i.e.* on condition that material ends are subordinate to the moral end.

Up to a certain point every one will agree with this elementary truth. Every one would grant that it is wrong to enrich oneself at the cost of a crime, or to enrich a friend, one's own or his family, or even one's town or province at the cost of a crime. But this elementary moral truth which is as clear as day suddenly becomes dim and altogether obscure as soon as we get to *one's country.* Everything becomes permissible in the service of its supposed interests, the end justifies the means, black becomes white, falsehood is preferred to truth, violence is extolled as a virtue. Nationality here becomes the final end, the highest good and the standard of good for human activity. Such undue glorification is, however, purely illusory, and is in truth degrading to the nation. The highest human goods cannot, as we have seen, be attained by immoral means. By admitting bad means into our service of the nation and by *justifying* them we limit the national interest to the lower material goods which may be obtained and preserved by wrong and evil methods. This is a direct *injury* to the very nation we wish to serve. It means transferring the centre of gravity of the national life from the higher sphere to the lower, and serving national *egoism* under the guise of serving the nation. The moral worthlessness of *such* nationalism is proved by history itself. There is abundant evidence that nations prospered and were great only so long as they did not make themselves their final end, but served the higher, the *universal* ideal ends. History shows also that the very conception of the nation as a final and ultimate bearer of the collective life of humanity is ill-founded.

II

The division of humanity into definite and stable groups possessing a national character is a fact which is neither universal nor first in the order of time. Not to speak of savages and barbarians, who are still living in separate families, clans or nomadic bands, division into nations did not exclusively predominate even in the civilised part of humanity when the tribe was finally superseded by the 'city' or 'country.' The country and the nation, though more or less closely associated, do not altogether coincide. In the ancient world we find hardly any clear division into nations at all. We find either independent civic communities, *i.e.* groups smaller than the nation and united politically only and not by the bond of nationality — such as the cities of Phœnicia, Greece and Italy — or, on the contrary, groups larger than the nation — the so-called 'world empires' which included many peoples, from the Assyro-Babylonic down to the Roman. In these crude precursors of the universal unity of mankind national considerations had merely a material significance and were not the determining factor. The idea of nationality as the supreme principle of life virtually found neither the time nor the place for its application in the ancient world. The opposition between one's own people and aliens was then far more sharp and ruthless than it is now, but it was not determined by nationality. In the kingdom of Darius and Xerxes men of different race and nationality were all regarded as members of one body, since they were equally subject to one common authority and one supreme law. Enemies or aliens were the men who were *not yet* brought under the rule of 'the great king.' On the other hand, in Greece, the fact that Spartans and Athenians spoke the same language, had the same gods and realised that they belonged to the same nation, did not prevent them from treating each other as foreigners throughout their history, or even from being mortal enemies. Similar relations held between other cities or civic communities of Greece, and only once in a thousand years did the true national or pan-Greek patriotism actively show itself, namely, during the Persian war. The coincidence — and that only an approximate one — between practical solidarity and national character hardly lasted for forty years, and was superseded by a fierce and prolonged slaughter of the Greeks by the Greeks during the Peloponnesian war. This state of deadly struggle between small communities belonging to one and the same nation was considered perfectly normal and continued up to the moment when all these communities together lost their independence. They lost it not in order to form a national unity, but in order that the Greek nation might, under the power of foreign kings, immediately pass from its state of political disruption to becoming the uniting and civilising element in the whole of the ancient world. The opposition between fellow-citizens and aliens (*i.e.* inhabitants of another city, though a Greek one) had now lost its meaning as a supreme political principle, and was not replaced by the opposition between their own and other nations. What remained was the wider opposition between Hellenism and barbarism, where the former meant participation in the higher intellectual and æsthetic culture, and not necessarily the fact of being a Greek by birth, or of using the Greek language. Not even the most arrogant of Greeks ever regarded Horace and Vergil, Augustus or Mæcenas as barbarians. Indeed the founders of the Hellenic 'world empire' themselves — the Macedonian kings Philip and Alexander, were not Greeks in the ethnographical sense. And it was owing to these two foreigners that Greeks immediately passed from the narrow local patriotism of separate civic communities to the consciousness of themselves as bearers of a world-wide culture, without ever returning to the stage of the national patriotism of the Persian wars. As to Rome, the whole of Roman history was a continuous transition from the policy of a city to the policy of a world Empire — *ab urbe ad orbem*[1] — without pausing at a purely national stage. When Rome was defending herself against the Punic invasion, she was merely the most powerful of the Italian cities. When she crushed her enemy, she imperceptibly overstepped the ethnographical and the geographical boundaries of Latinism and became conscious of herself as a moving force in world-history, anticipating by two centuries the poet's reminder —

> But, Rome, 'tis thine alone, with awful sway,
> To rule mankind and make the world obey,
> Disposing peace and war thy own majestic way,
> To tame the proud, the fetter'd slave to free.[2]

Roman citizenship soon became accessible to all, and the formula 'Rome for the Romans' appealed to no one on the banks of the Tiber: Rome was for the world.

While Alexanders and Cæsars were politically abolishing in East and West the vague limits of nationality, cosmopolitanism as a philosophical doctrine was developed and disseminated by the representatives of the two most popular schools of thought — the wandering Cynics and the dispassionate Stoics. They preached the supremacy of nature and reason, the unity underlying all existence and the insignificance of all artificial and historical limita-

---

1. "From the city to the world." — *Editor's note.*
2. Virgil, *Aeneid* VI, 851. — *Editor's note.*

tions and divisions. They taught that man by his very nature and therefore *every* man had a supreme destination and dignity, consisting in freedom from external affections, errors and passions, in the steadfast courage of the man who "if the whole world were dashed to fragments, would remain serene among the ruins."[3] Hence they inevitably recognised all the externally given determinations, social, national, etc., as conventional and illusory. Roman jurisprudence,[4] in its own sphere and from its own point of view, also supported the philosophical ideas of natural and therefore universal reason, of virtue which is the same for all, and of the equality of human rights. As a result of this collective intellectual work the conception 'Roman' became identical with the conception of 'universal,' both in its external range of application and in its inner content.[5]

III

At the beginning of the Christian era the Jewish people were the only one within the civilised world of antiquity who had a strong national consciousness. But in their case it was intimately associated with their religion, with the true feeling of its inner superiority and a presentiment of world-wide historical destiny. The national consciousness of the Jews had no real satisfaction; it lived by hopes and expectations. The short-lived greatness of David and Solomon was idealised and transformed into a golden age. But the vital historical instinct of the people who were the first to evolve a philosophy of history (in the book of Daniel on the world empires and on the kingdom of truth of the Son of man)[6] did not allow them to stop at the glorified image of the past and made them transfer their ideal into the future. This ideal, however, had from the first certain features of universal significance, and when, by the inspiration of the prophets, it was transferred to the future it became finally free from all narrow nationalistic limitations. Isaiah proclaimed the Christ as the banner that is to gather all nations round Himself, and the author of the book of Daniel entirely adopted the point of view of *universal* history.

3. Si fractus illabatur orbis
    Impavidum ferient ruinae.   [Horace, *Odes* III 3, 6-7. — *Editor's note.*]
    4. For confirmation of these statements see the last chapter of Part I of "The National Question" by the present author.
    5. Although the Stoic philosophy originated in Greece, independently of Rome, it developed only in the Roman era, was particularly prevalent among the Romans, and manifested its practical influence chiefly through Roman lawyers.
    6. See Daniel 7:13-14. — *Editor's note.*

This universalistic conception of the Messiah, expressing the true national self-consciousness of the Jews as the finest ideal flower of the spirit of the people, was held only by the elect few. When the banner for all the peoples was, as foretold by the prophets, raised in Jerusalem and Galilee, the majority of the Jews with their official leaders (the Sadducees), and partly with their unofficial teachers (the Pharisees), proved to be on the side of national and religious exclusiveness as against the highest realisation of the prophetic ideal. The inevitable conflict and breach between these two tendencies — these 'two souls,'[7] as it were — of the Jewish people sufficiently explains (from the purely historical point of view) the great tragedy of Golgotha, with which Christianity began.[8]

It would, however, be an obvious mistake to associate Christianity with the principle of cosmopolitanism. There was no occasion for the Apostles to preach against nationality. The dangerous and immoral aspect of national divisions, namely, mutual hatred and malignant struggle, no longer existed within the limits of the 'universe'[9] of that day; Roman peace — *pax Romana* — had abolished wars between nations. Christian universalism was directed against other and more profound divisions, which remained in full force in practical life in spite of the ideas of the prophets, the philosophers, and the jurists. There remained the distinction of religion between Judaism and paganism, the distinction of culture between Hellenism (which included educated Romans) and barbarism, and, finally, the worst distinction — the socio-economic one — between freemen and slaves. It had retained all its force in practice, in spite of the theoretical protests of the Stoics. These divisions were in direct opposition to the moral principle — which was not the case with the national distinctions of that time. The latter had in the Roman Empire as innocent a character as, for instance, the provincialism of Gascogne or Brittany has in modern France. But the opposition between the Jews and the Gentiles, the Hellenes and the barbarians, freemen and slaves, involved the denial of all solidarity between them; it was an opposition of the higher beings to the lower, the lower having their moral dignity and hu-

7. Two souls live in my breast,
   They struggle, and long to be parted.   Goethe [*Faust*, Part I. — *Editor's note.*]
8. That the best among the Pharisees took no part in the persecution of Jesus Christ, and were favourable to primitive Christianity, is shown in Professor Chwolson's excellent article in the *Memuari Akademii Nauk (Proceedings of the Academy of Sciences)*, 1893. [D. Chwolson, *Das letze Passamahl Christi und der Tage seines Todes* (Christ's last paschal meal and the day of his death), *Mémoires de l'Académie Imperiale des Sciences de Saint-Petersbourg.* VII Série. T. XLI, SPb, 1893, pp. 1-132. — *Editor's note.*]
9. Οἰκομένη (*i.e.* γῆ), the Greek name for the Roman Empire.

man rights denied to them.[10] This is the reason why St. Paul had to proclaim that in Jesus Christ there is neither Jew nor Greek, neither bond nor free,[11] but a new creation — a *new* creation, however, and not simple reduction of the old to one denominator. In the place of the negative ideal of the dispassionate Stoic unmoved by the downfall of the world, the Apostle puts the positive ideal of a man full of compassion and at one with all that lives, who shares in the sufferings of the universal man, Christ, and in His death that redeems the world, and therefore participates in His triumph over death and in the salvation of the whole world. In Christianity the mind passes from the abstract *man in general* of the philosophers and jurists to the concrete *universal* man. The old hostility and estrangement between different sections of humanity is thereby completely abolished. *Every* man, if only he lets 'Christ be formed in him,'[12] *i.e.* if he enters into the spirit of the perfect man, and determines all his life and activity by the ideal revealed in the image of Christ, participates in the Godhead through the power of the Son of God abiding in him. For the regenerated man individuality, like all other characteristics and distinctions, including that of nationality, ceases to be a *limit,* and becomes the basis of positive union with the collective all-embracing humanity or Church (in its true nature), which is complementary to him. According to the well-known saying of St. Paul,[13] the peculiarities of structure and of function which distinguish a given bodily organ from other organs do not separate it from them and from the rest of the body, but on the contrary are the basis of its definite positive participation in the life of the organism, and make it of unique value to all the other organs and the body as a whole. Likewise in the 'body of Christ' individual peculiarities do not separate one person from others, but unite each with all, being the ground of his special significance for all and of his positive interaction with them. Now this obviously applies to nationality as well. The *all-embracing humanity* (or the Church which the Apostle preached) is not an abstract idea, but is *a harmonious union of all the concrete positive characteristics of the new or the regenerated creation.* It therefore includes the *national* as well as the *personal* characteristics. The body of Christ is a *perfect* organism and cannot consist of simple cells alone; it must contain larger and more complex organs, which in this connection are naturally represented by the different nations. The dif-

10. In speaking of the opposition between Judaism and paganism, I am referring, of course, not to the teaching of Moses and the prophets and sages — they all recognised in principle that the pagans had human rights — but to the spirit of the crowd and its leaders.

11. See Colossians 3:11. — *Editor's note.*

12. St. Paul's expression. [See Galatians 4:19. — *Editor's note.*]

13. See 1 Corinthians 12:12-27. — *Editor's note.*

ference between the personal and the national character is not one of principle[14] but of greater stability and wider range in the case of the latter. Since Christianity does not demand absence of individual character, it cannot demand absence of national character. The spiritual regeneration it demands both of individuals and of nations does not mean a loss of the natural qualities and powers; it means that these qualities are transformed, that a new direction and a new content are given them. When Peter and John were regenerated by the spirit of Christ, they did not lose any of their positive peculiarities and distinct characteristic features. So far from losing their individuality, they developed and strengthened it. This is how it must be with entire nations converted to Christianity.

Actual adoption of the true religion containing the unconditional principle of morality must sweep away a great deal from the national as well as from the individual life. But that which is incompatible with the unconditional principle and has therefore to be destroyed does not constitute a positive characteristic or peculiarity. There is such a thing as collective evil will, as historical sin burdening the national conscience, as a wrong direction of the life and activity of a nation. From all these wrongs a nation must set itself free, but such freedom can only strengthen it, and increase and widen the expression of its positive character.

The first preachers of the Gospel had no reason to occupy themselves with the national question which the life of humanity had not yet brought to the fore, since there were hardly any distinct, independent nations conscious of themselves as such on the historical stage of the time. Nevertheless we find in the New Testament definite indications of *a positive* attitude to nationality. The words spoken to the Samaritan woman, *"salvation is of the Jews,"*[15] and the preliminary direction to the disciples, "go rather to the lost sheep of the

14. This is brought out by the fact that the only rational way of accounting for the genesis of a stable national character, such as the Jewish — which is not affected by the external influences of climate, history, etc., is to suppose that it is the inherited, personal character of the national ancestor. The inner truth of the Biblical characteristic of Jacob — the ancestor of the Jews — and also of Ishmael, the ancestor of the Northern Arabs, will be recognised by any impartial reader, whatever his attitude toward the historical side of the narrative may be. Even granting that the man named Jacob, who did all that in the book of Genesis he is said to have done, never existed at all, anyway the Jews, or at any rate the chief tribe of Judah, must have had a common progenitor; and starting with the national character of the Jews we must conclude that that progenitor had precisely the typical peculiarities which the Bible ascribes to Jacob. See S. M. Solovyov's *Observations on the Historical Life of Nations,* and also my "Philosophy of Biblical History." [The latter was published in Zagreb in 1887, and it appeared later in a revised form with the title *The History and Future of Theocracy (Works,* volume IV). — *Editor's note*

15. John 4:22.

house of Israel,"[16] clearly show Christ's love for His own people. And His final command to the Apostles, "Go ye therefore, and teach *all nations*,"[17] implies that even outside Israel He contemplated not separate individuals only, but entire peoples.[18] When St. Paul became the Apostle of the Gentiles he did not thereupon become a cosmopolitan. Though separated from the majority of his compatriots in the all-important question of religion, he was not indifferent to his people and their special destination:

"I say the truth in Christ, I lie not, my conscience also bearing me witness in the Holy Ghost, that I have great heaviness and continual sorrow in my heart. For I could wish that myself were accursed from Christ for my brethren, my kinsmen according to the flesh: who are Israelites; to whom pertaineth the adoption, and the glory, and the covenants, and the giving of the law, and the service of God, and the promises; whose are the fathers, and of whom, as concerning the flesh, Christ came. . . . Brethren, my heart's desire and prayer to God for Israel is, that they might be saved."[19]

IV

Before they could realise the ideal of universal humanity, nations had first to be formed as distinct independent bodies. Let us consider this process with special reference to Western Europe, where it is finally completed. The Apostles' successors, to whom the command to teach all nations was handed down, soon came to deal with nations in their infancy, standing in need of elementary upbringing before they could be taught. The Church nurtured them conscientiously and with self-sacrificing devotion, and then continued to act as their guardian, making them pass through a school that was somewhat one-sided though not bad. The historical childhood and youth of the Romano-Germanic nations under the guardianship of the Roman Catholic Church — the so-called Middle Ages — did not end in anything like a normal way. The spiritual authorities failed to observe that their nurslings had come of age, and, from natural human weakness, insisted on treating them in the same old way. The anomalies and changes that arose from this fact have no bearing on

16. Matthew 10:6.

17. Matthew 28:19.

18. The words in the Acts of the Apostles (1:8), "Ye shall be witnesses unto me both in Jerusalem, and in all Judea, and in Samaria, and unto the uttermost part of the earth," show still more clearly that the Saviour of the world recognised a definite, local and national starting-point for His world-wide work.

19. Romans 9:1-5; 10:1.

our subject. What is of importance to us is the phenomenon which took place in the development of every European nation. It undoubtedly indicates a certain general ethico-historical law, for it was manifested under the most various and often directly opposed conditions.

For reasons sufficiently obvious Italy was the first of the European countries to attain to national self-consciousness. The Lombard League in the middle of the twelfth century clearly indicates national awakening. The external struggle, however, was only an impetus that called to life the true forces of the Italian genius. At the beginning of the next century the newly-born Italian language was used by St. Francis to express ideas and feelings of universal significance that could be understood by Buddhists and Christians alike. At the same period began Italian painting (Cimabue), and at the beginning of the fourteenth century appeared Dante's all-embracing poem, which would alone have been sufficient to make Italy great. From the fourteenth to the seventeenth centuries Italy, torn asunder by the hostilities between the cities and the podestas, the Pope and the Emperor, the French and the Spanish, produced all the works for which humanity loves and values her, and Italians may justly feel proud of these works. All these immortal works of the philosophical and scientific, poetical and artistic genius had the same value for other nations, for the world as a whole as for the Italians themselves. Men to whom Italy's true greatness was due were no doubt real patriots. They set the greatest value upon their country, but it was not in their case an empty claim leading to false and immoral demands — they embodied the lofty significance of Italy in works of absolute value. They did not consider it true and beautiful to affirm themselves and their nationality, but they *directly* affirmed themselves in what is true and beautiful. Their works were good not because they glorified Italy, but rather they glorified Italy because they were good in themselves — good *for all*. Under such conditions patriotism stands in no need of defence and justification. It justifies itself in practice, evincing itself as creative *power* and not as fruitless reflection or 'excitement of idle thought.' Corresponding to the inner intensity of the creative work at this blossoming time of Italy was the wide extension of the Italian race at that period. Its civilising influence extended to the Crimea in the East and Scotland in the North-West. The first European to penetrate to Mongolia and China was Marco Polo, an Italian. Another Italian discovered the new world, and a third, enlarging that discovery, left it his name. The literary influence of Italy was for several centuries prevalent throughout Europe. Italian poetry, epic and lyric, and the Italian novel were examples for imitation. Shakespeare took from the Italians the subjects and the form of his plays. The ideas of Giordano Bruno roused philosophical reflection both in England and in Germany. The Italian language and Italian fashions universally prevailed in the higher classes of society. And while the national creative work and influence were at their highest, Italians were obviously concerned not with keeping Italy for themselves — at that time indeed it was for any one who liked to take it — but only with things which made them be something for others and gave them a universal significance. They cared for the objective ideas of beauty and truth, which through their national spirit received a new and worthy expression. What conception of nationality can be logically deduced from this? It cannot be said, with Italy's national history before us, that nationality is something self-existent and self-contained, living in itself and for itself, for this great nation proves to be simply a special form of universal content, living *in* that content, filled with it and embodying it not for itself only but *for all.*

The *Spanish* nation developed under very peculiar conditions. For seven centuries Spain was the vanguard on the right flank of the Christian world in its struggle with Mohammedanism. And just when the left flank — Byzantium — was overthrown by the enemy, on the right flank Spaniards won a final and decisive victory. This long and successful struggle was justly regarded as the national glory of Spain. It is not permissible for a Christian people to hate and despise Mohammedans — or any one else — or seek to exterminate them; but to defend Europe against invasion by them was a direct Christian duty. For in so far as Christianity, in spite of all its historical perversions, contains absolute truth, to which the future belongs, in so far the defence even of the external boundaries of Christian faith and culture against the destructive violence of the armed hordes of unbelievers is an unquestionable merit from the point of view of humanity. Apart from the question of religious belief, would it have been a gain for historical progress had Western Europe met with the fate of Western Asia or of the Balkan Peninsula?[20] In defending themselves against the Moors the Spaniards were serving the common cause of humanity, and they

20. At one time the Moorish culture in Spain was not inferior, and in some respects it was superior to the Christian culture of the period. But history clearly proves how short-lived all Mohammedan culture is. The end with which it met in the Middle Ages in Damascus, Baghdad and Cairo would no doubt have been repeated once more in the West. There too it would have been replaced by stable barbarism, such as the Turkish. And if the Bashi-Bazouks were to overrun London, and Saxony were to be constantly raided by the Kurds, what would become of the British Museum and the Leipzig Press? This is an argument *ad homines.* But speaking quite seriously and wholly admitting the comparative merits of Mohammedanism and the historical tasks it still has to accomplish in Asia and Africa, it must be remembered that this religion professedly renounces the absolute moral ideal, *i.e.* the principle of the perfect manifestation of God in man, and has no right therefore to dominate Christian peoples. To repulse the Mohammedan invasion of Europe was therefore both a historical necessity and a historical merit for the Christian nations which took a leading part in the struggle.

knew it. They would not dream of saying 'Spain is for the Spaniards,' for in that case why should they not go further and say 'Castile is for the Castilians, Aragon is for the Aragonians,' etc.? They felt, they thought, and they proclaimed that Spain was for all Christendom, as Christianity was for all the world. Their feeling was perfectly genuine, they really wished to serve their religion as a universal religion, as the highest good for all, and one can only reproach them with having a wrong or a one-sided conception of Christianity. The continuous struggle for a common and just cause lasted for seven centuries, and, being chiefly an external struggle waged by the force of arms,[21] it created both the strength and the narrowness of the national spirit of Spain. More than any other nation the Spaniards distorted the truth of Christianity in their practical conception of it and in their actions; more decisively than any one they associated it with violence. According to the general custom of the Middle Ages, the Spaniards based their practical view of the world upon the distinction between the two swords — the spiritual sword of the monks under the rule of the Pope, and the worldly sword of the knights under the rule of the king. But in their case — more than in the case of any other nation — the two swords were so closely connected as to become essentially alike. The spiritual sword proved in the end to be as material and violent as the worldly, though more painful and less noble than the latter. The special part played by the Spanish nation in this respect is shown by the fact that the Inquisition had twice been started by Spaniards — by the monk Dominique in the thirteenth, and by the king Ferdinand in the fifteenth century.[22]

The struggle of Spanish knights with the bellicose Mohammedan invaders was a gain to Christianity and the source of the greatness of Spain. The

21. Chiefly, but not exclusively, for Spain too had some truly spiritual champions of Christianity. Such, *e.g.*, was Raymond Lullius, who devoted his life to spreading the true religion by means of rational persuasion. He worked out a special method, which he thought could render the dogmas of the faith as self-evident as the truths of pure mathematics and formal logic. Later on he became a missionary, and was assassinated in the Bastarian Colonies for peaceful preaching of the Gospel.

22. It is a curious coincidence that in both the East and the West the first persecution for religious beliefs — namely, the persecution of the Manichean heresy in the fourth century — was due to a *Spaniard* — Theodosius the Great. It is curious too that the heresy of the Albigenses, against which the Dominican inquisition was originally intended, was a direct development of Manicheism, on account of which the Emperor Theodosius had appointed his 'inquisitors' ten centuries before. Shortly before that time the deplorable part which the Spanish nation was to play with regard to religious persecutions was foreshadowed by the fact that the first execution for religious belief (viz. that of the Priscillian heretics) was due to the instigation of two Spanish bishops. This unheard-of action called forth protests both in Italy (St. Ambrose of Milan) and in France (St. Martin of Tours).

work of the 'spiritual sword' against the *conquered* Moors and defenceless Jews was treason to the spirit of Christ, a disgrace to Spain and the first cause of its downfall. The bitter fruits of the fatal historical sin did not ripen at once. In following its old path of external service to the Christian faith Spain did one good thing more for the common cause — namely, she spread Christianity beyond the ocean. Spanish knights and pirates acquired for Christian culture, such as it was, the greater part of the new world. They saved a whole country (Mexico) from such abominations and horrors of satanic heathendom[23] as cause even the horrors of the Inquisition to fade (and the Inquisition itself was abolished soon after). They founded in Southern and Central America a dozen new States which take some part in the common historical life of humanity. At the same time Spanish missionaries — a real saint like the Jesuit Francis Xavier among them — were the first to carry the Gospel to India and Japan. Spain, however, still regarded as its main task the defence of Christianity (as she understood it, *i.e.* of the Roman Church) from its immediate and most dangerous enemies. In the sixteenth century it found such enemies no longer in the Mohammedans but in the Protestants. At the present time we can look upon the Reformation as a necessary moment in the history of Christianity itself. But for people who lived at that epoch it was impossible to take this view. They either themselves became Protestants or regarded Protestantism as a hostile attack, proceeding from the devil, against the Christian truth embodied in the Church. For Spain, whose whole history was bound up with the Catholic idea, there could be no choice. All the strength of the most powerful country of the time was directed to crushing the new religious movement. It was a work wrong in principle, revoltingly cruel in practice, and a hopeless failure in its result. The moral guilt of Spain, which made the Duke of Alba her national and 'Christian' hero, is beyond all doubt. One can only point to some extenuating circumstances. The Spanish were sincerely, though blindly, convinced that they were standing up for a good that is universal, for what is most important and precious to humanity — the one true religion, of which godless renegades, possessed by the spirit of evil, wanted to rob mankind. In this national struggle against Protestantism the Spanish defended a certain universal principle, namely, the principle of the external guardianship of a divine institution over humanity. It was a false and untenable universalism, but its champions sincerely believed in it and served it disinterestedly without any selfish considerations, whether

23. For an impartial statement of the facts see A. Réville's book on the religion of Mexico and Peru. [A. Réville, *Histoire des religions*, volume VII: *Les religions du Mexique, de l'Amérique centrale et du Perou* (Paris, 1885). — *Editor's note.*]

nationally-political or personal. At the same time the Spanish genius of Ignatius Loyola founded, with the purpose of combating Protestantism by peaceful means, the order of Jesuits — an order of which people may think what they like, but to which one thing can certainly not be denied — viz. its universal and international character. So that in making the struggle with Protestantism into a national idea the Spanish did not separate it from the interests of the common good, as they understood it. The unsuccessful external struggle for Roman Catholicism undermined the kingdom of Spain, but did not exhaust the spiritual forces of the Spanish nation. Moral energy shown in the defence of a universal though a wrongly conceived cause found another and a better expression in the realm of the spirit. In the sixteenth and seventeenth centuries Spain made considerable national contributions to the general treasury of higher culture in the domain of art, poetry, and contemplative mysticism. In all these things the Spanish genius was occupied with objects important not for the Spanish nation only but for all mankind. Its work was extremely national in character, but this came about naturally, without any deliberate intention on the part of the authors. It undoubtedly had a universal interest, and supported the glory of Spain at a time when her external power was on the wane and her arms were justly suffering defeat. The influence of Spanish culture rivalled that of the Italian in the sixteenth and seventeenth centuries, precisely at a time when half Europe entertained a natural hostility towards the defenders of the old religion.

The highest development of the *English* national spirit may, for the sake of brevity, be designated by five names: Bacon, Shakespeare, Milton, Newton, and Penn. These five names have nothing to do with the demands and pretensions of exclusive nationalism. They stand for what is of importance and value to all mankind, and express the common debt of humanity to England. The men who created the national greatness of England never thought of nationalism as such. One was concerned with the true knowledge of nature and of man, and was occupied with the problem of a new and better scientific method; another sought artistically to represent the human soul, human passions, characters and destinies, and did not hesitate to borrow his subjects from foreign literature and transfer the place of action to foreign countries. The great leaders of the Puritan movement, who found their prophet in Milton, thought above all things of ordering life in accordance with the Biblical ideal, equally binding, in their view, upon all nations. These Englishmen did not hesitate to recognise for *their own* and to carry beyond the ocean an ideal which was Hebrew in its origin and German in its Protestant form. And the greatest representative of modern science discovered with his English intellect a universal truth about the physical world as an interconnected whole, containing, as a principle of its unity, that which he called the 'sensorium of the Deity.'

A broadly conceived world of scientific experience, open on all sides to the intellect; profound artistic humanism; high ideas of religious and political freedom and a grand conception of the physical unity of the universe — this is what the English nation produced through her heroes and men of genius. 'England for the English' was not enough for them; they thought that the whole world was for the English, and they had a right to think so, because they themselves were for the whole world. The wide diffusion of the English race was in close correlation with the good qualities of the national character. British merchants, of course, always observed their own interests; but it is not any merchants who could succeed in colonising North America and forming a new great nation of it. For the United States were built up, not by the Redskins or Negroes, but by English people and English political and religious ideas — ideas of universal significance. Nor is it *any* merchants who could take firm possession of India and build a civilised Australia on a perfectly virginal soil.[24]

The culminating point in the national history of *France* is the epoch of the great Revolution and of the Napoleonic wars, when the universal significance of that country was most clearly apparent. The national life was then at its highest, not perhaps from the point of view of its content, but of its intensity and of the breadth of external influence. No doubt, the rights of man and of citizen proclaimed to all the world proved to be largely fictitious; no doubt the all-embracing revolutionary trinity — *liberté, egalité, fraternité* — was realised in a very peculiar fashion. But in any case the fact that the people were carried away by these universal ideas showed that the spirit of narrow nationalism was foreign to them. Did France want to be 'for the French' only when she surrendered herself to a half-Italian in order that he should direct her powers and sweep away in the whole of Europe the old order of things, introducing everywhere the principles of civic equality, religious and political freedom? Apart from this epoch, indeed, France was always noted for a special kind of universal receptivity and communicativeness, by a power and a desire to grasp the ideas of others, give them a finished and popular form, and

---

24. Hindus taught in English schools begin to complain — in the English and their own newspapers, after the English style — that the English yoke is burdensome and to say that their nation must be united and obtain freedom for itself. Why is it that this had never occurred to them before? The fact is that they obtained ideas, such as that of nationality, national spirit, national dignity, patriotism, solidarity, development, exclusively from the English. Left to themselves they had not been able to arrive at them during the two and a half thousand years of their history, in spite of their ancient wisdom.

then to send them forth into the world. This power makes the history of France a vivid and emphatic *résumé* of universal history, and is too obvious and too well known to dwell upon.

Having first shown the greatness of her national spirit in the Reformation, *Germany* has in modern times (from the middle of the eighteenth to the middle of the nineteenth century) occupied the foremost place in the domain of higher culture, intellectual and æsthetic — the place which Italy had held at the end of mediæval and at the beginning of modern history. The universal character and significance of the Reformation, of the poetry of Goethe, of the philosophy of Kant or Hegel, stands in no need of proof or demonstration. I will only observe that for Germany, as for Italy, the period of the highest development of the spiritual forces of the nation coincided with the period of political weakness and disruption.

The broad idealism of the *Polish* spirit, receptive of foreign influences to the point of enthusiasm and devotion, is only too obvious. The universalism of the Poles caused the narrow nationalists to reproach them for 'treason to the cause of the Slavs.' But those who are familiar with the shining lights of Polish thought — Mickiewicz, Krasinski, Tovianski, Slowacki — know how greatly the power of the national genius showed itself in their universalistic work. As to our own country, the Russian spirit has hitherto found no embodiment more vivid and powerful than the Tsar, whose powerful arm has demolished our national exclusiveness for ever, and the poet who had a special gift to identify himself with the genius of other nations and yet remain wholly Russian.[25] Peter the Great and Pushkin — these two names are sufficient to prove that the dignity of our national spirit found its realisation only in unreserved communion with the rest of humanity, and not apart from it.

Without enumerating all the other nations, I will only mention Holland and Sweden. The national glory and prosperity of the first were due to her struggle for the faith against Spanish despotism. As a consequence of it, the little country did not shut itself up in its dearly bought independence, but became the abode of free thought for all Europe. Sweden manifested her national greatness when, under Gustavus Adolphus, she devoted herself to the service of the common cause of religious freedom against the policy of compulsory uniformity.

---

25. The well-known remark of Dostoevsky, who at his best was himself equally all-embracing.

V

The history of all nations which have had a direct influence upon the destinies of humanity in ancient and modern times teaches one and the same thing. At the period when their powers were unfolded to the utmost, they took the greatness and the value of their nationality to lie not in itself taken in the abstract, but in something universal, *supernational* that they believed in, that they served and that they realised in their creative work — a work national in its origin and means of expression, but wholly universal in its content and in its objective result. Nations live and act not for their own sakes, nor for the sake of their material interests, but for the sake of their idea, *i.e.* for the sake of what is most important to them and *can be of service to the world as a whole* — they live not for themselves only, but for all. That which a nation believes in and does in faith it is bound to regard as *unconditionally* good — not as its own good, but as good in itself and therefore as good for all; and such it generally proves to be. Historical representatives of a nation may wrongly understand this or that aspect of a nationally-universal idea which they serve, and then their service is bad and fruitless. Philip II and the Duke of Alba had a very wrong idea of ecclesiastical unity, and the Paris Convention understood the idea of human rights no better. But the bad understanding passes away and the idea remains, and, if it is really rooted in the soul of a people, it finds new and better expression free from the old imperfections.

The creative work of a nation, *i.e.* that which a nation concretely realises in the world, is universal; the object of true national *self-consciousness* is universal also. A nation is not aware of itself in the abstract, as of an empty subject separate from the content and the meaning of its life. It is conscious of itself in relation to that which it does and wants to do, in relation to what it believes in and what it serves.

It is clear from history that a nation does not regard itself, taken in the abstract, as the purpose of its life. In other words, it does not set an absolute value upon its material interest apart from its supreme ideal condition. But if this be so, the individual too has no right in his love for his nation to separate it from the meaning of its existence and to put the service of its material advantages above the demands of morality. A nation in and through its true creative work and self-consciousness affirms itself in the universal — in that which is of value for every one and in which all are united. How then can a true patriot, for the sake of a supposed 'advantage' to his nation, destroy its solidarity with other nations, and despise or hate foreigners? A nation finds its true good in the common good; how then can a patriot take the good of his nation to be something distinct from and opposed to everything else? It will clearly not be the ideal moral good which the nation itself desires, and the supposed patriot will prove to be opposed not to other nations but to his own in its best aspirations. National hostility and opposition no doubt exist, just as cannibalism once existed everywhere; they exist as a zoological fact, condemned by the best consciousness of the peoples themselves. Made into an abstract principle this zoological fact hangs over the life of nations, obscuring its significance and destroying its inspiration — *for the significance and the inspiration of the particular are only to be found in its connection and harmony with the universal.*

As against false patriotism or nationalism, which supports the predominance of the animal instincts of a people over its higher national self-consciousness, cosmopolitanism is right in demanding that the moral law shall be unconditionally applied to all, apart from all difference of nationality. But it is the moral principle itself which, when consistently worked out, prevents us from being satisfied with the negative demand of cosmopolitanism.

Let it be granted that the immediate object of the moral relation is the individual person. But one of the essential peculiarities of that person — direct continuation and expansion of his individual character — is his nationality (in the positive sense of character, type, and creative power). This is not merely a physical, but also a psychical and moral fact. At the stage of development now reached by humanity the fact of belonging to a given nationality is to a certain extent confirmed by the individual's self-conscious will. Thus nationality is an inner, inseparable property of the person — is something very dear and close to him. It is impossible to stand in a moral relation to this person without recognising the existence of what is so important to him. The moral principle does not allow us to transform a concrete person, a living man with his inseparable and essential national characteristics, into an empty abstract subject with all his determining peculiarities left out. If we are to recognise the inner dignity of this particular man this obligation extends to all positive characteristics with which he connects his dignity; if we love a man we must love his nation which he loves and from which he does not separate himself. The highest moral ideal demands that we should love all men as we love ourselves. But since men do not exist outside of nations (just as nations do not exist apart from individual men), and since this connection has already become moral and inward as well as physical, the direct logical deduction is that *we must love all nations as we love our own.* This commandment affirms patriotism as a natural and fundamental feeling, as a direct duty of the individual to the collective whole immediately above him, and at the same time it frees that feeling from the zoological properties of national egoism or nationalism, and makes it the basis of and the standard for a positive relation to all other nations in accordance with the absolute and all-embracing principle of morality. The significance of this demand of loving other nations does not in any way depend upon the metaphysical question as to whether nations are independent collective entities. Even if a nation exists only in its visible individual representatives, at any rate *in them* it constitutes a positive peculiarity which one may value and love in foreigners just as much as in men belonging to our own people. If such a relation actually becomes a rule, national *differences* will be preserved and even intensified, while hostile *divisions* and aggressiveness, that are so fundamental an obstacle to the moral organisation of humanity, will disappear.

The demand to love other nations as our own does not at all imply a *psychological identity* of feeling, but only an *ethical identity* of conduct. I must desire the true good of all other nations as much as that of my own. This 'love of benevolence' is identical if only because the true good is one and indivisible. Such ethical love involves, of course, a psychological understanding and approval of the positive characteristics of other nations. Once the senseless and ignorant national hostility has been overcome by the moral will, we begin to know and to value other nations — we begin *to like* them. This 'approving love,' however, can never be identical with the love we feel for our own people, just as the sincerest love for our neighbours (according to the commandment of the Gospel) can never be psychologically identical with the love for oneself, although it is ethically equivalent to it. One's own *self*, just as *one's own* nation, always retains the priority of a starting-point. When this difficulty is cleared away, no serious objections can be raised against the principle: *love all other nations as your own.*[26]

---

26. I cannot regard as serious the objection made by one of my critics that it is impossible to love one's own and other nations equally, because in war it is necessary to fight for one's own people against the others. I would have thought it obvious that *the moral norm* of international relations must be deduced from some other fact than that of war. Otherwise we might be driven to take as the norm for personal relations such facts as, *e.g.,* a furious fight between an actor and a Government clerk, which recently engaged the attention of the newspapers.

CHAPTER VI

The Penal Question
from the Moral Point of View

Having accepted the unconditional principle of morality as the standard of all human relations we shall find no real inner difficulty in applying it to international morality, *i.e.* to the question as to how we ought to regard foreigners as such; neither the characteristics of this or that people nor the general fact of belonging to a foreign nation contains any moral limitation in virtue of which we might *a priori* regard a given foreigner as a worse man than any of our compatriots. There is therefore no moral ground for national inequality. The general demand of altruism — to love one's neighbour as oneself and another nation as one's own — remains here in full force. The fact of international hostility must be unconditionally condemned as directly opposed to the absolute norm and as essentially anti-Christian.[1] The normal or the right attitude toward foreign nations is directly demanded by the unconditional principle of morality. Its application involves great practical difficulties, both historical and psychological, but it does not give rise to any inner moral difficulties, complications, or questions. Such difficulties arise when instead of the morally indifferent fact of nationality we have to deal with a fact which undoubtedly belongs to the moral sphere, namely, that of criminality.

The connotation and the denotation of this idea vary with regard to detail according to time and place. Much that was formerly regarded as criminal is no longer recognised as such. The very fact of criminality which had once extended to the criminal's family and relatives is, at a certain stage of spiritual

---

1. The question of *war* is historically connected with the fact of international hostility but is not exhausted thereby. Apart from international wars there have been, and may be in the future, intestine wars — social and religious. The problem of war must be considered separately, and one of the subsequent chapters will be devoted to it.

development, recognised as exclusively a personal characteristic. But these historical changes do not affect the nature of the case. Apart from *supposed* criminals of different kinds, in all human societies there have always been and to the end of the world there will be real criminals, *i.e.* men with an evil will sufficiently strong and decided to be directly realised in practice to the detriment of their neighbours and the danger of the community as a whole. How then are we to regard these avowedly *bad* people? It is clear that from the point of view of the absolute moral principle the demands of altruism which received their final expression in the Christian commandments of love must extend to these men too. But the question, in the first place, is how we are to combine love for the evil-doer with love for his victim, and secondly, what should be the *practical* expression of our love for the evil-doer or criminal so long as he is in this obviously abnormal moral condition. No one can avoid this moral question. Even if a person never came into personal contact with unquestionable crimes and criminals, as a member of society he must know that there exists a very complex administrative, legal and penal organisation intended for dealing with crime. He must, therefore, in any case, determine his moral relation to these institutions — and this in the last resort depends on his attitude toward the criminal. What *ought* this attitude to be from the purely moral point of view? In dealing with this important question, I will begin with the simplest case, which lies at the basis of all further complications.

I

When one man is doing injury to another, *e.g.* when the stronger man is beating the weaker, a person witnessing the injury — if he takes the moral point of view — experiences a *double* feeling and an impulse to a twofold course of action. In the first place, he wants to *defend the victim,* and in the second, *to bring the injurer to his senses.* Both impulses have the same moral source — the recognition of another person's life and the respect for another person's dignity, psychologically based upon the feeling of pity or compassion. We experience direct pity for the being who undergoes physical and mental suffering; the mental suffering, of which he is more or less clearly conscious, consists in the fact that human dignity has been violated in his person. Such external violation of human dignity in the injured is inevitably connected with the inward degradation of that dignity in the injurer; in both cases it demands to be re-established. Psychologically, our feeling for the victim is very different from our feeling for the aggressor — the first is pure pity, and in the second anger and moral indignation predominate. But to be moral, that indignation must not pass into injustice towards the wrong-doer, into denying his human right, although that right materially differs from the right of the victim. The latter has a right to our defence, the former has a right to be brought to reason by us. The moral basis of the two relations is, however, in the case of rational beings, one and the same — the absolute worth or dignity of human personality, which we recognise in others as well as in ourselves. The twofold violation of that dignity taking place in criminal assault — violation passive in the injured and active in the injurer — calls forth a moral reaction in us, which is essentially the same in both cases, in spite of the fact that its psychological expression is different and even opposed. Of course, when the injury directly or indirectly causes physical pain to the victim, the latter excites a stronger and more immediate feeling of pity; but speaking generally, the injurer ought to rouse even greater pity, for he inwardly loses his moral dignity. However this may be, the moral principle demands that we should recognise the right of both to our help in re-establishing the violated norm both in the one and in the other.

This deduction from the moral principle, demanding that in the case of crime, *i.e.* of injury to man by man, we should take up a moral attitude toward both parties, is far from being universally recognised. It must be defended against two kinds of adversaries. Some — and they are in the majority — recognise only the right of the victim or of the injured person (or community) to be defended and avenged. The wrong-doer or the criminal, once his guilt has been proved, they regard, at any rate in practice, as a rightless, passive object of retribution, *i.e.* of more or less complete crushing or extermination — 'hanging is too good for him,' 'to the dog a dog's death,' is the popular sincere expression of this point of view. Its direct opposition to the moral principle and its incompatibility with any degree of developed human feeling[2] explain and psychologically excuse the extreme opposite view, which is beginning to gain ground in our time. This view recognises the right of the injurer to be brought to reason by means of verbal persuasion only, and admits of no compulsion with regard to him — which practically amounts to depriving the injured person or society of their right to defence. Their safety is made to depend upon the *success* of persuasion, *i.e.* on something quite problematical, which no one can control or be held responsible for. Let us carefully consider the two opposed doctrines, which, for the sake of brevity, I will describe respectively as the doctrine of *retribution* and the doctrine of *verbal persuasion*.

---

2. This is shown, among other things, by the fact that among the people, at any rate among the Russian people, criminals are called *the unfortunate*.

II

The doctrine of retribution admits of a very real explanation and of fictitious proof, and when dealing with it, it is very important not to mix the one with the other. When an animal is attacked by another about to devour it, the instinct of self-preservation urges it to defend itself with its claws and teeth, or, if these are not strong enough, to seek safety in flight. No one would look for moral motives in this case any more than in the physical self-defence of man, whose natural means of defence are replaced or supplemented by artificial weapons. Even the savage, however, does not as a rule live by himself, but belongs to some social group — a family, a clan, a band. Therefore when he encounters an enemy the affair does not end with their single combat. Murder or any other injury inflicted upon a member of a group is felt by the group as a whole and rouses in it a feeling of resentment, In so far as that feeling includes pity for the victim, we must recognise the presence of a moral element in it. But no doubt the predominant part is played by the instinct of collective self-preservation, as among bees and other social animals. In defending one of its members, the clan or the family is defending itself; in avenging one of its members, it is avenging itself. But for the same reasons the aggressor too is defended by his clan or family. Single combats thus develop into wars between entire communities. The Homeric poems have preserved for us this stage of social relations by immortalising the Trojan war, which arose out of a private injury inflicted by Paris upon Menelaus. The history of the Arabs before Mohammed is full of such wars. The ideas of crime and punishment do not really exist at this stage at all; the injurer is an enemy to be revenged upon, not a criminal to be punished. The place which later on is occupied by legal justice is here entirely taken up by the universally recognised and absolutely binding custom of blood-vengeance. This custom applies, of course, to injuries between members of different clans or tribes. But, speaking generally, other kinds of injuries are not found at this stage of the communal life. The cohesion of the social group bound together by kinship is too strong, and the prestige of the patriarchal power too great, for the individual to rebel against it. It is almost as impossible as the conflict of an individual bee with the rest of the hive. No doubt even at the primitive stage man retained his power of arbitrary choice and did in some few instances manifest it. But these exceptional cases were dealt with by exceptional measures on the part of the patriarchal authority, and did not call forth any general regulations. Things were changed with the transition to the order of the state. When many clans and tribes for any reason chose or were compelled to unite in one way or another under one common leader with a more or less definite power they lost their independence and forfeited the right of blood-vengeance.

It is curious that philosophers and jurists, from ancient times and almost down to our own day, made *a priori* theories with regard to the origin of the state, as though all actual states had arisen in some remote prehistoric times. This is due, of course, to the extremely imperfect state of historical science. But what may be permissible to Hobbes and even to Rousseau cannot be allowed on the part of modern thinkers. The kinship-group stage through which all nations have passed in one way or another is not anything enigmatic: the clan is a direct consequence of the natural blood-tie. The question is, then, as to the transition from the stage of kinship to that of the state — and this can be an object of *historical observation*. It is sufficient to mention the transformation which took place in quite historical times of the disconnected tribes and clans of Northern Arabia into a powerful Mohammedan state. Its theocratic character is not an exception: such were to a greater or lesser extent all the important states of antiquity. Consider the way in which a state comes to be formed. A leader, military or religious, or most frequently both, impelled by the consciousness of his historic calling and also by personal motives, gathers round himself men from different clans and tribes, thus forming an *inter-tribal* nucleus. Around this nucleus entire clans and tribes come to be grouped voluntarily or by compulsion, receiving from the newly formed supreme power laws and government, and to a greater or lesser extent losing their independence. When a social group has a government organised on the principle of hierarchy with a supreme central authority at the head, a regular army, a financial system based upon taxation, and laws accompanied by penal sanctions, such a group has the essential characteristics of a state. All the characteristics enumerated were present in the Mohammedan community during the later years of Mohammed's life. It is remarkable that the history of the original formation of this state confirms to a certain extent the 'social contract' theory. All the chief actions of the Arab prophet in this connection were signalised by formal treaties, beginning with the so-called 'oath of women,' and ending with the conditions he dictated at Mecca after his final victory over the tribe of the Koreishites and their allies. It should be noted, too, that the fundamental point of all these treaties is the abolition of blood-vengeance between the tribes and clans which are to enter the new political union.

Hence arises the distinction, which did not exist before, between private and public right. With regard to blood-vengeance and other important matters, the interests of the collective group were identical with the interests of the individual. This was all the more natural as in a small social group such as the clan or the tribe all, or at any rate most, of its members could know each other personally, and thus each was for all, and all for each — a concrete unit. In the state, however, the social group embraces hundreds of thousands or even millions of men, and the concrete personal relation between the parts and the whole becomes impossible. A clear distinction is drawn between private and public interests and between the corresponding rights. In opposition to our modern legal notions, at that stage murder, robbery, bodily injuries, etc., are treated as the violations of private rights. Formerly, at the kinship-group stage, all such crimes were regarded as directly affecting the interests of the community, and the whole clan retaliated against the culprit and his kinsmen. When a wider political union was formed, this right and duty of blood-vengeance was taken away from the clan, but did not pass, unchanged, to the state. The new common authority, the source of government and of law, could not at once enter into the interests of all its numerous subjects to such an extent as to defend them like its own. The head of the state cannot act and feel like the elder of a clan. And we find that with regard to the defence of private persons and property the state is at first content with very little. For bodily injury or other violence to a free man, and even for the murder of one, the culprit or his relatives pay to the family of the victim compensation in money, the amount of which is settled by mutual agreement *(compositio),* and is generally very moderate. Ancient law-codes, *e.g.* the Salic Law, or our own *Russkaya Pravda,* which are relics of a primitive political order, are full of the enumerations of fines differing according to the sex of the person and to other circumstances. The direct and rapid transition from merciless blood-vengeance, often accompanied by long and devastating wars between entire tribes, to simple money compensation is remarkable; but from the point of view indicated it is perfectly natural.

At this stage of social development the only capital offences are, strictly speaking, political crimes;[3] all other, murder included, are regarded as private quarrels rather than crimes.

Such elementary opposition between public and private rights could not be stable. Money-fine for every kind of injury to a private person does not satisfy the injured party (*e.g.* the family of the murdered man), nor does it deter the wrong-doer, especially if he be rich, from committing further crimes. Under such conditions blood-vengeance for private offences, abolished by the state as opposed to its very conception, is renewed *de facto* and threatens

3. The scope of this notion became broader or narrower depending on the historical circumstances. In the Middle Ages, when the capital character of simple murder was not yet clear to the legal consciousness, coining false money was punished by painful death, as a crime detrimental to society as a whole, infringing upon the privileges of the central authority and, in this sense, political.

to destroy the *raison d'être* of the state: if each has to avenge his own wrongs, why should he bear the hardships imposed by the new political order? To justify the demands that private persons make upon it, the state must really take upon itself to protect their interests; in order to abolish the private right of blood-vengeance, the state must make it a public right, *i.e.* must itself exercise it. At this new and higher stage the solidarity of the central power with its individual subjects becomes more clear. The distinction between crimes directed against the government (political crimes) and those infringing upon private interests only is still retained, but it is now merely a distinction of degree. Each free man becomes a citizen, *i.e.* a member of the state which undertakes to protect his safety; every violation of it is regarded by the state authority as an attack upon its own rights, as a hostile action against the social whole. All attacks against person and property are regarded as violations of the law of the state, and no longer as private offences, and are therefore, like political crimes, for the *state* itself *to avenge.*

III

The legal doctrine of retribution has then a historical foundation in the sense that legal punishments still in use in our day are a historical transformation of the primitive principle of blood-vengeance. Originally, the injured person was avenged by a more narrow social union called the clan, then by a wider and more complex union called the state. Originally, the criminal lost all human rights in the eyes of the clan he injured; now he became the rightless subject of punishment in the eyes of the state, which revenges itself on him for the violation of its laws. The difference consists chiefly in the fact that at the patriarchal stage the act of vengeance itself was accomplished very simply — the aggressor was, at the first opportunity, killed like a dog — but the consequences were very complex, and took the form of endless inter-tribal wars. In the state, on the contrary, the act of vengeance, which the public authorities took upon themselves, was performed slowly and with all sorts of ceremonies, but no further complications ensued, for the criminal had no one sufficiently strong to avenge him — he was defenceless before the power of the state.

But can the unquestionable fact that legal executions are a historical transformation of blood-vengeance be used as an argument in favour of the executions themselves, or in favour of the principle of retaliation? Does this historical basis justify us in determining our attitude towards the criminal by the idea of vengeance, the idea, *i.e.*, of paying evil for evil, pain for pain? Speaking generally, logic does not allow us to make such deductions from the genetic connection between two events. Not a single Darwinian, so far as I am aware, drew the conclusion that because man is descended from the lower animals he ought to be a brute. From the fact that the urban community of Rome had been originally established by a band of robbers, no historian has yet concluded that the true principle of the Holy Roman Empire ought to have been brigandage. With regard to the question before us, it is clear that since we are dealing with the *evolution* of blood-vengeance there is no reason to regard this evolution as completed. We know that the relation of society and of law to the criminal has undergone great changes. Pitiless blood-vengeance was replaced by money-fines, and these were replaced by 'civil executions,' extremely cruel at first, but, beginning with the eighteenth century, becoming more and more mild. There is not the slightest rational ground to suppose that the limit of mercy has already been reached and that the gallows and the guillotine, penal servitude for life, and solitary confinement must for ever remain in the penal code of civilised countries.

But while historical progress clearly tends to eliminate the principle of vengeance or of exact retaliation from our treatment of criminals, and finally to abolish it altogether, many philosophers and jurists still continue to urge abstract arguments in defence of it. These arguments are so feeble that no doubt they will be an object of astonishment and ridicule to posterity, just as Aristotle's arguments in favour of slavery, or the ecclesiastical proofs of the flatness of the earth, are a source of wonder to us now. The pseudo-arguments used by the champions of the doctrine of retribution are not in themselves worth considering. But since they are still repeated by authors worthy of respect, and since the subject is of vital importance, the refutation of them ought also to be repeated.

"Crime is a violation of right; right must be re-established; punishment, *i.e.* equal violation of the criminal's right, performed in accordance with a definite law by public authority (in contradistinction to private vengeance), balances the first violation, and thus right is re-established." This pseudo-argument turns on the term 'right.' But concrete right is always *somebody's* right (there must be a *subject of rights*). Whose right is then here referred to? In the first place, apparently, it is the right of the injured person. Let us put this concrete content in the place of the abstract term. Peaceful shepherd Abel has no doubt a right to exist and to enjoy all the good things of life; but a wicked man, Cain, comes and deprives him of this right by murdering him. The violated right must be re-established; to do so public authority comes on the scene and, against the direct warning of Holy Writ (Genesis 4:15), hangs the murderer. Well, does this re-establish Abel's right to live? Since no one but an inmate of Bedlam would affirm that the execution of the murderer raises the victim from the dead, we must take the word 'right' in this connection to mean, not the right of the injured person, but of somebody else. The society or the state[4] may be the subject of the right violated by the crime. All private rights (of life, of property, etc.) are guaranteed by the state; it answers for their inviolability in placing them under the defence of its laws. The law forbidding private persons to take the life of their fellow-citizens at their own discretion is proclaimed by the state in its own right, and therefore the violation of the law (a murder) means violation of the right of the state. The execution of the murderer reestablishes the right of the state and the dignity of the law — not the right of the murdered man.[5]

What justice this argument contains has nothing to do with the case. There is no doubt that once laws exist, their violation must not be overlooked, and that it is the business of the state to see to it. But we are not dealing here with the general question of the punishability of crime, for in this respect all crimes are identical. If a law is sacred in itself as proceeding from the state, this is true of all laws in an equal degree. They all equally express the right of the state; and the violation of any law whatever is the violation of this supreme right. Material differences between crimes have to do with the particular interests which are infringed; but on its formal side, in relation to what is *universal,* that is, to the state *as such,* and to its law and power, every crime, if, of course, it is committed by a responsible agent, presupposes a will opposed to the law, a will that sets it at nought and is therefore criminal — and from this point of view all crimes ought logically to require the same punishment. But the difference in punishments for the different crimes exists in all legal codes, and it obviously presupposes, in addition to the general principle of punishability, a certain other specific principle which determines the particular connection between *this* crime and *this punishment.* The doctrine of retribution discovers this connection in the fact that the right violated by a particular criminal action is re-established by a corresponding or *equal* ac-

---

4. In this connection either term may be used indifferently.

5. In the opinion of one of my critics, I am wrong in supposing that a crime must necessarily be the violation of *somebody's* right. Apart from any subject of rights — individual or collective, private or public — and also apart from the moral norm or the absolute good, there exists, it is urged, right as such, — an independent objective essence, and the proper object of punishment is the satisfaction of this self-existent right. The critic is mistaken in thinking that I am ignorant of this metaphysical impersonation of the ancient Moloch. But there is no need for me to go into it, since no serious criminologist has for a long time past upheld it. It is obvious that 'right' is by its very meaning a relation between subjects, conditioned by certain moral and practical norms, and that therefore a subjectless and unrelated right is an *Unding* — *a thought that has no content.*

267

tion — for instance, a murderer must be killed. There can, however, be no real correspondence or equality. The most famous champions of the doctrine conceive of the matter as follows: Right is something positive, a *plus;* the violation of it is something negative, a *minus.* If the negation in the form of crime has taken place (*e.g.* a man has been deprived of life), it must call forth equal negation in the form of punishment (taking the murderer's life). Then such double negation, or the negation of the negative, will once more bring about a positive state, *i.e.* re-establish the right: *minus multiplied by minus makes plus.* It is difficult to take this 'play of mind' seriously; it should be noted, however, that the idea of the *negation of the negative* logically expresses a direct inner relation between two opposed acts. Thus, for instance, if an impulse of ill-will in man is 'negative,' is, namely, a negation of the moral norm, the opposite act of will, suppressing that impulse, will indeed be a 'negation of the negative,' and the result will be a positive one — man's affirmation of himself as normal. Similarly, if crime as an active expression of ill-will is negative, the criminal's active repentance will be a negation of the negative (that is, not of the fact, of course, but of the inner cause that produced it), and the result will again be positive — his moral regeneration. But the execution of the criminal has obviously no such significance; in this case the negation is directed, as in the crime itself, upon something positive — upon human life. It cannot indeed be maintained that the execution of the criminal negates his crime, for that crime is an irrevocably accomplished fact, and, according to the remark of the Fathers of the Church, God Himself cannot undo what has been done. Nor does it negate the criminal's evil will, for the criminal has either repented of his crime — and in that case there is no longer any evil will — or he remains obdurate to the end, and then his will is inaccessible to the treatment he is receiving; and in any case an external enforced action can neither cancel nor change the inner state of will. What, then, is negated by the execution of the criminal is not his evil will, but the positive good of life, — and this is once more a simple negation, and not a 'negation of the negative.' But a simple succession of two negatives cannot lead to anything positive. The misuse of the algebraic formula makes the argument simply ridiculous. In order that two minuses, that is, two negative quantities, should make a plus, it is not sufficient to place them one after another, but it is necessary to *multiply* one by the other. But there is no intelligible meaning in *multiplying crime by punishment.*[6]

6. It is obvious that we cannot in this case go further than *addition* (of the material results). The corpse of the murdered victim may be added to the corpse of the hanged murderer and then there will be two corpses — *i.e.* two negative quantities.

IV

The inherent absurdity of the doctrine of retribution or 'avenging justice' is emphasised by the fact that, with a few exceptions, it has no relation whatever to the existing penal laws. Strictly speaking, there is only one case in which it appears to be applicable — that of the death penalty for murder. Therefore the pseudo-philosophical arguments in favour of this doctrine, the gist of which has been considered above, refer to this single instance only — a bad omen for a principle which lays claim to universal significance. In Russia, where capital punishment is the penalty for certain political crimes only, there is not even this one case of apparent correspondence. No trace of equality between crime and punishment can be detected in the case of parricide and penal servitude for life, or simple murder with a view to robbery and twelve years' penal servitude. The best argument against the doctrine is the circumstance that it finds its fullest application in the penal codes of some half-savage peoples, or in the laws prevalent at the epoch of barbarism, when, *e.g.,* for inflicting a certain injury the culprit underwent a similar injury, for speaking insolent words a person had his tongue cut out, etc. A principle the application of which proves to be incompatible with a certain degree of culture and refinement is condemned by the verdict of history.

In modern times the doctrine of re-establishing right by means of equal retribution was, if I am not mistaken, defended by abstract philosophers more than by jurists. The latter understand the equalisation of crime with punishment in the relative and quantitative sense only (the *measure* of punishment). They demand, *i.e.,* that a crime more grave than another should be punished more severely, so that there should be a scale of punishments corresponding to the scale of crimes. But the basis and, consequently, the apex of the penal ladder remain indefinite, and therefore the punishments may be either inhumanly cruel or extremely mild. Such a scale of penalties has existed in the penal codes in which all, or almost all, simple crimes were punished by a fine: a larger fine was paid for the murder of a man than for the murder of a woman, for a serious bodily injury than for a slight one, etc. On the other hand, codes in which the penalty for theft was hanging punished more heinous crimes by capital punishment accompanied by various degrees of torture. What is in this case immoral is the cruelty of the punishments, and not, of course, their graduated character.

From the moral point of view it is of interest that the penal laws show a tendency to preserve the cruel punishments as far as possible. This tendency has no doubt become weaker, but it has not yet disappeared altogether. Not finding a sufficiently secure foundation in the pseudo-rational principle of 're-established right,' it seeks empirical support in the principle of *intimidation*. In truth, the latter has always formed part of the doctrine of retribution. The popular aphorism, 'To a dog a dog's death,' has always been accompanied by the addition, 'as a warning to others.'

This principle can hardly be said to be wholly valid even from the utilitarian and empirical point of view. No doubt fear is an important human instinct, but it has no decisive significance for man. The perpetually increasing number of suicides proves that, in many, death itself inspires no fear. Prolonged solitary confinement or penal servitude may in themselves be more terrible but they do not produce an immediate intimidating effect. I will not dwell upon these and other well-known arguments against the theory of intimidation, such as the contention that the criminal always hopes to avoid detection and escape punishment, or that the enormous majority of crimes are committed under the influence of some passion which stifles the voice of sagacity. The relative force of all these arguments is open to dispute. Indisputable refutation of the deterrent theory is only possible from the moral point of view. It is refuted, first, on the ground of principle, as directly opposed to the fundamental law of morality, and, secondly, by the fact that this opposition compels the champions of intimidation to be inconsistent and gradually to relinquish, on the strength of moral motives, the most clear and effective demands of their own theory. It is understood, of course, that I am referring here to intimidation as a fundamental principle of legal justice and not merely as a psychological fact, which naturally accompanies any method of dealing with crime. Even supposing it were intended to reform criminals by means of moral exhortation alone, the prospect of such tutelage, however mild and rational, might intimidate vain and self-willed men and deter them from criminal actions. Obviously, however, this is not what is meant by the theory which regards intimidation as the essence and the direct object of punishment, and not as an indirect consequence of it.

The moral principle asserts that human dignity must be respected in every person, and that therefore no one may be made merely a *means* of or an *instrument* for the advantage of others. According to the deterrent theory, however, the criminal who is being punished is regarded as merely a means for intimidating others and safeguarding public safety. The penal law may, of course, intend to benefit the criminal himself, by deterring him, through fear of punishment, from committing the crime. But once the crime has been committed, this motive obviously disappears, and the criminal in being punished becomes solely a means of intimidating others, *i.e.* a means to an end external to him; and this is in direct contradiction to the unconditional law of morality. From the moral point of view a punishment inspiring fear would be permissible only as a threat; but a threat which is never fulfilled loses its meaning. Thus, the principle of penal intimidation can be moral only on condition of being useless, and can be materially useful only on condition of being applied immorally.

In point of fact the theory of intimidation finally lost its sting from the time when all civilised and half-civilised countries abolished cruel corporal punishments and capital punishment accompanied by torture. It is clear that if the object of punishment is to intimidate both the criminal and others, these means are certainly the most effective and rational. Why then do the champions of intimidation renounce the true and the only reliable means of intimidation? Probably because they consider these means immoral and op-posed to the demands of pity and humanity. In that case, however, intimida-tion ceases to be the *determining* factor in punishment. It must be one or the other: either the meaning of punishment is intimidation — and in that case execution accompanied by torture must be admitted as pre-eminently intimi-dating; or the nature of punishment is determined by the moral principle — and in that case intimidation must be given up altogether, as a motive essen-tially immoral.[7]

V

The circumstance that the most consistent forms of retribution and intimida-tion have disappeared from modern penal codes, in spite of the fact that from the first point of view such forms must be recognised as the most just, and from the second as the most effective, is sufficient to prove that a different, a moral point of view has penetrated into this sphere and made considerable progress in it. This undoubted and fairly rapid progress has failed to affect only the penal codes of savage or barbarian peoples — such as the Abyssini-ans or the Chinese; and even they, indeed, are about to enter into the general life of civilised humanity. Nevertheless, our own penal systems — I mean those of Europe and America — still retain much unnecessary violence and cruelty, which can only be explained as a dead legacy of the defunct principles of retribution and intimidation. Among these vestiges of the past are capital

---

7. In the eighteenth century, when the movement against the cruelty of penal laws was at its height, several writers sought to prove that torturing prisoners is both inhuman and useless as a deterrent, for it does not prevent any one from committing crimes. If this contention could be substantiated it would deprive the theory of intimidation of all meaning whatever. It is obvi-ous that if even painful executions are insufficient to intimidate criminals, punishments more mild are still less likely to do so.

punishment, which is still being obstinately defended though it has lost its grounds; indefinite deprivation of liberty; penal servitude; exile into distant countries with unbearable conditions of life, etc.

All this systematic cruelty is revolting to the moral feeling and brings about a change in our original attitude towards the criminal. Pity for the injured person and the impulse to defend him set us against the injurer (the criminal). But when society, which is incomparably stronger than the individual criminal, turns upon him its insatiable hostility after he has been disarmed, and makes him undergo prolonged suffering, it is *he* who becomes the injured party and excites in us pity and a desire to protect him. Although legal theory and legal practice have decidedly renounced *consistent application* of the principles of retribution and intimidation, they have not given up the principles themselves. The system of punishments that exists in civilised countries is a meaningless and lifeless compromise between these worthless principles on the one hand and certain demands of humanity and justice on the other. In truth, what we find are simply the more or less softened vestiges of the old brutality, with no uniting thought, no guiding principle involved. The compromise cannot help us to solve the question that is essential for the moral consciousness: does the fact of crime deprive the criminal of his human rights, or does it not? If it does *not,* how can we rob him of the first condition of any right — of existence, as is done in the case of capital punishment? And if the fact of crime does deprive the criminal of his natural rights, what need is there of legal ceremony with rightless beings? Empirically this dilemma is solved by a distinction being drawn between crimes, some of which are taken to deprive the criminal of human rights, and others merely to *limit* them to a greater or lesser extent. Both the principle and the degree of such limitation are, however, changeable and indefinite, and the very distinction between the two kinds of crime proves to be arbitrary and to differ according to time and place. Thus, for instance, in Western Europe political crimes do not involve the loss of human rights, while in Russia the old view is still in full force, and these crimes are regarded as the most heinous of all. One would have thought that so important a fact as the transformation of man from an independent being fully possessed of rights into passive material for punitary exercises must depend upon some objective reason or determining principle, the same for all times and at all places. In fact, however, it appears that in order to change from a person into a thing, a man must in one country commit a simple murder; in another, a murder with aggravating circumstances; in the third, some political crime, etc.

Such an extremely unsatisfactory state of this important question, such a frivolous attitude toward the life and destiny of men, is revolting to the intellect and conscience, and produce a reaction of the moral feeling. Unfortunately, however, this reaction leads many moralists to the opposite extreme, and induces them to reject the idea of punishment in general, *i.e.* in the sense of real opposition to crime. According to this modern doctrine, violence or compulsion towards any one is never permissible, and therefore the criminal may only be dealt with by rational persuasion. The merit of this doctrine is the moral purity of its purpose; its defect is that the purpose cannot be realised in the way advocated. The principle of taking up a passive attitude towards criminals not only rejects retribution and intimidation (which is the right thing to do), but also excludes measures intended to *prevent* crimes and to improve criminals. From this point of view the state has not the right to lock up, even only for a time, a vicious murderer, though the circumstances of the case make it clear that he will continue his crimes; nor has it a right to place the criminal in a more normal environment, even if it were exclusively for his own good. Similarly, it is contended that a private person has no right forcibly to detain a would-be murderer from rushing at his victim, but may only address him with words of exhortation. In criticising the theory I will consider this instance of individual opposition to crime, as it is more simple and fundamental.

It is only in extremely rare, exceptional cases that men who are depraved and capable of deliberate crime are affected by words of rational persuasion. To ascribe beforehand such *exceptional* power to one's own words would be morbid self-conceit; to be content with words without being certain of their success when a man's life is at stake would be inhuman. The victim has a right to all the help we can render him, and not to verbal intercession only, which, in the vast majority of cases, can be nothing but comical. In the same way, the aggressor has a right to all the help we can give to restrain him from a deed which is for him even a greater disaster than for his victim. Only after having *stopped his action* can we with calm conscience address *words of exhortation* to him. If I see the criminal's arm raised to murder his victim and I seize hold of it, will this be a case of immoral violence? It will no doubt be violence, but so far from being immoral, it will be *binding* on me, and will directly follow from the demands of the moral principle. In restraining a man from murder I *actively* respect and support his human dignity, which is seriously menaced by his carrying out his intention. It would be strange to believe that the very fact of such violence — *i.e.* a certain contact of the muscles of my arm with the muscles of the murderer's arm, and the necessary consequences of the contact — contains an element of immorality. Why, in that case it would be immoral to pull a drowning man out of water, for it too cannot be done without much physical exertion and some physical pain to the person who is being saved. If it is permissible and a moral duty to pull a drowning man out of the water, even if he resists, it is all the more permissible to pull a criminal away from his victim, even if it means bruises, scratches, and dislocations.[8]

It must be one or the other. Either the criminal whom we restrain has not yet lost all human feeling, and then he will, of course, be grateful for having been saved in time from sin — no less than the drowning man is grateful for having been taken out of the water; in that case, the violence which he suffered was done with his own tacit consent, and his right has not been violated, so that, strictly speaking, there has been no violence at all, since *volenti non fit injuria*.[9] Or the criminal has lost human feeling to such an extent that he is annoyed at having been prevented from cutting his victim's throat. But to address a man in such a condition with words of rational persuasion would be the height of absurdity; it would be the same as preaching to one who is dead-drunk the advantages of abstinence, instead of pouring cold water over him.

Were the fact of physical violence, *i.e.* of the application of muscular force, in itself bad or immoral, it would, of course, be wrong to use this bad means even with the best of intentions — it would be admitting the immoral rule that the end justifies the means. To resist evil by evil is wrong and useless; to hate the evil-doer for his crime and therefore to *revenge* oneself on him is childish. But there is no evil in restraining the evil-doer from crime for the sake of his own good and *without any hatred* of him. Since there is nothing bad in muscular force as such, the moral or the immoral character of its application depends in each case upon the intention of the person and the circumstances of the case. Physical force rationally used for the real good of others, both moral and material, is a *good* and not a bad means, and such application of it, so far from being forbidden, is directly prescribed by the moral principle. The dividing line between the moral and immoral use of physical compulsion may be a fine one, but it is perfectly clear and definite. The whole point is the attitude we take towards the evil-doer in resisting evil. If we retain a human, moral relation to him and are thinking of his own good, there will obviously be nothing immoral in our enforced violence — no trace of cruelty or revenge. The violence will, in that case, be simply an inevitable condition of our helping the man, just like a surgical operation or the locking up of a dangerous lunatic.

8. What, however, if in restraining the murderer we may in the struggle unintentionally cause him grave injuries and even death? It will be a great misfortune for us, and we will grieve over it as over an *involuntary* sin; but, in any case, unintentionally to kill a criminal is a lesser sin than deliberately to allow an intentional murder of an innocent person.

9. 'There is no injury to the willing,' *i.e.* an action which is in accordance with the will of the person who suffers it cannot be a violation of his right.

The moral principle forbids one to make a human being merely a means to extraneous purposes, *i.e.* to ends which do not include his own good. If, therefore, in resisting crime we regard the criminal simply as a means for the defence or the satisfaction of the injured person or society, our action is immoral, even though its motive might be unselfish pity for the victim and genuine anxiety for public safety. From the moral point of view this is not sufficient. We ought *to pity both* the victim and the criminal; and if we do so, if we really have the good of them both in view, reason and conscience will tell us what measure and what form of physical compulsion are necessary.

Moral questions are finally decided by conscience, and I confidently ask every one to turn to his own inner experience (imaginary, if there has not been any other) and say in which of the two cases does conscience reproach us more: in the case when, being able to prevent a crime, we had callously passed by, saying a few useless words, or when we had actually prevented it even at the expense of inflicting *certain* physical injuries? Every one understands that in a *perfect society* there must be no compulsion at all. But the perfection has yet to be *attained;* and it is quite obvious that to let evil and irrational men exterminate, unhindered, the normal people is not the right method of creating the perfect society. What is desirable is the organisation of the good, and not the freedom of evil. "But," the modern sophists will urge, "society has often taken for evil what afterwards proved to be a good, and has persecuted innocent men as criminals; therefore legal justice is worth nothing, and all compulsion must be given up." This argument is not my invention — I have read and heard it many times. Reasoning in this way we should have to say that the mistakes in the astronomical theories of Ptolemy are a sufficient ground for giving up astronomy, and that the errors of the alchemists prove chemistry to be worthless.

It is difficult to understand how men of a different stamp from obvious sophists can defend so poor a doctrine. The truth is, I think, that its real foundation is mystical and not ethical. The idea underlying the doctrine seems to be this: "That which seems to us to be evil, may not be evil at all; the Deity or Providence knows better than we do the true connection of things and the way to produce real good out of apparent evil. We can know and judge only our own inner states and not the objective significance and consequences of our own and other people's actions." It must be confessed that to a religious mind this view is extremely attractive; nevertheless, it is a mistaken view. The truth of a theory is tested by the fact whether it can be consistently carried out without landing us in contradictions and absurdities. The view in question cannot bear this test. If our ignorance of all the objective consequences of our own and other people's actions were a sufficient ground for remaining inactive, we ought not to resist our own passions and evil impulses. For aught we know, the all-merciful Providence might derive wonderful results from a person's profligacy, drunkenness, ill-feeling to his neighbours, etc.

Suppose, for instance, that for motives of abstinence a man stayed away from a public-house. But had he not resisted his inclination and gone, he would on his way back have found a half-frozen puppy. Being in a condition when one is inclined to be sentimental, he would have picked up the puppy and warmed it back to life. The puppy, upon growing up into a big dog, would have saved a little girl from drowning in the pond; and the little girl would eventually become the mother of a great man. Now, however, the misplaced abstinence has interfered with the plans of Providence. The puppy was frozen, the little girl drowned, and the great man is doomed to remain for ever unborn. Another person, given to anger, felt inclined to slap in the face the man he was arguing with, but thought that this would be wrong, and restrained himself. And yet, had he not controlled his anger, the injured person would have taken the opportunity to turn him the other cheek, and would have thus softened the heart of the aggressor. Virtue would have doubly triumphed, while, as it was, their meeting ended in nothing.

The doctrine which absolutely rejects all forcible resistance to evil, or all defence of one's neighbours by means of physical force, is really based upon an argument of this nature. A man has saved another's life by using force and disarming the brigand who attacked him. But, later on, the person saved became a terrible malefactor, far worse than the brigand; therefore it would have been better not to have saved him. Exactly the same disappointment, however, might ensue if the man were threatened by a rabid wolf instead of by a brigand. Does it follow, then, that we are not to defend any one even from wild beasts? Besides, when I save people in a fire or in an inundation, it may very well happen that the saved may subsequently be extremely unhappy or prove to be terrible scoundrels, so that it would have been better for them to have been burnt or drowned. Does it follow that one ought not to help any one in any calamity whatsoever? Actively helping one's neighbours is a direct and positive demand of morality. If we renounce the duty of kindness on the ground that actions inspired by that feeling *may* have bad consequences *unknown* to us, we can just as well for the same reason renounce the duty of abstinence and all others, because these, too, may prompt us to actions which may lead to evil consequences, as in the examples cited above. If, however, that which appears to us to be good leads to evil, then, *vice versa*, that which appears to us to be evil may lead to good. Perhaps, then, the best plan would be to do evil straight away in order that good might ensue. Fortunately, this whole line of thought is self-destructive, for the series of unknown events may go further than we think. Take the first instance, in which Mr. X., by resisting his inclination for strong drink, indirectly prevented the birth of a great man. We cannot tell whether this great man would not have caused great disasters to humanity; and if he would, it is just as well that he has not been born; therefore Mr. X. did very well in making himself stay at home. In the same way, we do not know what further consequences might ensue from the triumph of virtue due to a slap in the face magnanimously endured. It is highly probable that this extreme magnanimity would eventually lead to spiritual pride, which is the worst of all sins, and thus ruin the man's soul. Therefore Mr. Y. did well in controlling his anger and preventing the magnanimity of his opponent from showing itself. Altogether, since we know nothing for certain, we have equal right to make all sorts of suppositions with regard to possibilities. But it by no means follows that because we do not know what consequences our actions may lead to, we ought to refrain from all action. This conclusion would be correct only if we knew for certain that the consequences would be bad. Since, however, they may equally be good or bad, we have equal ground (or, rather, equal absence of ground) for action or inaction. All these reflections on the indirect results of our actions can then have no practical significance. They could be a real determining force in our life only if we could know more than the immediate links in the series of consequences. The immediate links may be always supposed to be followed by further links of an opposite character and destructive of our conclusion. It would therefore be necessary to know the *whole series of consequences* down to the end of the world, which is impossible for us.

Our actions or refusal to act must then be determined, not by the consideration of their possible indirect consequences unknown to us, but by impulses *directly* following from the positive demands of the moral principle. This is true not only from the ethical but also from the mystical point of view. If everything be referred back to Providence, it is certainly not without Its knowledge that man possesses reason and conscience, which tell him in each concrete case what direct good he can do, independently of all indirect consequences. And if we believe in Providence, we certainly believe also that It cannot allow that actions conformable to reason and conscience should ultimately lead to evil. If we know that it is immoral or opposed to human dignity to stupefy oneself with strong drink, our conscience will not permit us to consider whether in the state of intoxication we might not do something which would subsequently lead to good results. Similarly, if from a purely moral motive, apart from any malice or revenge, we prevented a brigand from killing a man, it will never occur to us to argue that this may perhaps lead to some evil, and that it might have been better to let the murder take place.

Through our reason and conscience we know for certain that carnal passions — drunkenness or profligacy — are bad in themselves and ought to be restrained. The same reason and conscience tell us with equal certainty that active love is good in itself and that one must act in the spirit of it — to help our neighbours, to defend them from the elements, from wild beasts, and also from men who are evil or insane. Therefore the man who from a pure impulse of pity snatches away the knife from a would-be murderer's hand and thus saves him from an extra sin and his victim from a violent death, or the man who uses physical violence to prevent a patient ill with delirium tremens from freely running about the streets, will always be justified by his own conscience and by the universal verdict of humanity as one who carried out in practice the moral demand: Help all as much as in thee lies.

Providence certainly extracts good from our evil, but from our good it derives a still greater good. And what is of especial importance is that this second kind of good comes about with our direct and active participation, while the first, that derived from our evil, does not concern us nor belong to us. It is better to be a helper than a dead instrument of the all-merciful Providence.

VI

Punishment as *intimidating revenge* (the typical instance of which is capital punishment) cannot from the moral point of view be justified, for it denies the criminal his human character, deprives him of the right of existence which belongs to every person, and makes him a passive instrument of other people's safety. No more, however, can we justify from the moral point of view an indifferent attitude toward crime, the attitude of not resisting it. It does not take into account the right of the injured party to be protected nor the right of the whole society to a secure existence, and makes everything depend upon the arbitrary will of the worst people. The moral principle demands real resistance to crimes, and determines this resistance (or punishment in the wide sense of the term, as distinct from the idea of retribution) as *a rightful means of active pity, legally and forcibly limiting the external expressions of evil will, not merely for the sake of the safety of the peaceful members of society, but also in the interests of the criminal himself.* Thus the true conception of punishment is many-sided, but each aspect is equally conditioned by the universal moral principle of pity, which includes both the injured and the injurer. The victim of a crime *has a right* to protection and, as far as possible, to compensation; society *has a right* to safety; the criminal *has a right* to correction and reformation. Resistance to crimes that is to be consistent with the moral principle must realise or, at any rate, aim at an equal realisation of those three rights.

Protection of individuals, public safety, and the subsequent good of the criminal, demand in the first place that the person guilty of a crime should be for a time deprived of liberty. In the interests of his relatives and his own, a spendthrift is rightly deprived of freedom in the administration of his property. It is all the more just and necessary that a murderer or a sexual abuser should be deprived of freedom in his line of activity. For the criminal himself deprivation of freedom is especially important as a *pause* in the development of the evil will, as an opportunity to reflect and repent.

At the present time, the criminal's fate is finally decided by the court, which both determines his guilt and decrees his punishment. If, however, the motives of revenge and intimidation are consistently banished from penal law, the conception of punishment as a measure *determined beforehand* and, in truth, *arbitrarily*, must disappear also. The consequences of the crime for the criminal must stand in a natural and inner relation with his real condition. The law court, having established the fact of guilt, must then determine its nature, the degree of the criminal's responsibility and of his further danger to society; that is, it must make a diagnosis and a prognosis of the moral disease. But it is opposed to reason to prescribe unconditionally the means and the length of the period of treatment. The course and the methods of treatment must differ according to the changes in the course of the illness, and the court must leave this to penitentiary institutions, into the hands of which the criminal should pass. A short time ago this idea would have been thought an unheard-of heresy, but of late attempts have been made to realise it in a few countries (*e.g.* in Belgium and Ireland), in which *conditional sentences* may be passed. In certain cases the criminal is sentenced to a definite punishment, but undergoes it only if he repeats his crime. If he does not, he remains free, and his first crime is regarded as accidental. In other cases, the sentence is conditional with regard to the length of imprisonment, which may be shortened according to the subsequent behaviour of the criminal. From the point of view of principle these conditional sentences are an advance of enormous importance.

VII

There had been a time when men suffering from mental disease were treated like wild beasts, chained, beaten, etc. Less than a hundred years ago it was considered to be the right thing; but now we remember it with horror. Since the rate of progress is continually increasing, I hope to live to a time when prisons and penal servitude of the present day will be looked upon in the same way as we now look upon the old-fashioned asylums with iron cages for the patients. Although the penal system has undoubtedly progressed of late, it is still largely determined by the old idea of punishment as *torment* deliberately inflicted on the criminal, in accordance with the principle, 'The thief deserves all he gets.'

In the true conception of punishment its positive end, so far as the criminal is concerned, is not to cause him physical pain, but to heal or reform him morally. This idea was accepted long ago (chiefly by theologians, partly by philosophers, and by a very few jurists), but it calls forth strong opposition on the part of jurists and of a certain school of anthropologists. From the legal side it is urged that to correct the criminal means to intrude upon his inner life, which the state and society have no right to do. There are two misconceptions involved here. In the first place, the task of reforming criminals is, in the respect we are here considering, merely an instance of the positive influence which the society (or the state) ought to exert upon such members of it as are in some respects deficient, and therefore not fully possessed of rights. If such influence is rejected on principle as intrusion into the individual's inner life, it will be necessary to reject also public education of children, treatment of lunatics in public asylums, etc.

And in what sense can it be said to be an intrusion into the inner world? In truth, by the fact of his crime the criminal has *bared* or *exposed* his inner world, and is in need of influence in the opposite direction which would enable him once more to withdraw into the normal boundaries. It is particularly surprising that although the argument recognises the right of society to put a man into *demoralising* conditions (such as our present prisons and penal servitude, which the jurists do not reject), it denies the right and the duty of society to put him into conditions that might render him *moral*.

The second misunderstanding consists in imagining that reformation of the criminal means forcing upon him ready-made principles of morality. But why regard incompetence as a principle? When a criminal is capable of reformation at all, it consists, of course, chiefly in *self-reformation*. External influences must simply put the man into conditions most favourable for it, help him and support him in this inner work.

The anthropological argument is that criminal tendencies are innate and therefore incorrigible. That there exist born criminals and hereditary criminals, there is no doubt. That some of them are incorrigible it is difficult to deny. But the statement that all criminals or even the majority of them are incorrigible is absolutely arbitrary and does not deserve to be dwelt upon. If, however, all we may admit is that some criminals are incorrigible, no one can or has a right to be certain beforehand that this particular criminal belongs to that group. *All* therefore ought to be put into conditions most favourable for possible reformation. The first and the most important condition is, of course, that at the head of penal institutions should stand men capable of so high and difficult a task — the best of jurists, alienists, and men with a religious calling.

Public guardianship over the criminal, entrusted to competent persons with a view to his possible reformation, — this is the only conception of 'punishment' or positive resistance to crime compatible with the moral principle. A penal system based upon it will be more just and humane than the present one, and will, at the same time, be certainly more efficient.

CHAPTER VII

The Economic Question
from the Moral Point of View

I

If individuals and nations learnt to value the national peculiarities of foreign peoples as much as they value their own; if within each nation individual criminals were, as far as possible, reformed by re-education and rational guardianship, from which all vestige of legal ferocity was eliminated, — this moral solution of the national and the penal questions would still leave untouched an important cause both of national hostility and of criminality, namely, the economic cause. The chief reason why Americans hate the Chinese is certainly not that the Chinese wear plaits and follow the moral teaching of Confucius, but that they are dangerous rivals in the economic sphere. Chinese labourers in California are persecuted for the same cause for which Italians are ill-treated in southern France, Switzerland, and Brazil. In exactly the same way the feeling against the Jews, whatever the inmost causes of it may be, clearly rests upon and is obviously due to economic considerations. Individual criminality is not created by environment, but it is largely kept up and encouraged by pauperism, excessive mechanical labour, and the inevitable coarsening that follows therefrom. The influence of the most rational and humane penal system upon individual criminals would have but little general effect so long as these conditions prevailed. The bad effect of the economic conditions of the present day upon the national and the criminal questions is obviously due to the fact that these conditions are in themselves morally wrong. Their abnormality is manifested in the economic sphere itself, since the struggle between the different classes of society for the possession of material goods is becoming more and more acute, and in many countries of Western Europe and America threatens to become a deadly strife.

For a man who takes the moral point of view it is as impossible to take part in this social-economic struggle as to participate in the hostility between races and nations. But at the same time it is impossible for him to remain indifferent to the material position of his neighbours. If the elementary moral feeling of pity, which has received its highest sanction in the Gospel, demands that we should feed the hungry, give drink to the thirsty, and warm the cold, this demand does not, of course, lose its force when the cold and hungry number millions instead of dozens. And if *alone* I cannot help these millions, and am not therefore morally bound to do so, I *together with others* can and must help them. My personal duty becomes a collective one — it still remains my own, although it becomes wider in so far as I participate in the collective whole and its universal task. The very fact of economic distress proves that economic conditions are not connected with the principle of the good as they should be, that they are not morally organised. A whole pseudo-scientific school of conservative anarchists in economics directly denied, and still denies, though without the old self-confidence, all ethical principles and all organisation in the sphere of economic relations. The prevalence of this school had much to do with the birth of revolutionary anarchism. On the other hand, the many varieties of socialism, both radical and conservative, do more to detect the presence of the disease than to offer a real cure for it.

The defect of the orthodox school of political economy — the liberal or, more exactly, the anarchical school — is that it *separates* on principle the economic sphere from the moral. The defect of socialism is that it more or less *confuses* or wrongly identifies these two distinct, though indivisible, spheres.

II

All practical affirmation of a thing apart from its due connection or correlation with everything else is essentially immoral. To affirm a particular, conditional, and relative activity as a thing by itself, as absolutely independent and self-contained, is wrong in theory and immoral in practice, and can lead to nothing but disaster and sin.

To regard man as merely an economic agent — a producer, owner, and consumer of material goods — is a wrong and immoral point of view. These functions have in themselves no significance for man, and do not in any way express his essential nature and worth. Productive labour, possession and enjoyment of its results, is one of the aspects of human life or one of the spheres of human activity. The truly human interest lies only in the fact as to *how* and *with what object* man acts in this particular domain. Free play of chemical processes can take place only in a corpse; in a living body these processes are connected and determined by organic purposes. Similarly, free play of economic factors and laws is possible only in a community that is dead and is decomposing, while in a living community that has a future, economic elements are correlated with and determined by moral ends. To proclaim *laissez faire, laissez passer* is to say to society 'die and decompose.'

No doubt economic relations as a whole are based upon a simple and ultimate fact, which cannot as such be deduced from the moral principle — the fact, namely, that work, labour, is necessary to the maintenance of life. There has never been, however, a stage in the life of humanity at which this material necessity was not complicated by moral considerations — not even at the very lowest stage. Necessity compels the half-brutal savage to procure means of livelihood; but in doing so he may either think of himself alone or include in his need the need of his mate and his young. If the hunt has been unsuccessful he can either share his scarce booty with them, hardly satisfying his own hunger, or take everything for himself, leaving them to fare as best they can; or, finally, he may kill them so as to satisfy his hunger with their flesh. Whichever course he adopts, even the most orthodox devotee of political economy would not be likely to ascribe his action to the effect of inexorable economic 'laws.'

The necessity to work in order to obtain the means of livelihood is indeed a matter of fate and is independent of human will. But it is merely an impetus which spurs man to activity, the further course of that activity being determined by psychological and moral, and not by economic, causes. When social structure becomes somewhat more complex, not only the distribution of the products of labour and the manner of enjoying them, or 'consumption,' but the labour itself is determined by motives other than those of physical need — motives which have no element of compulsion or natural necessity about them. It is sufficient to name as an instance the most prevalent among them — the greed for acquisition and the thirst for pleasure. There is no economic law which determines the degree of cupidity or voluptuousness for all men, and there is indeed no law that these passions should be necessarily inherent in man at all, as inevitable motives of his actions. Therefore in so far as economic activities and relations are determined by these mental propensities they do not belong to the domain of economics and do *not* obey any 'economic laws' with necessity.

Take the most elementary and the least disputable of these so-called laws, namely, the law that the price of goods is determined by the relation between supply and demand. This means that the more demand there is for a particular article and the less there is of it, the more it costs — and *vice versa*.

Suppose, however, that a rich but benevolent trader who has a constant supply of some article of the first necessity decides, in spite of the increased demand for that article, not to raise his prices or even decides to lower them for the good of his needy neighbours. This will be a violation of the supposed economic 'law,' and yet, however unusual the case may be, certainly no one would think it impossible or supernatural.

Let us grant that if everything depended upon the good will of private individuals, we might, in the domain of economics, regard magnanimous motives as a negligible quantity, and build everything upon the secure foundation of self-interest. Every society, however, has a central government, a necessary function of which is to limit private cupidity. There are a good many historical instances in which the state made the habitual and — from the point of view of self-interest — the natural order of things unnatural and unusual, sometimes indeed rendering it altogether impossible, and transforming the former exceptions into a universal rule. Thus, for instance, in Russia for two and a half centuries landowners who set all their serfs free and, in doing so, gave them land were the most rare and extraordinary exception, the usual order or 'law' of relations between the landed gentry and the peasants being that the latter, together with the land on which they lived, were the property of the former. But with remarkable completeness and rapidity this universal law was, by the good will of the government, made illegal and impossible in practice, while the former rare exceptions were transformed into an absolutely binding rule, admitting of no exception at all. Similarly, the exceptional case of the tradesman who does not put up the price of the articles of first necessity with the increase in demand, becomes a universal rule as soon as the government deems it necessary to regulate the price of goods. In that case this direct violation of the supposed 'law' actually becomes law, — not a 'natural' one, but positive law or law of the state.

It should be noted that notwithstanding the difference between the two conceptions of the law of nature and the man-made law of the state, the latter resembles the former in that within the sphere of its application it has a universal force and admits of no unforeseen exception.[1] But the alleged economic laws never have such a significance and can at any moment be freely violated and annulled by the moral will of man. *In virtue of* the law of 1861 *not a single* landowner in Russia may buy or sell peasants otherwise than in his dreams.[2] On the other hand, *in spite of* the 'law' of supply and demand, noth-

---

1. Direct violation of the law by evil will is foreseen by the law itself and is treated as a crime which calls forth a corresponding punishment.

2. Solovyov is referring to the emancipation of the serfs. — *Editor's note.*

ing prevents any virtuous Petersburg landlord, even when fully awake, from lowering the rent of his flats out of philanthropic motives. The fact that only a very few take the opportunity of doing so, proves not the power of economic factors, but the weakness of individual virtue. For as soon as this lack of personal benevolence is supplanted by the demand of the law of the state, rents will be immediately lowered, and the 'iron' necessity of economic laws will at once prove to be as fragile as glass. This self-evident truth is at the present time admitted by writers altogether foreign to socialism, such as Laveleye,[3] for instance. In earlier days, J. S. Mill, anxious to preserve for political economy the character of an exact science and at the same time to avoid too obvious a contradiction with reality, invented the following compromise. Admitting that the economic *distribution* of the products of labour depends upon the human will and may be subordinated to moral purposes, he insisted that *production* is entirely determined by economic laws which have in this case the force of the laws of nature — as if production did not take place in the same general conditions and depend upon the same human powers and agents as distribution! This anti-scientific and scholastic distinction met, indeed, with no success, and was equally rejected by both opposed camps which Mill had sought to reconcile by means of it.

Freedom of the individual and society from the supposed natural laws of the material-economic order stands, of course, in no immediate connection with the metaphysical question of free will. When I say, *e.g.*, that Petersburg landlords are free from the supposed law which determines price by the relation of supply and demand, I am far from maintaining that any one of these landlords *whatever his character may be* can at any given moment lower the rent of his flats in spite of the increased demand for them. I only urge the obvious truth that given a *sufficiently* strong moral impulse, no alleged economic necessity can prevent the individual, especially in his public capacity, from subordinating material considerations to the moral in this or in that instance. Hence it logically follows that in the realm of economics there exist no natural laws acting independently of the individual will of the given agents. I do not deny the presence of law in human activity; I only argue against a special kind of material-economic necessity invented a hundred years ago, and taken to be independent of the general conditions that determine volition through psychological and moral motives. The character of objects and events which fall within the province of economics is on the one hand due to

---

3. Solovyov is referring to Emile de Laveleye (1822-1892), a Belgian writer, known chiefly for his book *De la propriété et de ses formes primitives* (translated into English as *Primitive Property*). — *Editor's note.*

physical nature, and is therefore subject to material necessity (to the mechanical, chemical, and biological laws), and on the other hand is determined by human activity, which is subject to moral and psychological necessity. And since no further causality, in addition to the natural and the human, can be found in the phenomena of the economic order, it follows that there can be in that domain no independent necessity and uniformity of its own.

It has been pointed out that the lack of moral initiative in private individuals is successfully supplemented by state legislation, which regulates economic relations in the moral sense with a view to the common good. Reference to this fact does not prejudge the question as to the extent to which such regulation may be desirable in the future and as to the form it should take. Of one thing only there can be no doubt: the very fact of state interference in the domain of economics (*e.g.* the legislative regulation of prices) unmistakably proves that the given economic relations do not express any natural necessity. For it is clear that laws of nature could not be cancelled by laws of the state.

III

Subordination of material interests and relations in human society to some special economic laws *acting on their own account* is the fiction of bad metaphysics, and has not the least foundation in reality. Therefore the general demand of reason and conscience remains in force — the demand, namely, that this province too should be subordinated to the supreme principle of morality, and that in its economic life society should be the organised realisation of the good.

There are not and there cannot be any independent economic laws, any economic necessity, for economic phenomena can only be thought of as activities of man who is a moral being, and is capable of subordinating all his actions to the pure idea of the good. There is only one absolute and independent law for man as such — the moral law, and only one necessity, namely, the moral. The peculiarity and independence of the economic sphere of relations lie not in the fact that it has ultimate laws of its own, but in the fact that from its very nature it presents a special and peculiar *field for the application* of the one moral law. Thus earth differs from other planets, not by having an independent source of light all to itself, but by receiving and reflecting the one universal light of the sun in a special and definite way, dependent upon its place in the solar system.

This truth is fatal both to the theories of the orthodox economists and to the socialist doctrine which seems at first sight to be opposed to them. When the socialists denounce the existing economic system and declaim against the unequal distribution of property, the cupidity and callousness of the rich, they appear to adopt the moral point of view, and to be inspired by the good feeling of pity towards those who labour and are heavy laden. The positive side of their doctrine, however, clearly shows that they take up, to begin with, an ambiguous and, subsequently, a directly hostile attitude toward the moral principle.

The inmost essence of socialism for the first time found expression in the remarkable doctrine of the followers of Saint-Simon, who proclaimed as their motto the rehabilitation of matter in the life of humanity. There is no doubt that matter has its rights, and the less they are respected in principle the more they assert themselves in practice. The nature of these rights, however, may be interpreted in two different and, indeed, directly contradictory ways. According to the first meaning — a perfectly true and an extremely important one — the sphere of material relations (more immediately of the economic ones) has a right to become the object of man's moral activity. It has a right to have the supreme spiritual principle realised or incarnate in it — *matter has a right to be spiritualised*. It would be unjust to maintain that this meaning was entirely foreign to the early socialistic systems. But they did not dwell upon it or develop it, and very soon this glimmer of a higher consciousness proved to be merely a deceptive light over the quagmire of carnal passions which gradually sucked in so many noble and inspired minds.

The other and more prevalent meaning given to the principle of the rehabilitation of matter justifies the degradation of the Saint-Simonists, and indeed makes it into a principle. The material life of humanity is not regarded as merely a special province of human activity or of the application of moral principles. It is said to have an entirely independent material principle of its own, existing in its own right both in and for man, namely, the principle of instinct or passion. This element must be given full scope so that the normal social order should naturally follow from personal passions and interests supplementing and replacing one another (Fourier's fundamental conception). This 'normal' order neither need nor can be moral. Alienation from the higher spiritual interests becomes inevitable as soon as the material side of human life is recognised to have an independent and unconditional value. One cannot serve two masters; and socialism naturally gives predominance to the principle under the banner of which the whole movement had first originated, *i.e.* to the material principle. The domain of economic relations is entirely subordinated to it, and is recognised as the chief, the fundamental, the only real and decisive factor in the life of humanity. At this point the *inner* opposition between socialism and the bourgeois political economy disappears.

In truth, the morally abnormal condition of the civilised world at the present day is due, not to this or that particular institution, but to the general conception and trend of life in modern society. Material wealth is becoming all-important, and social structure itself is distinctly degenerating into a *plutocracy*. It is not personal and hereditary property, division of labour and capital, or inequality of material possessions that is immoral. What is immoral is plutocracy, which distorts the true social order, raising the lower and the essentially subservient factor — the economic one — to the supreme and dominant position, and relegating all other things to be the means and instruments of material gain. Socialism leads to a similar distortion, though in a different way. From the plutocratic point of view the normal man is in the first place a capitalist and then, *per accidens*, a citizen, head of a family, an educated man, member of some religious union, etc. Similarly from the socialist point of view all other interests become insignificant and retreat into the background — if they don't disappear altogether — before the economic interest. In socialism, too, the essentially lower, material sphere of life — industrial activity — becomes decidedly predominant and overshadows all else. Even in its most idealistic forms socialism has from the first insisted that the moral perfection of society wholly and directly depends upon its economic structure, and sought to attain moral reformation or regeneration exclusively by means of an economic revolution. This fact clearly shows that socialism really stands on the same ground as the bourgeois régime hostile to it, namely, the supremacy of the material interest. Both have the same motto: 'man liveth by bread alone.' For a plutocrat the worth of man depends upon his possessing or being capable of acquiring material wealth. For a consistent socialist the worth of man depends upon his producing material wealth. In both cases man is taken as an economic agent, apart from other aspects of his being. In both cases economic welfare is taken to be the final end and the highest good. The struggle between the two hostile camps is not one of principle; or, rather, the struggle is waged, not about the content of a principle, but only about the extent of its realisation. One party is concerned with the material welfare of the capitalist minority, and the other with the also material welfare of the labour majority. And in so far as that majority, the working classes themselves, begin to care exclusively about their material welfare they obviously prove to be as selfish as their adversaries, and lose all moral advantage over the latter. In certain respects indeed socialism applies the principle of material interest more fully and consistently than do its opponents. Although plutocracy really cares for the economic interest alone, it admits the existence, though in a subordinate sense only, of other spheres of life, with independent institutions — such as the state and the Church — corresponding to them. Socialism in its pure form, however, rejects all this. For it man is exclusively a producer and consumer, and human society is merely an economic union — a union of workmen proprietors involving no substantial distinctions. And since the *predominance* of the material interests — of the economic, industrial and financial elements — constitutes the characteristic feature of the bourgeois régime, consistent socialism which intends finally to limit the life of humanity to these lower interests alone is certainly not an antithesis to, but the extreme expression, the crowning stage of the one-sided bourgeois civilisation.

Socialists and their apparent opponents — the plutocrats — unconsciously join hands on the most essential point. Plutocracy subjugates the masses of the people to its own selfish interests, disposes of them to its own advantage, for it regards them merely as labour, as producers of material wealth. Socialism protests against such 'exploiting,' but its protest is superficial and is not based upon principles, since socialism itself in the long-run regards man as *merely* (or in any case as mainly and primarily) an economic agent — and if he is only that, there is no *inherent* reason why he should not be exploited. On the other hand, the exclusive importance which attaches to material wealth, in the commercial state of the present day, naturally leads those who directly produce this wealth, the working classes, to demand an equal share in the enjoyment of the goods which, but for them, could not exist and which they are brought up to regard as the chief thing in life. Thus the practical materialism of the ruling classes themselves calls forth and justifies socialistic tendencies in the subjugated working classes. And when fear of social revolution brings about an insincere conversion of the plutocrats to the idealistic principles, it proves to be a useless game. The masks of morality and religion hastily put on do not deceive the masses, who know perfectly well what the true worship of their masters is.[4] And having learnt this cult from their superiors, working people naturally want to be the priests and not the victims.

The two hostile parties mutually presuppose one another and cannot escape from the vicious circle until they acknowledge and adopt in practice the unquestionable truth, forgotten by them, that the significance of man, and therefore of human society, is not essentially determined by economic relations, that man is not primarily the producer of material goods or market val-

4. A remarkably characteristic specimen of plutocratic hypocrisy is an article by the well-known Jules Simon (now deceased) which appeared some years ago without attracting notice. The article deals with the three chief evils of modern society: the decline of religion, of family, and of . . . *rentes!* The treatment of religion and family is dull and vague, but the lines dealing with the fall of interest on capital (from 4 per cent to 2½ per cent, if I remember rightly) are written with the blood of the heart.

ues, but is something infinitely more important, and that consequently society, too, is more than an economic union.[5]

IV

For the true solution of the so-called 'social question' it must in the first place be recognised that economic relations contain no special norm of their own, but are subject to the universal moral norm as a special realm in which they find their application. The triple moral principle which determines our due relation towards God, men, and the material nature is wholly and entirely applicable in the domain of economics. The peculiar character of economic relations gives a special importance to the last member of the moral trinity, namely, the relation to the material nature or *earth* (in the wide sense of the term). This third relation can have a moral character only if it is not isolated from the first two but is conditioned by them in their normal position.

The realm of economic relations is exhaustively described by the general ideas of *production* (labour and capital), *distribution* of property, and *exchange* of values. Let us consider these fundamental ideas from the moral point of view, beginning with the most fundamental of them — the idea of *labour*. We know that the first impulse to labour is given by material necessity. But for a man who recognises above himself the absolutely perfect principle of reality, or the will of God, all necessity is an expression of that will. From this point of view labour is a *commandment* of God. This commandment requires us to work hard ('in the sweat of thy face') to cultivate the ground, *i.e.* to perfect material nature. For whose sake? In the first place for our own and that of our neighbours. This answer, clear at the most elementary stages of moral development, no doubt remains in force as humanity progresses, the only change being that the denotation of the term 'neighbour' becomes more and more wide. Originally my neighbours were only those to whom I was related by the blood tie or by personal feeling; finally it is all mankind. When Bastiat,[6] the most gifted representative of economic individualism, advocated the principle 'each for himself' he defended him-

---

5. The contention that socialism and plutocracy are based upon one and the same materialistic principle was put forward by me eighteen years ago (in chapter xiv of the *Critique of Abstract Principles*, first published in *Russky Viestnik* in 1878) and led my critics to accuse me of having a wrong conception of socialism and of misjudging its value. I need no longer answer these criticisms, for they have been brilliantly disproved by the history of the socialistic movement itself, the main current of which has decidedly evinced itself as *economic materialism*.

6. See F. Bastiat, *Les harmonies économiques* (Paris, 1850). — *Editor's note.*

self against the charge of selfishness by pointing to the economic harmony in virtue of which each man in working solely for himself (and his family), unconsciously, from the very nature of social relations, works also for the benefit of all, so that the interest of each harmonises in truth with the interest of all. In any case, however, this would be merely a natural harmony, similar to that which obtains in the non-human world where certain insects, seeking nothing but sweet food for themselves, unconsciously bring about the fertilisation of plants by transferring the pollen from one flower to another. Such harmony testifies, of course, to the wisdom of the Creator, but does not make insects into moral beings. Man, however, *is* a moral being and natural solidarity is not sufficient for him; he ought not merely to labour for all and participate in the common work, but *to know* that he does so and *to wish* to do it. Those who refuse to recognise this truth as a matter of principle will feel its force as a fact in financial crashes and economic crises. Men who are the cause of such anomalies and men who are the victims of them, both belong to the class of people who work for themselves, and yet the natural harmony neither reconciles their interests nor secures their prosperity. The merely natural unity of economic interests is not sufficient to secure the result that each, in working for himself, should also work for all. To bring this about economic relations must be *consciously directed towards the common good.*

To take selfishness or self-interest as the fundamental motive of labour means to deprive labour of the significance of a universal commandment, to make it into something accidental. If I work solely for the sake of my own and my family's welfare, then as soon as I am able to attain that welfare by other means I must lose my only motive for work. And if it were proved that a whole class or group of persons can prosper by means of robbery, fraud, and exploitation of other people's labour, no theoretically valid objection could be urged against this from the point of view of unrestrained self-interest. Is it for the natural harmony of interests to abolish such abuses? But where was the natural harmony in the long ages of slavery, feudalism, serfdom? Or perhaps the fierce intestine wars which abolished feudalism in Europe and slavery in America were the expression — though somewhat a belated one — of natural harmony? In that case it is difficult to see in what way such harmony differs from disharmony, and in what way the freedom of the guillotine is better than the restrictions of state socialism. If, however, natural harmony of interests, seriously understood, proves to be powerless against economic abuses due to the unrestrained selfishness of individuals and classes whose freedom in this respect has to be restricted in the name of higher justice, it is unfair and impermissible to appeal to justice in the last resort only, and to put it at the end and not at the beginning of social structure. In addition to being unfair and impermissible it is also quite useless. For such morality *ex machina* has no power to attract or to inspire. No one will believe in it or be restrained by it from anything, and the only thing left will be bare compulsion — one day in one direction, and the next in another.

When the principle of the individualistic freedom of interests is adopted by the strong, it does not make them work more but gives rise to the slavery of ancient times, to the seigniorial right of the Middle Ages, and to modern economic slavery or plutocracy. When adopted by the weak, who, however, are strong as the majority, as the masses, this principle of unrestrained selfishness does not make them more *united* in their work, but merely creates an atmosphere of envious discontent, which produces in the end the bombs of the anarchists. Had Bastiat, who was fond of expressing his ideas in the form of popular dialogues, lived to our day, he might have played the chief part in the following conversation:

Anarchist. Out of especial friendliness for you, Mr. Bastiat, I warn you to take yourself away from here, as far as ever you can — I am just going to blow up all this neighbourhood, for there are lots of tyrants and exploiters about.

Bastiat. What a terrible position! But consider: you are doing irreparable damage to the principle of human liberty!

Anarchist. On the contrary — we are putting it into practice.

Bastiat. Who has put these devilish ideas into your mind?

Anarchist. You yourself.

Bastiat. What an absurd slander!

Anarchist. It is perfectly true. We are your pupils. Have you not proved that the root of all evil is the interference of public authority with the free play of individual interests? Have you not ruthlessly condemned all intentional organisation of labour, all compulsory social order? And that which is condemned as evil must be destroyed. We translate your words into practice and are saving you from dirty work.

Bastiat. I struggled only against the interference of the state in the economic life, and against the artificial organisation of labour advocated by socialists.

Anarchist. Socialists are no concern of ours; if they are deluded by fancies, so much the worse for them. *We* are not deluded. We fight against one organisation only — one which really exists and is called social order. Towns and factories, stock exchanges and academies, administration, police, army, Church — all these did not spring from the ground of themselves; they are the product of artificial organisation. Therefore on your own premises they are an evil and ought to be destroyed.

Bastiat. Even if this were true, things ought not to be destroyed by violent and disastrous means.

Anarchist. What is disaster? You have yourself beautifully explained that apparent calamities lead to the real good of all, and you have always very subtly distinguished between the unimportant things that are *evident* and the important things that *cannot be seen.* In the present case what is visible are the flying sardine boxes, demolished buildings, disfigured corpses — this is evident but unimportant. And that which is not seen and which alone is important is the future humanity which will be free from all 'interference' and all 'organisation' — since the persons, classes, and institutions which might interfere and organise will be exterminated. You preached the principle of anarchy, we carry out anarchy in practice.

Bastiat. Policeman! policeman! seize him quick before he blows us up. What are you thinking about?

Policeman. Well, I was wondering whether, from the point of view of self-interest, which I too have adopted after reading your eloquent arguments, it is of more advantage to me to seize this fellow by the scruff of the neck or to make haste and establish a natural harmony of interests between us.

V

In opposition to the alleged economic harmony, facts compel us to admit that starting with private material interest as the purpose of labour we arrive at universal discord and destruction instead of universal happiness. If, however, the principle and the purpose of labour are found in the idea of the common good, understood in the true moral sense — *i.e.* as the good of all and each and not of the majority only — that idea will also contain the satisfaction of every private interest within proper limits.

From the moral point of view every man, whether he be an agricultural labourer, a writer, or a banker, ought to work with a feeling that his work is useful to all, and with a desire for it to be so; he ought to regard it as a duty, as a fulfilment of the law of God and a service to the universal welfare of his fellow-men. But just because this duty is universal, it presupposes that every one else must regard the person in question in the same way, *i.e.* treat him not as a means only but as an end or purpose of the activity of all. The duty of society is to recognise and to secure to each of its members the *right* to enjoy unmolested *worthy* human existence both for himself and his family. Worthy existence is compatible with voluntary poverty, such as St. Francis preached and as is practised by our wandering pilgrims; but it is incompatible with work which reduces all the significance of man to being simply a means for producing or transferring material wealth. Here are some instances.

"We watch the *kriuchniks* at work: the poor half-naked Tatars strain every nerve. It is painful to see the bent back flatten out all of a sudden under a weight of eight to eighteen puds (the last figure is not exaggerated). This terrible work is paid at the rate of five roubles per thousand puds. The most a *kriuchnik* can earn in the twenty-four hours is one rouble, and that if he works like an ox and overstrains himself. Few can endure more than ten years of such labour, and the two-legged beasts of burden become deformed or paralytic" (*Novoe Vremya*, N. 7356).[7] Those who have not seen the Volga *kriuchniks* are sure to have seen the porters in big hotels who, breathless and exhausted, drag to the fourth or fifth floor boxes weighing several hundred-weight. And this in our age of machines and all sorts of contrivances! No one seems to be struck by the obvious absurdity. A visitor arrives at a hotel with luggage. To walk up the stairs would be a useful exercise for him, but instead he gets into a lift, while his things, for which, one would have thought, the lift was expressly meant, are loaded on the back of the porter, who thus proves to be not even an instrument of another man but an instrument of his things — the means of a means!

Labour which is exclusively and crudely mechanical and involves too great a strain of the muscular force is incompatible with human dignity. But equally incompatible with it and equally immoral is work which, though in itself not heavy or degrading, lasts all day long and takes up *all* the time and *all* the forces of the person, so that the few hours of leisure are necessarily devoted to physical rest, and neither time nor energy is left for thoughts and interests of the ideal or spiritual order.[8] In addition to hours of leisure, there are, of course, entire days of rest — Sundays and other holidays. But the exhausting and stupefying physical work of the week produces in holiday time a natural reaction — a craving to plunge into dissipation and to forget oneself, and the days of rest are devoted to the satisfaction of that craving.

"Let us not, however, dwell on the impression which individual facts susceptible of observation produce upon us, even though such facts be numerous. Let us turn to statistics and inquire as to how far wages satisfy the necessary wants of the workers. Leaving aside the rate of wages in the different industries, the quality of food, the size of the dwelling, etc., we will only ask of

7. This is from the article entitled "Arrest on a Ship," which appeared in the newspaper *Novoe Vremya* on 20 August 1896. A *kriuchnik* was a laborer who carried heavy loads on his back with the aid of a hook. A *pud* is equal to 36 pounds. — *Editor's note.*

8. Tram conductors in Petersburg work more than eighteen hours a day for twenty-five or thirty roubles a month (see *Novoe Vremya*, N. 7357).

statistics the question as to the relation between the length of human life and the occupation pursued. The answer is as follows: Shoemakers live on the average to the age of 49; printers, 48.3; tailors, 46.6; joiners, 44.7; blacksmiths, 41.8; turners, 41.6; masons, 33. And the average length of life of civil servants, capitalists, clergymen, wholesale merchants, is 60-69 years.[9] Now take the figures referring to the death-rate in relation to the size of the dwellings and the amount of rent in the different parts of town. It will be seen that in parts of the town with a poor population, belonging chiefly to the working class and paying low rents, mortality is far higher than in the neighbourhood with a relatively larger number of rich people. For Paris this relation was established by Villarmé as early as the twenties of the present century. He calculated that during the five years from 1822 to 1826, in the II. arrondissement of Paris, where the average rent per flat was 605 francs, there was one death per 71 inhabitants, while in the arrondissement XII., where the average rent was 148 francs, there was one death per 44 inhabitants. Similar data are to hand for many other towns, Petersburg among them."[10] Hence the following true conclusion is deduced: "If a workman is not regarded as a means of production, but is recognised, like every other human being, to be a free agent and an end in himself, the average forty years of life cannot be regarded as normal, while men belonging to richer classes live on the average till sixty or seventy years. This life, the longest possible under the social conditions of the present day, must be regarded as normal. All deviation below this average, unless it can be ascribed to the peculiarities of the particular work in question, must be entirely put down to excessive labour and insufficient income which does not allow to satisfy the most essential needs and the minimum demands of hygiene with regard to food, clothing, and housing."[11]

The absolute value of man is based, as we know, upon the *possibility* inherent in his reason and his will of infinitely approaching perfection or, according to the patristic expression, the possibility of becoming divine (θέωσις). This possibility does not pass into actuality completely and immediately, for if it did man would be already equal to God — which is not the case. The inner potentiality *becomes* more and more actual, and can only do so under definite real conditions. If an ordinary man is left for many years on an uninhabited island or in strict solitary confinement he cannot improve morally or intellectually, and indeed, exhibits rapid and obvious regress to-

9. The author quoted refers here to Hanshofer's book, *Lehrbuch der Statistik.* All the figures quoted are apparently for the countries of Western Europe.

10. A. A. Isaev, *Nachala politicheskoi economii (Principles of Political Economy),* 2nd ed., pp. 254-255.

11. *Ibid.,* p. 226.

wards the brutal stage. Strictly speaking, the same is true of a man wholly absorbed in physical labour. Even if he does not deteriorate he is certainly unable to think of actively realising his highest significance as man. The moral point of view demands, then, that every one should have the means of existence (*e.g.* clothes and a warm and airy dwelling) and sufficient physical *rest* secured to him, and that he should also be able to enjoy *leisure* for the sake of his spiritual development. This and *this alone* is *absolutely* essential for every peasant and workman; *anything above this is from the evil one.*

Those who are opposed to improving the socio-economic relations in accordance with the demands of morality urge the following consideration. They maintain that the only way in which the working people can, in addition to a secured material existence, have leisure to pursue their moral and intellectual development, is by reducing the number of hours of work, without reducing the wages. And this, they argue, will lead to a decrease of output, *i.e.* to economic loss or regress. Let it be *provisionally* granted that shorter hours of work with no reduction in wages will indeed inevitably lead to a diminution in productivity. But a *temporary* diminution of output does not necessarily mean regress or loss. When the hours of work have been reduced to a certain norm, positive reasons conditioning the increase of productivity will continue to operate. Such causes are to be found in technical improvements, greater proximity between different districts and countries owing to new means of communication, a closer intercourse between the different classes — causes all of which are wholly or partly independent of wages and hours of work. Thus the general quantity of output will again begin to increase; and even at the time when the increase will not yet have attained the former level, production of the objects of first necessity for individuals and the state will obviously not be decreased at all, and the decrease will entirely affect objects of luxury. It will be no great hardship to society if gold watches, satin skirts, and velvet chairs become twice or even three times as dear as they are now. It may be said that shorter hours of work with the same pay means a direct loss to the factory owners. It is impossible, however, to do anything without loss to some one or other; and it could hardly be called a calamity or an injustice if certain manufacturers were to get half a million instead of a million, or fifty instead of a hundred thousand dividend. This social class, no doubt an important and necessary one, does not inevitably consist of avaricious, greedy, and selfish men. I know several capitalists entirely free from these vices; and those of them who are not have a right to demand that society should pity them and not condone their abnormal and dangerous state of mind.

The hackneyed philippics, prompted by low envy, that socialists indulge in against the rich are perfectly sickening; demands for equalisation of property are unreasonable to the point of absurdity.[12] But it is one thing to attack private wealth as though it were an inherent evil, and another to demand that wealth, as a relative good, should harmonise with the common good understood in the light of the unconditional moral principle. It is one thing to strive for an impossible and unnecessary equalisation of property, and another, while preserving the advantages of larger property to those who have it, to recognise the right of every one to the necessary means of worthy human existence.

Apart from the false conclusions which the opponents of the moral regulation of economic relations deduce from their fundamental assertion, they are wrong in that assertion itself. Regulation of the hours of work and of the amount of wages need not necessarily curtail production at all (not even of the articles of luxury) or cause corresponding losses to the factory owners. This would be the case if the quantity — not to speak of quality — of the production entirely depended upon the number of hours expended upon it. No thoughtful and conscientious economist would, however, venture to maintain such a crying absurdity. It is easy to see that a worker exhausted, dulled, and embittered by excessive labour can produce in sixteen hours less than he can produce in eight hours if he works zealously and cheerfully, with a consciousness of his human dignity and a faith in his moral connection with the society or the state which looks after his interests instead of exploiting him. Thus a moral adjustment of economic relations would at the same time make for economic progress.

VI

In considering the organisation of human relations — in this case, of the economic ones — moral philosophy is not concerned with the concrete particu-

---

12. The diametrical opposition between socialism and Christianity has often been noted, but the essence of it is generally wrongly understood. The popular saying that socialism demands that the poor should take from the rich, while Christianity wants the rich to give to the poor, is more witty than profound. The opposition is far deeper than this, and lies in the moral attitude towards the rich. Socialism *envies* them and Christianity *pities* them — pities them because of the obstacles which connection with Mammon puts in the way of moral perfection: it is hard for the rich to enter the kingdom of heaven. But socialism takes that kingdom itself — *i.e.* the highest good and blessedness — to consist in nothing other than wealth, provided it is differently distributed. That which for Christianity is an obstacle, for socialism is an end; if this is not an antithesis I do not know what else to call by that name.

lar forms and determinations. These are dictated by life itself, and find realisation through the work of specialists and of men endowed with authority — men of theory and men of practice. Moral philosophy is only concerned with the immutable *conditions* which follow from the very nature of the good, and apart from which no concrete organisation could be moral. From the ethical point of view every social organisation is valuable and desirable only in so far as it embodies the moral principle, only in so far as it *justifies the good*. To make projects or prophecies is not the business of philosophy. It can neither offer definite plans of social organisation, nor even know whether individuals and nations will seek to adjust their relations according to the demands of the absolute moral principle at all. Its problem is as clear and as independent of any external circumstances as the problems of pure mathematics. Under what conditions is a fragment of a three-sided prism equal to three pyramids? Under what conditions do social relations in a given sphere correspond to the demands of the moral principle and ensure the stability and the constant moral progress of a given community?

We already know two conditions under which social relations in the domain of material labour become moral. The first general condition is, that the sphere of economic activity should not be isolated or affirmed as independent and self-contained. The second, more special condition is that production should not be at the expense of the human dignity of the producers; that not one of them should become merely a means of production, and that each should have secured to him material means necessary for worthy existence and development. The first demand has a religious character: not to put Mammon in the place of God, not to regard material wealth as an independent good, and the final purpose of human activity,[13] not even in the economic sphere. The second is a demand of humane feeling: to pity those who labour and are heavy laden, and not to set a lower value upon them than upon soulless things. To these two a third condition is necessarily added, which, so far as I am aware, has never yet been insisted upon in this connection. I am referring to the duties of man as an economic agent towards material nature itself, which he is called upon to cultivate. This duty is directly indicated in the commandment of labour: Till the ground.[14] To cultivate the ground means not to misuse, exhaust, or devastate it, but to improve it, to bring it to greater power and fulness of being. Neither our fellow-men nor

---

13. The recognition of material wealth as the *end* of economic activity may be called the original sin of political economy, since it dates back to Adam Smith.

14. The Hebrew words *la'ăbod 'et ha'ădāmâ* (Gen. 3:23) literally mean 'to serve the earth' — not, of course, to serve in the sense of a religious cult (although the word *'ābad* is used in this sense also) but in the sense in which angels serve humanity or a teacher serves children, etc.

material nature must be a mere passive or impersonal instrument of economic production or exploitation. Taken in itself or in isolation it is not the end of our activity, but it is a distinct and independent part of that end. Its subordinate position in relation to the Deity and humanity does not render it rightless: it has a right to our help in transforming and uplifting it. Things are rightless, but nature or earth is not merely a thing but an objectified essence, which we can and therefore must help to become spiritualised. The end of labour, so far as material nature is concerned, is not to make it an instrument for obtaining things and money, but to perfect it — to revive the lifeless, to spiritualise the material in it. The *methods* whereby this can be achieved cannot be indicated here; they fall within the province of *art* (in the broad sense of the Greek τέχνη). But what is essential is the point of view, the inner attitude and the direction of activity that results from it. *Without loving nature for its own sake it is impossible to organise material life in a moral way.*

Man's relation to material nature may be of three kinds: passive submission to it as it now exists; active struggle with it, its subjugation and the using of it as an indifferent instrument; and finally, the affirmation of it in its ideal state — of that *which it ought to become through man.* The first relation is wholly unjust both to man and to nature — to man, because it deprives him of his spiritual dignity by making him the slave of matter; to nature, because, in worshipping it in its present imperfect and perverted condition, man deprives it of the hope of perfection. The second, the negative, relation to nature is relatively normal, as a transitory and temporary stage; for it is clear that in order to make nature what it ought to be, we must first condemn it as it is, as it ought *not* to be. But absolutely normal and final is of course only the third, the positive relation, in which man uses his superiority over nature for the sake of uplifting it as well as of raising himself. It will be easily noted that man's threefold relation to earthly nature is a repetition, though on a wider scale, of his relation to his own material nature. Here, too, we necessarily distinguish the abnormal (passive) and the normal (positively active) relation and the transition from the first to the second (the negatively active relation). The carnal man submits and surrenders himself to the material life in its undue, perverted state. The ascetic struggles with the flesh in order to conquer it. The perfect man, having passed through such a struggle, does not destroy his bodily life but attains to its transfiguration, resurrection, and ascension. Asceticism or the subjugation of the flesh in individual life, struggle with external earthly nature and the subjugation of it in the common life of humanity, is merely a necessary transition and not the ideal form of activity. The ideal is to cultivate the earth, to minister to it, so that it might be renewed and regenerated.

VII

The efficient or producing cause of labour is found in the *needs* of man. This cause holds good for all the factors of production which appear now as the subjects and now as the objects of needs. The worker, as a living being, has need of the means of livelihood, and, as labour, he is the object of need to the capitalist, who in his turn, as employer, is an object of need to the worker, and in this sense is the immediate efficient cause of his labour. The same persons, as producers, stand in a similar relation to consumers, etc.

The *material* (and instrumental) cause of labour and production is found on the one hand in the forces of nature, and on the other in the various faculties and forces of man. But these twofold (efficient and material) economic causes, studied by political economy and statistics from different points of view, are physically unlimited and morally indefinite. The needs may increase in number and complexity *ad infinitum;* both needs and faculties may be of different worth, and, finally, the forces of nature may be used in the most various directions. All this leads to practical questions to which political economy, as a science limited to the material and existent aspect of things, can give no answer. Many persons have a *need* of pornography. Should this need be satisfied by the production of indecent books, pictures, immoral spectacles? Some demands, as well as some faculties, are obviously perverted in character; thus in the case of many persons certain positive qualities of intellect and will degenerate into a peculiar capacity for clever swindling within the limits of legality. Should we allow this capacity to develop freely and become a special profession or branch of work? Political economy as such can obviously answer nothing to questions such as these — they in no wise concern it. They directly concern, however, the recognised interests of society which cannot confine itself to matters of fact alone, but must submit them to a higher causality, by drawing a distinction between the normal and abnormal needs and faculties, the normal and abnormal use of the forces of nature. Since the fact of the existence of needs on the one hand and of forces and faculties on the other does not solve the practical question as to the extent to which the former should be satisfied and the manner in which the latter should be used, appeal has to be made to the moral principle as determining that which *ought* to be. It does not create the factors and elements of labour, but indicates how those already in existence should be used. Hence follows a new conception of labour, both more general and more definite than that given by political economy as such. For political economy labour is an activity of man ensuing from his needs, conditioned by his faculties, applied to the forces of nature, and having for its purpose the production of the greatest possible wealth. From the moral point of view *labour is interaction between men in the material world; it must, in accordance with moral demands, secure to each and all the necessary means of worthy existence, enabling man to bring to perfection all his powers, and is finally destined to transfigure and spiritualise material nature.* Such is the essence of labour from the point of view of the higher causality — of the formal and final cause — apart from which the two lower causes remain practically indefinite.

Further conditions of the normal economic life become clear in analysing the conceptions of *property* and *exchange.*

VIII

All the acute questions of the economic life are closely connected with the idea of property, which in itself, however, belongs to the sphere of jurisprudence, morality, and psychology rather than to that of economic relations. This fact alone clearly shows how mistaken is the attempt to conceive of economic phenomena as entirely independent and self-contained.

The inalienable basis of property, as all serious philosophers of modern times rightly recognise, is to be found in the very nature of man. Even in the contents of inner psychical experience we necessarily distinguish *ourselves* from what is *ours:* all our thoughts, feelings, desires, we regard as belonging to us, in contradistinction to ourselves as thinking, feeling, desiring. The relation is twofold. On the one hand, we necessarily put ourselves above what is ours, for we recognise that our existence is not by any means exhausted by or limited to any particular mental states — that *this* thought, *this* desire may disappear while we ourselves remain. This is the fundamental expression of human personality as formally unconditional, quite apart from the metaphysical question of the soul as substance. On the other hand, however, we are aware that if we are deprived of all mental states altogether we shall become a blank; so that for the reality and fulness of being it is insufficient to be 'oneself,' but it is necessary to have 'one's own.' Even in the inner psychical sphere that which belongs to the self is not always the absolute property of the person and is not always connected with him to the same extent.

Some mental states express by their content in the most intimate, direct, and immediate way that which is essential and fundamental to the given individual, and are in a sense inseparable from him. Thus, for instance, when a person has an implicit steadfast faith in God, such faith is his inalienable property — not in the sense that he must always actually have in mind a positive thought of God with corresponding thoughts and impulses, but only in the sense that every time when the idea of God actually arises in his mind, or when he is faced with a question concerning God, a definite positive answer accompanied by corresponding states of feeling and will is bound to follow. Other mental states are, on the contrary, merely superficial and transitory reactions of the person to external influences — accidental both in content and in origin, though conditioned by a more or less complex association of ideas and other mental and bodily processes. Thus when a person happens to think of the advantages or disadvantages of cycling, or to wish for a drink of beer, or to feel indignation at some lie in the newspapers, etc., it is obvious that such accidental states are but feebly connected with the person to whom they belong, that he loses nothing and experiences no essential change when they disappear. Finally, some mental states cannot, apart from their content and manner of origin, be regarded as reactions on the part of the individual who experiences them at all, so that their belonging to him must be recognised as fictitious. To this category belong *suggested* (*hypnotically* or otherwise) ideas, desires and feelings, and actions ensuing therefrom. It is very difficult to offer a theoretical account of them, but they unquestionably exist. Without going into these exceptional phenomena, however, it is sufficient to indicate the fact that both in theory and in practice certain actions are not laid to the responsibility of the persons who commit them. In view of the circumstance that, for the most part, these actions are conditioned by corresponding ideas, feelings, and impulses on the part of the agent, the recognition that he is not responsible for them implies that certain mental states do not belong to or form the property of the person who experiences them.

Thus even in the sphere of the inner psychical life we find that property is but relative and different in degree, beginning with the 'treasure' in which man 'puts his very soul'[15] and which may nevertheless be taken from him, and ending with states which prove to belong to him in an utterly fictitious sense. Similar relativity obtains with regard to external property. The immediate object of it is man's own body, which, however, belongs to man only more or less. This is true, first, in the natural sense that the individual himself cannot regard as in an equal measure his own those organs or parts of the body without which earthly life is altogether impossible (*e.g.* the head or the heart), those without which it is possible but not enjoyable (*e.g.* 'the apple of the eye'), and those the loss of which is no misfortune at all (*e.g.* an amputated finger or an extracted tooth, not to speak of nails, hair, etc.). If, however, the real connection of the person with his body is thus relative and unequal, there is no natural ground for regarding the body as his absolute property or

---

15. See Matthew 6:21. — *Editor's note.*

as absolutely inviolable. And from the point of view of the unconditional moral principle the bodily inviolability of a person is not anything distinct and on its own account, but is connected with universal and generally binding norms, and is therefore incompatible with the violation of these norms. If it is both my right and my duty forcibly to prevent a man from injuring a defenceless being, it must be the right and the duty of other persons to exercise such bodily compulsion over myself too in a similar case.

If, on the other hand, property is understood in the strict sense as the 'jus utendi and *abutendi* re sua' (the right to the use and to the *abuse* of one's own thing), such a right is not absolute so far as one's body is concerned. On this side too it is limited by just considerations of the common good which have found expression in legal codes of all epochs and nations. If the whole of man's physical powers are needed, for instance, for the defence of his country, even so slight an 'abuse' of one's body as cutting off a finger is recognised as criminal. And even apart from such special conditions, not by any means every use that man may make of his body is regarded as permissible.

But whatever the moral and social limitations of man's rights over his own body may be, in any case it unquestionably belongs to him, just as his mental states do, in virtue of a direct and natural connection, independent of his will, between *himself* and *what is his*. As to external things, the ground upon which they belong to this or that person, or are appropriated by him, is not immediately given and calls for explanation. Even when there appears to be the closest connection between a person and a thing, as for instance between necessary clothing and the person who is wearing it, the question as to property still remains open, for the clothes may not be his own but may have been stolen from somebody else. On the other hand, a person living in Petersburg or London may have immovable property in East Siberia which he has never seen nor ever will see. If, then, the presence of the closest real connection between a person and a thing (as in the first case) is in no sense a guarantee of property, while the absence of any real connection (as in the second instance) is no obstacle to property, it follows that the real connection is altogether irrelevant and that the right of property must have an ideal basis. According to a current philosophical definition, property is the ideal continuation of the person in things or the extension of the person to things. In what way, however, and upon what ground is the self thus extended to and does it appropriate what is other than it? Such extension cannot be due to the act of personal will alone; an act of will can transfer the already existing right of property (through gift or legacy, etc.), but it cannot create the right itself. The right of property is usually held to arise in two ways only, through possession and work. Possession in the strict sense, *i.e.* apart from any special work (such as military work), through simple seizure resulting from a direct act of will gives rise to a special right of property, 'the right of the first occupier' *('jus primi occupantis'),* but does so only in exceptional cases, more and more rarely met with, when that which is seized belongs to no one *('res nullius').*

Work thus remains, in the general opinion, the essential basis of property. The product of one's work and effort naturally becomes one's own, one's property. This ground, however, also proves to be insecure. If it were sufficient, children would have to be recognised as the property of the mother who brought them into the world with no little labour and effort. Reservations have to be made and human beings must be *a priori* excluded from the class of objects of property; and this can only be done in virtue of principles utterly foreign to the economic sphere as such. At this point, however, a new and more important difficulty arises. It has been granted that things alone can be objects of property, and that the ground of property is labour which produces them. This would be all very well if labour could produce things; but in truth labour produces not things but *utility* in things. Utility, however, is a relation and not a thing and cannot therefore be the object of property. In common parlance, dating from primitive times, it is usual to speak of workmen making things; but even persons ignorant of political economy understand that workmen merely produce in the given material changes which communicate to it some relatively new qualities corresponding to certain human needs. There is no doubt that they work for their own sake as well as for other people's, and that their work must give satisfaction to their own needs. "The workman is worthy of his meat,"[16] — this is a moral axiom which no one would honestly challenge. The question, however, is what can be the ground of the workman's ownership of the so-called products of labour. Labour which does not produce a thing, but only a certain particular quality in it, inseparable from the thing itself, cannot justify the ownership of that which it did not produce, and which does not depend upon it. The employer is responsible for the workman's labour but not for the reality of its products, and is therefore in the same position as the workman with regard to the latter.

Thus there exists no real ground why the product of labour should be the property of any one, and we must therefore turn to the ideal grounds.

---

16. 'Meat' should, of course, be understood in the wide sense explained above. [See Matthew 10:10. — *Editor's note.*]

IX

In virtue of the absolute significance of personality every man has a right to the means of a worthy existence. Since, however, the individual as such has this right potentially only, and it depends upon society actually to realise or to secure it, it follows that the individual has a corresponding duty towards society — the duty to be useful to it or to work for the common good. In this sense work is the source of property: the worker has an unquestionable right of property over what he has *earned*. Within certain limits demanded by the moral principle, wages may be regulated by society — *i.e.* by the central authority or the Government — and not be allowed to fall below a certain minimum, but they cannot be prescribed with absolute exactness. On the other hand, the needs and the conditions of a worthy existence are even in a normal society only an *approximately* constant and definite quantity. Hence it becomes possible for individual persons to save or to accumulate material means, *i.e.* to form *capital*. There is, of course, still less visible and real connection between capital and the person who has saved it than there is between the workman and the thing he has made, but the close and complete ideal connection is obvious. Capital as such, in its general nature — apart from the circumstances owing to which it may in individual cases have been built up — is a pure product of human will, for originally it depended upon that will to save a part of the earnings or to use it too for current needs. Capital, therefore, ought in justice to be recognised as property *par excellence*.[17]

The conception of property involves the conception of freely disposing of the object of property. Ought this freedom to be absolute and include both the use and the abuse of property? Since the realisation of any right at all is possible only if society guarantees it, there is no reason why society should guarantee personal misuse of a right that conflicts with the common good. From the fact that, according to the moral principle, the individual has absolute and inalienable rights, it by no means follows that every act of his will is the expression of such an inalienable right. Apart from being irrational such a supposition would be practically self-destructive, since a will which trespasses upon all rights would also in that case be inviolable, and therefore there would be no inalienable right left. And if it is both permissible and obligatory

---

17. I have indicated the source of capital in the simplest normal scheme. But whatever anomalies may accompany the formation and growth of capital in actual life, the part played by the will or the strength of spirit remains in any case essential. Since there is no doubt that all wealth may be squandered, the mere fact of *saving* it is an obvious *merit of will* on the part of the saver; it is null in comparison with merits of a different and higher order, but in their absence it undoubtedly has an importance of its own.

to prevent a person from misusing his hands (for instance, from committing a murder), it is also permissible and obligatory to prevent him from misusing his property to the detriment of the common good or social justice.[18]

The only question is as to what we are to understand by misuse that calls for the intervention of the state. Socialism recognises as misuse all transfer of earned property to another person by legacy or testament. This transference of economic advantages to persons who have not personally deserved them is alleged to be the main wrong and the source of all social evils. But although inheritance of property has some real drawbacks, they disappear in the face of the positive side of this institution, which necessarily follows from the very nature of man. The continuous chain of progress in humanity is kept together by the conscious successiveness of its links. While the all-embracing unity of the future is still in the making, the very process whereby it comes about demands mutual moral dependence between generations, in virtue of which one does not merely follow the other but also *inherits* from it. If it were not for the intentional and voluntary handing down of what has been acquired, we should have only a physical succession of generations, the latter repeating the life of the former, as is the case with animals. The most important thing, of course, is the continuous accumulation of spiritual inheritance; but since it is given to only a few to hand down to universal posterity permanent spiritual acquisitions, and since moral demands are the same for all, it is the right and the duty of the majority of men to try to improve the material conditions of life for their immediate successors. Those who wholly devote themselves to the service of the universal future and already anticipate it as an ideal have a right to refer to the precept of taking no thought for the morrow advocated in the Gospels. To imitate the lilies of the field one must be as pure as they are, and to be like the fowls of the air one must be able to fly as high. But if either purity or loftiness be lacking, practical carefreeness likens us not to the lilies or the birds of the air, but to the animal which, careless of the future, grubs up the roots of the kindly oak tree, and even, on occasion, devours its own offspring instead of acorns.[19]

When dealing with an institution which is not immoral and is based upon ideal foundations though it corresponds only to the medium level of morality, no serious moralist ought to forget the unquestionable truth that it

---

18. Even Roman law, thoroughly individualistic as it was in this respect, introduced an important reservation into the formula quoted above: *proprietas est jus utendi et abutendi re sua quatenus juris ratio patitur* — property is the right to the use and to the abuse of one's thing in so far as *it is compatible with the meaning* (or the rational basis) *of justice*. But the meaning of justice demands precisely that private caprice should be limited by the common good.

19. Solovyov is referring to Ivan Krylov's fable "The Pig Beneath the Oak." — *Editor's note.*

is far more difficult for society to rise above this level than to sink below it. Even if socialism and theories akin to it did intend to turn every human being into an angel, they would certainly fail to do so; but to bring the human mass down to the brutal stage is not at all difficult. To reject in the name of the absolute moral ideal the necessary social conditions of moral progress means, in the first place, in defiance of logic, to confuse the absolute and eternal value of that *which is being realised* with the relative value of the degree of realisation as a process in time. Secondly, it means a thoughtless attitude towards the absolute ideal which, apart from the concrete conditions of its realisation, becomes for man an empty phrase. Thirdly, this pseudo-moral uncompromising straightforwardness means the absence of the most fundamental and elementary moral impulse — *pity*, and pity precisely for those who are most in need of it — for 'these little ones.'[20] To preach absolute morality and reject all moralising institutions, to lay burdens too heavy to be borne upon the weak and helpless shoulders of average humanity, *is illogical, thoughtless, and immoral.*

Inherited property is the abiding realisation of moral interaction in the most intimate and the most fundamental social group — namely, in the family. Inherited wealth is, on the one hand, the embodiment of pity, reaching beyond the grave, of the parents for their children, and, on the other, a concrete point of departure for a pious memory of the departed parents. With these two is connected, at any rate with regard to the most important kind of property — the property in land, a third moral factor, viz, man's relation to external nature, *i.e.* to the earth. For the majority of men this relation can become moral only on condition of their having inherited landed property. To understand earthly nature and to love it for its own sake is given to a few only; but every one becomes naturally attached to his own native spot, to the graves of his fathers and the haunts of his childhood. It is a moral bond, and one which extends human solidarity to material nature, thus making a beginning of its spiritualisation. This fact both justifies the institution of inherited property in land and serves as a basis for making it more conformable to the demands of morality. It is not sufficient to recognise the ideal character which obviously attaches to such property: it is necessary to strengthen and develop this character, protecting it from the low and selfish motives which are natural enough at the present stage of human progress and may easily gain the upper hand. Decisive check must be put upon the treatment of the earth as a lifeless instrument of rapacious exploitation; the plots of land handed down from one generation to another must, in principle, be made inalienable and suffi-

20. Matthew 10:42. — *Editor's note.*

cient to maintain in each person a moral attitude towards the earth. It will be said that, with the population constantly increasing, enough land cannot be found both to preserve to each what he has got, or even a part of it, and to give some to those who have not got any. This objection appears to be a serious one, but is in truth either thoughtless or unfair. It would certainly be very absurd to suggest as an absolute, separate, and independent measure that an inalienable plot of land should be secured to each and all. This measure may and ought to be taken only in connection with another reform — the cessation, namely, of that rapacious method of cultivation which will end in there not being enough land for any one, let alone for all. And if land is treated in the moral way and *looked after* like a being whom one loves, the minimum amount of land sufficient for each person may become so small that there will be enough for those who have not got any, without doing injustice to those who have.

As to the unlimited increase of population, it is not ordained by any physical, and, still less, by any moral law. It is understood, of course, that normal economics are possible only in connection with the normal family, which is based upon rational asceticism and not upon unchecked carnal instincts. The immoral exploitation of land cannot stop so long as there is immoral exploitation of woman. If man's relation to his inner *house* (this is the name applied by the Scriptures to the wife) is wrong, his relation to his external house cannot be right either. A man who beats his wife cannot care for the earth as he should. Speaking generally, the moral solution of the economic question is intimately connected with the whole life-task of the individual and of humanity.

X

Just as there can be no physiological life without the interchange of substances, so there can be no social life without the interchange of things (and of signs representing them). This important domain of human material relations is studied on its technical side by political economy, financial and commercial law, and falls within the scope of moral philosophy only in so far as *exchange* becomes *fraud*. To judge economic phenomena and relations as such — to affirm, *e.g.*, as some moralists do, that money is an evil, that there must be no commerce, that banks ought to be abolished, etc. — is unpardonable childishness. It is obvious that objects which are thus condemned are morally indifferent or neutral, and become good or evil only according to the quality and direction of the will that uses them. If we are to give up money as an evil because many people use money for evil purposes, we ought also to give up the power of articulate speech, since many use it for swearing, idle talk, and slander; we should also have to give up using fire for fear of conflagrations, and water for fear of persons committing suicide by drowning. In truth, however, money, commerce, and banks are not in themselves an evil but become an evil, or, more exactly, become the consequence of an already existing evil and the cause of a new one, when, instead of necessary interchange, they serve the purposes of selfish fraud.

The root of evil in this case, as in the whole of the economic sphere, is one and the same, namely, that the material interest is made dominant instead of subservient, independent instead of dependent, an end instead of a means. From this poisonous root three noxious stems spring in the domain of exchange — falsification, speculation, and usury.

A modern text-book of political economy gives as a current definition of commerce that it is a trade "consisting in the buying and selling of goods with the object of gain."[21] The description of commerce as the buying and selling of goods is purely verbal, the important thing is the purpose, which is here said to consist entirely in the gain of the trader.[22] If, however, the one object of commerce is gain, all profitable falsification of goods and all successful speculation are justified. And if gain is the purpose of commerce, it is certainly also the purpose of money-lending, and since the latter is more profitable the higher the rate of interest, unlimited usury is also justified. If, on the other hand, such facts are recognised as inconsistent with the moral norm, it must also be recognised that commerce and exchange in general may be a means of private gain only *on condition* that they should in the first place serve the community as a whole and fulfil a social function for the good of all.

From this point of view the economic anomalies indicated can be abolished only if their immoral root is destroyed. But every one understands that the unchecked growth of a plant strengthens its roots and extends them in breadth and in depth, and that if the roots are very deep, the stem must be cut down first. To speak without metaphors: apart from the inner, purely ideal and verbal struggle with the vice of cupidity, normal society can and ought decisively to oppose by means of concrete external measures such luxurious growths of unlimited cupidity as commercial falsification, speculation, and usury.

Falsification of goods, especially of the objects of necessary consump-

---

21. Isaev, *Principles of Political Economy,* 2nd ed., p. 430. — *Editor's note.*

22. I do not, of course, hold the author of the book responsible for this definition, since he only gives expression to the popular idea.

tion, is a menace to public welfare and is not merely immoral but positively criminal. In some cases it is regarded as such even at the present day, but this view must be worked out more consistently. When the whole legal procedure and system of penalties[23] are reformed, increased persecution of these special offences will not be an act of cruelty but of justice. Two things ought to be remembered in this connection: in the first place, that people who suffer most from this evil are the poor and ignorant, who are unfortunate enough as it is; and secondly, that the unchecked performance of these crimes, as of all others, is injurious not only to the victims but to the criminals themselves, who may feel that their immorality is justified and encouraged by the condonation of society.

Financial operations with fictitious values (the so-called 'speculations') are certainly a social disease rather than a personal crime, and the first remedy is absolute prohibition of institutions whereby this disease is nurtured. As to usury, the only sure method of abolishing it is, obviously, universal development of normal credit, not with the object of gain but as a charitable institution.

In discussing economic relations which ought to hold in the domain of labour, property, and exchange, I have spoken throughout of justice and right, conceptions which have also been presupposed in the treatment of the penal question. For the most part the terms 'justice' and 'right' carry the same meaning. The idea of justice, however, expresses a purely moral demand, and therefore belongs to the ethical sphere, while right determines a special sphere of relations — namely, the legal one. Is this distinction merely a misunderstanding or, if it is well grounded, what is the meaning and the degree of it? Turning now to the question as to the relation of morality and legal justice or right, we may note, without prejudging the content of our inquiry, that the question is an extremely wide one, for the idea of right inevitably involves a series of other ideas — law, authority, legal compulsion, state. In discussing the *organisation* of just social relations I took these ideas for granted, since such an organisation can obviously not be realised through moral preaching alone.

---

23. See above, Part III, Chap. VI.

CHAPTER VIII

Morality and Legal Justice

I

The *absolute* moral principle, the *demand,* namely, or the *commandment* to be perfect as our Father in heaven is perfect, or to realise in ourselves the image and likeness of God, already contains in its very nature the recognition of the *relative* element in morality. For it is clear that the demand for perfection can be addressed only to a being who is imperfect; urging him to *become* like the higher being, the commandment presupposes the lower stages and the relative degrees of advance. Thus, the absolute moral principle or the perfect good is for us, to use Hegel's language, a unity of itself and its other, a synthesis of the absolute and the relative. The existence of the relative or the imperfect, as distinct from the absolute good, is a fact not to be got over, and to deny it, to *confuse* the two terms, or, with the help of dialectical tricks and on the strength of mystical emotions, to affirm them as identical, would be false. Equally false, however, is the opposite course — the *separation,* namely, of the relative from the absolute, as of two wholly distinct spheres which have nothing in common. From this dualistic point of view man himself, whose striving towards the absolute is inseparably connected with relative conditions, proves to be the incarnation of absurdity. The only rational point of view, which both reason and conscience compel us to adopt, consists in recognising that the actual duality between the relative and the absolute resolves itself for us into a free and complete unity (but not by any means into an empty identity of indifference) through the real and moral process of approaching perfection — a process ranging from the inert stone to the glory and freedom of the sons of God.

At each stage the relative is connected with the absolute as a means for *concretely* bringing about the perfection of all, and this connection justifies the lesser good as a condition of the greater. At the same time it justifies the absolute good itself, which would not be absolute if it could not connect with itself or include in one way or another all concrete relations. And indeed, nowhere in the world accessible to us do we find the two terms in separation or in their bare form. Everywhere the absolute principle is clothed with relative forms, and the relative is inwardly connected with the absolute and held together by it. The difference lies simply in the comparative predominance of one or the other aspect.

When some two species of concrete relations or some two domains within which they are exemplified are separated from and opposed to one another, one being regarded as absolute and the other as purely relative in meaning, we may be certain that the opposition itself is purely relative. Each of the two domains is simply a special instance of the relation between the absolute and the relative, — a relation different in form and degree, but identical in nature and supreme purpose. And it is in this relation of both to the absolute that the positive connection or the unity of the two consists.

Within the limits of the active or practical life of humanity there is apparent opposition between the moral sphere in the strict sense and the sphere of legal justice. From ancient times, beginning with the pagan Cynics and the Christian gnostics, and down to our own day, this opposition has been taken to be unconditional. Morality alone has been regarded as absolute, and legal justice, as a purely conventional phenomenon, has been rejected in the name of the absolute demands. One immediately feels that this view is false, but moral philosophy compels us to disregard this feeling which may, after all, be deceptive, and to consider the true relation between morality and legal justice from the standpoint of the absolute good. Is this good justified by its relation to justice? A person interested in etymology may note that the answer is already contained in the terms of the question. This philological circumstance will be discussed further on, but it must not as such prejudge the philosophic problem.

II

In his lectures on Criminal Law Professor N. S. Tagantsev quotes, among other things, the following Prussian enactment of the year 1739:

"If an advocate or a procurator or any similar person ventures to present any petition to his Royal Majesty, either personally or through somebody else, it is the pleasure of his Royal Majesty that the aforesaid person should be hanged without mercy, and a dog be hanged by the side of him."

Of the legality or conformity to law of the enactment in question there can be no doubt; and there can be equally no doubt of its being opposed to the most elementary demands of justice. The opposition seems to be intentionally emphasised by extending the punishment of the advocate or procurator to the perfectly innocent dog. Similar, though not such glaring cases of disagreement between morality and positive right, between justice and law, are frequently met with in history. The question must then be asked, how is this fact to be regarded, and which of the two conflicting principles are we to adopt in practical life? The answer appears to be clear. Moral demands have an inherent character of being absolutely binding, which may be entirely absent from the enactments of positive law. Hence the conclusion seems legitimate that the question as to the relation between morality and legal justice is settled by a simple rejection of the latter as a binding principle of action. All human relations must accordingly be reduced to purely moral interaction, and the sphere of the legal or juridical determinations and relations must be entirely rejected.

This conclusion is very easily thought of, but is also extremely thoughtless. This 'antinomy,' or the absolute opposition between morality and law, has never subjected its fundamental assumption to any consistent or far-reaching criticism.

That a formally legal enactment, such as the edict of the king of Prussia, quoted above, is opposed to the demands of morality is only too obvious. But it may well be that it is also opposed to the demands of legal justice itself. The possibility of conflict between the formal legality of certain actions and the essence of legal justice will become clearer to the reader if I give a concrete instance of an analogous conflict between the formally-moral character of an action and the true nature of morality.

It was reported in the papers a little while ago that a woman suspected of causing the illness of a boy by means of a bewitched apple was terribly injured and almost killed by the crowd in the centre of Moscow — near St. Panteleimon's Chapel in Nikolsky Street. Now these people acted independently of any interested motives or external considerations; they had no personal enmity toward the woman and no personal interest in beating her; their sole motive was the feeling that so outrageous a crime as the poisoning of an innocent babe by means of sorcery ought to meet with just retribution. Thus it cannot be denied that their behaviour had a formally-moral character, though every one will agree that it certainly was essentially immoral. If, however, the fact that revolting crimes may be committed from purely moral motives does not lead us to reject morality as such, there is no reason why such essentially unjust, though legal, enactments as the Prussian law of 1739 should be regarded as sufficient ground for rejecting legal justice. In the case of the crime in Nikolsky Street it is not the moral principle that is at fault, but the insufficient development of the moral consciousness in the half-savage crowd; in the case of the absurd Prussian law it is not the idea of legal justice or law that is at fault, but only the small degree to which the idea of justice was developed in the consciousness of King Friedrich-Wilhelm. It would not be worth while to discuss the subject were it not for the bad habit, which has become established of late, especially with reference to legal questions, to deduce, contrary to logic, general conclusions from concrete particular instances.

III

It is not legal justice and morality that conflict and are incompatible with one another, but the different states both of the legal and the moral consciousness. Apart from these states and their concrete expressions, there exist, however, in the domain of legal justice, just as much as in the domain of morality, abiding and essential norms, the presence of which is unconsciously admitted even by the spirit of lies, in his sophistic attack on jurisprudence:

> All rights and laws are still transmitted
> Like an eternal sickness of the race, —
> From generation unto generation fitted
> And shifted round from place to place.
> Reason becomes a sham, Beneficence a worry:
> Thou art a grandchild, therefore woe to thee.
> The right born with us, ours in verity
> This to consider, there's, alas! no hurry.[1]

Even Mephistopheles recognises this *natural right*, and merely complains that it is ignored.[2] In truth, however, it is referred to whenever a question of right arises. No fact belonging to the legal sphere, no expression of legal justice, can be judged of except by reference to a general conception or norm of justice. Mephistopheles himself applies this conception or norm when he says

1. From Goethe's *Faust*.
2. Apart from the direct meaning of this remark, it may be regarded as a kind of prophecy of the persecution which, a quarter of a century after Goethe's death, the idea of the natural right suffered in jurisprudence. There are signs which show that this persecution is coming to an end.

that certain rights and laws, once rational and beneficial, have become sense-less and mischievous. He indicates here one aspect of the case only, namely, the so-called *conservatism* of legal justice. This fact, too, has its rational foundation, and the disadvantages which it involves, and upon which Mephistopheles exclusively dwells, are cancelled by another fact, not mentioned by the spirit of lies for his own reasons — the fact, namely, that legal consciousness gradually develops, and that legal enactments are, as a fact, improved. This unquestionable *progress* in the domain of legal justice can be shown even in the case of the unjust law quoted above. I do not simply mean that enactments like the Prussian edict of 1739 have become utterly impossible in any European country, and that the penalty of death even for the worst and unquestionable crimes has long been condemned by the best representatives of the legal profession. I contend that this edict itself meant unquestionable progress in comparison with the state of things which had once prevailed in Brandenburg and Pomerania, as in the rest of Europe, when every powerful baron could calmly put peaceful people to death for motives of personal vengeance, or for the sake of seizing their property. At the time of Frederick the Great's father it was the king alone who had the power to take a man's life, and, in doing so, he had no personal or selfish purpose in view. It is obvious, indeed, that Friedrich Wilhelm's object in composing his edict was to put down denunciation and slander by the threat of the penalty of death, and not actually to deprive of life advocates, procurators, and dogs. The barons of the old times were unquestionably guilty of murder and robbery, but the king, even when publishing the revolting edict, was still acting as the guardian of justice, though at a very low level of legal consciousness.

This difference of degree, this actual progress in legal justice, the steady advance of the legal enactments towards legal norms, conformable to, though not identical with, the moral demands, sufficiently proves that the relation between the two principles is not merely negative. It shows that it is impermissible from the point of view of morality itself to dismiss the whole range of legal facts and problems by a simple and meaningless rejection of them.

IV

The relation between the moral and the legal sphere is one of the fundamental questions of practical philosophy. It is really the question as to the relation between the ideal moral consciousness and actual life. The vitality and the fruitfulness of the moral consciousness depend upon this relation being understood in a positive sense. Between the ideal good on the one hand and the evil reality on the other lies the intermediate sphere of law and justice, whose function is to give concrete embodiment to the good, and to limit and to correct the evil. Justice and its embodiment — the state — condition the actual organisation of the moral life of humanity. Moral preaching which takes up a negative attitude towards justice as such could have no objective basis or means of expression in the real environment that is foreign to it, and would remain at best an innocent pastime. If, on the other hand, the formal conceptions and institutions of legal justice were completely severed from moral principles and purposes, legality would lose its absolute basis and become purely arbitrary.

Indeed, in order consistently to carry out the separation between legal right and morality it would be necessary to give up the ordinary use of speech, which, in all languages, unmistakably testifies to the fundamental inner relation between the two ideas. The conception of right and the correlative conception of duty form so essential a part of the system of moral ideas that they may serve as a direct expression of them. Every one understands and no one would dispute such moral affirmations as: I am conscious of the *duty* to abstain from everything shameful, or, what is the same thing, I recognise that human dignity (in my own person) has a *right* to my respect; it is my *duty* to help my neighbours as much as in me lies and to serve the common good, *i.e.* my neighbours and society as a whole have a *right* to my help and service; finally, it is my *duty* to harmonise my will with what I regard as the highest of all, or, in other words, the absolutely highest has a *right* to a religious attitude on my part (which is the ultimate basis of all religious worship).

There is not a single moral relation which could not be correctly and intelligibly expressed in terms of right. One would think that nothing could be more remote from the juridical order of ideas than love for one's enemies. And yet if the supreme moral law proclaims it my *duty* to love my enemies, it is clear that my enemies have a *right* to my love. If I deny love to them, I act unjustly, I sin against what is *right*. Here we have a term which alone embodies the essential unity of the juridical and the moral principles.[3] For rights are nothing more than the expression of what is right, and, on the other hand, all

---

3. In all languages, moral and juridical conceptions are expressed either by the same terms or by terms derived from the same root. The Russian *dolg*, like the Latin *debitum* (hence the French *devoir*) and the German *Schuld*, has both a moral and a juridical meaning; in the case of δική and δικαιοσύνη, *jus* and *justitia*, the Russian *pravo* and *pravda*, the German *Recht* and *Gerechtigkeit*, the English *right* and *righteousness*, the two meanings are distinguished by the use of suffixes. Cp. also the Hebrew *ṣedeq* and *ṣĕdāqâ*.

virtues[4] are reducible to the idea of right or justice, *i.e.* to what is right or due in the ethical sense. This is not a case of accidental similarity of terms, but of essential homogeneity and inner connection of the ideas themselves.

It does not, of course, follow that the spheres of legal justice and morality coincide, or that the moral and the juridical conceptions should be confused. One thing only is indisputable, namely, that there is a positive and intimate relation between the two spheres, which does not permit of one being rejected in the name of the other. The question, then, is in what precisely do the connection and the difference between them consist.

V

The fact that we speak of *moral right* and moral duty, on the one hand proves the absence of any fundamental opposition or incompatibility of the moral and the juridical principles, and, on the other, indicates an essential difference between them. In designating a given right (*e.g.* the right of my enemy to my love) as *moral* only, we imply that in addition to the moral there exist other rights, *i.e.* rights in a more restricted sense, or that there exists *right as such,* which is not directly and immediately characterised as moral. Take, on the one hand, the duty of loving our enemies and their corresponding right to our love, and on the other, take the duty to pay one's debts, or the duty not to rob and murder one's neighbours and their corresponding right not to be robbed, murdered, or deceived by us. It is obvious that there is an essential difference between the two kinds of relation, and that only the second of them falls within the scope of justice in the narrow sense of the term.

The difference can be reduced to three main points:

(1) A purely moral demand, such, *e.g.,* as the love for one's enemies, is unlimited or all-embracing in nature; it presupposes moral perfection, or, at any rate, an unlimited striving towards perfection. Every limitation admitted as a matter of *principle* is opposed to the nature of the moral commandment and undermines its dignity and significance. If a person gives up the absolute moral ideal as a principle, he gives up morality itself and leaves the moral ground. Juridical law, on the contrary, is essentially limited, as is clearly seen in all cases of its application. In the place of perfection it demands the lowest, the minimum degree of morality, that is, simply, actual restraint of certain manifestations of the immoral will. This distinction, however, is not an opposition leading to real conflict. From the moral point of view it cannot be de-

4. See above, Part I, Chapter V: 'Virtues.'

nied that the demand conscientiously to fulfil monetary obligations, to abstain from murder, robbery, etc., is a demand for what is good — though extremely elementary — and not for what is evil. It is clear that if we ought to love our enemies, it goes without saying that we ought to respect the life and property of all fellow-men. The higher commandments cannot be fulfilled without observing the lower. As to the juridical side of the matter, though the civil or the penal law does not demand the supreme moral perfection, it is not opposed to it. Forbidding every one to murder or be fraudulent, it cannot, and indeed has no need to, prevent any one from loving his enemies. Thus with regard to this point (which in certain moral theories is erroneously taken to be the only important one), the relation between the two principles of the practical life may be expressed by saying that *legal justice is the lowest limit or the minimum degree of morality.*

(2) The unlimited character of the purely moral demands leads to another point of difference. The way in which such demands are to be fulfilled is not definitely prescribed, nor is it limited to any concrete external manifestations or material actions. The commandment to love one's enemies does not indicate, except as an example, what precisely we ought to do in virtue of that love, *i.e.* which particular actions we ought to perform and from which we ought to abstain. At the same time, if love is expressed by means of definite actions, the moral commandment cannot be regarded as already fulfilled by these actions and as demanding nothing further. The task of fulfilling the commandment, which is an expression of the absolute perfection, remains infinite. Juridical laws, on the contrary, prescribe or prohibit perfectly definite external actions, with the performance or non-performance of which the law is satisfied and demands nothing further. If I produce in due time the money I am owing, and pass it to my creditor, if I do not murder or rob any one, etc., the law is satisfied and wants nothing more from me. This difference between the moral and the juridical law once more involves no contradiction. The demand for the moral inner disposition, so far from excluding external actions, directly presupposes them as its own proof or justification. No one would believe in the inward goodness of a man if it never showed itself in any works of mercy. On the other hand, the request to perform definite actions is in no way opposed to the inner states corresponding to them, though it does not demand them. Both the moral and the juridical laws are concerned with the inner being of man, with his will; but while the first takes this will in its universality and entirety, the second has only to do with particular expressions of it in respect of certain external facts, which fall within the province of justice in the narrow sense, — such as the inviolability of the life and property of each person, etc. What is of importance from the juridical point of view is pre-

cisely the objective expression of our will in committing or in refraining from certain actions. This is another essential characteristic of legal justice, and, in addition to the original definition of it as a certain minimum of morality, we may now say that legal justice is the demand for the *realisation* of this minimum, *i.e.* for *carrying out a certain minimum of the good*, or, what is the same thing, for doing away with a certain amount of evil. Morality in the strict sense is immediately concerned, not with the external realisation of the good, but with its inner existence in the heart of man.

(3) This second distinction involves a third one. The demand for moral perfection as an inner state presupposes free or voluntary fulfilment. Not only physical but even psychological compulsion is here, from the nature of the case, both undesirable and impossible. External realisation of a certain uniform order, on the contrary, admits of direct or indirect *compulsion*. And in so far as the direct and immediate purpose of legal justice is precisely the realisation or the external embodiment of a certain good — *e.g.* of public safety — to this extent the compelling character of the law is a necessity; for no genuine person could seriously maintain that by means of verbal persuasion alone all murders, frauds, etc., could be immediately stopped.

VI

Combining the three characteristics indicated we obtain the following definition of legal justice in its relation to morality: *legal justice is a compulsory demand for the realisation of a definite minimum of the good, or for a social order which excludes certain manifestations of evil.*

The question has now to be asked, what is the ground for such a demand, and in what way is this compulsory order compatible with the purely moral order, which apparently by its very nature excludes all compulsion? It may be urged that once the perfect good is established in consciousness as an ideal, every man ought to be allowed freely to realise it as much as in him lies. Why, it will be said, make into a law the compulsory minimum of morality, when we ought freely to fulfil the maximum? Why declare under penalty, 'Thou shalt not kill,' when we ought mildly to exhort people not to be angry?[5]

All this would be perfectly true were the moral problem a theoretical one and were the perfect good compatible with egotistical impassibility or indifference to the sufferings of others. But since the true conception of the good *necessarily* includes the principle of altruism, which demands corresponding

5. See Matthew 5:21-22. — *Editor's note.*

behaviour on our part, *i.e.* demands that compassion for the ills of others should prompt us actively to save them from evil, moral duty certainly requires us to do more than simply to profess the perfect ideal. In the natural course of things, which ought not to be approved of or acquiesced in, but which it is childish not to take into account, what would happen is this: whilst some would be freely striving towards the supreme ideal and grow perfect in impassibility, others would exercise themselves, unhindered, in every conceivable crime and would certainly exterminate the first before they could attain a high degree of moral perfection. But even supposing that men of good will were by some miracle saved from extermination by the bad ones, these good men themselves would obviously prove to be *insufficiently* good if they would be content with pious conversations about the good, instead of actively helping their neighbours and protecting them against the extreme and destructive forms of evil.

Moral interest demands personal freedom as a condition apart from which human dignity and higher moral development are impossible. But man cannot exist, and, consequently, cannot perfect his freedom and his moral nature apart from society. Moral interest therefore demands that personal freedom should not conflict with the conditions which render the existence of society possible. This demand cannot be carried into effect by means of the ideal of moral perfection, which the individual is to attain by his own free efforts. For the essential practical purpose before us this ideal gives both too much and too little — its demands are too great and its concrete results too small. Of the person who recognises it, the ideal demands that he should love his enemies; but it cannot compel those *who do not recognise* its demands to abstain even from murder and robbery. The strict moralist will perhaps say, "We don't want people to abstain from crimes unless they do so voluntarily"; but in saying this he would be guilty of obvious injustice. He will have forgotten to ask the opinion of the plundered people themselves and of the families whose members have been murdered — as though the injury they had suffered is the ground for regarding them as completely rightless.

The moral law has been given to man "that he might live thereby";[6] and if human society did not exist, morality would remain merely an abstract idea. The existence of society, however, depends not on the perfection of some, but on the security of all. This security is not guaranteed by the moral law, which is non-existent for persons in whom anti-social instincts predominate, but it is safeguarded by the compulsory law which has actual power over every one. To appeal to the gracious power of Providence to restrain and exhort lunatics

6. See Romans 10:5. — *Editor's note.*

and criminals is sheer blasphemy. It is impious to lay upon the Deity that which can be successfully performed by a good legal system.

The moral principle demands, then, that men should freely seek perfection. To this end the existence of society is necessary. Society cannot exist if each person wishing to do so may, without let or hindrance, rob and murder his neighbours. Hence the compulsory law, which actually prevents these extreme expressions of the evil will, is a *necessary condition of moral perfection;* as such it is demanded by the moral principle itself, though it is not a direct expression of it.

Let it be granted that the highest morality, on its ascetic side, demands that I should be indifferent to the prospect of being killed, mutilated, or robbed. But the same supreme morality on its altruistic side does not permit me to remain indifferent to the fact that my neighbours may, without interference from any one, become murderers or be murdered, robbers or the robbed, and that society, apart from which the individual cannot live and develop, should run the risk of being destroyed. Such indifference would be a clear sign of moral death.

The demand for personal liberty presupposes for its realisation the restriction of that liberty to the extent to which, at the given state of humanity, it is incompatible with the existence of society or with the common good. From the point of view of abstract thought there appears to be an opposition between these two interests, both of which are equally binding morally. In reality, however, they coincide, and legal justice is the offspring of their union.

VII

The principle of legal justice may be considered in the abstract, and in that case it is simply a direct expression of moral justice. I affirm my freedom as my right in so far as I recognise the freedom of others as their right; but the conception of right necessarily involves, as we have seen, an objective element, or a demand to be realised. Right must be capable of realisation: that is, the freedom of others, whether recognised by me or not, must, independently of my personal feeling of justice, restrict my freedom within limits equally binding upon every one. This demand for compulsory justice follows from the idea of the common good or public interest, or, what is the same thing, from the idea of the realisation of the good, which inevitably requires that justice should be an actual fact and not an idea merely. The degree and the means of the realisation depend, of course, upon the state of the moral consciousness in the given society and upon other historical conditions. The natural right thus becomes the positive right, and can, from this point of view, be formulated as follows: *legal justice is the historically changeable determination of the necessary and compulsory equilibrium of two moral interests — personal freedom and the common good.*

It would be a fatal confusion of ideas to believe that justice has for its purpose material equalisation of private interests. Justice as such has nothing to do with this. It is concerned only with the two main factors of human life — the freedom of the individual and the good of society. When legal justice limits itself to this and does not introduce the element of compulsion into private relations, it does the best service to morality. The individual must be moral by his free choice, and for that he must have *a certain freedom to be immoral.* Within certain limits justice secures this freedom for him, though it in no way inclines him to take advantage of it. Had not the creditor the right to compel his debtor to pay the money owing to him, he would not be able by a free moral act to renounce his right and to forgive a poor man his debt. On the other hand, the fact that the debtor is compelled to abide by the obligation he has freely entered upon, preserves his freedom and his full rights in relation to the creditor: he is not dependent upon the creditor's will but upon his own decision and the law of the land. The interest of individual freedom coincides in this case with the interest of the common good, since without the security of free contracts there can be no normal social life.

The harmony of the two moral interests is still more obvious in the case of the penal law. It is clear that the freedom of the individual, or his natural right to live and to strive for perfection, would be an empty sound if it depended upon the whim of any individual who might want to murder or to cripple his neighbour, or to deprive him of the means of subsistence. It is our moral right to defend our freedom and safety from the attacks made upon it by the evil will of others, and it is our moral duty to help other people to do the same. This common duty is discharged for the benefit of all by the penal law.

Legal compulsion in this sphere secures the freedom of peaceful citizens, but it leaves sufficient room for the exercise of evil propensities and compels no one to be virtuous. A malicious man may, if he likes, give vent to his malice in evil-speaking, intrigues, slander, quarrels, etc. It is only when the evil will attacks the objective public rights of individuals, and threatens the security of society itself, that it becomes necessary for the sake of the common good, which coincides with the freedom of peaceful citizens, to limit the freedom of evil. In the interests of freedom, legal justice allows men to be wicked, and does not interfere with their free choice between good and evil. But in the interests of the common good it prevents the evil man from becoming an *evil-*

doer, dangerous to the very existence of society. The purpose of legal justice is not to transform the world which lies in evil into the kingdom of God, but only to prevent it from changing *too soon* into hell.

Such premature hell has threatened and, to a certain extent, still threatens humanity *on two sides.* The normal society, that is, a society that leads a secure and worthy existence and progresses towards perfection, is conditioned by the proper balance being maintained between the individual and the collective interest. Hence, anomalies perilous to society may arise either from the excess of individual power, breaking up the social solidarity, or, on the contrary, from the excess of social control crushing the individual. The first anomaly menaces humanity with the burning hell of anarchy; the second, with the icy hell of despotism, *i.e.* of the same anarchy or arbitrariness concentrated at one point and pressing upon society from without.

In actual history the balance between free individual powers and the collective power of the social organisation is, of course, movable and variable, made up of a number of particular deviations and rectifications. But the very fact that we *note* these variations is sufficient to prove that above them lie the abiding norms of social and individual relations — the eternal boundaries which spring from the very nature of morality, and cannot, without fatal consequences, be overstepped by society either in the one direction or in the other. The most universal and in this sense the most important of these boundaries is that which limits the *compelling* power of social organisations to the domain of the objective or practical good, leaving all the rest, *i.e.* all the inner or spiritual world of man, to the entire responsibility of individuals and of free associations. To defend the life and property of every one against the attacks of external and internal enemies, to secure to all the necessary education, food, medical assistance, and all that is connected therewith (means of communication, post, etc.), — this is the practical good which can and ought to be realised by the organised power of the society. For this end society must inevitably impose certain restrictions or liabilities. The *compulsory* character of these restrictions is *specific* only, for it is clear that a person who, for instance, voluntarily abstains from crimes does not experience any personal inconvenience from the legal and penal institutions. Speaking generally, all restrictions due to the necessary organisation of social forces are as little opposed to individual freedom as the fact that if I intend to buy a thing I must pay for it, or that if I do not want to get wet in the rain I must take an umbrella.

The *essential* characteristic of the good which is conditioned by the organisation of legal justice in society is not its compulsory character — which is merely a possible consequence of it — but *the direct objectivity of its aim.* What is above all things important is that certain things should and certain things should not *exist as a fact*. It is important that there should be protection against savage peoples, so that they should not burn and destroy towns and villages; it is important that evil men should not rob and murder the wayfarers; it is important that the population should not be exterminated by diseases; it is important that every one should have access to intellectual education and enlightenment.

These necessary goods are external in character, and the way to obtain them is also external, admitting of compulsion where it is inevitable. To the immediate, essential work of the law courts, hospitals, schools, it makes no difference whatever whether they are supported by voluntary subscriptions or by compulsory taxation. The same thing, however, cannot be said of spiritual goods, which from their very nature cannot be compulsory. There are, in the last resort, two such goods for man: virtue, *i.e. the inner inclination of our will to the good as such*, and truth or right belief, *i.e. the inner agreement of our reason with truth as such*. It is clear from these definitions alone that freedom or lack of constraint forms an essential part of both spiritual or inward goods. Therefore all compulsory external action in this sphere is, in the first place, *a fraud*. The end of *externally* compelling or forcing a man to have an inner, *i.e.* an *inwardly* determined, disposition for the good, or an inner receptivity for the true, cannot possibly be achieved, and is indeed a logical contradiction or absurdity; and to use compulsion to no purpose is obviously an evil. Hence, all compulsory measures with regard to spiritual things in the supposed interests of truth and virtue are nothing other than the use of evil means for a false purpose — an abuse in the fullest sense.

There are three kinds of violence in our world: (1) *brutal* violence, such as is committed by murderers, highwaymen, corrupters of children; (2) *human* violence, necessarily permitted by the compulsory organisation of society for safeguarding the external goods of life; and (3) violent intrusion of the external social organisation into the spiritual life of man, with the false purpose of safeguarding the inner goods — a species of violence which is *wholly* false and evil, and may therefore justly be called *diabolical*.

VIII

From the nature of legal justice, which serves the external or the objective good, it follows that truth and virtue must always remain a private concern, and one which is perfectly free. In addition to the principle of unlimited religious tolerance, certain other consequences follow from this.

In the domain of the penal as well as of the civil law the freedom of the individual is limited, not by the private or subjective interest of other individuals *taken separately,* but by the good of all. Many vain and self-conscious people would rather be plundered or even crippled than suffer secret abuse, slander, and heartless condemnation. If, therefore, legal justice aimed at the protection of private interest as such, it would in cases of this kind have to limit the freedom of slanderers and evil-speakers even more than the freedom of robbers and men of violence. But it does not do so, for verbal insults are not so detrimental to the safety of society, and do not indicate so menacing a degree of evil will as the crimes against person and property. Even if the law intended to cope with such actions, it would be impossible for it to take into account all the forms and degrees of individual sensitivity to insults. And if it could do so, it would be unjust, for it is impossible to prove that the guilty person intended to cause the high degree of suffering which he did cause in reality. *Common* law may be guided only by definite intentions and objective actions which can be verified by every one. Besides, in the cases which do not fall within the scope of penal law, the injured person may, if he likes, avenge himself on the injurer by the same means. His freedom in this respect is respected as much as that of his adversary. And if he is morally superior to the latter, and thinks that he ought not to avenge himself, he would not in any case have appealed to the law, however sensible he may have been of the injury. If he abstains from personal revenge, so much the better for him and for society, which is at liberty freely to express its moral judgment. What matters from the legal point of view is not the evil will *as such,* and not the result of action, which may, *as such,* be accidental, but only the connection of the intention with the result, or the extent to which the evil will is realised in action. This is because the degree of realisation and the corresponding degree of danger to society may be determined objectively and are an external evil, the protection from which is an external good, admitting of legal compulsion.

IX

Since the essence of legal justice consists in maintaining the balance between two moral interests — that of individual liberty and of the common good, it is clear that though the latter interest may *limit* the former it may not under any circumstances *abolish it.* For in that case the balance would obviously be disturbed and disappear through the destruction of one of the terms of the relation. Therefore measures against the criminal should never go so far as to deprive him of life or to take away his freedom for ever. Laws which permit capital punishment, lifelong penal servitude, or lifelong solitary confinement cannot be justified from the legal point of view — they contradict the very nature of legal justice. Besides, the contention that in certain cases the common good requires that a given person should be completely done away with, involves a logical self-contradiction. Common good is *common* just because in a certain sense it contains the good of *all* individual persons *without exception;* if it did not, it would be the good of the majority. It does not follow that it therefore is a mere sum of private interests, or that it allows of unlimited individual freedom. This would be another contradiction, since the unlimited freedom of one individual may, and actually does, conflict with the liberty of others. But the conception of the *common good* implies with logical necessity that in *restricting* particular interests and activities within common bounds it cannot *do away with* a single bearer of such interests and activities by depriving him of life or of all possibility of free action. The common good must, in one way or another, be the good of *this individual also.* But if it deprives him of existence and of the possibility of free action — that is, of the possibility of any good at all — it ceases to be a good for him; it itself then becomes merely a private interest, and therefore loses its right to limit personal liberty.[7]

With reference to this point, too, we see that the demands of morality entirely coincide with the essence of legal justice. Speaking generally, although legal justice in exercising compulsion to secure the minimum of the good differs from morality in the strict sense, yet in its exercise of compulsion it observes the demands of morality, and must on no account conflict with it. If, therefore, some positive law is opposed to the moral consciousness of the good, we may be *a priori* certain that it does not satisfy the essential demands of justice either. So far as such laws are concerned, it is not in the interests of justice that they should be retained, but that they should be *lawfully* repealed.

X

External compulsion is one of the essential characteristics of the norms of legal justice as distinct from moral norms in the strict sense. Hence, justice from its very nature requires *guarantees, i.e.* sufficient power to enforce the realisation of its norms.

Every person in virtue of his absolute moral worth has an inalienable

---

7. After what has been said in Chapter VI on the penal question, I need not explain that the moral principle not only permits but in certain cases actually demands that the criminal should for a time be deprived of liberty, both for his own good and for the sake of public safety. But it is morally impossible to inflict the penalty of death, or to pass a sentence depriving a man of liberty for the rest of his life.

right to exist and to strive for perfection. This moral right would, however, be an empty word were its actual realisation to depend entirely upon external happenings and the arbitrary will of others. To be real, a right must contain within itself the conditions of its own realisation, *i.e.* it must be safeguarded from violation. The first and essential condition of this is communal life, since a solitary man is obviously powerless against the forces of nature, wild beasts, and brutal men. But being the necessary *defence* of individual liberty, or of the natural rights of man, communal life involves at the same time a *limitation* of these rights — not an accidental or arbitrary limitation, but one that follows from the nature of the case and is inwardly binding. Making use of the social organisation to safeguard my existence and free activity, I must recognise in my turn the right of that organisation to exist and to exercise its authority over me — that is, I must submit my activity to conditions that are necessary to the existence and the development of society. In this case the two interests coincide, for if I desire to realise my right, or to secure for myself a sphere of free activity, I must determine the degree of the realisation or the extent of the freedom in accordance with the fundamental demands of the social good, apart from which there can be no realisation of my rights at all nor *any* safeguards of my freedom. The individual's subordination to society is in perfect agreement with the absolute moral principle which does not sacrifice the particular to the universal, but unites them by an inner bond of solidarity. In surrendering to society his unlimited but insecure and unreal freedom, the individual has his determined or rational freedom secured to him — the sacrifice is as profitable as the exchange of a dead lion for a living dog.[8]

The definite limitation of personal freedom in given conditions of time and place, in accordance with the demands of the common good, or, what is the same thing, a certain balance or a constant harmony between these two principles, is a positive right or *law* in the strict sense.

Law, as such, is a universally recognised and impersonal — *i.e.* independent of personal opinions and desires — determination of right, or an expression of a proper balance (under given conditions and in certain respects) between individual liberty and the good of the whole. It is a definition or a *general* notion which finds concrete realisation through particular judgments in *individual* cases or instances.

Hence the three necessary characteristics of law are: (1) its *publicity;* an enactment that is not made *generally* known cannot be universally binding, *i.e.* cannot be a positive law; (2) its *concreteness;* it is the norm of some particular definite relations in a given real environment and not the expression of

8. See Ecclesiastes 9:4. — *Editor's note.*

any abstract truth or ideal;[9] (3) its *real applicability* in each *individual* case; this is ensured by the law being always accompanied by a 'sanction,' *i.e.* by its holding out the threat of compulsory and punitive measures if its demands are unfulfilled or its prohibitions violated.[10]

In order that the sanction might not remain an empty threat the law must be supported by some real power sufficient to carry its demands into execution. In other words, justice must have its actual bearers or representatives in society who would be sufficiently powerful to give a binding force to the laws they publish and to the sentences they pass. Such actual representatives of justice or agents of the law are called *authorities*.

I am bound to demand that the social whole should safeguard my natural rights in a way in which I myself am unable to safeguard them, and in doing so I am bound in reason and conscience to recognise the positive right of this social whole to use means and methods of action without which it could not fulfil this necessary and desirable task. Namely, I must leave to the social whole, (1) the power to issue generally binding laws; (2) the power to judge, in accordance with these laws, private affairs and actions; and (3) the power to compel each and all to fulfil the legal verdicts and all other measures necessary for general security and welfare.

It is clear that these three different powers — the legislative, the judicial and the executive, though necessarily *distinct*, cannot be *separate*, and ought on no account to conflict with one another: they all have one and the same purpose — to serve the common good in accordance with the law. Their unity finds its real expression in their being equally subordinate to one supreme authority, invested with all the positive rights of the social whole as such. This central power finds immediate expression as legislative authority. Judicial authority is conditioned by the first, since a court of justice is not autonomous, but acts in accordance with a law that is binding upon it. The first two authorities condition the third, which is concerned with enforcing laws and verdicts. In virtue of this inner connection, without the one supreme authority in one form or another there could be neither universally binding laws, nor regular functioning of justice, nor effective administration, and the purpose of social organisation could not be attained. It is clear, of course, that the due relationship between the three authorities is violated both by separat-

---

9. Certain law-codes still preserve — on paper — enactments which require that people should abstain from drunkenness, be pious, honour their parents, etc. But such spurious laws are merely a vestige of the primitive state in which the moral and the juridical conceptions were confused or merged into one.

10. The pious wishes of the lawgiver referred to in the last note are not accompanied by any sanction, which fact sufficiently proves that they are spurious laws.

ing and placing them in hostile opposition to one another, and by confusing them and distorting their natural order. This happens, for instance, when the second authority, the judicial one, is subordinate not to the first but to the third, and is dependent not upon the law but upon the different organs of the executive power.

The social body with a definite organisation, containing in itself the fulness of positive rights or the one supreme authority, is called *the state*. In every organism it is necessary to distinguish the organising principle, the system of the organs or of the instruments whereby the organisation is carried out, and the totality of elements to be organised. Corresponding to this, we distinguish in the collective organism of the state, taken in the concrete, (1) the supreme authority; (2) its different organs or subordinate authorities; and (3) the substratum of the state, *i.e.* the mass of the population of a given territory, consisting of individuals, families and other more or less broad private unions subordinate to the authority of the state. In the state alone does justice find all the conditions necessary for its concrete realisation, and from this point of view the state is the *embodiment of justice*.

Without dwelling here upon the question as to the actual historical origin and the supreme sanction of the state authority,[11] I have simply indicated its *formal basis* as the necessary condition of a just organisation of society. In its simplest practical expression the meaning of the state consists in subordinating, within its limits, violence to justice, arbitrariness to legality, and replacing the chaotic and destructive conflict of the particular elements of natural humanity by a regular order of existence. Compulsion is exercised by the state only in the last extremity, the extent of it is determined beforehand in accordance with law, and it is justified by the fact that it proceeds from a common and impartial authority. This authority, however, extends only to the boundaries of the given state's territory. There is no supreme authority above individual states, and therefore conflicts between them are in the last resort decided by means of violence only — by *war*. That this fact contradicts the *absolute* principle of morality, there can be no question. The *relative* significance of war and the best means of abolishing it are the last of the fundamental practical questions which the collective life of historical humanity puts before the moral consciousness.

11. See above, Part III, Chapters I and VI, and below, Chapters IX and X.

CHAPTER IX

The Meaning of War

I

No one, I fancy, doubts that, speaking generally, health is a good thing and disease a bad one, that the first is normal and the second anomalous. The only way to define health, indeed, is to call it the normal state of the organism, and disease 'the deviation of the physiological life from its normal condition.' This anomaly of the physiological life, called disease, is not however a meaningless accident or an arbitrary product of external evil forces. Not to speak of the in-evitable diseases of growth or development, the opinion of all thoughtful medical men is that the true cause of all disease lies in the inner deep-lying changes of the organism itself, and the external immediate causes of illness (*e.g.* catching cold, exhaustion, infection, etc.) are merely the *occasions* for the inner cause to manifest itself. Similarly, the abnormal phenomena which ig-norant people usually identify with the disease itself (*e.g.* fever and shivering fits, cough, various pains, abnormal secretion) in truth simply express the successful or the unsuccessful *struggle* of the organism against the destructive effect of the inner disturbances in which the disease really consists; their ulti-mate nature for the most part remains unknown, though they undoubtedly exist as a fact. Hence follows the practical conclusion that medical art must have for its main object not the external symptoms of a disease but its inner causes. At any rate it must detect their presence and then assist the healing work of the organism itself, by hastening and encouraging the natural pro-cesses and not doing violence to them.

The situation of the chronic disease of humanity — international hostil-ity, expressing itself in wars, is analogous. Its symptomatic treatment, a treat-ment, that is, directed upon its external symptoms rather than its inner causes, would be at best a doubtful procedure; a simple and absolute rejection of war would have no definite meaning whatever. So long as there is moral disturbance within humanity, external wars may be useful and necessary, just as in the case of profound physical disturbance such abnormal phenomena as fever or sickness may be useful and necessary.

In strictness, we ought to ask with regard to war three different questions instead of one only. In addition to the moral assessment of war in general, there is another question, namely, its significance in the history of humanity — a history which is not *yet completed,* and finally there is a third personal question as to how I (that is, how any human being), recognising with reason and conscience the binding character of moral demands, must regard *here* and *now* the fact of war and the practical consequences that follow from it. The confusion or the wrong division of these three questions — the generally moral or theoretical, the historical, and, finally, the personally-moral or the practical — is the chief cause of all misunderstandings and misconceptions with regard to war which have of late become particularly prevalent.

Theoretical condemnation of war has long been a commonplace among civilised people. Every one agrees that peace is a good and war an evil. Our tongue automatically speaks of *the blessings of peace and the horrors of war,* and no one would venture to say the opposite — 'the blessings of war' or 'the horrors of peace.' In all churches prayers are offered for peaceful times and for deliverance from the sword or wars, which are placed along with fire, famine, pestilence, earthquake and flood. With the exception of savage paganism all religions condemn war in principle. The Jewish prophets had preached the coming of peace among men and peace in the whole realm of nature. The Buddhist principle of compassion toward all living beings requires the same thing. The Christian commandment of loving one's enemies excludes war, since a *loved enemy* ceases to be an enemy and cannot be made war upon. Even the bellicose religion of Islam regards war only as a temporary necessity and condemns it from the point of view of the ideal. "Fight your enemies until Islam is established," and then "let all hostility cease" for "God abominates the aggressor" (*Koran,* sura ii).

II

Thus to the first question with regard to war there exists only one indisputable answer: *war is an evil.* Evil may be either absolute (such as deadly sin, eternal damnation) or relative, that is, it may be less than some other evil, and, as compared with it, may be regarded as a good (*e.g.* a surgical operation to save a patient's life).

The significance of war is not exhausted by the negative definition of it as an evil and a calamity. There is also a positive element in it — not in the sense that it can itself be normal, but in the sense that it may be actually necessary in the given conditions. *This* way of regarding abnormal phenomena in general is not to be avoided and must be adopted in virtue of the direct demands of the moral ideal and not in contradiction to it. Thus, for instance, every one will agree that, speaking generally, it is godless, inhuman, and unnatural to throw children out of the window on to the pavement. Yet in case of a fire, if there were no other means of extricating the unfortunate babes from the burning house, this terrible action would become permissible and even obligatory. It is obvious that the rule to throw children in extreme cases out of the window is not an independent principle on a level with the moral principle of saving those in danger; this latter moral demand still remains the *only* motive of action. It is not a case of deviation from the moral norm but of actual realisation of that norm in a way which, though dangerous and irregular, proves from real necessity to be the only possible one *under given conditions.*

It may be that war too depends upon a necessity which renders this essentially abnormal course of action permissible and even obligatory *under certain conditions.* This question can be settled only by an appeal to history. Sometimes, however, it is mistakenly treated from the wider naturally-scientific point of view, and the necessity of war is connected with the alleged universal principle of struggle for existence.

In truth, however, the struggle for existence neither in the human nor in the animal kingdom has anything to do with war. When it is said that a certain species was *victorious* in the struggle for existence, this does not at all mean that it had overcome any enemies in direct encounters or real battles. It simply means that sufficient adaptation to the external environment enabled the species in question to survive and to multiply — which all do not equally succeed in doing. In the struggle for existence mammoths in Siberia disappeared and martens were victorious. But this does not mean, of course, that martens were braver than mammoths and exterminated the latter in open fight with the help of their teeth and paws. In a similar way the Jewish nation, which is comparatively small and was disarmed long ago, has proved to be unconquerable in the struggle for existence, whilst many centuries of military successes did not save from downfall the huge Roman Empire, as well as other warlike states that had preceded it.

Just as the struggle for existence is independent of war and carried on by methods which have nothing in common with fighting, so, on the other hand, war has grounds of its own distinct from the struggle for the means of livelihood. If the latter were the only ground of war, the primitive epoch of history would have been the most peaceful of all. For men were then few in number, their demands were of the simplest, and each had ample room for satisfying them. Fighting and mutual extermination would in that case involve great risks and bring no advantages. In this respect the normal issue of all quarrels suggested itself naturally. "And Abraham said unto Lot, Let there be no strife, I pray thee, between me and thee, and between my herdmen and thy herdmen; for we be brethren *(kî 'ănāšîm 'aḥîm 'ănaḥnû)*. Is not the whole land before thee? Separate thyself, I pray thee, from me: if thou wilt take the left hand, then I will go to the right; or if thou depart to the right hand, then I will go to the left. And Lot lifted up his eyes, and beheld all the plain of Jordan, that it was well watered everywhere, before the Lord destroyed Sodom and Gomorrah, even as the garden of the Lord, like the land of Egypt, as thou comest unto Zoar. Then Lot chose him all the plain of Jordan; and Lot journeyed east: and they separated themselves the one from the other" (Gen. 13:8-11).

If such friendly agreement was, however, but a rare occurrence in those days, and, speaking generally, the mutual relations of primitive humanity were more like 'bellum omnium contra omnes,'[1] according to the well-known theory of Hobbes, this was due, not to the inevitable struggle for existence, but to the free play of evil passions. The fratricide with which history begins was caused by *envy* and not by *hunger*. And the most ancient poetical work that has been handed down — the savage song of Lamech, a grandson of Cain, recorded in the Bible — bears witness not to material need but to savage malice, vindictiveness and ferocious pride. "And Lamech said unto his wives, Adah and Zillah, Hear my voice; ye wives of Lamech, hearken unto my speech: for I have slain a man to my wounding, and a young man to my hurt. If Cain shall be avenged sevenfold, truly Lamech seventy and sevenfold" (Gen. 4:23-24).

III

The predominance of such feelings at a time when the human race, multiplying slowly as compared with the majority of other animals, was small in number, would have menaced it with speedy extermination were not the war of all against all counterbalanced from the first by the tie of kinship. This tie has its

---

1. "The war of all against all." — *Editor's note.*

root in the maternal instinct, is developed by means of family feelings and relations, and receives its final sanction in the religion of ancestor-worship. The
kinship-group organisation (in the wide sense[2]), which resulted from all
these circumstances, may be regarded as the primitive stage in the historical
development of humanity, which had never consisted of separate isolated entities at war with one another. The tie of kinship had existed from the first,
and the 'war of all against all' expresses the mutual relation not between separate individuals, but between distinct groups, each of which was held together
by kinship. This does not mean, of course, that each clan was as a fact at continual war with other clans, but only that no clan was secure against, or protected from, the possibility of war with any other clan. This state of things,
however, could not be permanent. It was only in rare cases that war between
clans ended in the extermination of the weaker. Given a certain equality of
power, the issue of war was a treaty or contract sanctioned by religion. On the
other hand, the weaker groups, to avoid extermination in an unequal struggle, either severally joined a stronger clan and became subordinate to it, or
many of them together formed a federated union. Thus war itself gave rise to
rights and treaties as a security of peace. Such unions of tribes are the beginning of the *state*.

At the period with which continuous historical records begin for us, a
considerable part of humanity was already organised into states. There were
two fundamental types of state: the Western or Greek *republic, i.e.* a small
city commune, and the Eastern *despotic monarchy,* an extensive organisation
embracing either one (as in Egypt) or many nations (the so-called world
empires).

Without the state there could be no progress in human culture, which is
based upon a complex co-operation of many forces. Such cooperation was
impossible to any large extent for disconnected tribes, at constant blood-feud
with one another. In the state we find human masses for the first time in history acting in concord. War has already been banished from within these
masses and transferred to the wider circumference of the state. In the primitive social group all grown-up men are always under arms. In the state warriors either form a special caste or profession, or, in the case of conscription,
military service is merely a temporary occupation of the citizens. *The organisation of war* by the state is the first great step towards the *establishment of
peace.* This is particularly clear in the history of large states built up by conquest — the so-called world empires. Each conquest meant in this case the
spreading of peace, that is, a widening of the circle within which war ceased to

2. See below, Chap. X.

be a normal event and became a criminal feud — a rare and reprehensible accident. 'The world empires' undoubtedly strove, though only half consciously, to give peace to the world by subjugating all nations to one common power. The greatest of the states founded upon conquest, the Roman Empire, directly described itself as *peace* — '*pax Romana.*'

But the older monarchies also aimed at the same thing. Inscriptions of the Assyrian and Persian kings, discovered in the nineteenth century, leave no doubt that these conquerors considered it their true vocation to subdue all nations for the sake of establishing peace on earth, though their conception of the task and of the means of fulfilling it was, as a rule, much too simple. More complex and more fruitful were the world-wide historical plans of the Macedonian Empire, which rested upon the superior power of Greek culture deeply and firmly rooted among the conquered races of the East. The idea of universal and eternal peace became perfectly definite among the Romans, who firmly believed that they were destined to subjugate the universe to the power of one single law. This idea was particularly dwelt upon by Virgil. Apart from the well-known '*tu regere imperio populos,*' etc.,

> But Rome! 'tis thine alone, with awful sway
> To rule mankind and make the world obey.
> Disposing peace and war thy own majestic way
> To tame the proud, the fetter'd slave to free —

he returns to it at every opportunity in his *Aeneid,* as the inspiring motive of the whole poem. Thus, for instance, he represents Jupiter as saying to Venus about her descendants:

> "The people Romans call, the city Rome.
> To *them* no bounds of empire I assign,
> Nor term of years to their immortal line. . . .
> Then dire debate, and impious war, shall cease,
> And the stern age be softened into peace.
> Then banish'd faith shall once again return,
> And Vestal fires in hallow'd temples burn;
> And Remus with Quirinus shall sustain
> The righteous laws, and fraud and force restrain."
>
> *Aeneid* i. 278-294

The same god tells Mercury that the ancestor of the Romans, Aeneas, is destined to conquer Italy throbbing with war, and to install in power the noble line of the Teucri, who "shall on the conquered world impose the law" (*Aeneid* iv. 229-231).

In comparing the four 'world empires' we find that as they succeeded one another they gradually approached the ideal of *universal* peace both from the point of view of their extension and of their inner principles. The first empire, the Assyro-Babylonian, did not extend beyond near Asia, was supported by constant devastating wars, and its legislation was limited to military decrees. The second empire, that of Cyrus and the Achaemenides, added to near Asia a considerable part of Central Asia on the one hand and extended to Egypt on the other; its inner force was the light religion of Ormuzd, which sanctioned morality and justice. In the third empire, that of Alexander and his successors, historical East was for the first time united to historical West, and the two were welded together not merely by the force of the sword but also by the ideal elements of Greek culture. Finally, the progress made by the fourth — the Roman Empire, consisted both in the fact that Romans extended the former unity as far as the Atlantic Ocean, and that they gave it a firm political organisation and a stable juridical form. War was inevitably the means and the armed powers the necessary support of this work of establishing peace. War and peace were correctly symbolised by the opposed but inseparable faces of the Roman god Janus.

War unites more powerfully than anything else the inner forces of each of the warring states and at the same time proves to be the condition for the subsequent coming together and mutual interpenetration of the opponents themselves. This is most clearly seen in the history of Greece. It was only three times in the course of their history that the majority of independent Greek tribes and city-states united for the sake of a common cause and manifested their inner national unity in a practical way — and every time it was due to a war: the Trojan war at the beginning, the Persian wars in the middle, and the expedition of Alexander the Great as the culminating achievement, owing to which the creations of the national genius of Greece finally became the common property of humanity.

The Trojan war established the Greek element in Asia Minor, where, nurtured by other civilising influences, it blossomed out for the first time. It was on the shores of Asia Minor that Greek poetry was born (the Homeric epos) and that the most ancient school of their philosophy arose and developed (Thales of Miletus, Heracleitus of Ephesus). The quickening of the united national forces in the struggle with the Persians gave rise to another and a still more rich manifestation of the creative genius of the Greeks. And the conquests of Alexander, throwing as they did these ripe seeds of Hellenism on to the ancient soil of civilised Asia and Egypt, produced that great

Helleno-oriental synthesis of religious and philosophical ideas which, together with the subsequent unity established by the Roman Empire, was the necessary historical condition for the spread of Christianity. Without the Greek language and Greek ideas, as well as without the 'Roman peace' and Roman military roads, the work of preaching the Gospel could not have been accomplished so quickly as it was and on so wide a scale. The Greek words and ideas became common property solely thanks to the warlike Alexander and his generals; the Roman 'peace' was attained through many centuries of wars, and was guarded by legions; and it was for these legions that the roads were made along which walked the apostles. "Their line is gone out through all the earth, and their words to the end of the world" (Ps. 19:4), sings the Church. This 'earth,' these 'ends of the world,' were no other than the wide circle *(orbis)* which Rome drew round itself with its blood-stained sword.

Thus all the wars in which ancient history abounds served to increase the sphere of peace. The heathen 'kingdoms of the *beast*' prepared the way for the messengers proclaiming the kingdom of the Son of *man*.[3]

Apart from this, however, the military history of antiquity shows important progress in the direction of peace in another respect. Not only did war serve the purposes of peace; as time went on, lesser and lesser numbers of active military forces were required for the attainment of these purposes, while the peaceful results became, on the contrary, more and more important and far-reaching. This paradoxical fact is beyond dispute. In order to take Troy it was necessary for almost all the Greek population to be under arms for a period of ten years,[4] and the direct result of this terrible effort was next to nothing. But to accomplish the great catastrophe — the conquest of the East by Alexander the Great, which crowned the whole of the Greek history and had immediate consequences for the civilisation of the world, all that was needed from the military point of view was a three-year-long expedition of an army of thirteen thousand men. If we compare the results and, on the other hand, take into account the greater population of Greece and Macedon under Alexander compared to the Achaean population which sent to Troy so large a military contingent, we shall be struck by the relative *diminution* that has taken place in the course of these seven centuries in the number of lives that had to be sacrificed for the attainment of historical purposes. Another comparison

---

3. See Daniel 7. — *Editor's note.*

4. The number of Greek forces given in the *Iliad* cannot, of course, be taken as literally exact, but as an approximate estimate. This number (110,000 men) seems to be entirely probable. It should be noted with reference to the *Iliad* generally that recent excavations have re-established the historical value of the poem, allowing, of course, for its mythological setting.

leads to the same conclusion. The Persian Empire, whose millions of soldiers could not secure to it military success in the struggle with tiny Greece, was hardly able to exist for two centuries. The Roman Empire, three times as great and with a population of at least 200 millions, kept under arms some 400 thousand legionaries to defend its endless frontiers, and existed three times as long as the kingdom of Darius and Xerxes. And how immeasurably more important to humanity were the blessings of culture guarded by those few legions than the objects for the sake of which gathered the innumerable hordes of the king of kings! The nature of military progress exemplified in the advantages of the Macedonian phalanx and the Roman legion over the Persian hordes consisted, generally speaking, in the preponderance of quality over quantity and of form over matter. It was at the same time a great moral and social progress, since it led to an enormous decrease in the number of human lives swallowed up by war.

IV

When the Roman world — and peace — came to be replaced by the Christian, the problem of war remained essentially unchanged on its externally historical side. True, by its absolute condemnation of all hatred and enmity, Christianity abolished the principle, the moral root of war. But cutting down the roots does not mean felling the tree; and indeed the preachers of the Gospel did not wish to fell this Nebuchadnezzar's tree, for they knew that the earth needed its shade until out of the small seed of true faith there would grow up, to replace it, 'the greatest of plants,' under the boughs of which there would be secure shelter both for men and beasts of the field.[5]

The teachers of Christianity did not reject the state and its calling to 'bear the sword against the wicked,'[6] and therefore they did not reject war. The followers of the new faith saw great triumph in the fact that two victorious wars allowed Caesar Constantine to plant the cross of Christ over the old unchanged building of the Roman Empire. Under the unchanged external appearance of the state, however, secret spiritual forces were at work. The state, even when surmounted by the cross, ceased for the Christian to be the supreme good and the final form of life. Faith in the eternal Rome, that is, in the absolute significance of political unity, was replaced by the expectation of 'the new Jerusalem,' that is, of the inner spiritual union of regenerated men and

---

5. See Daniel 4; Matthew 13:32. — *Editor's note.*
6. See Romans 13:4. — *Editor's note.*

nations. Apart, however, from human consciousness being thus ideally raised to a higher level, the process of external realisation of unity in the body of humanity continued unceasingly, though at first slowly.

The Christian world *(tota christianitas, toute la chrétienté)*, which in the Middle Ages took the place of the ancient Roman Empire, was considerably wider than it. True, there were frequent wars within it — just as in the Roman Empire there had been insurrections of peoples and mutinies of military leaders; but the representatives of the Christian principles looked upon these wars as upon lamentable feuds, and in every way tried to put a stop to them. As to the constant struggle between the Christian and the Muhammadan world (in Spain and the Levant), it undoubtedly was in the interests of progress and culture. The defence of Christianity against the advance of Islam preserved for historical humanity the possibility of higher spiritual development which was in danger of being submerged by the comparatively lower religious principle.[7] Besides, the interaction between the two worlds, though based on hostility, could not be limited to bloodshed alone and gradually led to a widening of the intellectual horizon on both sides. It thus prepared the ground in the case of Christians for the great epoch of the Renaissance of arts and learning, and later on for the Reformation.

In modern history three general facts have the most important bearing upon the question we are considering — namely, (1) the development of nationality; (2) the corresponding development of international relations of all kinds; and (3) the extension of the unity of culture to the whole of the globe.

Having freed themselves from the tutelage of the Roman Church, and rejected the impotent pretensions of the Holy Roman Empire, European nations became differentiated into independent political wholes. Each national state recognised itself and was recognised by others as a *perfect body*, as possessed, *i.e.*, of supreme authority or absolute fulness of power and therefore as unsubordinated to any other power on earth. The direct consequences of this national segregation were not favourable to the cause of peace. In the first place, it legitimised war even among Christian states, since war proved to be the sole means of settling disputes between separate and absolutely independent wholes which had no supreme arbiter to appeal to, after the manner in which in the Middle Ages they always could, and sometimes did, appeal to the Pope and to the Emperor. Secondly, the national idea, when taken to be the supreme principle in the life of nations, naturally became national pride; patriotism lost its true character; active love for one's own people became idolatrous worship of it as of the supreme good, and this in its turn passed into ha-

7. See above, Part III, Chap. V.

tred and contempt for other nations, and led to unjust aggressive wars and oppression of other peoples.

Concealed by these negative features, however, lies the positive significance of nationality. Nations must live and develop in their essential peculiarities as the living organs of humanity; apart from them its unity would be dead and devoid of content, and this peace of death would be worse than war. The true unity of mankind and the hoped-for peace must be based not upon the weakness and subjugation of nations but upon the highest development of their powers and a free interaction between nationalities which serve as a complement to one another. And in spite of all the efforts of national selfishness which strives to bring about hostile estrangement between nations, positive interaction among them exists, and is constantly increasing in depth and in breadth. The former international relations have not disappeared but have gained in inner force, and new ones have been added to them. Thus in the West the Roman Church, in spite of losing its external power, has considerately gained in spiritual authority; it has been purged of many of the crude abuses of the Middle Ages, and has made good by other conquests the damage it deservedly suffered at the hands of the Reformation. By the side of this Church and in opposition to it arose the equally wide-embracing and powerful brotherhood of the freemasons, which, however enigmatic it may be in other respects, is unquestionably international and universal in character. Relations of another kind came to be established on an unprecedented scale in the economic sphere. A world-market came into existence. There is not a single country which is economically self-sufficient, producing everything necessary for itself, getting nothing from others and giving them nothing in return, so that the idea of the state as 'a perfect body,' *i.e.* an absolutely independent social organism, proves in this fundamental respect to be the purest fiction. Further, constant co-operation of all educated countries in scientific and technical work, the results of which immediately become common property; inventions whereby distance is annulled; the daily press, with its continual news from everywhere; finally, the remarkable improvement in the means of international communication — all this makes civilised humanity one whole which actually, even though involuntarily, lives one common life.

And civilised humanity tends more and more to become *the whole* of humanity. When at the beginning of modern history Europeans extended their activity on all sides, taking America in the West, India in the South-east, and Siberia in the North-east, the greater part of the globe proved to be in their power. Now this power may be said to have extended to the whole of the globe. The Muhammadan world is surrounded and permeated through and through with European culture, and it is only in the tropical deserts of the Sudan that it can, and that without any hope of success, maintain its primitive independence (the kingdom of the Dervishes). The whole of the African coast has been divided between European Powers, and now the centre of the black continent has become the arena of their rivalry. Mongolian Asia — China and Japan — had alone remained outside the boundary of European influence, but this last barrier between human races is being removed before our eyes. With astonishing success and rapidity the Japanese, in the course of a quarter of a century, acquired the entire material and positively scientific side of European civilisation and then at once proceeded to prove to their Mongolian brethren, in the most convincing way possible, the necessity of following their example. The Chinese, who had already been shaken in their self-confidence by the English, but were still rather slow at understanding these foreigners, understood a fellow-nation at once; and henceforth the famous wall of China is no longer a symbol of a continuing isolation but only a relic of the irrevocable past.

We must now consider what bearing this curious process of 'gathering together of lands' by means of a single material culture had upon war. On the one hand, war played an *active* part in it. The wars of the Revolution and the Napoleonic wars are well known to have had a powerful influence upon the advance and the dissemination of universally-European ideas which conditioned the scientific, technical, and economic progress of the nineteenth century and thus brought about the material unification of humanity. In a similar way the final act of that unification — its extension to the last stronghold of isolated barbarism, China — began, in our eyes, with war and not with peaceful persuasion. On the other hand, the universality of material culture, realised partly through means of war, itself becomes a powerful means and ground of peace. At the present time the enormous majority of the population of the globe constitutes one connected body, between the parts of which there is physical, if not moral, solidarity. This solidarity shows itself in the sphere from which none can escape — the economic sphere. Some industrial crisis in New York immediately makes itself felt in Moscow and Calcutta. The body of humanity has evolved a common sense-organ *(sensorium commune)*, owing to which every particular stimulus *sensibly* produces a general effect.

Every prolonged and serious war is inevitably accompanied by profound economic disturbances which are bound to be *worldwide*, now that the different parts of the earth have become so closely connected. This state of things was being evolved throughout the nineteenth century, though it became clear to all only at the end of it. It is a sufficient foundation for the *fear of war*, completely unknown in earlier times, which has now taken possession of all civilised nations. During the first half of the century wars became shorter and more rare. Between Waterloo and Sebastopol, Europe had forty years of peace — a thing which had not happened during the whole of its previous history. Later on, special historical causes brought about several comparatively short European wars in 1859, 1864, 1866, and 1870; the Russo-Turkish war of 1877-78 could not be made into a general European war. The most important of these wars — the Franco-Prussian — is very characteristic. It left in the most civilised nation of Europe a feeling of national injury and a thirst for vengeance — and yet for the last twenty-eight years these feelings have not been able to pass into action solely from fear of war. In the seventeenth or eighteenth century, not to speak of epochs more remote, such prudence would have been quite inconceivable. And what do the monstrous armaments of European countries indicate if not the terrible, overwhelming fear of war, and consequently the approaching end of wars?[8]

It would be irrational, however, to think and to act as though that approaching end had already come. Although the common economic sensorium does at present unite all the parts of the earth with a tie of which the people themselves are conscious, yet this tie is not everywhere of the same strength and the parts are not all equally sensitive. There are still some nations left which in the case of a world war risk little — and there are some which are prepared to risk a great deal. The introduction of the Mongolian race into the sphere of the material European culture has a twofold significance. This race, the chief representatives of which, the Chinese people, number at least two hundred million souls, are noted for great racial pride and extreme contempt for life, both their own and other people's. It is more than probable that the now inevitable acquisition of the technology of European culture by the yellow race will only serve it as a means for proving in a decisive struggle the superiority of its spiritual powers over the spiritual powers of Europe. This forthcoming armed struggle between Europe and Mongolian Asia will certainly be the last war, but it will on that account be all the more terrible. It will indeed be a world war, and it is not a matter of indifference to the destinies of humanity which side will prove victorious.

---

8. The three last half-European wars do not contradict this statement. The Serbo-Bulgarian war of 1885, the Greco-Turkish of 1897, and the Spanish-American of 1898 all came to an end before they had really begun.

V

There is a wonderful system and unity in the general history of human wars, the chief moments of which I have indicated. From the rosy mist of historical childhood there stands out in the first place the clear though half-fantastical image of the Trojan war — that first great encounter of East and West, of Europe and Asia. This is how Herodotus regarded the Trojan war, with which his history begins; and it is not for nothing that the first inspired work of purely human poetry (the *Iliad*) is connected with it too. This war was indeed the beginning of the earthly, worldly history of humanity which throughout its course turns round the fateful struggle between East and West, while its arena is becoming wider and wider. Now that arena has reached its utmost limit — the whole surface of the globe. In the place of the deserted Skamander there is the Pacific Ocean, in the place of the smoking Troy — the ominous mass of China, and the struggle is still as before between the opposing principles of East and West. There was a moment of crisis, a pause in the struggle, when, following upon the external union of the historical East with the West in the Roman Empire — under the power of the descendants of Aeneas of Troy, — the light of Christianity abolished the ancient hostility from within:

> And streaming afar the light that came
> Out of the East arose,
> And glimmering with portent and celestial power
> It reconciled East and West.[9]

But the old material and cultural union proved to be unstable, and the spiritual is still awaiting its final realisation. True, in the place of the political unity of the Roman Empire, modern humanity has evolved another unity — the economic one, which, like the first, puts great external obstacles in the way of armed struggle. But these obstacles which have of late saved us from a *European* war are unable to prevent the last and the greatest struggle between the two worlds — of Europe and of Asia. These now are no longer represented by separate peoples, such as the Acheans and the Trojans, or even the Greeks and the Persians, but appear in their true proportions as the two great and hostile halves into which *the whole of humanity* is divided. The victory of one side or another will indeed give peace to the whole world. There will be no more struggle between nations; but the question still remains whether this political peace, this establishment of international unity in the shape of a world em-

9. Lines from Solovyov's poem *"Ex oriente lux." — Editor's note.*

pire — be it a monarchy or some other form of state, — will indeed mean a real and lasting peace, whether it will stop the struggle — sometimes an armed struggle — between other, non-political elements of humanity. Or, maybe, it will simply be a repetition on a vast scale of what has happened, within our memory, in more narrow limits. Germany had once consisted of many states at war with one another. The national body suffered from lack of real unity, and the creation of such a unity was the cherished dream of the patriots. It came to be realised after several wars — and it proved to be insufficient. The Germans, of course, will never relinquish their political unity, but they clearly see that it was only one necessary step forward and not the attainment of the supreme goal. The political struggle between small states came to be replaced throughout the empire by a more deep-rooted struggle — religious and economic. The Ultramontanes and the social democrats are proving to be more formidable foes than the Austrian and the French. When the whole of humanity is politically united, whether in the form of a world empire or a world-wide federation of states, the question still remains whether such union will put an end to the struggle of freemasonry with clericalism, or appease the hostility of socialism against the propertied classes and of anarchism against all social and political organisation. It is clear that the struggle between religious beliefs and material interests survives the struggle between states and nations, and that the final establishment of external political unity will clearly show its inner insufficiency. It will make plain the moral truth that external peace is not necessarily a true good *in itself* and that it becomes a good only in connection with an inner regeneration of humanity. And it is only when the insufficiency of external union will have been known *by experience* and not merely in theory that the time will be ripe for spiritualising the united body of the universe, and for realising in it the Kingdom of Truth and of Eternal Peace.

VI

War, as we have seen, has been the chief historical means of bringing about the external political unification of humanity. Wars between clans and tribes led to the formation of the state, which abolished war within its own limits. External wars between separate states gave rise to vaster and more complex political bodies possessing a unity of culture, and seeking to establish peace and equilibrium within their limits. At one time the whole mass of humanity, broken up and divided, was permeated through and through with war which never ceased between innumerable small groups. War was everywhere; but gradually driven further and further back it now appears to be an almost in-evitable danger at one point only — at the dividing line between the two chief races into which historical humanity is divided. The process of unification is drawing towards its end, but that end has not yet come. It is extremely im-probable that the yellow race will peacefully enter within the circle of Euro-pean culture, and, from the historical point of view, there is no reason to be-lieve that war is to be immediately and completely abolished. Is, however, this point of view binding upon the moral consciousness?

The matter appears as follows: "Whatever the historical significance of war may be, it is in the first place murder of men by men. But our conscience condemns murder, and therefore we ought conscientiously to refuse to take any part in war, and ought to persuade others to do the same. To spread such a view by word and example is the true and the only certain means of abolishing war, since it is clear that when every one refuses to do military service, war will become impossible." In order that this argument might be convincing, it would have in the first place to be proved that war and even military service are the same as murder. But this is not the case. Military service means only a *possibility of war*. During the forty years between the wars of Napoleon I and Na-poleon III several million men in Europe underwent military training, but only an insignificant part of them had actual experience of war. Even when war does break out, however, it cannot be reduced to murder, that is, to a crime which presupposes evil intention directed upon a certain object, upon this particular man whose life I take. In war the individual soldier has, generally speaking, no such intention, especially with the present method of fighting by means of guns and cannons against an enemy who is too far off to be *seen*. Only in cases of actual hand-to-hand fighting does the question of conscience arise for the individual, and then it must be decided by each according to his conscience. Speaking generally, war as a conflict between collective organisms (states) and their collective organs (armies) is not the work of individuals who play a passive part in it, and for them possible murder is *accidental* only.

It might be said, however, that it is better to avoid the very possibility of accidental murder by refusing to do military service. This is undoubtedly true if it is a question of free choice. A man who has attained a certain level of moral consciousness, or one whose feeling of pity is strongly developed, will certainly not choose the army as a profession, but will prefer to follow a peaceful calling. But so far as compulsory military service required by the state is concerned, it must be admitted that so long as it exists a refusal on the part of the individual to submit to it is a *greater evil* than the institution itself, however much we may disapprove of the modern system of universal military service, the disadvantages of which are obvious and the efficiency doubtful.

The person who refuses to serve his time in the army *knows* that the requisite number of recruits will *in any case* be gathered and that *somebody else* will be called in *his* stead. Therefore he *consciously* forces his neighbour, who would otherwise be free, to all the hardships of military service. Besides, the whole meaning of such a refusal satisfies the demands neither of logic nor of morality, since this is what it comes to. For the sake of avoiding a remote *future* possibility of accidentally killing an enemy in a war which will not depend upon me, I myself declare war to the state *now* and *compel* its representatives to take a number of violent measures against me *at once*, in order that I might save myself from committing problematic and accidental violence in the unknown future.

The purpose of military service is defined in our law by the formula 'to defend the throne and the fatherland,' that is, the political whole to which a given individual belongs. The state may, as it often has done in the past, abuse its armed forces, and, instead of self-defence, undertake unjust and aggressive wars but this is not a sufficient ground for determining my own present actions. Such actions must be solely determined by *my own* moral duties and not by those of others. The question then in the last resort comes to this: *Is it my moral duty to take part in the defence of my country?*

Theories which take up an absolutely negative attitude towards war and maintain that it is the duty of every one to refuse the demand of the state for military service, altogether deny that the individual has any duties towards the state. From their point of view the state is simply a band of brigands who hypnotise the crowd in order to keep it in subjection and to use it for their own purposes. But seriously to believe that this account exhausts or in the least expresses the *true nature of the case* would be altogether too naïve. This view is particularly ill-founded when it appeals to Christianity.

Christianity has revealed to us our absolute dignity, the unconditional worth of the inner being or of the soul of man. This unconditional worth imposes upon us an unconditional duty — to realise the good in the whole of our life, both personal and collective. We know *for certain* that this task is impossible for the individual taken separately or in isolation, and that it can be realised only if the individual life finds its *completion* in the universal historical life of humanity. One of the means of such completion, one of the forms of the universal life — at the present moment of history the chief and the dominant form — is the *fatherland* definitely organised as the *state*. This form is not, of course, the supreme and final expression of human solidarity, and the fatherland must not be put in the place of God and of His universal kingdom. But from the fact that the state is not everything, it by no means follows that it is unnecessary and that it would be right to aim at abolishing it.

Suppose that the country in which I live is visited by a calamity such as famine. What is in this case the duty of the individual as an unconditionally moral being? Both reason and conscience clearly say that he must do one of two things — either feed all the hungry or himself die of starvation. It is impossible for me to feed millions who are starving, and yet my conscience does not in the least reproach me for remaining alive. Now this is naturally due to the fact that the state takes upon itself my moral duty to provide bread for all the starving, and that it can fulfil it owing to its collective resources and to its organisation intended for prompt action on a wide scale. In this case the state proves to be an institution which can successfully perform work that is morally binding but physically impossible for the individual. If, however, the state fulfils for me my direct moral duties, it cannot be said that I owe nothing to it and that it has no claim upon me. If it had not been for it I would have been in conscience bound to give my very life; can I then refuse to contribute my small share towards the means which it needs for carrying out my own work?

But, it will be said, the rates and taxes collected by the state may be expended upon things which appear to me to be useless, and even pernicious, instead of upon obviously useful work. In that case it will be my duty to expose such abuses, but certainly not to deny, by word and deed, the very principle of taxation by the state, the recognised destination of which is to serve the general welfare.

Now the military organisation of the state is really based upon the same principle. If savages such as the Caucasian mountaineers of the old days, or the Kurds and the Black Flags of the present times, attack a traveller with the obvious intention of murdering him and his family, it is no doubt his *duty* to fight them — not out of hostility or malice against them, not to save his life at the expense of his neighbour's life, but to save the defenceless beings entrusted to his protection. To help others in such circumstances is an absolute moral duty, and it cannot be limited to one's own family. But successfully to defend all the weak and innocent against the attacks of evil-doers is impossible for isolated individuals or even for groups of many men. Collective organisation of such defence is precisely the purpose of the military force of the state, and to support the state in one way or another in this work of pity is the moral duty of every one, which no abuses can render void. Just as the fact that ergot is poisonous does not prove that rye is injurious, so the burdens and the dangers of *militarism* are no evidence against the necessity of armed forces.

The military or indeed any compulsory organisation is not an evil, but a consequence and a symptom of evil. There was no trace of such an organisation at the time when the innocent shepherd Abel was killed by his brother out of malice. Justly fearing lest the same thing should happen to Seth and other peaceful men, the guardian angels of humanity mixed the clay with copper and iron and created the soldier and the policeman. And until Cain's feelings disappear from the hearts of men, soldier and policeman will be a good and not an evil. Hostility against the state and its representatives is, after all, *hostility* — and this fact would alone be sufficient to justify the *necessity* of the state. And it is strange, indeed, to be hostile to it for the sole reason that the state merely limits by external means and does not inwardly abolish in the whole world the malice which we are unable to abolish in ourselves!

VII

Between the historical necessity of war on the one hand, and the abstract denial of it on the other, lies the duty of the individual to the organised whole — the state — which, down to the end of history, conditions both the existence and the progress of humanity. The unquestionable fact, however, that the state possesses the means both for preserving human society in its present condition, and also for moving it forward, imposes upon the individual other duties with regard to the state than a mere fulfilment of its lawful demands. Such fulfilment would be sufficient were the state a perfect embodiment of the normal social order. But since in truth it is only the condition and the means of human progress, and is itself gradually becoming more perfect in different respects, it is the duty of the individual to take, so much as in him lies, active part in this general political progress. The individual is the bearer of the absolute moral consciousness, of the perfect ideal of truth and peace, or of the kingdom of God. This consciousness he received, not from the state, but from above and from within. The ideal, however, cannot be actually *realised* in the collective life of humanity except by means of a *preparatory* state organisation. Hence for every individual who really adopts the moral point of view there follows the direct positive duty of helping the state by persuasion or preaching to fulfil in the best possible way its preliminary function. *After* this function has been discharged — but not *until* then — the state itself will of course become superfluous. The individual both can and must thus influence society both with reference to war and to all other aspects of the political life.

The evil of war lies in the extreme hostility and hatred between the *disjecta membra* of humanity. In personal relations bad feelings are not justified by any one, and it is useless to denounce them. In the case of international hatred, however, the bad feeling is usually associated with false opinions and erroneous reasoning, and is indeed often created by them. To struggle against this deception is the first duty of every man who truly desires to bring humanity nearer to a good peace.

As to the future decisive struggle between Europe and Asia, probable as it is, it does not threaten us as an unavoidable impending doom. The future is still in our hands. The first condition which could render the peaceful inclusion of the Mongolian race within the circle of Christian culture possible — though not very probable — is that the Christian nations should themselves become more Christian, and that in *all* relations of the collective life they should be more guided by moral principles than by shameful selfishness and evil economic and religious hostility.

Not long ago at the world congress of religion in Chicago[10] some Asiatic men — Buddhists and Brahmanists — addressed the Europeans with the following words, expressive of the popular opinion of the East: "You send to us missionaries to preach your religion. We do not deny its merits, but having got to know you during the last two centuries we see that your whole life is opposed to the demands of your faith. You are moved, not by the spirit of love and truth which your God revealed to you, but by the spirit of greed and violence, natural to all bad people. It must then be one of two things: either your religion, in spite of its inner excellence, cannot be practically realised, and therefore is of no use even to you who profess it; or you are so bad that you do not want to fulfil the demands which you can and you ought to fulfil. In either case you have no advantage over us and you should leave us in peace."[11] The only convincing answer to this criticism are deeds and not words. Asia would be neither justified in fighting nor capable of conquering a Europe that was inwardly united and truly Christian.

War has been the direct means of the external and the indirect means of the inward unification of humanity. Reason forbids us to give up this weapon so long as it is needed, but conscience compels us to strive that it should be *needed no longer,* and that the natural organisation of the human race divided into hostile parts should really become a moral or spiritual organisation. Such an organisation has its source in the nature of man, is inwardly based upon the absolute good, and attains complete realisation through means of world history. The description of this moral organisation, or of the totality of the moral conditions which justify the good in the world, must serve as the conclusion of moral philosophy.

10. This congress was held in 1893. — *Editor's note.*

11. These words are Solovyov's summary of Swami Vivekananda's remarks at the Chicago congress. — *Editor's note.*

CHAPTER X

The Moral Organisation
of Humanity as a Whole

I

The *natural* organisation of humanity consists in the fact that different individuals and groups are compelled by nature to interact in such a way that their private needs and activities lead to results of universal significance and to comparative progress of the whole. Thus from ancient times the needs of shepherds and agriculturists, the warlike spirit of chieftains, and the self-interested enterprise of merchants created material culture and were the means of historical progress. This natural arrangement, owing to which private interests lead to the common good, expresses a certain real unity of the human race. But this unity is both inwardly and outwardly imperfect. It is outwardly imperfect because, as a fact, it is incomplete; it is imperfect inwardly because it is not the object of the conscious will of the individuals and the groups which enter into it. Such unconscious and involuntary solidarity is already found in the pre-human world in the unity of the genus and the development of organic species. To advance no further is unworthy of man in whom the objective and generic reason — the universal *predicate* of nature — becomes the individual *subject*. What is needed is a moral, conscious, and voluntary organisation of humanity for the sake of, and inspired by, the all-embracing good. It became the direct object and purpose of life and thought from the moment when, in the middle of the historical development, this good was revealed as absolute and complete. Unity in the good means not only a coexistence of private interests and actions and a harmony between them in the general result, but a direct co-fellowship of individuals and of social groups in unanimous striving to attain a universal purpose — it means that absolute perfection is taken and understood by each as *his own* purpose.

351

The purpose of the moral organisation of human life is to realise the absolute norm of the good or of active (practical) perfection, and life as morally organised may be defined as the process of *growing perfect*. This logically involves the question, *Who is growing perfect? i.e.* the question as to the subject of moral organisation. We know that *isolated individuals* do not exist and therefore do not grow in perfection. The true subject of moral progress — as well as of historical progress in general — is the individual man *together with and inseparably from the collective man* or society. Not every configuration of molecules forms a living cell, and not every conglomeration of cells forms a living being. Similarly not every gathering of individual men or of social groups constitutes a true and living bearer of the moral organisation. In order to possess such a significance, *i.e.* in order to be an organic complement of the moral personality, the collective whole must be no less real than the individual, and, in this sense, it must possess the same worth and the same rights as the latter.

The natural groups which actually widen the life of the individual are the family, the nation, and humanity — the three abiding stages in the development of the collective man. Corresponding to them we have in the historical order the kinship-clan stage, the national-political stage, and the spiritually universal stage. The latter may be revealed only on condition that the first two become spiritualised.

It will be asked whether the family is to form part of the final and universal organisation of morality or whether it is simply a transitory limitation in the development of human life. But the individual person *in his given condition* and in his selfish striving for exclusive separateness is also only a transitory stage, just like the nation or even humanity itself. It is not a question of idealising and preserving for all eternity the corruptible aspect of this or that living subject, but of discovering and setting aglow the spark of divinity hidden under the corruption, of finding the absolute and eternal significance inherent in the conditional and the temporal, and of affirming it not as a fixed idea only, but as the beginning of fulfilment, as a token of perfection. The positive elements of life in their relative and temporary manifestations must be understood and recognised as *conditional data for the solution of an unconditional problem*. In the case of the family these natural data are the three generations successively connected by the fact of birth: grandparents, parents, and grandchildren. The continuous and the relative character of the bond does not abolish its triple character as an abiding norm. The members of the series which extend beyond it on either side — great-grandparents and great-grandchildren — constitute no independent element in the idea of the family relation. The supreme task is to spiritualise the relative natural connection of the three generations and to make it unconditionally moral. This purpose is achieved in three ways — through family religion, marriage, and the bringing up of children.

II

Family religion is the most ancient, deeply rooted, and stable institution of humanity. It has survived the patriarchal stage and all the religious and political changes. The object of family religion is the older generation, the departed fathers or forefathers. According to the most ancient ideas, the forefathers must necessarily be dead; this was so inevitable that, by a natural process of thought, all the dead, independently of their age and sex, were called forefathers (the Lithuanian and Polish *dziady* — a relic of remote antiquity). If a real grandfather happened to live too long, it was out of order, it violated the religiously moral norm, which, however, was easily re-established by the voluntary sacrifice of the old man. This barbarous practice really contained a true idea, or, rather, two true ideas — in the first place that a being who is on the same level as man and has the same needs and faculties cannot be a true *object* of reverence and worship, and, secondly, that in order to have a powerful and beneficial *influence* in the earthly sphere, such as is characteristic of a higher being, one must *withdraw* from that sphere and sever one's immediate physical connection with it. If family worship of the older generation was to be maintained in the epoch when force predominated, it could not be allowed to be associated with the spectacle of debility and weakness. The old men understood it themselves and with noble wisdom parted in good time with their enfeebled life for the sake of another, powerful and mysterious existence.

> "My day is drawing to its close," the Konung thus began,
> "Mead does not taste sweet to me, my helmet weighs me down.
>
> . . . . .
> "Make then two mounds for us, O sons,
> On the banks of the bay, by the wave-beaten shore.
>
> . . . . .
> "When the rocks are white with the light of the moon,
> And wet our graves with the dew,
> We shall rise from the hills, from the waters, O Thorsten,
> And whisper of the days to be."[1]

1. Verses from E. Tegner's epic poem after the Norse saga of Fridthjof. Solovyov is using a

Even in the heathen ancestor-worship the natural bond between the successive generations tended to acquire a spiritual and moral meaning. A complete realisation of this religious bond with the forefathers is made possible through the revelation of the absolute significance of life in Christianity. Instead of the material sacrificial feeding of the departed who on their side help the living in affairs of this world, there is established a spiritual interaction in prayer and sacrament. Both sides pray for one another, both help one another in attaining an *eternal good*. Both are concerned with an unconditional good — the salvation of the soul. Eternal memory,[2] rest with the saints, universal resurrection of life — this is what the living desire *for the departed,* what they help them to attain, and it is in this that they expect help from the departed *for themselves.* The mutual relation, as it enters the sphere of the absolute, ceases to be self-interested and becomes purely moral, being understood and carried out as part of the perfect good.

Eternal memory does not mean, of course, that people on earth will eternally remember the dead as those who have been and are no more. To begin with, it would not be of much importance for the dead, and, secondly, it is impossible, since earthly humanity itself ought certainly not to expect an *eternal* continuation of its *temporal* existence — if there is any meaning in the world. We ask eternal memory of God and not of men, and it means dwelling in the eternal mind of God. 'To grant eternal memory' means to make a man conformable to his eternal idea — to God's eternal thought about him, and to raise him to the sphere of the absolute and the changeless. By comparison with the anxieties of the world, it is eternal rest. Death as such is not rest, and the dead among natural humanity may be more appropriately described as restless (the French *revenant,* the German *Poltergeister*) than as those at rest. The rest we ask for our departed depends upon God's eternal memory of them. Affirmed in their absolute idea, they find in it a secure and indefeasible token that the perfect good will be finally realised in the world, and therefore they cannot be troubled. The distinction between the present and the future still exists for them, but no element of doubt or anxiety attaches to that future. It is separated from them only by an inevitable delay, and they may already contemplate it *sub specie aeternitatis.* But for those who die in the natural humanity, the future, though it becomes their main interest, still remains an awe-inspiring riddle and mystery.

Russian translation of Tegner's Swedish poem (*Fridthjof, Norse Hero* [Voronezh, 1874], pp. 51, 55). — *Editor's note.*

2. The prayer for granting 'eternal memory' to the departed forms an important part of the funeral and the requiem services in the Orthodox Church. — *Editor's note.*

We shall rise from the hills, from the waters, O Thorsten,
And whisper of the days to be.

Eternal rest is not inactivity. The departed remain active, but the character of the activity is essentially changed. It no longer springs from an anxious striving towards a distant and uncertain end. It proceeds on the basis and in virtue of the already attained and the ever-abiding connection with the absolute good. Therefore in this case activity is compatible with serene and happy rest. And just as the beneficial influence of the departed expresses their moral connection with their *neighbours in nature,* their living posterity, so in their blessed rest they are inseparable from their *neighbours in God and in eternity.* It is rest with *the saints.*

This is the ideal. If it is not attained by all, if the departed are not all at rest, if not all to whom 'eternal memory' is sung deserve it of God, this fact in no way affects our religious attitude toward the 'forefathers,' which is the foundation of family morality, and, through it, of all morality. For in the first place the actual destiny of each of the departed remains for us, after all, problematical only. Secondly, even if the unfavourable supposition is the more probable one, our religious attitude simply acquires a different character, and the feeling of pity which comes to be added to it prompts us to more active intercession. Finally, in the case of each person the majority, or at any rate a certain number, of his ancestors satisfy the demands of the 'eternal memory' and of 'rest with the saints.' Therefore every man in addition to all other relations is bound to have a generic bond, a bond of kinship with the world of God's eternity. In this essential respect the family may have an absolute significance for every one, and, through the abiding past, be the true complement of our moral personality.

On the other hand, the fulness of life for the forefathers, even when they are eternally remembered by God and are at rest with the saints, depends upon the work of their descendants who bring about the earthly conditions under which the end of the world process may come, and, with it, the bodily resurrection of the departed. Each of the departed is naturally connected with the final humanity of the future through the blood tie of successive generations.[3] By spiritualising his bodily organism and the external material nature, each fulfils his duty in relation to his forefathers, and pays his moral debt to

---

3. I cannot enlarge upon the details of this connection and upon other cognate questions without passing into the sphere of metaphysics and mystical aesthetics. But the general necessity of resurrection as the fulness of spiritual and bodily existence is sufficiently clear from the point of view of the absolute moral principle and of the moral order of reality.

them. Having received from them physical existence and all the legacy of the past ages, the new generation continues further the work which will finally make the fulness of life possible for the departed also. Thus from this new point of view, the natural bond with former generations, or the family religion of the past, acquires an absolute significance and becomes an expression of the perfect good.

It is only when the goal shall have been reached that man's work of spiritualising his body and the earthly nature in general will be reflected *backwards* and exercise its beneficial influence upon the past. It is only in the future that the past will attain the fulness of reality. But until this task is accomplished, until the perfection of life is attained in which the spiritual being and the corporeal being will entirely interpenetrate one another, until the gulf between the visible and the invisible world is bridged and death becomes impossible both for the living and for the dead — until then the necessary condition of this future perfection and the moral problem of the present state are the struggle of the spirit with the flesh, its strengthening and concentration. The *present* means of bodily resurrection is the subjugation of the flesh; the necessary condition of the fulness of life is asceticism or the suppression of the unlimited vitality. True asceticism, *i.e.* spiritual power over the flesh leading to the resurrection of life, has two forms — *monasticism* and *marriage.* The first, exclusive and exceptional, has already been discussed elsewhere;[4] the explanation of the second forms part of the argument now before us.

III

It is not for nothing that the relation, which appears to be so simple, and the physical basis of which is found in the animal and even in the vegetable kingdom, is called 'a great mystery,' and is recognised as the abiding symbol, sanctified by the word of God, of the union of the God of Israel with His people, of Christ crucified with the earthly church, and of Christ the King of Glory with the New Jerusalem. Reverence for the forefathers and religious interaction with them connect man with the perfect good through the past; true marriage has the same significance for the present, for the central period of life. It is the realisation of the absolute moral norm in the vital centre of human existence. The opposition of the sexes, which in the world of pre-human organisms expresses simply a general interaction between life that gives form and life that receives form, between the active and the passive principles, ac-

4. See above, Part I, Chapter II, 'The Ascetic Principle in Morality.'

quires a more definite and profound meaning in the case of man. Woman, unlike the female of animals, is not merely the embodiment of the passively receptive aspect of the material reality. She is the concentrated substance of nature as a whole, the final expression of the material world in its *inward* passivity, as ready to pass into a new and higher kingdom and be morally spiritualised. And man in his relation to woman does not merely represent the active principle as such, but is the bearer of the purely human activity, determined by the absolute meaning of life, in which woman comes to participate through him. And he in his turn owes to her the possibility of *realising* that meaning or the absolute good in a direct and immediate way.

The highest morality, proceeding from the absolute principle and determined by it (that which in theology is called *grace*), does not annihilate nature but imparts true perfection to it. The natural relation between man and woman involves three elements: (1) the *material,* namely, physical attraction, due to the nature of the organism; (2) the *ideal,* that exaltation of feeling which is called being in love; and, finally, (3) the *purpose* of the natural sexual relation or its final result, namely, reproduction.

In true marriage the natural bond between the sexes does not disappear but is transmuted. Until, however, this transmutation becomes a fact, it is a moral problem, for which the elements of the natural sexual relation are the data. The chief significance belongs to the intermediate element — the exaltation or the ecstasy of love. In virtue of it man sees his natural complement, his material other — the woman, — not as she appears to external observation, not as others see her, but gains insight into her true essence or idea. He sees her as she was from the first destined to be, as God saw her from all eternity, and as she shall be in the end. Material nature in its highest individual expression — the woman — is here truly recognised as possessed of absolute worth; she is affirmed as an end in herself, an entity capable of spiritualisation and 'deification.' From such recognition follows the moral duty — so to act as to realise in this actual woman and in her life that which she ought to be. The highest form of love in woman has a corresponding character. The man whom she has chosen appears to her as her true saviour, destined to reveal to her and to realise for her the meaning of her life.

Marriage remains the satisfaction of the sexual want, which, however, no longer refers to the external nature of the animal organism, but to the nature that is human and is awaiting to become divine. A tremendous *problem* arises which can only be solved by constant *renunciation*. To be victorious in the struggle with the hostile reality the soul has to pass through *martyrdom*.[5]

---

5. D. P. Yurkevich, Professor of Philosophy, now deceased, told me that a young scholar,

From this point of view the fullness of life-satisfaction which includes the bodily senses is connected not with the preceding lust but with the subsequent joy of realised perfection.

It is obvious, of course, that in a *perfect* marriage in which the inner completeness of the human being is finally attained through a perfect union with the spiritualised material essence, reproduction becomes both unnecessary and impossible. It becomes unnecessary because the supreme purpose has been achieved, the final goal attained. It becomes impossible, just as it is impossible that when two equal geometrical figures are placed one upon the other there should be a remainder that does not coincide. The perfect marriage is the beginning of a new process which does not reproduce life in time but re-creates it for eternity. But we must not forget that perfect marriage is not necessarily the original condition of, but only the *final means* for, the moral union of man and woman. One cannot assume this higher stage in advance, just as one cannot begin to build a house by starting with the roof, or call the roof a real house. The true human marriage is one which consciously *aims* at the perfect union of man and woman, at the creation of the complete human being. So long, however, as it merely aims at this and has not yet actually realised the idea, so long as there still is a duality between the idea and the empirical material reality opposed to it — external, physical reproduction is both the *natural consequence of the perfection not yet attained and the necessary means for its future attainment.* It is clear that so long as the union of man and woman is not wholly spiritualised, so long as it is complete in idea and subjective feeling only, and in objective reality continues to be superficial and external like that of animals, it can have *no other* result. But it is equally clear that in the present imperfect condition this result is of supreme importance, for the children will do what the parents failed to accomplish. The external, temporal succession of generations exists *because* marriage has not yet attained perfection, because the union of individual man and woman is not sufficiently spiritual and inwardly complete to re-create in them the perfect human being in the image and likeness of God. But this *'because'* also proves to be *'in order that'* — namely, in order that the task which has been too great

---

son of an evangelical pastor in Moscow, was present once at the marriage ceremony in the Russian Church, and was very much struck by the fact that in the service the bridal crowns are compared to crowns of the martyrs. This profound idea affected him so deeply that it caused a complete revolution in his mind. As a result of it, the young philologist gave up worldly learning and the university chair he was going to occupy, and, to the distress of his relatives, went into a monastery. He was the well-known Father Clement Sederholm, of whose life and character the late K. N. Leontyev wrote so excellent an account. [See K. N. Leontyev, *Father Clement Sederholm* (Moscow, 1882). — *Editor's note.*]

for the strength of this individual being (man and woman) should be realised by him indirectly, through a series of future generations taking their start from him. Thus the inward completeness and the unconditional meaning of family are re-established; man even in his imperfect state retains his absolute significance, and the living bond between the temporal members of the series, extending to eternity, remains unbroken.

For the moral organisation of humanity the connection with the past through heredity alone, through the fact of descent, *i.e.* from a particular line of ancestors, is insufficient; there must also be an abiding moral bond, and this is found in the family religion. Further, so far as the present is concerned, the natural fact of the sexual relation is also insufficient for that organisation; the relation must be raised to the spiritual level, which is done in true marriage. Finally, from the point of view of the future, it is not enough for the moral organisation of the collective man that the children should be simply a *new* generation, with an unknown future before it; in addition to the fact of external succession there must be inner moral succession as well — the parents must not merely produce the children for the future, but are in duty bound to *bring them up* so that they could work in the future for the realisation of their world-wide historical task.

IV

The natural moral feeling of pity which does not permit us to injure our neighbours and compels us to help them is naturally concentrated upon those of them who are most intimately related to us and at the same time need our help most — that is, on the children. This relation has a moral character when the family is simply an empirical factor in the natural life of man; it acquires an absolute significance when the family becomes the basis of a new, spiritually-organised life.

The moral significance of marriage consists in the fact that woman ceases to be the instrument of natural desires but is recognised as a being possessed of absolute worth, as a complement necessary to make the individual man truly whole. When the marriage fails or does not completely succeed in realising this absolute significance of human individuality, the task acquires a different object and is transferred to the children as bearers of the future. With the simple natural pity for the weak and suffering offspring come to be associated the world-woe for the evils and troubles of life, the hope that these new beings shall be able to lighten the universal burden, and, finally, the duty to preserve them for this work and to prepare them for it.

In a spiritually-organised family the relation of the parents to children is chiefly determined by the conception of the supreme destiny of man. The purpose of education is to connect the temporal life of this future generation with the supreme and eternal good which is common to all generations, and in which the grandparents, parents, and children are indivisibly one. For it is only through abolishing the temporal disintegration of humanity into generations that exclude and expel one another from existence that the Kingdom of God can be revealed and the resurrection of life accomplished. But until the perfection is reached, the moral bond between generations and the absolute supertemporal unity of man are maintained by reverent regard for the forefathers on the one hand, and by the bringing up of children on the other.

There is a great argument going on in man between Time and Eternity as to who is the stronger — the Good or Death. "Your fathers," says the Prince of this world to man, "those through whom you have received everything you possess, were and are no more, nor ever shall be; but, if so, where is the Good? You are reconciled to the death of your fathers, you sanction it by your consent, *you live and enjoy yourself, whilst those to whom you owe your existence are gone forever.* Where, then, is the good, where is the very source of piety — gratitude, where is pity, where is shame? Have they not been completely conquered by selfishness, self-seeking, sensuality? Yet do not despair. This condemnation of your life has meaning only from the point of view of the Good, only on the supposition that the Good exists. But this is just where the fundamental error lies: there is no Good. If there were, either your fathers would not have died, or you could not have been reconciled to their death. And now it is clear that the Good, with its fictitious demands and standards of piety, shame, and pity, is but an empty claim. If you want to live, live forgetful of the Good, for it has been swallowed up by death, is no more and never shall be." "Your fathers died, but they have not ceased to exist, for the keys of life are in *my* hands," says Eternity. "Believe not that they disappeared. That you might behold them again bind yourself to the unseen by the secure bond of the Good: revere them, pity them, be ashamed to forget them." "Illusion!" says the Prince of Time again. "You may believe in their hidden subjective existence if you like; but if you are not content with such a counterfeit of life for yourself, and cling to the fulness of the visible objective life, then, if the Good exists, you must demand the same for your fathers. But the visible objective existence — the only one worth speaking about — has been lost by your fathers, and shall never more be returned to them. Renounce, then, the impotent Good, the exhausting struggle with chimeras, and enjoy life to the full." But the last word is with Eternity, which, admitting the past, appeals all the more confidently to the future. "The Good does not depend upon the degree of your power, and your weakness is not the impotence of the Good. And you yourself are impotent only when you do not go beyond your own self; the incompleteness of your life is your own doing. In truth all is open to you. Live in all things, be a unity of yourself and your other, not only in relation to the past, to your forefathers, but also in relation to the future. Affirm yourself in new generations that with active help from you they might bring the world to that final stage in which God will give back the fulness of life to all — to them themselves, to you, and to your fathers before you. By doing this you can at the present moment show the absolute power of the Good over time and death, not by idly denying them, but by making use of them for the full and perfect revelation of the immortal life. Make use of the death of your forefathers, so as to preserve, in the religious regard for the departed, a sure token of their resurrection. Make use of your temporal existence, so that, by giving it to posterity, by transferring the centre of your moral gravity into the future, you might anticipate and bring nearer the final revelation of the Kingdom of God in the world."

V

Even the conventional everyday morality demands that man should hand down to his children not only the goods he has acquired, but also the capacity to work for the further maintenance of their lives. The supreme and unconditional morality also requires that the present generation should leave a twofold legacy to the next, — in the first place, all the positive acquisitions of the past, all the savings of history; and, secondly, the capacity and the readiness to use this capital for the common good, for a nearer approach to the supreme goal. This is the essential purpose of true education, which must be at once both *traditional* and *progressive*. The division and opposition between these two factors of the true life — between the ground and that which is built upon it, between the root and that which grows out of it — is absurd and detrimental to both sides. If the past that is good is self-contained and is no longer a real foundation for the new that is better, it means that the old has lost its vital force. In regarding it as *finished* and worshipping it in this form as an external object, we make *religion* into a *relic* — dead, but not working miracles. This is the besetting sin of popular conservatism which strives to replace the living fruits of the spirit by artificial preserves. In so far as it finds expression in religion, this pseudo-conservatism produces men who are hostile and indifferent to religion. Faith cannot be the *consequence* of such bringing up, since it is absent from the *ground* of it. It is obvious, indeed, that exclusive zeal for preserving faith can only be due to the lack of faith in the zealots themselves, They would have neither time nor occasion to be so distressed and worried about faith if they *lived by faith*.

When *tradition* is put in the place of *its object* — when, *e.g.,* the traditional conception of Christ is preserved in absolute purity, but the presence of Christ Himself and of His spirit is not felt — religious life becomes impossible, and all efforts artificially to evoke it only make the fatal loss more clear.

But can the life of the future grow out of a past that is really dead? If there is no real connection between the parts of time, what is the meaning of progress? *Who* is it that progresses? Could a tree actually grow if its roots and trunk existed in thought only, and its branches and leaves alone were actually real? Without dwelling at present upon the logical absurdity involved in this point of view, let us deal with its ethical aspect alone. Man as a moral being has absolute worth; his present condition, taken as such, does not correspond, or is inadequate to that worth. Hence arises the moral problem, not to separate oneself, one's own personality and existence, from the absolute good which abides as the one in all. In so far as a moral being is inwardly related to all, he really has absolute worth and his dignity is satisfied. In the order of time the *all* from which we must not separate ourselves, and to which we must be inwardly united, appears in two immediate ways, as our *past* and as our *future*, as ancestors and as posterity. In order to realise our moral dignity in time, we must spiritually become that which physically we are already, namely, a uniting and intermediate link between the two. And to do so we must recognise the abiding reality of the departed and the unconditional future of the posterity. We must not regard the deceased as ended. They are bearers of the absolute principle, which must be completely realised for them also. The departed, the forefathers, living in the memory of the past, have also a hidden existence in the present, which will become manifest in the future. *They have both future and actuality.*

It is on this basis alone that true education is possible. If we are indifferent to the future of our forefathers, we can have no motive for caring about the future of the new generation. If we can have no absolute moral solidarity with those who *died,* there can be no ground for such solidarity with those who certainly *will die.* In so far as education mainly consists in handing down moral duty from one generation to another, the question arises *what* duty can this be and in relation to *whom* are we to hand it down to our successors, if our own bond with our ancestors be severed. It would be a mere play of words to say that it is the duty to move humanity forward, for neither 'forward' nor 'humanity' has in this case any real meaning. 'Forward' must mean to the good, but there can be no good if we start with evil — the most elementary and unquestionable evil of ingratitude to the fathers, acquiescence in their disappearance, callous separation and estrangement from them. And what is the humanity which our pupils and successors are to move forward? Do last year's leaves, scattered by the wind and rotten on the ground, form part, together with the new leaves, of one and the same tree? From this point of view there is no humanity at all, and what exists are merely separate generations of men that replace one another.

If this external relation, which is constantly passing away, is to be replaced by the real and abiding moral tie, this obviously must be done in two directions. The form of time, in itself morally indifferent, cannot really determine our moral relations. Compromise here is impossible — there cannot be two absolute principles of life. The question whether we attach absolute significance to the temporal order of events or to the moral order, that is, to the inner bond between beings, must be settled finally and once for all. If the first alternative be adopted, humanity, irremediably broken up in time, is devoid of real unity; there can be no common task and therefore no duty to bring up future generations that they might carry it on further. In case of the second alternative, however, education inevitably involves reverence for the past, of which it is the natural complement. This traditional element in education conditions its progressive character, since *moral progress can consist only in a better and more far-reaching fulfilment of the duties which follow from tradition.*

The absolute worth of man — his capacity to be the bearer of eternal life and to participate in the divine fulness of being — which we religiously revere in the departed, we morally educate in the coming generation by affirming that the two are connected by a bond that triumphs over time and death. Special problems, the technique of education, belong to a sphere of their own which I need not touch upon here. But if pedagogy is to be based upon a positive universal principle, indisputable from the moral point of view and bestowing absolute worth upon its aims, it can find it only in the indissoluble bond between generations which support one another in furthering one common task — the task of *preparing for the revelation of the kingdom of God and for universal resurrection.*

VI

Reverence for the forefathers and family education based upon it overcome the immoral separateness and re-establish the moral solidarity of men in the order of time or in *the succession of existence.* It is a victory of the good over individual selfishness — the affirmation of the personality as a positive element in the family union which abides in spite of time and death. But if it is to be the basis of a moral and, therefore, a universal organisation, if it is to be the incipient form of the absolute and therefore all-embracing good, this union cannot be self-contained, limited, and exclusive. The family directly re-establishes the moral wholeness in one fundamental relation — that of the succession of generations. This wholeness, however, must also be re-established in the order of *coexistence.*

The linear infinity of the family can become morally complete only in another wider whole — just as a geometrical line becomes real only as the limit of a surface, which has the same relation to the line as the line itself has to a point. The moral point — the single individual — has actual reality only as the bearer of generic succession. The whole line of this succession becomes truly real only in connection with a multitude of collectively coexisting families which constitute a *nation.* We received all our physical and moral possessions from our fathers, and *the fathers had them only through the fatherland.* Family traditions are fractions of the national traditions; the future of the family is inseparable from the future of the nation. Therefore reverence for the fathers necessarily passes into reverence for the fatherland or into patriotism, and family education is linked with national education.

The good which is in its essence inexhaustible and ungrudging bestows upon every subject of moral relations, whether individual or collective, an inner dignity and absolute worth of its own. For this reason the moral bond and the moral organisation differ essentially from every other by the fact that in them the subject of the lower, or, more strictly, of the narrower order in becoming the subordinate member of a higher or a wider whole, is not absorbed by it, but preserves its own individual peculiarity. Indeed, it finds in this subordination both the inner condition and the external environment for realising its highest dignity. Just as the family does not blot out its individual members, but gives them, within a certain sphere, the fulness of life, and lives not by them only, but also in and for them, so the nation absorbs neither the individual nor the family, but *fills* them with living content in a definite national form. This definite form, which constitutes the particular significance or the positive quality of a nation, is to be found, in the first place, in *language.* As a definite expression, as a special characteristic of universal reason, language unites those who speak some one particular language without separating them, however, from people who speak another language — for all languages are but special qualifications of the *all-embracing word;* in it all languages are commensurate with or understandable by one another.

The multiplicity of languages is in itself something as positive and normal as the multiplicity of grammatical elements and forms in each of these languages. What is abnormal is mutual lack of understanding and the alienation that follows therefrom. According to the sacred story of the tower of Babel, the divine punishment for, and at the same time the natural consequence of seeking external and godless unity, consists in the loss of inner unity and solidarity and in being unable to understand one another's *speech* (which is possible even when the vocabulary is identical). Had not the inner moral unity been lost, the difference of languages would not have mattered; one might have learnt them, and there would have been no need to scatter upon the face of the earth. The important point was not the creation of new languages, but *confusion* of them. "Go to, let us go down, and there confound *(nāblâ)* their language *(šĕpātām)*, that they may not understand one another's speech. So the Lord scattered them abroad from thence upon the face of all the earth" (Gen. 11:7-9). It is clear that the story does not refer to the origin of the many languages, for in order that they might be confused they must have existed already.

The profound significance of this remarkable ancient revelation can be fully understood only by comparing the book of Genesis with the New Testament book of the Acts of the Apostles. "And when the day of Pentecost was fully come, they were all *with one accord* in one place. And suddenly there came a sound from heaven, as of a rushing mighty wind, and it filled all the house where they were sitting. And there appeared unto them cloven tongues, like as of fire, and it sat upon each of them. And they were all filled with the Holy Ghost, and began to speak with other tongues, as the Spirit gave them utterance. And there were dwelling at Jerusalem Jews, devout men, out of every nation under heaven. Now when this was noised abroad, the multitude came together, and were confounded, because that every man heard them speak in his own language. And they were all amazed, and marvelled, saying one to another, Behold, are not all these which speak Galilaeans? And how hear we every man in our own tongue, wherein we were born? Parthians, and Medes, and Elamites, and the dwellers in Mesopotamia, and in Judaea, and Cappadocia, in Pontus, and Asia, Phrygia, and Pamphylia, in Egypt, and in the parts of Libya about Cyrene, and strangers of Rome, Jews and proselytes, Cretes and Arabians, we do hear them speak in our tongues the wonderful works of God" (Acts 2:1-11).

True unity does not annul multiplicity but finds its realisation in it, setting it free from the limitations of exclusiveness. One language inspired by the Spirit of God means communicability and understanding between many *distinct languages, which are divided but do not divide.* This is not the idea of the inventors and adherents of various Volapüks and Esperantos, who consciously or unconsciously imitate the builders of the Tower of Babel.[6]

The normal relation between languages is at the same time the normal relation between nations (in Slavonic the two conceptions are expressed by the same word). The true unity of languages is found not in a *single* language but in an *all-embracing* language, that is, in an interpenetration of all languages which would make them equally understandable to all while the peculiarity of each would be preserved. Similarly the true unity of nations does not mean a single nationality, but an all-embracing nationality, that is, interaction and solidarity of all nations for the sake of each having an independent and full life of its own.

VII

When, having learnt a new language, we understand a foreigner whose language it is, when we not only understand the meaning of the words he speaks but by means of them enter into a real communion of feelings, thoughts, and aspirations with him, we clearly prove thereby that true unity of men is not limited to persons belonging to the same people. It is impossible to deny the fact of this inter-lingual and international and therefore universally-human communion, but it may be maintained that the communion is purely a superficial relation based upon no real unity. This contention is often urged by those who maintain that although a nation is a real whole, humanity is purely a general idea, abstracted from the fact of interaction between separate nations essentially external to one another. Leaving it to metaphysics to decide to what extent all interaction involves an underlying unity of those that interact, I will only note here that the peculiarity of the particular interaction which obtains between different nations or between individuals belonging to different nations, presupposes, apart from all metaphysics, at least the same kind of real unity which is assumed to hold within each nation between the groups and individual persons who compose it.

What ground is there for regarding nationality as a real power and a nation as a real unit rather than a mere conglomeration of human entities? With regard to the family the question is answered by pointing out the *evident* physical bond. With regard to the nation three grounds are indicated.

6. The inner relation and contrast between the confusion of Babel and the meeting of the Apostles in Zion, as the violation and the restitution of the norm, are clearly indicated in the Church anthems sung at Pentecost.

1. *The supposed physical bond,* or the unity of descent. — This *supposition,* however, has equal and, indeed, far greater force in reference to humanity as a whole than to distinct nations. The original unity of mankind is a dogma of three monotheistic religions and the prevailing opinion of philosophers and naturalists — while a direct unity of physical descent within the limits of a nation is, in the vast majority of cases, obvious fiction.

2. *Language.* — Identity of language unites those who speak it, but we know that difference of language does not prevent men from being of the same mind, thinking the same thoughts, and even using the same words. For such difference does not abolish but makes manifest the one inner language undoubtedly common to all men, who can under certain conditions understand each other whatever their particular tongue may be. This is not a superficial result of external interaction, for that which is here mutually understood refers not merely to accidental objects but embraces the inmost contents of the human soul. This fundamental and profoundly real fact expresses the actual connection and unity of all men. Difference of tongue is the difference between the essential forms of the mental life, and is important, since every such form represents a particular quality of the soul. Yet still more important is the content which each form expresses in its own way and which though present in all is not exhausted by, nor is exclusive of, any. That content is the positive and independent principle of the hidden unity and of the visible unification of all.

Language is the deepest and most fundamental expression of character. But just as differences of individual character do not destroy the unity of the nation which includes all the different people, so differences of national character cannot destroy the real unity of all nations in humanity, which is also a 'character.'

3. *History.* — If national history is the basis of national unity, universal or world-history is the basis of a wider, but not less stable, all-human unity. Moreover, national history is altogether unthinkable except as an inseparable part of world-history. Try to think of Russian history from the exclusively national point of view. Even if the Scandinavian origin of our state could somehow be explained away, it cannot be denied that the introduction of Christianity into Russia by the Greeks at once brought our nation into the sphere of the supernational life of the world. Christianity as such or in its content is an absolute truth and is therefore superhuman, and not merely supernational. Even from the purely historical point of view, however, it cannot be traced to any one particular nationality. It is impossible to separate the Jewish nucleus from the Chaldean and Persian, Egyptian and Phoenician, Greek and Roman setting. And yet without this national nucleus and this na-

tional setting there could have been no Christianity as positive revelation, and the foundation for the world-wide Kingdom of God would not have been laid. But whatever the significance of the national elements in the historical formation of the world religion may be, new nations such as Russia, which appeared after Christianity became established and accepted it in its crystal-lised form as the final revelation of the supreme and absolute good, cannot look to themselves for the true source of their life. Their history can have meaning only as a more or less perfect acquisition of the given, as a more or less successful preparation for fulfilling the task Christianity had put before them. It is obvious that during such a preparatory process not a single Chris-tian nation can or ought to be separate from, alien or hostile to other nations, for such a relation is opposed to the very essence of Christianity — and it is impossible to prepare for carrying out a given task while remaining in direct opposition to its inner meaning. Russia definitely confirmed her faith in Christian universalism when in the most glorious and important epoch of her new history she finally abandoned her national isolation and showed her-self to be a living member of the international whole. And it was not till then that the national strength of Russia found expression in what is still the most significant and precious thing we have — and not for ourselves only, but for other nations as well. On the powerful stem of the state, 'Europeanised' by Pe-ter, grew the beautiful flower of our pensive, deep, and tender poetry. Russian universalism — which resembles cosmopolitanism as little as the language of the Apostles resembles Volapük — is connected with the names of Peter the Great and Pushkin. What other national Russian names can be said to equal these?

Just as the individual man finds the meaning of his personal existence through the family, through his connection with his ancestors and posterity, just as the family has an abiding living content in the nation and national tra-dition, so the nation lives, moves, and has its being only in a supernational and an international environment. Just as the whole series of successive gen-erations live in and through the individual man, just as the whole nation lives and acts in and through the totality of these series, so the whole humanity lives and works out its history in the totality of nations.

If a nation be a real fact and not an abstract general idea, if the inward or-ganic nature of the bond which unites nations with one another in the uni-versal history be a fact also, humanity as a whole, too, must be recognised as a fact. Real living organs can only be organs of a real living organism, and not of an abstract idea. The absolute moral solidarity in the good, uniting man with his ancestors and his descendants, and thus forming the normal family, also unites him, by means of this elementary and immediate bond of liberation, to the world-whole concentrated in humanity. Humanity is the complete collective subject or 'recipient' of the perfect good, the full image and likeness of the Deity, the bearer of the actual moral order — the Kingdom of God. But, as has already been said, it follows from the very nature of the moral order or the moral organisation that every part or every member of the great collective man participates in the absolute completeness of the whole, since he is as necessary to that completeness as it is to him. The moral bond is perfectly mutual. Humanity is unthinkable apart from the nations that compose it, the nation is unthinkable apart from families and the family apart from individuals, and, *vice versa*, the individual cannot exist, either physically or morally, apart from the succession of generations, the moral life of the family is impossible apart from the nation, and the life of the nation is impossible apart from humanity. This truism used to be readily accepted by all. Recently, however, for reasons which the existing systems of the philosophy of history have not yet been able to discover, it has become customary to separate, contrary to all logic, this elementary truth from its necessary apex, and to declare that the inner dependence of nations upon humanity is a fancy and a chimera. It is granted that a bad son and a bad father, a man who has no reverence for his ancestors and does not care about the upbringing of his descendants (whether physical or spiritual), cannot he a good patriot, and that a bad patriot cannot truly serve the common good. It is also granted that, *vice versa*, a bad patriot cannot be a good member of a family, and that a bad member of a family cannot be a really good man. But it is not allowed that in virtue of the same solidarity between the different degrees of organisation a man indifferent to the one supreme good of all nations taken together cannot be a really good patriot (and consequently cannot be a good member of a family, and, finally, cannot be individually good). And yet it is perfectly clear that if a man has for his supreme purpose the good of his own nation, taken separately and independently of others, he in the first place deprives the highest good of its essential characteristic of universality, and therefore distorts the purpose itself. Secondly, in dividing the interest of one nation from the interests of the others, while in reality they are intimately connected, he distorts the idea of his own nation. Thirdly, it follows from this double distortion that such a man can only be serving a distorted nation by communicating to it a distorted good — that is, he can only be serving evil, and, since he does nothing but harm to his fatherland, he must be pronounced a bad patriot.

The good embraces all the details of life, but in itself it is *indivisible*. Patriotism as a virtue is part of the right attitude toward everything, and in the moral order this part cannot be separated from the whole and opposed to it. In the moral organisation not a single nation can prosper *at the expense of* others;

it cannot positively affirm itself to the detriment or the disadvantage of others. Just as the positive moral dignity of a private person is known from the fact that his prosperity is truly useful to all others, so the prosperity of a nation true to the moral principle is necessarily connected with the universal good. This logical and moral axiom is crudely distorted in the popular sophism that we must think of our own nation only, because it is good, and therefore its prosperity is a benefit to every one. It either thoughtlessly overlooks or impudently rejects the obvious truth that this very alienation of one's own nation from others, this *exclusive* recognition of it as pre-eminently good, is in itself evil, and that nothing but evil can spring from this evil root. It must be one or the other. Either we must renounce Christianity and monotheism in general, according to which "there is none good but one, that is, God,"[7] and recognise our nation *as such* to be the highest good — that is, put it in the place of God — or we must admit that a people becomes good not in virtue of the simple fact of its particular nationality, but only in so far as it conforms toward and participates in the absolute good. And it can do so only if it has a right attitude toward everything, and, in the first place, toward other nations. A nation cannot be really good so long as it feels malice or hostility against other nations, and fails to recognise them as its neighbours and to love them as itself.

The moral duty of a true patriot is then to serve the nation in the good, or to serve the true good of a nation, inseparable from the good of all, or, what is the same thing, *to serve the nation in humanity, and humanity in the nation.* Such a patriot will discover a positive aspect in every foreign race and people, and by means of it will seek to relate this race or people with his own for the benefit of both.

When we hear of a *rapprochement* between nations, of international agreements, friendships, and alliances, we must, before rejoicing or being grieved about it, know *in what* it is that the nations are being united, in good or in evil. The fact of union as such decides nothing. If two individuals or two nations are united by the hatred of a third, their union is an evil and a source of fresh evil. If they are united by mutual interest or by common gain, the question still remains open. The interest may be unworthy, the gain may be fictitious, and in that case the union of nations, as well as of individuals, even if it is not a direct evil, can certainly not be a good desirable for its own sake. The union of men and of nations can be positively approved only in so far as it furthers the moral organisation of humanity, or the organisation of the absolute good in it. We have seen that the ultimate *subject* of this organisation, the real bearer of the *moral order,* is the collective man or humanity, succes-

---

7. Mark 10:18. — *Editor's note.*

sively differentiated into its organs and elements — nations, families, persons. Having determined *who* it is that is morally organised, we must decide *what* he is organised *in* — that is, we must consider the question as to the *universal forms of the moral order.*

VIII

The right or the due relation of man to the higher world, to other men, and to the lower nature is collectively organised in the forms of the Church, the state, and the economic society or the zemstvo [local assembly].

Individual religious feeling finds its objective development and realisation in the universal Church, which thus may be said to be *organised piety.*

From the point of view of religious morality, man lives in three different spheres: the worldly or the conditional (this world), the Divine or the unconditional (the Kingdom of God), and the sphere which is intermediary between the two, and binds them together — the religious sphere in the strict sense (the Church).

To stop at a direct opposition between the world and the Deity, between earth and heaven, is contrary to sound religious feeling. Even supposing that we are genuinely prepared to regard the universe as worthless dust, that dust does not fear our contempt — it *remains. On whom or what?* To say that it remains on the Deity would obviously be impious. To declare the world dust to be an illusion of our imagination would mean that our own self, enslaved by the weary nightmare of phenomena and powerless before the phantoms it has created, is itself a worthless speck of dust which has somehow got into the eye of eternity and hopelessly mars its purity; and this second view would be still more impious than the first. Everything in the long run must be referred to God, and, therefore, the more contempt we have for the world, the more unworthy is our conception of the Absolute being. To declare that the world is pure nothing is the height of blasphemy, since in that case all the evil aspects of existence, which are not abolished by a verbal rejection of them, must be directly and immediately ascribed to God. This argument cannot be avoided so long as only two opposing terms are recognised. But there exists a third intermediary term, the historical environment in and through which the worthless dust of the earth is converted, by a skilful system of fertilisation, into a fruitful ground for the future Kingdom of God.

Sound religious feeling demands not that we should reject the world and seek to abolish it, but only that we should not accept the world as an absolutely independent principle of our life. Being *in the world* we must become *not of the world,* and in this capacity influence the world so that it too should cease to be on its own account and become more and more from God.

The essence of piety at the highest stage of universal consciousness consists in ascribing absolute worth to God alone and in valuing all else only as related to Him and as capable of having absolute worth not in itself and of itself, but in and through God. *All things acquire worth by establishing their positive relationship with the One that is worthy.*

If all men and nations were truly pious, that is, identified their own good with the one absolute good and blessedness, that is, God, they would obviously be united among themselves. And being at one in God, they would live in God's way; their unity would be holiness. The present humanity, however, which is not brought together and elevated by the one exclusive interest in God, is following its own will, and is divided between a multitude of relative and disconnected interests. The result is alienation and disruption; and since good actions cannot spring from an evil root, the activity of divided humanity can as such lead to nothing but sin. Therefore the moral organisation of humanity cannot begin until humanity is really united and its activity is consecrated.

Perfect unity and holiness are in God; sin and division are in worldly humanity; union and consecration are in the Church which harmonises and reconciles the divided and sinful world with God. But in order to unite and consecrate, the Church must itself be *one* and *holy,* that is, it must have its foundation in God, independently of the divided and sinful men who are *in need of* union and consecration, and therefore cannot obtain it of themselves. *The Church, then, is in its essence the unity and holiness of the Godhead,* not, however, of the Godhead as such, but *as abiding and acting in the world.* It is *the Godhead in its other,* the true substance of divine humanity. The unity and the holiness of the Church are expressed in space as its universality or *catholicity,* and in time as *apostolic* succession. The meaning of catholicity (καθ᾽ ὅλον — according to or in conformity with the whole) is that all the forms and activities of the Church unite individuals and nations with the whole of the divine humanity, both in its individual centre, Christ, and in the concentric circles around Him — the world of the incorporeal powers and the departed saints living in God, and of the faithful who are still fighting the battle here on earth. In so far as everything in the Church is catholic, conformable to the absolute whole, all exclusiveness of ethnic and personal characteristics and of social position disappear in it. All divisions or *separations* disappear, and all the *differences* are left — for piety requires that unity in God should be understood not as empty indifference and bare uniformity, but as the absolute fulness of every life. There is no division but there is difference between the invisible and the visible Church, since the first is the hidden moving power of the second, and the second the growing realisation of the first. The two are one in essence but different in condition. There is no division but there is difference in the visible Church between the many tribes and nations to which, in their unity, the one spirit speaks in different tongues of the one identical truth, and communicates by different gifts and callings one and the same good. Finally, there is no division but there is difference between the Church as teaching and as taught, between the clergy and the people, between the mind and the body of the Church. In a similar manner the difference between husband and wife is not an obstacle to, but the basis of, their perfect union.

IX

The catholicity of the Church — the fundamental form of the moral organisation of humanity — is the conscious and intentional unity between all the members of the universal body in relation to the one absolute purpose of existence, a unity, accompanied by complete division of 'spiritual labour,' of gifts and services, by which that purpose is expressed and realised. This moral unity essentially differs by its voluntary and conscious character from the natural unity of the organs in the body or the members in the various natural groups. It forms a true *brotherhood* which gives to man positive *freedom* and positive *equality.* The individual does not enjoy true freedom when his social environment weighs upon him as external and alien to him. Such alienation is abolished by the conception of the universal Church alone, according to which each must find in the social whole not the external limit but the inward completion of his liberty. Man *in any case* stands in need of such completion by the 'other'; for in virtue of his natural limitations he is necessarily a dependent being, and cannot by himself or alone be a sufficient ground of his own existence. Deprive man of what he owes to others, beginning with his parents and ending with the state and world-history, and nothing will be left of his existence, let alone his freedom. It would be madness to deny this fact of inevitable dependence. Man is not strong enough and he needs *help* in order that his freedom might be a real thing and not merely a verbal claim. But the help which man obtains *from the world* is accidental, temporal, and partial, whilst the universal Church promises him secure, eternal and all-sufficient help from God. It is with that help alone that he can be actually free, that is, have sufficient power to satisfy his will. Man obviously cannot be truly free so long as that which he does not want is inevitable, and that which is demanded by his will is impossible. Every object of desire, every good is possible for man only on condition that he himself lives, and those whom he loves live also. There is therefore one fundamental object of desire — the continuation of life, and one fundamental object of aversion — death. But it is precisely in the face of this that all worldly help proves to be of no avail. The calamity of calamities — death — proves to be inevitable; and the good of goods — immortality — utterly impossible. The world then can give no real freedom to man. It is only divine humanity, or the Church, based upon an inner unity and a perfect harmony of the visible and the invisible life in the kingdom of God — the Church affirming the essential primacy of spirit and promising the final resurrection of the flesh, that alone discloses to man the sphere in which his freedom can find positive realisation, and his will actual satisfaction. Whether we believe this or not does not depend upon philosophical arguments. But although the most perfect philosophy can neither give faith nor take it away, the simplest act of logical reflection is sufficient to show that man who wants to live and is sentenced to death cannot be seriously regarded as free, and from the standpoint of the world or of nature this no doubt is the position of every man and of all mankind. It is then through the universal Church alone that the individual can obtain positive freedom. In no other way is positive equality possible for him either.

The natural dissimilarity of people is as inevitable as it is desirable. It would be very regrettable if all men were spiritually and physically alike, and in that case the multiplicity of men would have no meaning. Direct equality between distinct particular men is altogether impossible. They can be equal not in themselves, but only in their common relationship to something other, supreme and universal. Such is the equality of all before the law, or equal civic rights. This equality of rights, important as it is in the order of worldly existence, remains essentially formal and negative. The law fixes certain general limits to human activity, equally binding upon all and each, but it does not form the content of any one's life, secures to no one the essential goods of life, and indifferently leaves to some their helpless nothingness, and to others the superabundance of all possible advantages. The world may recognise as an abstract possibility or a theoretical right the unconditional significance of each human being, but the realisation of this possibility and this right is given by the Church alone. It initiates each into the wholeness of the Divine life made manifest in man, communicates to each the absolute content of life, and thus equalises all — in the way similar to that in which all finite magnitudes are equal to one another in relation to infinity. If in Christ "dwelleth all the fulness of the Godhead bodily" in the words of the Apostle,[8] and Christ

8. Colossians 2:9. — *Editor's note.*

lives in every believer, there can be no room for inequality. Participation in the absolute content of life through the universal Church, liberating and equalising all in a positive way, makes of them one absolute whole or a perfect brotherhood.

In so far, however, as this brotherhood, perfect in nature, is conditioned in origin as established and coming into being in time, it requires a corresponding form for its divine-human connection with the past as such — it requires religious succession or *spiritual fatherhood*. This demand is satisfied by the definition of the Church as *apostolic*.

X

Since we live in time, the bond of our dependence upon the divine principle as manifested in history must also be preserved in time and handed down through it. In virtue of that bond our present spiritual life begins *not of itself*, but springs from the earlier or older bearers of the grace of God. The one holy catholic Church is of necessity an *apostolic* Church. Apostleship or messengership is the opposite of imposture. Messengership is a religious basis of activity, whereas imposture is an anti-religious basis of activity. It is precisely with reference to this point that Christ indicates the opposition between Himself and the antichrist. "I am come in My Father's name and ye receive Me not; if another shall come *in his own name,* him ye will receive."[9] The primitive basis of religion, namely, the pious recognition of one's dependence upon the progenitor, attains its perfect expression in Christianity. "The Father hath sent Me." "I do the will of Him Who sent me."[10] The only-begotten Son is pre-eminently a messenger, is essentially the apostle of God, and, strictly speaking, the profound and eternal meaning of calling the Church 'apostolic' refers to Him; and the other meaning of this — the direct historical one — also depends on this. "As My Father hath sent Me, even so send I you"[11] — the apostles born of Christ by the word and the spirit are sent by Him to give spiritual birth to new generations so that the eternal bond between the Father and the Son, the One Who sends and the One Who is sent, should be continually handed down through time.

Filial relationship is the archetype of piety, and the only-begotten Son of God — the Son by pre-eminence — is the individual embodiment of piety it-

---

9. John 5:43. — *Editor's note.*
10. John 5:36; 6:38. — *Editor's note.*
11. John 20:21. — *Editor's note.*

self. The Church as the collective organisation of piety must be entirely determined by Him in its social structure, in its doctrine and holy practices. Christ as the incarnation of piety is the way, the truth, and the life of His Church.

The way of piety for all that exists (with the exception, of course, of the First Beginning and the First Object of all piety) consists in starting not with oneself or with what is lower, but with the higher, the senior, the preceding. It is the way of hierarchy, of holy succession and tradition. Therefore whatever external forms the order of the Church government might assume under the influence of historical conditions, the strictly ecclesiastical religious form — ordination through the laying on of hands — always proceeds in the hierarchical order, from above downwards. Laymen may not ordain their spiritual fathers, and indeed the clergy themselves must necessarily be arranged in order of degrees so that those of the highest degree — the bishops — alone represent the *active* principle itself, and transfer the grace of consecration to the two other orders.

The *truth* of the Church depends upon the same piety, though in another way, or in another, theoretic respect. The truth of the Church, revealing to us the mind of Christ, is neither scientific nor philosophical, nor even theological — it contains nothing but *dogmas of piety*. This fact is the key to the understanding of Christian dogmatism, and of the Councils that were engaged in formulating it. With regard to religious teaching the interest of piety is obviously concerned with the fact that our conceptions of the Deity should not in any way detract from the fulness of our religious attitude toward it, a fulness given once for all in Christ as the Son of God and the Son of Man. All 'heresies' from which the Church protected itself by its dogmatic definitions denied, in one way or another, this religious fulness or the entirety and completeness of our adoption by God through the perfect God-man. Some regarded Christ as a half-god, others as a half-man; some put a kind of double personality in the place of the one God-man, others limited His nature as God-man to the intelligible side alone, and regarded the divinity as incapable of sensible expression, etc.[12]

The lawful *way* of the hierarchical order, as well as the *truth* of faith, finds its fulfilment and justification in the *life* of the Church. Human life must be

---

12. The profound and important significance of the dogmatic disputes dealing with the very essence of the Christian religion or piety I have more definitely indicated elsewhere. See my works "The Great Dispute and Christian Politics" (1883), "The Dogmatic Development of the Church" (1886) [this work has been incorporated in the first part of *The History and Future of Theocracy* — *Editor's note*], and *La Russie et l'Église universelle* (1889). This significance is particularly clear in the dispute concerning the ikons which in the Christian East completed the circle of the dogmatic development.

inwardly collected, united, and consecrated by the action of God and thus transformed into a divinely-human life. The nature of the case and the principle of piety demand that the process of regeneration should begin from above, from God, that it should be founded upon the effects of grace and not upon the natural human will alone — it demands that the process should be *divinely-human* and not humanly-divine. This is the meaning of sacraments as the special foundation of the new life. The moral significance of sacraments in general consists, from the point of view of religious morality or piety, precisely in this — that in sacraments man adopts his proper attitude of absolute dependence upon a perfectly real and yet perfectly mysterious, sensuously unknowable good which is given to him and not created by him. In the presence of the sacrament the human will renounces all that is *its own*, remains in a state of perfect potentiality or purity, and in virtue of it becomes capable, as pure form, of receiving superhuman content. Through sacraments the one and holy essence, which is the Church in itself (the *Ding an sich* or the *noumenon* of the Church, to use philosophic language), actually unites to itself or absorbs into itself the inner being of man and renders his life divine.

This life, supernatural so far as the other kingdoms of nature, including the rationally-human, are concerned, but perfectly natural for the kingdom of God, has its regular cycle of development, the chief moments of which are signalised by the Church in the seven sacraments especially so called. This life comes to birth (in baptism), receives the beginning of a right organisation and the power to grow and develop (in confirmation), is healed from accidental imperfections (in penitence), nurtured for eternity (in Eucharist); it completes or integrates the individual being of man (in marriage), creates spiritual fatherhood as the basis of the true social order (in ordination), and, finally (in extreme unction), sanctifies the diseased and dying bodily nature for the perfect wholeness of future resurrection.[13]

XI

The real and mysterious tokens of the higher life or the Kingdom of God, received in the sacraments of the Church, do not in their origin and their essence depend upon the will of man. But since this higher life is *the divinely-human life,* our part in it cannot be merely passive. It demands a conscious and voluntary co-operation of the human soul with the supreme Spirit. The

---

13. This is discussed more fully in my books *The Spiritual Foundations of Life* and *La Russie et l'Église universelle* (last chapter).

positive strength for such co-operation is from the very first given by the grace of God (disregard of this truth leads to the dangerous errors of semi-Pelagianism), but it is received by the will of man, which formally differs from the divine will; and it is manifested in actions which spring from the human will. Disregard of this second truth, which is as important as the first, found expression in the Monothelite heresy, so far as Christology is concerned, and in Quietism in the sphere of the moral doctrine.

The specifically-human actions conformable to the grace of God (and caused by its preliminary influence) must obviously express man's normal relation to God, to men, and to his own material nature, in accordance with the three general foundations of morality — piety, pity, and shame. The first concentrated active expression of the religious feeling or piety — its chief *work* — is *prayer;* in the same way, the work of pity is *almsgiving*, and the work of shame is abstinence or *fasting*.[14] These three works condition the beginning and the development of the new life of grace in man. This is depicted with wonderful clearness and simplicity in the holy narrative about the devout centurion Cornelius, "which gave much alms to the people, and prayed to God alway." In his own words, "I was fasting until this hour: and at the ninth hour I prayed in my house; and, behold, a man stood before me in bright clothing, and said, Cornelius, *thy prayer* is heard, and *thine alms* are had in remembrance in the sight of God" (then follows the command to send for Simon, who has the words of salvation). The hidden anticipatory effect of God's grace, which Cornelius did not reject, incited him to do human good and strengthened him in the works of prayer, almsgiving, and fasting; and these works themselves, as is here directly indicated, called forth new manifest effects of the Divine grace. It is noteworthy, too, that just as the appearance of the angel from heaven was simply an exceptional means of carrying out the established method of piety and sending for the earthly messenger of God, the earthly mediator of the higher life and truth, so the exceptional and abundant pouring out of the gift of the Holy Spirit on Cornelius and his household after Peter's preaching at his house did not render superfluous for them the usual and, so to speak, the organic method of beginning the life of grace through the real and mystical means of baptism.[15]

This typical narrative is still more remarkable for *what it does not contain*. Neither the angel of God nor Peter the apostle of *Christ's peace,* nor the voice of the Holy Spirit Himself, suddenly revealed in the newly converted, told the

---

14. These three religiously moral works are dealt with at length in the first part of the *Spiritual Foundations of Life*.

15. Acts 10.

centurion of the Roman centurion that which, according to the recent interpretation of Christianity, was the most important and urgently necessary thing for this Roman soldier. They did not tell him that in becoming a Christian he had *first of all* to lay down his arms, and *was bound to give up military service*. This supposed necessary demand of Christianity is not even hinted at in the narrative, although it is concerned with a soldier. Refusal to do military service does certainly not form part of the New Testament idea of what is required of a warrior of this world in order that he might become a citizen with full rights in the kingdom of God. In addition to the things the centurion Cornelius was already doing, namely, prayer, almsgiving, fasting, — he had "to call Simon, whose surname is Peter: . . . he shall tell thee what thou oughtest to do." And when Peter came, Cornelius said to him, "Now therefore are we all here present before God, to hear *all things that are commanded thee of God.*" But the things which God commanded the apostle to reveal to the Roman soldier for his salvation contained no reference to military service. "Then Peter opened his mouth and said, Of a truth I perceive that God is no respecter of persons but in every nation he that feareth him, and worketh righteousness, is accepted with him. The word which God sent unto the children of Israel, preaching peace by Jesus Christ: (he is Lord of all:) that word, I say, ye know, which was published throughout all Judæa, and began from Galilee, after the baptism which John preached; how God anointed Jesus of Nazareth with the Holy Ghost and with power; who went about doing good, and healing all that were oppressed of the devil: for God was with him. And we are witnesses of all things which he did, both in the land of the Jews, and in Jerusalem; whom they slew and hanged on a tree; him God raised up the third day, and shewed him openly not to all the people, but unto witnesses chosen before of God, even to us, who did eat and drink with him after he rose from the dead. And he commanded us to preach unto the people, and to testify that it is he which was ordained of God to be the Judge of quick and dead. To him give all the prophets witness, that through his name whosoever believeth in him shall receive remission of sins. While Peter yet spake these words, the Holy Ghost fell on all them which heard the word."[16]

I am dwelling upon the story of Cornelius the centurion, not because I want to raise once more the question of military service,[17] but because this story seems to me to throw clear light on the general question as to the relation of the Church to the state, of Christianity to the empire, of the Kingdom of God to the kingdom of this world, or, what is the same thing, on the ques-

16. Acts 10:34-44. — *Editor's note.*
17. See above, Chapter IX, 'The Significance of War.'

tion of the *Christian state*. If the centurion Cornelius, having become a real Christian, remained, nevertheless, a soldier, and was not divided into two alien and disconnected personalities, it is clear that he must have become a *Christian soldier*. A collection of such soldiers forms a Christian army. Now the army is both the extreme expression and the first real basis of the state; and if a Christian army is possible, a Christian state is therefore even more possible. That historical Christianity solved the question precisely in this sense there can be no doubt. The only thing that can be called in question is the inner ground for that solution.

XII

When the centurion Cornelius was a pagan, the same feeling of pity which impelled him 'to give much alms' also urged him, no doubt, to defend the weak from injuries and to force violent and aggressive men to obey the law. He knew that law, like every human utility, is only a relative good and may be abused; he may have heard of the revolting abuse of legal authority which the procurator Pontius allowed when, under the influence of the envious and vindictive priesthood of Jerusalem, he sentenced to death the virtuous Rabbi from Nazareth. But being a just man, Cornelius knew also that *abusus non tollit usum*,[18] and deduced no general conclusions from exceptional instances. A true Roman — to judge by his name, — he was conscious with noble pride of his own share in the destiny of the city that ruled the world:

> . . . to make the world obey,
> To tame the proud, the fetter'd slave to free.[19]

And it was not for him an abstract conviction. In Palestine, where his cohort was stationed, it was Roman arms alone that put a stop, for a time at any rate, to the fierce intestine wars between different dynasties and parties, accompanied by savage slaughter. And it was only under the ægis of the Roman power that the neighbouring clans of the Edomites and the Arabs gradually emerged out of the condition of continual wars and crude barbarism.

Cornelius then did not err in thinking highly of his vocation, and in considering the state and its chief organ, the army, a power necessary for the common good. Ought he to have changed his judgment when he became a

---

18. "Abuse does not abolish use." — *Editor's note*.
19. Virgil, *Aeneid*, VI, 851. — *Editor's note*.

Christian? A new, higher, and purely spiritual life was revealed *in him,* but this fact did not abolish the evil *outside* of him. The pity which justified his military calling referred precisely to those who were suffering from the *external* evil, which remained what it was. Or perhaps the higher life revealed in him, ought, without abolishing the external evil, to have abolished the inward good in him — the pity or charity which was 'remembered by God,' and to have replaced it by indifference to the sufferings of others. Such indifference or unfeelingness, however, is the distinctive mark of the stone — of the lower and not of the higher grade of being. But perhaps, in addition to compassion, the Christian receives, together with the new life, a special power to overcome every external evil without resisting it by force — to overcome it by immediate moral effect alone, or by the miracle of grace. This supposition is remarkably ill-founded and is based upon a complete misunderstanding both of the nature of grace and of its moral conditions. We know that Christ Himself encountered upon earth such a human environment that His grace could not work miracles 'because of their unbelief.'[20] We know that in the very best environment — in the midst of His apostles — He found 'the son of perdition.'[21] We know that of the two thieves who were crucified only one repented. It is uncertain whether he would have been susceptible to the Divine grace under other circumstances, but it is quite certain that his comrade remained inaccessible to it even under *these* circumstances.

Those who affirm that *every* evil-doer may be all at once converted to the good and restrained from crime by the immediate effect of the inner power of grace alone, do not in the least realise the meaning of what they are saying. So far as the inward, purely-spiritual power of the good is concerned, its distinctive characteristic lies precisely in the fact that it does not work like a mechanical agency which inevitably produces external physical changes, but that it acts only on condition of being inwardly received by the person upon whom it acts — a truth which, one would have thought, the case of Judas made obvious to the blind.

The power of the grace of Christ affected men who were sinful owing to the infirmity of the flesh and not owing to the firmness of evil will — men who were not happy in their sins, but suffered from them and felt the need of a physician. It was of these sick ready to be healed that Christ said that they will enter the kingdom of heaven before the self-righteous, and this precisely was the reason why the latter hated Him and reproached Him for condescending to mix with publicans and sinners. But even His enemies could find

---

20. Mark 6:6. — *Editor's note.*
21. John 17:12. — *Editor's note.*

no pretext to accuse Him of condoning bloodthirsty murderers, impious blasphemers, shameless seducers, and professional criminals of all kinds, enemies of human society. But, it will be said, He left them in peace. There was, however, no occasion for Him to deal with them since there existed Roman and Jewish authorities whose business it was precisely to restrain evil, as far as possible, by compulsion.

According to both the spirit and the letter of the Gospel we must not appeal to the powers that be for enforced defence of *ourselves* against attacks on our person or property. I ought not to drag into the law court and prison the man who strikes me or walks away with my fur coat. I ought with all my heart to forgive the wrong-doer for the wrong which he does me, and not to offer any resistance to him so far as I alone am concerned. This is clear and obvious. It is clear, too, that I must not give way to evil feeling against the person who wrongs my neighbours — him, too, I must forgive in my heart and regard him as a fellowman. What *practical* duty, however, does the moral principle impose upon us in that case? Can my duty be actually the same in the case of my own injury and that of another? To allow injury to myself means to sacrifice myself, and is a moral act; to allow injury to others means sacrificing others, and this can certainly not be called self-sacrifice. The moral duty towards others, psychologically based upon pity, must not in practice give rights to violent men and evil-doers alone. Peaceful and weak persons also have a right to our active pity or help. And since, as individuals, we are unable to give continual and sufficient help to all the injured, we must do this in our collective capacity, that is, through the state. Political organisation is a naturally-human good, as necessary to our life as our physical organism is necessary to it. In giving us a higher spiritual good Christianity does not deprive us of the lower, natural goods — it does not pull from under our feet the ladder which we are mounting.

With the coming of Christianity and the good news of the Kingdom of God, the animal, vegetable, and mineral kingdoms did not disappear. And if they have not been abolished, there is no reason why the naturally-human kingdom, embodied in political organisation, should be abolished either, since it is just as necessary in the historical process as the others are in the cosmical. Nothing could be more absurd than to maintain that although we cannot cease to be animals we ought to cease being citizens.

The fact that the purpose of Christ's coming to the earth could not consist in creating a kingdom of this world or a state — which had already been founded long ago — in no way proves that He took up a negative attitude with regard to the state. The circumstance that the Gospel does not deal with the external means of protecting humanity from the crudely-destructive effect of the powers of evil could entitle us to draw conclusions only if the Gospel had appeared before the foundation of the state, in a community that had neither law nor authority nor organised justice. There was no need to give in the Gospel over again the principles of civic and juridical order which had, many centuries before, been already given in the Pentateuch. If Christ did not intend to reject them, He could do nothing but confirm them, *and this was precisely what He did.* "One jot or one tittle shall in no wise pass from the law. . . . Think not that I am come to destroy the law. . . . I am not come to destroy, but to fulfil."[22]

But, it will be urged, the grace and truth manifested in Christ made the law void. Now, *when exactly* did this happen? Was it when Judas betrayed his master, or when Ananias and Sapphira deceived the Apostles, or when the deacon Nicolas introduced sexual laxity under the pretext of brotherhood, or when a Christian of Corinth was guilty of incest? Or was it when the Spirit wrote through the prophet of the New Testament to the Churches and said to the representative of one of them, "I know thy works, that thou hast a name that thou livest, and art dead" (Rev. 3:1); and to another, "I know thy works, that thou art neither cold nor hot: I would thou wert cold or hot. So then because thou art lukewarm, and neither cold nor hot, I will spue thee out of my mouth" (Rev. 3:15-16).

If then, from the time grace and truth first appeared and to this day, they have not taken possession either of the whole nor even of the majority of Christian humanity, the question is how and in whom has the law been made void. Could the law have been made void by grace in those who have neither law nor grace? It is obvious that for them, that is, for the majority of mankind, the law must, according to the word of Christ, remain in full force as the external limit of their liberty. And in order to be such a limit, the law must possess sufficient power of compulsion, that is, must be embodied in the organisation of the State with its law courts, police, armies. And in so far as Christianity did not abolish the law, it could not abolish the State. This necessary and rational fact does not, however, by any means prove that the inner relation of men to the external force embodied in the state, and consequently the general and particular character of its activity, remained unchanged. Chemical substance does not disappear in vegetable and animal bodies, but acquires new peculiarities in them, so that there exists a whole science of organic chemistry. The case of *Christian politics* is similar. A Christian state must, if it is not a mere name, distinctly differ from a heathen state, though as *states* both have the same basis and common aim.

---

22. Matthew 5:17-18. — *Editor's note.*

XIII

"A peasant goes forth into the fields to his husbandry; a Polovets falls upon him, slays him, and drives away his horse. Then in a crowd the Polovtsy come out against the village, kill all the peasants, set fire to the houses and lead the women away into captivity, while the princes are taken up with feuds among themselves."[23] If *pity* for these peasants was not to be confined to sentimental words alone, it was bound to lead to the organisation of a strong central authority sufficient to defend the peasants from intestine wars between the princes and the raids of the Polovtsi.

When, in another country, the greatest of her poets exclaimed with profound grief, which he showed not in words only:

Ahi, serva Italia dei dolor' ostello,
Nave senza nocchiero in gran tempesta![24]

— the same pity directly incited him to call from beyond the Alps a supreme representative of state authority, a strong protector against incessant and unbearable acts of violence. The pity for the actual calamities of Italy, expressed in many passages of the *Divine Comedy,* and the appeal for a state invested with the fulness of power as a necessary means of salvation took the form of a definite, well-thought-out conviction in Dante's book *On Monarchy.*

The troubles of anarchy or of a weakly-developed state, that called forth the pity of Vladimir Monomakh and of Dante, can be cured or remedied only by a powerful state, and would inevitably arise again if it disappeared. The purely moral motives were obviously insufficient in the thirteenth century to prevent men from trying to exterminate one another. And even granting that at the present day these motives have become stronger and more widely spread — though this is doubtful, — it would be ridiculous to maintain that they are in themselves sufficient for the maintenance of peace. It is obvious that Italian citizens no longer give vent to their party differences by cutting each other's throats solely because of the compulsory order of the state with its army and police. As to Russia — not to speak of the intestine wars among the princes, and of the people taking the law into their own hands, — there is no doubt that the savage races which the duchy of Moscow and the Russian empire had

23. From the *Instruction* of Vladimir Monomakh, one of the rulers of Russia in the eleventh century, to his children. A Polovets is a member of the Polovtsy, a steppe tribe that fought a series of wars against Russia in the eleventh to thirteenth centuries. — *Editor's note.*

24. "Italy, the slave and the abode of suffering, a ship without a pilot amidst terrible storms." [From Dante's *Divine Comedy: Purgatorio,* VI, 78. — *Editor's note.*]

with such difficulty gradually driven farther and farther away from the centre of the country, submitted to force rather than became regenerated. And if, God forbid, the lance and the bayonet were to disappear or to lose their force on the Caucasian, Turkestan, or Siberian frontier all moralists would become at once convinced of the true nature of these excellent institutions.[25]

Just as the Church is collectively organised piety, so the state is collectively organised pity. To affirm, therefore, that from its very nature the Christian religion is opposed to the state is to affirm that the Christian religion is opposed to pity. In truth, however, the Gospel not merely insists upon the morally binding character of pity or altruism, but decidedly confirms the view, expressed already in the Old Testament, that there can be no true piety apart from pity: "I will have mercy and not sacrifice."[26]

If, however, pity be admitted in principle, it is logically inevitable to admit also the historical organisation of social forces and activities, which raises pity from the stage of a powerless and limited feeling and gives it actuality, wide application, and means of development. From the point of view of pity it is impossible to reject the institution owing to which one can *practically pity,* i.e. *give help and protection* to tens and hundreds of millions of men instead of dozens or at most hundreds of people.

The definition of the state (so far as its moral significance is concerned) as organised pity can be rejected only through misconception. Some of these misconceptions must be considered before we go on to deal with the conception of the Christian state.

XIV

It is urged that the stern and often cruel character of the state obviously contradicts the definition of it as organised pity. But this objection is based on a confusion between necessary and sensible severity and useless and arbitrary cruelty. The first is not opposed to pity, and the second, being an abuse, *is opposed to the very meaning of the state,* and therefore does not contradict the

---

25. My father had as a boy heard first-hand reminiscences of how armed bands of Mongolians on the Volga engaged in open brigandage carried away into captivity whole families of Russian travellers and tormented them in all sorts of ways. At the present time this no longer happens on the Volga, but on the Amur such things are still known to take place. The perpetual war mission of the state is therefore not yet over for Russia, and, had the good centurion Cornelius lived in our day, no moral motives could prevent him from being a Cossack fighter in the Ussuriisky region.

26. Matthew 9:13. — *Editor's note.*

definition of the state — of the normal state, of course — as organised pity. The supposed contradiction is based upon grounds as superficial as the argument that the senseless cruelty of an unsuccessful surgical operation and the sufferings of the patient in the case even of a successful operation are in obvious contradiction to the idea of surgery as a beneficent art helpful to man in certain bodily sufferings. It is obvious that such representatives of state authority as Ivan the Terrible are as little evidence against the altruistic basis of the state, as bad surgeons are against the usefulness of surgery. I am aware that an educated reader may well feel insulted at being reminded of such elementary truths, but if he is acquainted with the recent movement of thought in Russia he will not hold me responsible for the insult.

But, it will be maintained, even the most normal state is inevitably pitiless. In pitying peaceful people whom it defends against men of violence, it is bound to treat the latter without pity. Such *one-sided* pity is out of keeping with the moral ideal. This is indisputable, but again it says nothing against our definition of the state, for, in the first place, even one-sided pity is pity and not anything else; and secondly, even the normal state is not by any means an expression of the moral ideal already attained, but only one of the *chief means* necessary for its attainment. The ideal condition of mankind, or the Kingdom of God, when *attained,* is obviously incompatible with the state, but it is also incompatible with pity. When everything will once more be good there will be no one to pity. And so long as there are men to be pitied, there are men to be defended; and the moral demand for organising such protection efficiently and on a wide scale — *i.e.* the moral significance of the state — remains in force. As for the pitilessness of the state toward those from whom or against whom it has to defend the peaceful society, it is not anything fatal or inevitable, and although it undoubtedly is a fact, it is not an unchangeable fact. In point of history there is no doubt that the relation of the state towards its enemies is becoming less cruel, and consequently more merciful. In old days they used to be put to painful death together with their family and relatives (as is still the case in China). Later, every one had to answer for himself; and subsequently the very character of the responsibility has changed. Criminals have ceased to be tormented solely for the sake of inflicting pain; and at the present time the positive task of helping them morally is recognised. What can be the ultimate reason of such a change? When the state limits or abolishes the penalty of death, abolishes torture and corporal punishment, is concerned with improving prisons and places of exile, it is obvious that in pitying and protecting peaceful citizens who suffer from crimes, it begins to extend its pity to the opposite side also — to the criminals themselves. The reference, therefore, to the one-sided pity is beginning to lose force as a fact. And it is through the state alone that the organisation of pity ceases to be one-sided, since the human crowd is still for the most part guided in its relation to the enemies of society by the old pitiless maxims, 'to the dog, a dog's death'; 'the thief deserves all he gets'; 'as a warning to others,' etc. Such maxims are losing their practical force precisely owing to the state, which is in this case more free from partiality either to the one side or the other. Restraining with an authoritative hand the vindictive instincts of the crowd, ready to tear the criminal to pieces, the state at the same time never renounces the humane duty to oppose crimes, — as the strange moralists, who in truth pity only the aggressive, violent, and rapacious, and are utterly indifferent to their victims, would have it do. This indeed is a case of one-sided pity![27]

XV

Our definition of the state may lead to a less crude misconception on the part of the jurists who regard the state as the embodiment of legality as an absolutely independent principle, distinct from morality in general and from motives of pity in particular. The true distinction between legal justice and morality has already been indicated.[28] It does not destroy the connection between them; on the contrary, it is due to that connection. If this distinction is to be replaced by separation and opposition, an unconditional principle must be found which shall ultimately determine every legal relation as such and be altogether outside of, and as far as possible removed from, the moral sphere.

Such an a-moral and even anti-moral principle is to be found in the first place in *might* or force: *Macht geht vor Recht.*[29] That in the order of history relations based upon right follow those based upon force is as unquestionable as the fact that in the history of our planet organic life appeared after the inorganic and on the basis of it — which does not prove, of course, that inorganic matter is the specific principle of organic forms as such. The play of natural forces in humanity is simply the *material* for relations determined by the conception of right and not the principle of such relations, since otherwise there could be no distinction between right and rightlessness. Right means the *limitation* of might, and the whole point is the *nature* of the limitation. Similarly, morality might be defined as *the overcoming of evil,* which does not imply that evil is the principle of morality.

27. See above, Part III, Chapter VI, 'The Penal Question from the Moral Point of View.'
28. See above, Part III, Chapter VIII, 'Morality and Legal Justice.'
29. "Might comes before right." — *Editor's note.*

We shall not advance any further in the definition of right it we replace the conception of might, derived from the physical sphere, by the more human conception of freedom. That individual freedom lies at the basis of all relations determined by law there can be no doubt, but is it really the unconditional principle of legality? There are two reasons why this cannot be the case. In the first place, because in reality it is *not unconditional,* and, secondly, because it is not the determining principle of *legality.* With regard to the first point, I mean not that human freedom is never unconditional, but that it is not unconditional in that sphere of concrete relations in which and for the sake of which law exists. Suppose that some man living in the flesh on earth actually possessed absolute freedom, that is, that he could by the act of his will alone, independently of any external circumstances and necessary intermediate processes, accomplish everything he wished. It is obvious that such a man would stand outside the sphere of relations determined by legality. If his unconditionally free will determined itself on the side of evil, no external action could limit it; it would be inaccessible to law and authority. And if it were determined on the side of the good it would make all law and all authority superfluous.

It is then irrelevant to speak of unconditional freedom in this connection, since it belongs to quite a different sphere of relations. Legality is concerned only with limited and conditional freedom, and the question is precisely as to what limitations or conditions are lawful. The freedom of one person is limited by the freedom of another, but not every such limitation is consistent with the principle of legality. If the freedom of one man is limited by the freedom of his neighbour who is free to wring his neck or chain him up at his pleasure, there can be no question of legality at all, and in any case such a limitation of freedom shows no specific characteristics of the principle of legality as such. These characteristics must be sought not in the mere fact of the limitation of freedom, but in the equal and universal character of the limitation. If the freedom of one person is limited to the same extent as the freedom of other people, or if the free activity of each meets with a restriction that is common to all, then only is the limitation of freedom determined by the conception of law.

The principle of legality is then freedom within the limits of equality, or freedom conditioned by equality — consequently a conditional freedom. But the equality which determines it is not an absolutely independent principle either. The essential characteristic of the legal norms is that, in addition to equality, they should necessarily answer, too, the demand for *justice.* Although these two ideas are akin, they are far from being identical. When the Pharaoh issued a law commanding to put to death all the Jewish new-born babes, this law was certainly not unjust on account of the unequal treatment of the Jewish and the Egyptian babes. And if the Pharaoh subsequently gave orders to put to death all new-born infants and not only the Jewish ones, no one would venture to call this new law just, although it would satisfy the demand for equality. Justice is not mere equality, but *equality in fulfilling that which is right*. A just debtor is not one who equally refuses to pay all his creditors but who equally pays them all. A just father is not one who is equally indifferent to all his children but who shows equal love for all of them.

Equality, then, can be just or unjust, and it is the just equality or, in the last resort, justice that determines the legal norms. The conception of justice at once introduces us into the moral sphere. And in that sphere we know that each virtue does not exist by itself; but all of them, justice among them, are different modifications of one principle or, rather, of the triune principle which determines our rightful relation to everything. And since justice is concerned with man's moral interaction with his fellow-beings, it is merely a species of the moral motive which lies at the basis of inter-human relations, namely of pity: *justice is pity equally applied.*[30]

In so far then as legality is determined by justice it is essentially related to the moral sphere. All definitions of law which try to separate it from morality leave its real nature untouched. Thus, in addition to the definition already mentioned, Jhering's famous definition declares that 'law is a protected or safeguarded interest.'[31] There can be no doubt that law does defend interest, but not every interest. It obviously defends only the just interests or, in other words, it defends every interest in so far as it is just. What, however, is meant by justice in this connection? To say that a just interest is an interest safeguarded by law is to be guilty of the crudest possible logical circle which can be avoided only if justice be once more taken in its essential, *i.e.* in its moral, sense. This does not prevent us from recognising that the moral principle itself, so far as the inevitable conditions of its existence are concerned, is realised in different ways, and to a greater or lesser degree. For instance there is the distinction between external, formal, or strictly-legal justice and inner, essential, or purely-moral justice, the supreme and ultimate standard of right and wrong being one and the same — namely, the moral principle. Possible conflict between 'outer' and 'inner' justice in particular cases is in itself no argument against their being essentially one, since similar conflict may arise in the carrying out of the simplest and most fundamental moral

---

30. See above, Part I, Chapter V, 'Virtues.'

31. See Rudolf von Jhering, *Geist des roemischen Rechts auf verschiedenen Stufen einer Entwicklung* (The spirit of Roman law in the different periods of its development), vols. 1-2 (Leipzig, 1891-94). — *Editor's note.*

demands. Thus, for instance, pity may demand that I should save two men who are drowning, but being unable to save both, I have to choose between the two. The cases of difficult choice between complex applications of legal justice and morality in the strict sense are no proof of there being any essential and irreducible opposition between the two. The argument that the conceptions of justice and morality change in the course of history is equally unconvincing. It might carry some weight if the rights and laws remained meanwhile unchanged. In truth, however, they change even more according to place and time. What conclusion, then, are we to adopt? There is change in the particular conceptions of justice, there is change in the rights and laws, but one thing remains unchangeable: the demand that the rights and laws should be just. The inner dependence of legal forms upon morality — independently of all external conditions — remains a fact. To avoid this conclusion one would have to go very far — to the country seen by the pilgrim women in Ostrovsky's play, where lawful requests to Mahmut of Persia and Mahmut of Turkey were to begin by the phrase "Judge me, O thou *unjust* judge."[32]

According to Jhering's definition, law *discriminates* between interests in contradistinction to morality which *evaluates* them. There can be no doubt that legal justice discriminates between people's interests and, equally, that it defends them. But this fact alone gives as yet no idea of the essence of legality. There may be discrimination of interests on grounds which have nothing to do with legality, and the definition thus proves to be too wide. Thus if robbers in a wood attack travellers and leave them their life but seize all their property, this will no doubt be a case of the discrimination of interests, but to see in it anything in common with legal right is only possible in the sense in which all violence is the expression of the right of the fist, or the right of brute force. In truth, legality is determined not of course by the fact of the discrimination between interests, but by the constant and universal norm of such discrimination. To be consistent with the conception of right, the discrimination of interests must be correct, normal, or just. In drawing a distinction between the normal and the abnormal discrimination of interests, and referring the first only to the province of legal justice, we obviously make a valuation of them, and therefore the supposed opposition between legality and morality falls to the ground. When we find some laws to be unjust and work for their repeal, then, though we do not leave the domain of legality, we are concerned not with any real discrimination of interests, but in the first place with valuing the already existing discrimination, which in its own day was

32. From Ostrovsky's *The Storm*, Act II, scene 1. — *Editor's note.*

also conditioned by judgments of value, though they were different from those we pass now and opposed to them.

If morality then be defined as the valuation of interests, legal justice forms an essential part of morality. This is by no means contradicted by the fact that the standard of value in morality in the strict sense and in the legal sphere is not the same. This difference, the necessity, namely, for recognising legal relations apart from the purely-moral ones, is itself based upon moral grounds — upon the demand, namely, that the highest, the final good should be realised apart from any external compulsion, and that, conse-quently, there should be some possibility of choice between good and evil. Or, to put it in a paradoxical form, the highest morality demands a certain freedom to be immoral. This demand is carried out by legal justice which compels the individual to do the minimum of good necessary for the social life, and, in the interest of the truly moral, that is, of free perfection, safe-guards him from senseless and pernicious experiments in compulsory righ-teousness and obligatory holiness.[33]

Thus if the state is the objective expression of right, it necessarily forms part of the moral organisation of humanity, which is binding upon the *good* will.

XVI

The connection of right with morality makes it possible to speak of the Christian state. It would be unjust to maintain that in pre-Christian times the state had no moral foundation. In the kingdoms of Judæa and of Israel, the prophets directly put moral demands to the state, and reproached it for not fulfilling these demands. In the pagan world it is sufficient to mention Theseus, for instance, who at the risk of his life freed his subjects from the cannibalistic tribute to Crete, in order to recognise that here too the funda-mental moral motive of the state was pity, demanding active help for the in-jured and the suffering. The difference between the Christian and the pagan state is not then in their natural basis but in something else. From the Chris-tian point of view the state is only a part of the organisation of the collective man — a part conditioned by another higher part, the Church, which conse-crates the state in its work of serving indirectly in its own worldly sphere and by its own means the unconditional purpose which the Church directly puts before it — to prepare humanity and the whole earth for the Kingdom of

33. See above, Part III, Chapter VIII, 'Morality and Legal Justice.'

God. From this follow the two chief tasks of the state — the conservative and the progressive: to *preserve the foundations of social life apart from which humanity could not exist,* and *to improve the conditions of its existence* by furthering the free development of all human powers which are to be the instrument of the future perfection, and apart from which the Kingdom of God could not be realised in humanity. It is clear that just as without the conservative activity of the state humanity would fall apart and there would be *no one left* to enter the fulness of life, so without its progressive activity mankind would always remain at the same stage of the historical process, would never attain the power finally to receive or to reject the Kingdom of God, and therefore there would be *nothing to live for.*

In paganism it was the conservative task of the state that was exclusively predominant. Although the state furthered historical progress, it did so involuntarily and unconsciously. The supreme goal of action was not put by the agents themselves; it was not *their* goal since they had not yet heard 'the gospel of the kingdom.' The progress itself, therefore, although it formally differed from the gradual perfecting of the kingdoms of physical nature, did not really have a purely-human character: it is unworthy of man to unwillingly move toward a goal he does not know. Scripture gives a splendid image of the great heathen kingdoms as powerful and wonderful *beasts* which rapidly appear and disappear. The natural, earthly men have no final significance, and cannot have it; and the state, created by such men, is their collective embodiment. But the pagan state, conditional and transitory in nature, affirmed itself as unconditional. Pagans began by deifying individual *bodies* (astral, vegetable, animal, and especially human) in the multitude of their various gods, and they ended by deifying the collective body — the state (the cult of kings in the Eastern kingdoms, the apotheosis of the Roman emperors).

The pagans erred not in ascribing positive significance to the state, but only in thinking that it possessed that significance *on its own account.* This was obviously untrue. Neither the individual nor the collective body of man has life on its own account but receives it from the spirit that inhabits it. This is clearly proved by the fact of the decomposition both of the individual and of the collective bodies. The perfect body is that in which dwells the spirit of God. Christianity, therefore, demands not that we should reject or limit the power of the state, but that we should fully recognise the principle which alone may render the significance of the state actually complete — namely, its moral solidarity with the cause of the Kingdom of God on earth, all worldly purposes being inwardly subordinated to the one spirit of Christ.

XVII

The question as to the relation of the Church to the state, which has arisen in Christian times, can be solved in principle from the point of view here indicated. The Church is, as we know, a divinely-human organisation, morally determined by piety. From the nature of the case the Divine principle decidedly predominates in the Church over the human. In the relation between them the first is pre-eminently active and the second pre-eminently passive. This obviously must be the case when the human will is in direct correlation with the Divine. The active manifestation of the human will, demanded by the Deity itself, is only possible in the worldly sphere collectively represented by the state and having reality prior to the revelation of the divine principle and without a direct dependence upon the latter. The *Christian* state is related to the Deity, as the Church is; it too is in a certain sense a divine-human organisation, but in it the human element predominates. This is only possible because the Divine principle is realised not *in* the state, but *for* it in the Church. So that in the state the Divine principle gives *full play* to the human and allows it *independently* to serve the supreme end. From the moral point of view both the independent activity of man and his absolute submission to the Deity as such are equally necessary. This antinomy can be solved and the two positions united only by distinguishing the two spheres of life (the religious and the political), and their two immediate motives (piety and pity), corresponding to the difference in the immediate object of action, the final purpose being one and the same. Pious attitude towards a perfect God demands pity for men. The Christian church demands a Christian state. Here as elsewhere *separation* instead of *distinction* leads to *confusion,* and confusion to dissension and perdition. Complete separation of the Church from the state compels the Church to do one of two things. It either has to renounce all active service of the good and to give itself up to quietism and indifference — which is contrary to the spirit of Christ; or, zealous actively to prepare the world for the coming of God's kingdom, but, in its separation and alienation from the state, having no means at its command for carrying out its spiritual activity, the Church, in the person of its authoritative representatives, has itself to seize the concrete instruments of worldly activity, to interfere in all earthly affairs and, absorbed in the question of means, forget its original purpose — an unquestionably pure and high one — more and more. Were such confusion allowed to become permanent, the Church would lose the very ground of its existence. The separation proves to be no less harmful to the other side. The state separated from the Church either gives up spiritual interests altogether, loses its supreme consecration and dignity, as well as the moral respect and the material submission of its subjects, or, conscious of the importance of spiritual interests for the life of man, but, in its separation from the Church, having no competent and independent institution to which it could entrust the supreme care of the spiritual good of its subjects, — the task of preparing the nations for the Kingdom of God, — it decides to take that task upon itself. To do so consistently the state would have to assume *ex officio* the supreme spiritual authority — which would be a mad and dangerous usurpation recalling the 'man of lawlessness' of the last days. It is clear that in forgetting its filial attitude towards the Church, the state would be acting in its own name, and not in the name of the Father.

The normal relation, then, between the state and the Church is this. *The state recognises the supreme spiritual authority of the universal Church, which indicates the general direction of the goodwill of mankind and the final purpose of its historical activity. The Church leaves to the state full power to bring lawful worldly interests into conformity with this supreme will and to harmonise political relations and actions with the requirements of this supreme purpose. The Church must have no power of compulsion, and the power of compulsion exercised by the state must have nothing to do with the domain of religion.*

The state is the intermediary social sphere between the Church on the one hand and the material society on the other. The absolute aims of religious and moral order which the Church puts before humanity and which it represents, cannot be realised in the given human material without the formal mediation of the lawful authority of the state (in the worldly aspect of its activity), which restrains the forces of evil within certain relative bounds until the time comes when all human wills are ready to make the decisive choice between the absolute good and the unconditional evil. The direct and fundamental motive of such restraint is pity, which determines the whole progress of legal justice and of the state. The progress is not in the principle, but in its application. Compulsion exercised by the state draws back before individual freedom and comes forward to help in the case of public distress. *The rule of true progress is this, that the state should interfere as little as possible with the inner moral life of man, and at the same time should as securely and as widely as possible ensure the external conditions of his worthy existence and moral development.* The state which chose on its own authority to teach its subjects true theology and sound philosophy, and at the same time allowed them to remain illiterate, to be murdered on the high-roads, or to die of famine and of infection, would lose its *raison d'être*. The voice of the true Church might well say to such a state: "It is I that am entrusted with the spiritual salvation of these men. All that thou art required to do is to have pity on their worldly difficulties and frailties. It is written that man does not live by bread *alone*, but it is not written that he lives without bread. Pity is binding upon all, and upon me also. If, therefore, thou wilt not be the collective organ of my pity, and wilt not, by rightly dividing our labour, make it morally possible for me to devote myself to the work of piety, I will once more have to set myself to do the work of pity, as I have done in the old days when thou, the state, wast not yet called Christian. I will myself have to see that there should be no famine and excessive labour, no sick uncared for, that the injured should receive reparation, and injurers be corrected. But will not then all men say: What need have we of the state, which has no pity for us, since we have a Church which took pity on our bodies as well as on our souls?" The Christian state, worthy of this name, is one which, without interfering in ecclesiastical affairs, acts within its own domain in the *kingly* spirit of Christ, who pitied the sick and the hungry, taught the ignorant, forcibly restrained abuses (driving out the money-changers), was kind to the Samaritans and the Gentiles, and forbade his disciples to use violence against unbelievers.

XVIII

Just as the fundamental moral motive of piety, determining our right attitude toward the absolute principle, is organised in the Church, and the other ultimate moral principle, that of pity, determining our right attitude toward our neighbours, is organised in the state, so with reference to the third essential aspect of human life our moral relation to the lower nature (our own and that of others) is organised objectively and in a collective form in society as an economic union or zemstvo.

The moral duty of abstinence based as a fact upon the feeling of shame inherent in human nature, is the true principle of the economic life of humanity and of the corresponding social organisation, so far as its own specific task is concerned. The economic task of the state which acts from motives of pity, is compulsorily to secure for each a certain minimum of material welfare as the necessary condition of worthy human existence. This is the right solution of the economic question with regard to one aspect of it, namely, with regard to relations between human beings. Economic activity as such is, however, vitally concerned with man's relation to material nature, and the unconditional character of the moral principle and the completeness of the moral order necessarily demand that this relation, too, should be brought under the norm of the good or of perfection. Humanity must therefore be morally organised not only in the ecclesiastical and the political, but also in the specifically economic sphere of relations. And just as between the Church and the state, so between the three parts of the collective moral organisation there must be *unity without confusion and distinction without separation.*

What form must, then, the good assume in the material-economic society as such? It is understood, of course, that moral philosophy can do no more than indicate what the informing principle and the final end of such a society ought to be. This principle is abstinence from the evil of inordinate carnality; this end is the transmutation of material nature, both our own and that external to us, into the free form of the human spirit, a form which does not limit it from without, but unconditionally completes its inward and external existence.

But what is there in common, it will be asked, between these ideas and the economic reality whose principle is the infinite multiplication of wants and whose end is an equally infinite multiplication of things that satisfy these wants? Shame and shamelessness, spiritualisation of the body and materialisation of the soul, resurrection of the flesh and death of the spirit, certainly do have something in common, but the common element is purely negative. This, however, is of no importance. The fact that a moral norm is rejected does not abolish, but, on the contrary, brings out its inner significance. There is no rational ground for supposing that economic life corresponds to the ideal from the first in a way in which neither the Church nor the state in its empirical reality corresponds to it. There undoubtedly is a certain contradiction between the feeling of shame and the operations on the stock exchange, but the contradiction is certainly not any greater, and perhaps is even less than that between piety in the spirit of Christ and the politics of the medieval Church. There is a lack of correspondence between the principle of abstinence and money speculations, but again it is not any greater, and, indeed, is less great than that between the principle of the state as based upon justice and morality and the institution of *lettres de cachet,* the dragonnades or the wholesale expulsions of persons belonging to a different religion. On the strength of what has happened and of what happens still, one may think that the whole of the economic sphere is simply the field for greed and self-interest, just as for some people the whole significance of religion and the Church is summed up by the ambition of the clergy and the superstitiousness of the masses, and for others the political world contains nothing but the tyranny of the rulers and the blind submissiveness of the crowd. Such views, no doubt, exist, but they are due either to a desire to misunderstand the true meaning of things, or to an incapacity to understand it. The following argument is of more weight. Even if we give up the immediate demand for the ideal of perfection in human relations, we still ought to insist upon two things before we recognise that the relations in question have any moral worth or significance. (1) The moral principle said to be involved in them must not be altogether foreign to them, but must show itself in them, even if in an imperfect way only. (2) In their historical development they must approximate to the norm or become more perfect. But economic life, if it is taken as a certain organisation of material relations, does not in any way satisfy these two necessary demands. In spite of all possible abuses in the ecclesiastical sphere, it could not be seriously denied that the moral principle of piety is inherent in the Church. It could not, for instance, be denied that the temples of God are, generally speaking, erected owing to the feeling of piety, and that the majority of people coming to the services are moved by it. It could not be denied, either, that in some, if not in all, respects the life of the Church is improving, and that many of the old abuses have now become impossible. In a similar way no just man will deny that state institutions — law courts, police, schools, hospitals, etc. — are intended for the moral purpose of defending men from injuries and calamities and of promoting their welfare, nor that the means of attaining that purpose by the state are gradually improving in the sense of becoming more merciful. But in the economic realm there exists no institution which would objectify the virtue of abstinence and serve to spiritualise material nature. The moral principle by which our material life ought to be determined, and our external environment transformed, has no reality whatever in the domain of the economic relations, and, therefore, there is in that domain nothing to improve.

This complete separation of the economic life from its own moral purpose is unquestionably a fact, but from our point of view it can be satisfactorily explained. The moral organisation of humanity, the principle of which was given in the Christian religion, could not be *equally* realised in all its parts. A certain historical successiveness followed from the very nature of the case. The religious task, the organisation of piety in the Church, was bound to occupy the foremost place, both because it was the most essential and, in a sense, the simplest thing, and the least conditioned by man. Indeed, man's relation to the unconditional principle revealed to him cannot be determined by anything other than that principle itself; since nothing can be higher than it; the relation rests upon its own foundation, upon what is given. The second task of moral organisation — the task of the Christian state — is, in addition to the motive of collective pity, also conditioned by the supreme religious principle which liberates that worldly pity from the limitations it had in the heathen state. And we see that the political task of historical Christianity, more complex and conditioned than the religious one, comes on the scene subsequently to the latter. There was a period in the Middle Ages when the Church acquired definite organic forms, while the Christian state was in the same condition of apparent non-existence as the Christian economic life is to-day. The right of the fist, which was predominant in the Middle Ages, no more corresponded to the ideal of the state than modern banks and stock exchanges correspond to the ideal of economic relations. Practical realisation of the latter is naturally the last in the order of time since the economic sphere is the furthest limit for the application of the moral principle. Its rightful organisation, *i.e.* the establishment of the moral relation between man and material nature, is inevitably conditioned in two ways: first, by the normal religious attitude of humanity organised in the Church; and, secondly, by the normal inter-human or altruistic relations organised in the state.

It is no wonder, therefore, that the true economic problem toward which some socialists of the first half of the nineteenth century vaguely groped their way, and from which modern socialists are as far removed as their opponents, has not yet received a stable and definite expression even in theory.

But however indefinite the last practical task may be, the changes in the moral sentiments that predominated in the history of the Christian world point with sufficient clearness to three main epochs. The *epoch of piety* was characterised by its exclusive aspiration to the 'divine,' its indifference and distrust of the human element, its hostility and fear of physical nature. This first epoch, in spite of its stability and long duration, contained in itself a seed of destruction: the spirit of the one-sided, intolerant piety of the Middle Ages was regarded as the absolute norm. When this contradiction found its direct and extreme expression in the inhuman and pitiless religious persecutions inspired by 'piety,' there was a reaction which found its first expression in idealistic humanism, and then showed itself in works of practical pity and mercy. This movement of *human morality* characteristic of the second epoch of Christian history — from the fifteenth to the nineteenth century inclusive — began to pass in the course of the nineteenth century into a third stage. Two preliminary truths appeared in the living consciousness of mankind. The first is that if mercy is to be fully carried out it must include the domain of *material life,* and the second is that the norm of material life is continence. To the philosophers this truth was clear in times of antiquity, but it has not yet shed its light upon the general consciousness for which it is but vaguely beginning to dawn. A glimmer of it can unquestionably be seen in the nineteenth century in such phenomena as the ascetic morality of the fashionable philosopher Schopenhauer, the spread of vegetarianism, the popularity of Hinduism and Buddhism which, though badly understood, are taken precisely on their ascetic side; the success of the *Kreuzer Sonata,*[34] the fear of the good people

34. A reference to a novella by Leo Tolstoy. — *Editor's note.*

lest the preaching of continence might lead to a sudden cessation of the human race, etc.

Economic relations and *asceticism* are the two apparently wholly heterogeneous orders of facts and ideas, which, in the beginning of the nineteenth century, were brought together in a perfectly crude and external way by Malthusianism. *The inner and essential connection between them consists in the positive duty of man to save material nature from the necessity of death and decay, and to prepare it for universal bodily resurrection.*

XIX

It is generally believed that the purpose of economic activity is the increase of wealth. But the purpose of wealth itself — unless one adopts the point of view of the *'avaricious knight'*[35] — is to possess the fulness of physical existence. This fulness no doubt depends upon man's relation to material nature, and here two ways are open before us. We can either selfishly exploit earthly nature or lovingly cultivate it. The first way has already been tried, and although it has been of some indirect benefit to the intellectual development of man and to external human culture, the main purpose cannot be attained by it. Nature yields to man on the surface, gives him the semblance of dominion over her, but the fictitious treasures, won by violence, bring no happiness and scatter in the wind like burnt-up cinders. By means of external exploitation of the powers of the earth man cannot secure that which is essential to his material welfare, — he cannot, that is, heal his physical life and render it immortal. And he cannot possess nature from within, for its true substance is unknown to him. But in virtue of his reason and conscience he knows the moral conditions, lying within his own control, which may place him in the right relation to nature. Reason reveals to him that every real fact or event is subject to the inexorable law of the conservation of energy. Carnal desires seek to bind the soul to the surface of nature, to material things and processes, and to turn the inner potential infinity of the human being into the evil external boundlessness of passions and lusts. Conscience even in its elementary form of shame condemns this path as *unworthy,* and reason shows that it is *perilous.* The more the soul expends itself outwardly, upon the surface of things, the less inner force it has left for penetrating to the inmost substance of nature and taking possession of it. It is clear that man can truly spiritualise nature, that is, call forth and develop its inner life, only by his own overflowing spiri-

---

35. A reference to Pushkin's verse-drama with this title. — *Editor's note.*

tuality; and it is equally clear that man himself can become spiritualised only at the expense of his external, outwardly directed mental powers and desires. The powers and desires of the soul must be *directed inward* and thereby increase in intensity. And the inwardly concentrated, powerful and spiritualised being of man will be in communion with the inner substance of nature and no longer with its material surface.

What is required is not that man should give up externally acting upon nature and carrying on the work of civilisation, but that he should change the purpose of his life and the centre of gravity of his will. External objects which most men passionately seek as ends in themselves, expending upon them their inner powers of feeling and will, must entirely become means and instruments, while the inner forces gathered and concentrated within must be used as a powerful lever to lift the weight of the material being which crushes both the scattered soul of man and the divided soul of nature.

The normal principle of economic activity is economy — the saving, the collecting of psychical forces by means of transmuting one species of mental energy (the external or extensive) into another kind of energy (the internal or the intensive). Man either scatters his sensuous soul or he gathers it together. In the first case he achieves nothing either for himself or for nature, in the second he heals and saves both himself and it. Speaking generally, organisation signifies that the means and instruments of the lower order are co-ordinated for the attainment of one general purpose of a higher order. Therefore the principle of economic activity that has hitherto been dominant — the indefinite multiplication of external and particular wants, and the recognition of the external means of satisfying them as ends in themselves — is the principle of disorganisation, of social decomposition, while the principle of moral philosophy — the collecting and the drawing in of all the external material purposes into one inward and mental purpose of the complete unification of the human being with the substance of nature, is the principle of organisation and universal resuscitation.

It must be remembered, however, that this task is *third* in the order of time in the general moral organisation of humanity, and that the real solution of it is conditioned by the first two. The practice of personal asceticism can be normal and rational only on condition of a pious attitude to God and pity toward men. If this were not so, the devil would be the pattern of asceticism. In a similar manner the collective organisation of the material life of man in accordance with the principle of gathering the inner forces and restraining the outer wants, cannot be rightly and successfully carried out by isolated agents in the economic realm taken by itself. It involves the recognition of the absolute purpose — the Kingdom of God — represented by the Church, and requires the help of the rightful methods of state organisation. Neither the individual nor the collective man can introduce normal order into his material or natural life if he does not fulfil the moral norm in his religious and inter-human relations.

Moral organisation of the human race or its regeneration into the divine humanity is an indivisible threefold process. Its absolute purpose is laid down by the Church as organised piety, collectively receptive of Divine grace; its formal means and instruments are supplied by the purely human, free principle of just pity or sympathy, collectively organised in the state; and it is only the ultimate substratum or material of the divine-human organism that is found in the domain of economic life, determined by the principle of abstinence.

XX

The individual factor is, from the nature of the case, inevitably involved in the social or the collective aspect of the moral organisation of humanity. It is only in and through the activity of the individual bearers of the supreme principles of life that humanity increases in perfection, or is morally organised in the various aspects of its existence. The unity, the completeness, and the right direction of the general moral progress depend upon a harmonious co-operation of the leading or 'representative' individuals. The normal relation between the state and the Church would find its essential condition and visible real embodiment in the abiding harmony of their supreme representatives, the high priest and the king. The power of the king would be consecrated by the authority of the priest, and the authoritative will of the latter would only find expression through the fulness of the power of the former. The high priest of the Church, the direct bearer of the Divine principle, the representative of the spiritual *parentage,* the father by pre-eminence, ought, every time that he is tempted to abuse his authority by turning it into a power of compulsion, to remember the words of the Gospel that the Father judges no one, but has passed all judgment to the Son, *for he is the Son of man.* The Christian king, pre-eminently the son of the Church, when tempted to raise his supreme temporal power to the level of the highest spiritual authority, and allow it to interfere with the affairs of religion and conscience, ought in his turn to remember that even the King of Heaven does the *will of the Father.*

The authority of the high priest or bishop, as well as the power of the king, are, however, inevitably connected with external advantages, and are open to temptations that may prove too strong. Disputes, encroachments and misunderstandings are bound to arise, and they obviously cannot be finally settled by one of the interested parties. All external limitations are, as a matter of principle or of ideal, incompatible with the supreme dignity of the high-priestly authority and of the royal power. But a purely moral control over them on the part of the free forces of the nation and society is both possible and extremely desirable. In the old Israel there had existed a third supreme calling, that of the prophet. Abolished by Christianity in theory, it practically disappeared from the stage of history, and came forward in exceptional cases only, for the most part in a distorted form. Hence all the anomalies of mediaeval and modern history. The restoration of the prophetic calling does not rest with the will of man, but a reminder of its purely moral significance is very opportune in our day, and is appropriate at the end of an exposition of moral philosophy.

Just as the high priest of the Church is the highest expression of piety, and the Christian monarch the highest expression of mercy and truth, so the true prophet is the highest expression of shame and conscience. This inner nature of the prophetic calling determines its external characteristics. The true prophet is a social activist who is absolutely independent, and neither fears, nor submits to, anything external. Side by side with the representatives of absolute authority and absolute power there must be in human society representatives of absolute freedom. Such freedom cannot belong to the crowd, cannot be an attribute of democracy. Every one, of course, desires to have moral freedom, as every one, perhaps, might wish to have supreme authority and power; but desiring is not enough. Supreme authority and power are given by the grace of God, while true freedom must be earned by man himself through an inner exploit of self-renunciation. *The right to be free* follows from the very nature of man and must be externally safeguarded by the state. But the degree to which this right may be *realised* entirely depends upon inner conditions, upon the level of the moral consciousness. The man who has complete freedom, both external and inward, is one who is not inwardly bound by anything external, and in the last resort knows of no other standard of judgment and conduct than good will and pure conscience.

Every high priest or bishop is only the apex of a numbrous and complex hierarchy of the clergy, through which he comes into contact with the whole of the laity; the king carries out his work among the people through a complex system of civil and military institutions represented by individual men; in a similar manner the free followers of the supreme ideal realise it in the life of the community through a number of men who more or less fully participate in their aspirations. The three services can be best distinguished by the fact that the office of the priest derives its main force from pious devotion to the true traditions of the past; the office of the king, from a correct understanding of the true needs of the present; and the office of the prophet, from faith in the true vision of the future. The difference between the prophet and the idle dreamer lies in the fact that in the case of the prophet the flowers and fruits of the ideal future do not hang in the air of personal imagination, but are supported by the visible stem of the present social needs and by the mysterious roots of religious tradition. And it is this same fact that connects the calling of the prophet with the office of priest and king.

The Final Definition of the Moral Significance of Life and the Transition to Theoretical Philosophy

Our life acquires moral worth and significance when, through striving after perfection, it becomes related to the perfect good. It follows from the very conception of the perfect good that all life and all existence are connected with it. There is meaning in the animal life, in its functions of nourishment and reproduction. But this meaning, important and unquestionable as it is, expresses only an involuntary and partial connection of a particular being with the universal good, and cannot satisfy the life of man; *his* will and his reason, being forms of the infinite, demand something more. The spirit is nurtured by the knowledge of the perfect Good and is propagated by doing good, by realising, that is, the unconditional and universal in all particular conditions and relations. In inwardly *demanding* a *perfect* union with the absolute good we show that that which is demanded by us has not yet been given us, and that, therefore, the moral significance of our life can only consist in *approaching* the perfect association with the good or in *rendering perfect* our actual inner connection with it.

The demand for moral perfection involves the general idea of the absolute good and of its necessary attributes. It must be all-embracing, that is, it must be the criterion of our moral relation to all things. All that exists or may exist is from the moral point of view exhausted by three categories: it is either above us, or on a level with us, or below us. It is logically impossible to find a fourth relation. Our inner consciousness testifies that above us is the absolute good or God and that which already is in perfect union with Him, a union we have not yet attained; on a level with us is everything which, like ourselves, is capable of spontaneously increasing in moral perfection, everything which, like us, is on the way to the absolute, and can conceive the purpose of its action, — that is, all human beings; below us is all that is incapable of inward spontaneous perfection and that can enter only through us into a perfect relation with the absolute — namely, material nature. This threefold relation in its most general form is a fact. We are, as a fact, subordinate to the absolute, by whatever name we might describe it. We are, as a fact, equal to other men in the essential attributes of human nature, and through heredity, history, and social life are one with them in our earthly destiny. We possess, as a fact, important advantages over the material creation. *The moral problem then can consist only in perfecting what is given.* The fact of the threefold relation must be transformed into a threefold norm of rational and voluntary activity. The inevitable submission to the supreme power must become the conscious and free service of the perfect good; the natural solidarity with other human beings must be transformed into sympathetic and harmonious co-operation; the actual advantages we have over material nature must become rational mastery over it for our good and its own.

The true beginning of moral progress is contained in the three fundamental feelings which are inherent in human nature and constitute natural virtue: the feeling of *shame* which safeguards our higher dignity against the encroachments of the animal desires, the feeling of *pity* which establishes an inner equality between ourselves and others, and, finally, the *religious* feeling which expresses our recognition of the supreme good. Inseparable from these feelings is the consciousness, even though it be a dim one, that they are the norm, and express what is good, while the opposite of them is bad — the consciousness that one ought to be ashamed of immoderate physical desires and slavery to the animal nature, that one ought to pity others, ought to do homage to the Divine. These feelings, representing the *good nature* which strives from the first towards that which *ought* to be, and the testimony of conscience that accompanies them, constitute the one or rather the triune foundation of moral progress. *Conscientious reason generalises the impulses of the good nature and makes them into a law.* The content of the moral law is that which is given in the good feelings, but it is clothed in the form of a universal and binding demand or imperative. Moral law grows out of the testimony of conscience, and conscience itself is the feeling of shame developed on its formal and not on its material side.

With regard to our lower nature the moral law, generalising the immediate feeling of modesty, commands us always to dominate all sensual desires, admitting them only as a subordinate element within the limits of reason; morality at this stage no longer takes the form — as in the elementary feeling of shame — of the mere instinctive rejection of the hostile element or of retreat before it, but demands actual *struggle* with the flesh. With regard to other human beings, the moral law gives to the feeling of pity or sympathy the form of justice, and demands that we should recognise each of our neighbours as having the same absolute significance as ourselves, or that we should regard others as we could consistently wish them to regard us, independently of this or that particular feeling. Finally, in relation to the Deity the moral law affirms itself as the expression of Its law-giving will, and demands that that will should be unconditionally recognised for the sake of its own dignity or perfection. But when this *pure* recognition of God's will as the all-embracing and all-sufficient good has been attained, it must be clear that the *fulness* of this will can be revealed only through its own inner *effects* in the soul of man. Having risen to this level, the formal or rational morality enters the domain of absolute morality — the good of the rational law is completed by the good of Divine *grace*.

According to the constant teaching of true Christianity, which correctly represents the essence of the matter, grace does not abolish nature and natural morality but 'perfects' it, that is, brings it to perfection; in like manner grace does not abolish the law, but fulfils it, and, only in so far as it does so, renders it unnecessary.

The fulfilment of the moral law, whether instinctive or deliberate, cannot, however, be limited to the personal life of the individual — for two reasons, a natural one and a moral one. The natural reason is that the individual taken separately does not exist at all. From the point of view of practice this reason is quite sufficient, but strict moralists who care not for what is but for what *ought to be* will attach greater weight to the moral reason — to the incompatibility, namely, between the idea of a separate isolated man and the idea of moral perfection. On natural and moral grounds the process of attaining perfection, which constitutes the moral significance of our life, can be conceived only as a collective process, taking place in the collective man, that is, in the family, in the nation, in humanity. These three aspects of the collective man do not replace but mutually support and complete one another, each following its own path towards perfection. Perfection is being attained by the family which spiritualises and preserves for eternity the meaning of the individual past in and through the moral bond with the forefathers, the meaning of the real present in true marriage and the meaning of the individual future in the upbringing of new generations. Perfection is being attained by the nation, which deepens and extends its natural solidarity with other nations by entering into moral communion with them. Perfection is being attained by humanity which organises the good in the general forms of the religious, political, and socio-economic culture, rendering them more and more conformable to the final end — the preparation of humanity for the unconditional moral order, or the kingdom of God. Religious good or piety is organised in the Church which seeks to make its human aspect more perfect by making it more and more conformable to the Divine. The inter-human good or justice and pity is organised in the State which grows more perfect by extending the domain of justice and mercy at the expense of violence and arbitrariness both within the nation and between nations. The physical good or man's moral relation to material nature is organised in the economic union, the perfection of which consists not in the accumulation of things, but in the spiritualisation of matter as the condition of normal and eternal existence in the physical world.

Constant interaction between personal moral effort and the organised moral work of collective man finally justifies the moral significance of life — that is, it justifies the good, which thus appears in all its purity, fulness, and power. The system of moral philosophy worked out in the present book is a conceptual reproduction of this process in its totality; it follows history in what has been attained already, and anticipates it in what is still left to be done. In reducing its contents to one formula we shall find that the perfection of the good finally shows itself as the *inseparable organisation of a triune love.* The feeling of reverence or piety, which means at first a timid and involuntary and then a free and filial submission to the supreme principle, comes to know its object as absolute perfection, and is transformed into a pure, all-embracing, and boundless love for it, conditioned solely by the recognition of its absolute character — an *ascending love.* In conformity with its all-embracing object this love includes all else in God, and, in the first place, those who, like us, can participate in it, *i.e.* human beings. Our physical and subsequently our moral and political pity for men become a spiritual love for them, or an *equalising love.* But the Divine and all-embracing love to which man attains does not stop at this; becoming a *descending love* it acts upon material nature, bringing it also within the fulness of the absolute good, making it the living throne of the Divine glory.

When this universal justification of the good, its extension to all the relations of life, is clearly seen as a historical fact by every mind, the only question for the individual will be the practical question of will, — to accept this perfect moral significance of life for oneself or to reject it. But as long as the end has not yet come, as long as the rightness of the good has not become self-evident in all things and to all, further theoretical doubt is still possible. That doubt cannot be resolved within the limits of moral or practical philosophy, although it in no way detracts from the binding character of the rules of this philosophy upon men of good will.

If the moral significance of life in the last resort consists in the struggle with evil and in the triumph of good over evil, there arises the eternal question as to the origin of evil itself. If evil springs from the good, struggle with it seems to be based upon a misconception; if it arises independently of the good, the good cannot be unconditional, since the condition of its realisation will be external to it. And if the good is not unconditional, wherein does its essential superiority consist, and what is the final guarantee of its triumph over evil?

Rational faith in the absolute good is based upon inner experience, and upon that which with logical necessity follows from it. But inner religious experience is a personal matter, and, from the external point of view, it is conditional. When, therefore, rational faith based upon it becomes a system of universal theoretic assertions, it must be theoretically justified.

The question as to the origin of evil is purely intellectual, and can be solved only by a true metaphysics, which, in its turn, presupposes the solution of the question as to the nature, the validity, and the means of knowing the truth.

The independence of moral philosophy in its own sphere does not prevent it from being inwardly connected with theoretical philosophy — the theory of knowledge and metaphysics.

It least of all befits believers in the absolute good to fear philosophical investigation, as if the moral significance of the world could lose by being finally explained, and as though union with God in love, and harmony with His will, could leave us no part in the Divine intellect. Having justified the good as such in moral philosophy, we must, in theoretical philosophy, justify the good *as Truth*.

Selective Index

Editor's note: This index is not exhaustive; it will emphasize the major figures, movements, and works of literature mentioned in the book. Solovyov's extensive table of contents can serve as a guide to the themes and concepts which he elaborates.